www.wadsworth.com

wadsworth.com is the World Wide Web site for Wadsworth and is your direct source to dozens of online resources.

At *wadsworth.com* you can find out about supplements, demonstration software, and student resources. You can also send email to many of our authors and preview new publications and exciting new technologies.

wadsworth.com
Changing the way the world learns®

Patterns of Transcendence

Religion, Death, and Dying

Second Edition

DAVID CHIDESTER

University of Cape Town

WADSWORTH

™

THOMSON LEARNING

Australia • Canada • Mexico • Singapore • Spain • United Kingdom • United States

Publisher: Eve Howard
Philosophy Editor: Peter Adams
Assistant Editor: Kara Kindstrom
Editorial Assistant: Chalida Anusasananan
Development Consultant: Jake Warde
Marketing Manager: Dave Garrison
Marketing Assistant: Adam Hofmann
Print/Media Buyer: Judy Inouye

Production Service: G&S Typesetters, Inc.
Permissions Editor: Bob Kauser
Copy Editor: Bruce Owens
Cover Designer: Yvo Riezebos
Cover Image: PhotoDisc
Compositor: G&S Typesetters, Inc.
Cover and Text Printer: Webcom Limited

Printed in Canada
1 2 3 4 5 6 7 05 04 03 02

For permission to use material
from this text, contact us by
Web: http://www.thomsonrights.com
Fax: 1-800-730-2215
Phone: 1-800-730-2214

For more information, contact
Wadsworth/Thomson Learning
10 Davis Drive
Belmont, CA 94002-3098
USA

For more information about our products, contact us:
**Thomson Learning Academic Resource
Center**
1-800-423-0563
http://www.wadsworth.com

International Headquarters
Thomson Learning
International Division
290 Harbor Drive, 2nd Floor
Stamford, CT 06902-7477
USA

UK/Europe/Middle East/South Africa
Thomson Learning
Berkshire House
168-173 High Holborn
London WC1V 7AA
United Kingdom

Asia
Thomson Learning
60 Albert Complex, #15-01
Singapore 189969

Canada
Nelson Thomson Learning
1120 Birchmount Rd.
Toronto, Ontario M1K 5G4
Canada

Library of Congress Cataloging-in-Publication Data
Chidester, David.
    Patterns of transcendence : religion, death, and dying / David Chidester.—2nd ed.
        p.   cm.
    Includes bibliographical references and index.
    ISBN 0-534-50607-0 (pbk.)
        1. Death—Religious aspects—Comparative studies.   I. Title.
    BL504.C45 2001
    291.2'3—dc21   2001026816

Contents

Preface

Death is the simplest fact of life: You are born, you live, and you die. Everyone does it. What could be simpler?

Of course, things are not so simple. This book is about the many complex ways that people have found to deal with the fact of death. As a historian of religions, I explore the religious symbols, myths, rituals, and traditions through which human beings all over the world have faced death. But I also pay attention to the ways people have worked to rise above and go beyond death's limit. In doing this, people have developed patterns of transcendence in relation to the process of dying and the reality of death. By entering into the simple, complex, and diverse human engagements with death and dying, I want to track those traces of transcendence.

Since finding ways to deal with death has been central to the human enterprise of religion, focusing on religion, death, and dying effectively provides a survey of the history of religions. We will travel far. After Chapter 1 introduces key issues in religious approaches to death, Chapter 2 explores the local, small-scale, and indigenous religions of Australia, Africa, and North America. In a profound sense, these indigenous religious traditions established the basic terms within which other religions have developed ways of living and dying. After all, everyone is indigenous somewhere. By reinforcing sacred ties of kinship, cultivating spiritual experience, remembering the dead, and imagining other worlds beyond death, indigenous religious ways of dealing with death and dying have developed into patterns of transcendence that appear in all religious traditions of the world.

Chapters 3 and 5 explore the symbols, myths, rituals, and traditions of death and dying in the religions of the East and West. In Chapter 3, we will enter the Hindu, Buddhist, Confucian, and Taoist traditions of Asia, focusing on Asian religious resources for dealing with death and dying. In Chapter 5, we will examine the approaches to death and dying in Judaism, Christianity, and Islam — religious traditions that have in different ways each located their origin in a common father, the patriarch Abraham, and are accordingly referred to as Abrahamic traditions.

As a counterpoint to these surveys of religious traditions, I dwell in detail on two religious texts—one Buddhist, the other Christian—that have presented different ways of understanding the process of dying, the reality of death, and the possibilities of the afterlife. Focusing on the *Tibetan Book of the Dead* in Chapter 4 and *The Divine Comedy* in Chapter 6, I single out the *Bardo Thödol* of the Buddhist teacher Padma Sambhava and the *Divina Commedia* of the Christian poet Dante Alighieri for special consideration. I focus on these two texts to raise the problem of comparison: How do we understand the similarities and differences in these Buddhist and Christian guidebooks for the process of dying, understanding death, and imagining the afterlife?

In Chapter 7, I conclude with the living, the survivors who find ways to transcend death in the midst of their grief, in the course of their ongoing exchanges with the deceased, and in the sacred space and time of their memories of the dead. In conclusion, this last chapter explores the ways in which the living and the dying can form communities of care and compassion that transcend death, even in a modern world that tries to avoid the reality of death. Redefining spirituality as a natural human faculty, new initiatives in compassionate care have found ways of rising above and going beyond death that evoke the power of religious symbols, myths, rituals, and traditions. These new developments in secular spirituality, or ordinary transcendence, recall the power of patterns of transcendence in the history of religions.

Throughout this book, I focus on four basic patterns of transcendence. First, ancestral transcendence, which arises out of family relations, affirms the ongoing bonds of kinship that remain unbroken by death. In this form of transcendence, people rise above and go beyond death by living on through the enduring connections that link ancestors with offspring. Although individuals certainly die, family relations live on through the beliefs and practices of ancestral transcendence.

Second, experiential transcendence, which originates out of a personal experience of rising above the limits of time and space, incorporates death into the ordinary course of life. For example, in their ecstatic states, shamans, mystics, or religious visionaries might achieve an experiential transcendence of death. But experiential transcendence might also appear in the calm, quiet acceptance of death as a necessary part of life. Whether appearing in ecstasy or acceptance, experiential transcendence can be a rehearsal for death, a way of assimilating the reality of death into the rhythms of life.

Third, cultural transcendence, which arises out of the social relations of a community, affirms ongoing social bonds, obligations, and exchanges that cannot be broken by death. These social bonds are not founded on kinship, as in ancestral transcendence, but are based on commitments to a shared cultural identity. Often enacted in public memorials for the dead, cultural transcendence is maintained in the memories of the living. By preserving the name, reputation, or fame of the deceased, cultural transcendence affirms important social connections and cultural continuities in the ongoing relations between the living and the dead.

Finally, mythic transcendence uses the medium of story-telling to establish ways of thinking and acting about death and dying. In narratives about death and the afterlife, religious traditions have produced rich, detailed accounts of other worlds. In rising above and going beyond death, these stories are resources for imagining transcendence. Although these mythic narratives provide maps for the afterlife, they also represent mirrors for this life, reflecting images of human identity that are crucial for the living.

All four of these patterns of transcendence—ancestral, experiential, cultural, and mythic—appear in every religious tradition. In surveying the religions of the world, this book explores the ways in which these patterns of transcendence have invested death and dying with human meaning. Although religions refer to realities that are more than human—to the supernatural, the sacred, the ultimate, or the transcendent—religion is at least human. Religion is something important that human beings do. In this book, we will investigate religious approaches to death and dying as ways of being human.

This book grew out of my experience as a teacher in the academic study of religion. During the early 1980s at the University of California, Santa Barbara, I taught a course titled "Religious Approaches to Death," which briefly earned me the designation "Dr. Death." In working out that course, I developed the basic outline of the story that appears in this book. I also learned about the challenges of balancing the demands of large-scale public performances, usually with about 300 students in the classroom, and the intensely personal engagements of individuals with the subject.

While developing "Religious Approaches to Death" for the first time, I was asked to co-teach another course with a visiting professor, Joseph Campbell, to be titled, "Visionary Journeys: The *Tibetan Book of the Dead* and *The Divine Comedy.*" I still have a copy of the flyer advertising the course. Although I can certainly guess what Joseph Campbell would have done with those texts, I cannot say anything for certain, because the course was cancelled due to lack of interest. Unfortunately, Campbell was not yet famous. However, as a result of that course that never happened, I became convinced that juxtaposing those two texts could generate an important creative tension in the study of religion, death, and dying. Therefore, I have given them a prominent place in this book.

After moving to South Africa in the mid-1980s, I continued to develop the basic story and the supporting materials for this book, but in an entirely different working environment. In a world of conflict and violence, the study of religion, death, and dying assumed a new urgency. In teaching at the University of Cape Town, I used the resources in this book not only in an introductory survey of the history of religions but also in courses on the psychology and sociology of religion. As I have found in my own teaching, this book can have many applications.

Although I published an earlier version of this book in 1990, I see this new edition as a new book. Besides updating the good parts and discarding the bad, I have recast the entire project by concluding with an exploration of religious approaches to living with loss, grief, memory, and pain. By ending with a new chapter on living transcendence, I have tried to reinforce the central theme of the book: Religious approaches to death are also religious approaches to life.

Over the years, both the book and I have benefited from the quality of care displayed by editors, colleagues, critics, friends, and family. At Wadsworth, I have received editorial support from Sheryl Fullerton and Leland Moss in an earlier era and from Peter Adams and Kara Kindstrom more recently. Apparently, the earlier edition of this book was both translated into and edited in Persian by Gholamhossein Tavacoly, but none of us associated with Wadsworth have benefited directly from that publication. During the course of the editorial process, I have truly appreciated the critical and supportive interventions by readers for the publisher: Charles E. Headington, Elizabeth Heitman, and Walter L. Moore for the first edition and David Batstone, University of San Francisco; Robert E. Goss, Webster University; June O'Connor, University of California—Riverside; and Sumner B. Twiss, Brown University, for this edition. Giving their time and attention, these critical colleagues have also been collaborators. I must single out June O'Connor for special thanks, however, because she motivated me to finish this project by asking a simple question: "Where is the book?"

Over the past twenty years, the Board of Directors has been one formal institution that has given my life continuity. As always, I thank Deborah Sills and Giles Gunn for being there, James McNamara for travel arrangements, and Edward T. Linenthal for demonstrating in new and always surprising ways the potency of religious studies. The Institute for Comparative Religion in Southern Africa—Viva, ICRSA, Viva!—is another formal institution that has sustained me over the past ten years. For helping to bring this book home, I especially thank my ICRSA colleague, Judy Tobler. For keeping alive the crucial institution that has given my life continuity—the institution of marriage—I thank Careen, as always, who has now lived through this book twice.

As time goes by, the losses mount. We have all known loss, grief, and bereavement. During the preparation of this edition of the book for publication, I have lost dear friends, family members, and beloved teachers. Since I am writing this book as a teacher, I will mention only my own teachers: Walter Capps, Robert Michaelsen, and Ninian Smart. Without them, I would not be possible. I miss them.

I dedicated the first edition of this book to my sister Cathy and my nephew Alex, referring to Alex as "Little Al, the People's Pal." I don't know how that dedication played out elsewhere in the world, but in my own classes in Cape Town I found that "Little Al" became a popular topic of discussion among students. They wanted to know: Who is this guy? Why is he famous? How did he become the pal of all the people? Now that Alex is taller than me, I have to be very careful not to cross him by stirring up such potentially embarrassing questions. I dedicate this second edition to Alex's grandmother, Jeanette, the mother of Cathy and me. Without her, of course, none of us would be. With her, we have been happy.

1

Religion, Death, and Dying

The earliest records for the history of religions are bones. Evidence of the intentional, careful burial of human remains has been dated as far back as 100,000 years before the common era (B.C.E.). Burial sites from 70,000 to 15,000 B.C.E. have been discovered all over the world. A child's body surrounded by a display of ibex horns, an adult male buried with flint tools, a woman's skull adorned with artificial eyes—these and many other archaeological discoveries attest to a measure of care in the final disposition of the dead.

Perhaps they also attest to religious beliefs and practices surrounding death and afterlife. Three features of prehistoric burials may hint at religious beliefs regarding death. First, the use of red ocher to paint the corpse has been found in burial sites in Europe, China, Africa, Australia, and the Americas. Possibly, this red dye was used to symbolize blood and life. Second, the placement of tools, food, and other objects in the graves was common, perhaps suggesting a belief in continued activity after death.

Finally, the effort that went into the burial practice itself may reflect a care and concern for the dead that had an essentially religious quality. Many Stone Age burials arranged the corpse so that it faced east, perhaps indicating an expectation of some type of rebirth with the rising sun. More frequently, corpses were intentionally placed or tied in a fetal position in the grave. Perhaps this practice was inspired by the expectation of a new birth for the deceased. Alternatively, the binding of the corpse may have been intended as a ritual protection of the living from the possibility of being visited by the dead. In either case, essentially religious beliefs about the survival of the dead—whether that survival might have been welcomed or feared—may very well have informed these earliest burial practices, which are the earliest records of the history of religions (Eliade, 1978: I:1; James, 1957: 23–30; Pearson, 2001).

Many nineteenth-century students of religion argued that the human encounter with death was the origin of religion. Influenced by evolutionary theory, scholars such as Herbert Spencer, John Lubbock, and E. B. Tylor looked for the origin and development of religion in prehistoric beliefs about death.

In his *Principles of Sociology,* Herbert Spencer imagined that religion began when prehistoric people dreamed of dead relatives. When those people saw their deceased fathers and mothers in dreams, they assumed that the ghosts of the dead survived in another world (1896: I:294–305). In 1871, John Lubbock and E. B. Tylor also posed this connection between dreams, death, and religion. Lubbock argued that dreams were the basis of belief in another life (1902: 226–27). Tylor, in his two-volume *Primitive Culture,* developed his influential theory of the origin of religion by arguing for an evolutionary progression from dreams to the notion of a surviving soul to the worship of those survivors as revered ancestors and finally to the gradual transformation of ancestors into deities (1920: II:110–13).

Students of religion eventually abandoned such evolutionary speculations, partially for lack of evidence but also because such theories implied that religion originated in a primitive mistake—a "primordial stupidity"—about the nature of dreams. Nevertheless, we can still observe the importance of death in the ongoing life of religious traditions and religious communities. As the anthropologist Bronislaw Malinowski noted, "Of all the sources of religion, the supreme and final crisis of life—death—is of the greatest importance" (1954: 47). Although we can conclude nothing about the birth of religion, we can observe the importance of death as a continuing source of religion's vitality.

At the beginning of the twentieth century, students of religion concentrated on two ways of analyzing the importance of death in the history of religions: focusing on the relation between death and fertility or focusing on the relation between death and society. The Scottish anthropologist James Frazer, in his monumental twelve-volume *The Golden Bough* (1911–15) and his three-volume work on *The Belief in Immortality and the Worship of the Dead* (1913–24), tried to understand religious approaches to death and dying in terms of the relation between death and new life. For Frazer, the history of religions was a catalog of attempts to transcend death, "no figurative or allegorical death, no poetical embroidery thrown over the skeleton, but the real death, the naked skeleton" (1911–15: VII:vi). Religion transcended death, this "real death," by imaginatively linking it with fertility.

Frazer collected countless versions of myths, legends, and folklore from all over the world that seemed to indicate this connection—out of death, new life. Agricultural myths of the life-and-death cycle of fertility, animal myths such as those about snakes shedding their skins, celestial myths of the waxing and waning moon, and political myths of kingship—"the king is dead, long live the king"—all seemed to point to a basic, underlying religious connection between dying and regeneration. From Frazer's perspective, religion was based on this imagined relation between death and new life.

Other students of religion, however, began to pay attention to the implications of religious approaches to death for human societies. In 1907, Robert Hertz published an important article on death rituals, arguing that religious beliefs and practices relating to death helped reconstruct a community disrupted by the loss of one of its members. The deceased continued to play an important role in restoring and maintaining the social order of the community.

Two years later, Arnold van Gennep developed the social analysis of death rituals by relating them to other rites of passage in the human life cycle. Birth, adulthood, marriage, and death were all examined as transitions in personal life that tend to be accompanied by collective ritual practices. These rituals contribute to the very definition of a society. Death rituals of passage construct a society that includes both the living and the dead in a continuous, unified social order.

The concerns of Hertz and van Gennep for the relation between death and society continue to interest anthropologists, sociologists, and historians of religion exploring religious beliefs and practices relating to death. We will return to them at the end of this chapter.

In the academic study of religion, religion may be regarded as beliefs in supernatural beings, forces, or realities (Spiro, 1966: 96; Tylor, 1920: II:424); as beliefs and practices relating to things that are sacred or set apart from ordinary life (Durkheim, 1965: 62; Eliade, 1961); or, in very broad definition, as anything that allows human beings to transcend the purely biological functioning of their physical organisms (Luckmann, 1967). Transcendence means to rise above or go beyond. Religion, in this last definition, would take shape in shared systems of meaningful communication—in symbols, myths, rituals, and traditions—that allow human beings to rise above or go beyond the merely animal functions of their bodies. In other words, religion might be regarded as a humanizing activity and religions as experiments in being human. As patterns of transcendence, religions provide opportunities for rising above or going beyond the limit placed on human life by the death of the body. Perhaps in that confrontation with death, human beings are most human, both in their limitations and in their potential for transcendence.

In this book, we will explore religious approaches to death and dying in a variety of religious traditions and communities, from small-scale, local, and tribal religions of Australia, Africa, and North America to the so-called world religions of the East and West. Although this survey necessarily will be preliminary and introductory, it will nevertheless suggest the rich diversity, as well as coherent patterns, in religious encounters with death. Before beginning that survey, however, it may be useful to outline some of the recurring themes we can expect in religious patterns of transcendence in relation to the death and dying of a human person.

DEATH AND HUMAN PERSONS

What is a human person? Because the very definition of a person depends on classifications operating within particular worldviews, we cannot take this question for granted. Usually, a worldview defines the class of human persons—in contrast to superhuman and subhuman persons—as that category of persons whose lives and deaths are most important and meaningful. In the modern world, four ways of defining a human person immediately come to mind—biological, psychological, sociological, and religious—that offer different terms and conditions for what it might mean to be human.

A *biological* definition would identify human beings as a species of animal life. A biologist can confidently assert, as if it were an obvious, scientific fact, that human beings are animals: "We are in fact animals, not vegetables or gods" (Reynolds, 1980: 45). Vegetables are subhuman, gods are superhuman. Human beings, however, are located in the animal kingdom.

Human animals can be distinguished from other animals based on three specialized features: They walk upright on two legs; they have opposable thumbs, resulting in the manual dexterity necessary for tool use; and they have a larger frontal lobe of the brain than other animal species. In a biological definition, therefore, humans may be walking animals, tool-using animals, and thinking animals, but they are nevertheless clearly identifiable as a species of animal life. When they die, human beings undergo the cessation of biological functions that occurs at the death of all animals.

A *psychological* definition of a human person would focus on individual, personal features of consciousness and will. A human being, in this sense, is an individual conscious agent—aware and acting as an individual—however much that conscious individual may be motivated by unconscious instincts, drives, and impulses. In this regard, a Freudian psychoanalyst can describe a person as a dark cellar where an old maiden aunt and a sex-crazed monkey are fighting a pitched battle, with a rather nervous bank clerk refereeing (Bannister, 1966: 363).

From the perspective of Freudian analysis, the human person may look like at least three different identities—superego, id, and ego—locked in an internal, psychological conflict. The conscious ego may be only the most apparent part of a much more complex psychological apparatus. Conscious awareness of death may distinguish human beings from other forms of animal life, but that awareness is also influenced by unconscious psychological forces when facing death.

A *sociological* definition locates human persons in a network of social relations. A person is a unit in a larger social system. Personal identity takes shape from detailed social interactions, in the framework of family, kinship, group, class, and other social institutions (Carrithers et al., 1985; Mauss, 1979). Specific social classifications of age, gender, status, and so on provide contexts within which a person emerges and operates. Important here is the mutual recognition of individuals within a human society. In many African traditions, for example, a person is a person because he or she regards others as persons. The Zulu definition of a person, *umuntu,* captures this notion that human persons exist as persons only in a context of interpersonal recognition.

Whereas mutual recognition defines an arena of social inclusion, a society also produces powerful forces of exclusion that effectively deny recognition of some persons as fully human members of that society. Strangers may be excluded, as illustrated by the many ethnographic reports of groups that reserve the title "human" for themselves while denying it to those outside. Even those assigned a place in society, however, may be excluded from fully human status. In many cases, children, women, slaves, and other subclassified persons may be denied a fully human status within a network of social relations. Dynamic forces of social interaction, therefore, may determine how a person lives, how a person dies, and the ways in which a community responds to the death of that person.

In the study of religion, it is possible to recognize that a human person may be all these things—a human animal, a conscious agent, and a social person—and to still appreciate the meaning and power of symbolic forms through which religious experiments in being human are conducted. *Homo religiosus* is *Homo symbolicus*—the religious person is a symbol-using, -owning, and -operating person. The symbolic forms of religion—symbols, myths, rituals, and traditions—provide a context in which a human life is not merely lived but lived meaningfully. Religious symbols represent opportunities for rising above or going beyond the biological, psychological, and social aspects of human life. As we will see, these aspects of human life and death may be transformed into patterns of transcendence through the power of religious symbolization.

Death may appear to be an easily identifiable event. One moment there is life, the next death. But because dying is at the same time a biological, psychological, and social process, a human death is a complex event. Because a human death is also a symbolized event, surrounded in the symbolic forms of religious imagination, discourse, and practice with which we will be concerned, death and dying appear even more complex in human experience. Some of the elements in that experience can be isolated in order to gain perspective on the complexity of human death and dying. We can begin by identifying some of the biological, psychological, and social factors involved in a human death.

Biological Death

In terms of human biology, death is the cessation of life. Vital signs used in many societies to indicate the end of life have been respiration, heartbeat, and pulse. The eyes may also be checked for lack of reflexes that might indicate the onset of death. The body begins to assume characteristic symptoms of the absence of life: Body temperature falls (*algor mortis*), areas of the skin take on a purple-red discoloration (*livor mortis*), and muscles become rigid (*rigor mortis*).

Nevertheless, some anxiety about the diagnosis of death may also be evident. During the great plagues of Europe, for example, bells were installed in coffins so that a person regaining consciousness after burial might ring for assistance. More recently, considerable interest has been aroused by the experiences of people who have been declared clinically dead but unexpectedly have revived, often to report extraordinary visions in these near-death events. However those experiences are understood, the fact that these people were declared dead suggests some margin for error in the biological determination of death.

Diagnosis of death by traditional vital signs has been considerably complicated in recent years by the development of technological means for sustaining breathing and heartbeat, even in cases where all brain activity has ceased. The medical use of life-support systems has led to a new biological definition of death—brain death—that may be diagnosed even when respiration and circulation are being artificially sustained. Potential for consciousness has become a new criterion for human life, while its irreversible absence indicates the death of a fully human person (Gervais, 1986; Lamb, 1996; Younger et al., 1999).

Medical specialists of biological death find themselves in a difficult moral position, as Clyde Nabes noted, "wherein we are uncertain we are dealing any longer with a human life; the morality of continuing to respirate a body that may or may not be a human being is unclear" (1981: 56). Hoping to resolve this dilemma, the Harvard Medical School Ad Hoc Committee to Examine the Definition of Brain Death has proposed standards for the biological determination of death that have been embodied in legislation governing medical practice in many states. A person can be declared dead if a physician finds no response to external stimuli, the absence of spontaneous muscle movement and breathing, the absence of observable reflexes, and the absence of brain activity, indicated by a flat electroencephalogram (EEG). These four criteria include traditional signs for the determination of death but also introduce the criterion of brain death. Irreversible loss of brain activity, therefore, has become the final indicator of the death of a human being in modern, Western medical practice.

Once the signs of death have been determined, a death certificate documents the end of a living person. That death certificate will also include the cause of death. Modern biological determinations of death tend to divide its causes into three classes: natural, accidental, and violent causes of death.

This medical, technological, and bureaucratic management of death, as we will see, is only one possible way of determining the signs and causes of death. Medical discourse and practice have been institutionalized in modern, Western societies but can be contrasted with other, traditional ways of managing death. In some traditions, persons may be classified as dead before (in medical terms) they "die." Often there is a difference between biological death and the religious or social recognition of death.

Many small-scale hunting-and-gathering societies, which depend on a relatively high degree of mobility for their survival, abandoned the aged and infirm to die so that they would not become a burden to the rest of the community. They were, therefore, "dead" to those societies even before their biological deaths.

Other examples of the discrepancy between biological death and the ritual certification of death could be cited: Among the Lugbara of central Africa, a dying father spoke his last words of blessing to his son; the son left the hut and sang the personal chant of his father. With this act, the cycle of death rituals began. Even if the father recovered, he would still be regarded by the community as dead, with no claims to the property or status he had held in the community (Middleton, 1982: 42–43). Among the Dogon of west Africa, funeral rituals could be carried out for someone who seemed dead but who unexpectedly recovered. Even if the "dead" person returned, he or she would not be recognized by family or community and would be forced to exist as a nameless beggar with no place in society (Bloch and Parry, 1982: 13).

Finally, some religious traditions support a renunciation of life as necessary for a particular spiritual discipline. In traditional India, Hindu ascetics might perform their own funeral rituals at the time they embarked on a life of self-denial, poverty, and meditation. If they tried to return to ordinary life, they were excluded as if they were unwelcome "ghosts" intruding on the world of the living (Parry, 1982: 86–101). These examples simply suggest that the "vital signs" in religious approaches to death and dying may be more complicated than the relatively simple and straightforward biological determinations of death.

In addition, the causes of death may also appear to be more complex. A medical, biological definition of the causes of death may confidently divide them into natural, accidental, and violent causes, but religious approaches to death tend to see these as intermediate causes in some larger, meaningful pattern of causation. For example, in the Australian and African traditions we will be examining, death was often attributed to witchcraft, to the evil influences of enemies, or to some disharmony in the community. If the ultimate cause of death was identified as a spell cast by an enemy sorcerer, then revenge could be enacted. In this way of symbolizing death, its ultimate cause was always an act of violence, even when intermediate causes might be disease or accident.

The symbolism of death in other religions may also identify ultimate causes. The popular Taoism of China, for example, imagined an Arbiter of Destiny who monitored human action and reduced the life spans of human beings by hours, days, months, or years, depending on the seriousness of their sins. When their time ran out, human beings died (Brokaw, 1991). Similarly, Christian symbolism of death often identified its cause as sin. "Death," according to Paul in the New Testament, "is the wages of sin" (Rom. 6:23). In both these examples, ethical causation is superimposed on the more immediate physical causes of dying to give biological death a larger meaning and significance. In this way, a human life might not simply be the presence of certain vital signs; it might depend on a particular quality of life that is articulated in religious symbolism of death.

Psychological Death

In an article written in the midst of the death and devastation of World War I, Sigmund Freud analyzed the psychological conditions of a human death. He wrote that human beings may be conscious of death but that consciousness is influenced by deep sources of resistance and denial in the unconscious. The unconscious denial of death makes one's own death unimaginable. "It is indeed impossible," Freud suggested, "to imagine our own death: and whenever we attempt to do so we can perceive that we are in fact still present as spectators" (1915: 305). Images of lying in a coffin, gatherings of friends and relatives, and observances performed by religious officials may all come to mind when contemplating death, as if the human consciousness could be a spectator at its own funeral. But it is impossible for consciousness to imagine its own extinction. Trying to imagine death, in this sense, is something like trying to make the mind blank but finding it filled instead with the thought of trying to make it blank.

The resistance to imagining one's own death, Freud argued, came from the deep recesses of the unconscious and its instinctual drives for life, survival, and self-preservation. "Hence," Freud concluded, "the psychoanalytic school could venture on the assertion that at bottom no one believes in his own death, or, to put the same thing in another way, that in the unconscious every one of us is convinced of his own immortality" (1915: 305). Beliefs in immortality, therefore, are nothing more than projections into consciousness of the denial of death that is so firmly locked in the defense mechanisms of the human unconscious.

Freud posed two options available in the psychological confrontation with death: acceptance or denial. Only two attitudes toward death were possible: "the one that acknowledges it as an annihilation of life and the other which denies it as unreal" (1915: 315). Freud was convinced that the only genuine scientific option was the acceptance of death as the extinction of the person, however much that extinction may defy imagination. Freud further argued that this acceptance should prove to be therapeutic. "If you want to endure life," he advised, "prepare yourself for death" (1915: 317).

The only other choice was to persist in an unconsciously motivated denial of death. Suppression of the unconscious mechanisms of denial caused the denial of death to surface in the many different forms of images, beliefs, and expectations of survival after death. All these could be dismissed as projections of the unconscious, merely symptoms of its resistance to imagining death. Religion—especially religious beliefs in survival after death—formed a vast collective, cultural neurosis. From Freud's perspective, psychological science could address the neurotic beliefs and behavior in religious approaches to death and dying only by insisting on an acceptance of death as extinction and an iconoclastic rejection of all images of human survival.

More recently, the Freudian psychologist Robert Jay Lifton argued for the psychological importance of images of transcendence in the human experience of death. He maintained that symbols of continuity, particularly religious ones, form an important ingredient in an authentically human death by allowing the person to identify with some form of collective, ongoing life. Lifton noted that "we, in fact, require symbolization of continuity—imaginative forms of transcending death—in order to confront genuinely the fact that we die."

Like a human life, a human death is meaningful. Death is invested with meaning by forms of symbolic transcendence that point above and beyond the limited ego identity to forms of connection and continuity that make personal life part of a greater living whole. Images of immortality, in this sense, may involve the denial of death, but they represent more than merely an unconscious repression. "A *sense* of immortality," Lifton argued,

> is by no means mere denial of death, though denial and numbing are rarely absent. Rather it is a corollary of the knowledge of death itself, and reflects a compelling and universal inner quest for continuous symbolic relationship to what has gone before and what will continue after our finite individual lives. (1979: 17)

Granting that psychological repression may be present, Lifton acknowledged a therapeutic role for religious symbolism of transcendence in the experience of an authentically human death. But more than this, symbols of transcendence—symbols that connect people with what has gone before and what will come after their individual lives—are essential for a life and death that are meaningful in fully human terms.

Psychological analysis of religion and death has frequently focused on the relation between religion and psychological processes of anxiety or acceptance in the face of death. Death anxiety has been treated as a measurable experience that can be calculated on various scales. Some of these scales—such as the Templer Death Anxiety Scale (Templer, 1970)—have been used in several studies to determine the effect of religious beliefs on anxieties about death and dying. Results have been inconclusive (Lester, 1967). Some have found that people deeply involved in religion seem to have less death anxiety (Templer, 1972), whereas others suggest that any coherent belief system, whether religious or not, tends to reduce anxiety about death (Kalish and Reynolds, 1976; Pressman et al., 1992).

Part of the problem in this analysis may be the assumption that anxiety is unhealthy and that religion, if it were therapeutic, would reduce or eliminate anxiety. The historian of religion Mircea Eliade, however, suggested a very different perspective on death anxiety by claiming that it should be interpreted as a signal of transcendence. "The anxiety aroused by the imminence of death," Eliade stated, "is already a promise of resurrection, reveals the presentiment of re-birth into another mode of being, and this is a mode which transcends death" (1967: 243). Also, the popular and influential work of Elisabeth Kübler-Ross (1969) on psychological stages in the process of dying suggests that an ultimate acceptance of death tends to be achieved through a process that involves a high degree of denial, internal conflict, and intense anxiety. From this perspective, anxiety may represent a serious confrontation with death that forms a necessary prelude for any authentic psychological adjustment, acceptance, or even transcendence.

The psychological approaches to death and dying mentioned here have been almost exclusively preoccupied with the experience of death in modern, Western societies. Different "death styles" may be cultivated within the cultural norms of different societies. The dynamics of emotion, anxiety, and acceptance in these varying styles may be difficult to interpret. Numerous reports from different societies and cultural groups have suggested that fear of death is not a universal emotion. Leonid Rzhevsky stated that Chinese "look upon death not with fear, but with pleasure" (1976: 38); William Douglass described Spanish Basque villagers as "calm in the face of death" (1969); and even in the United States, studies have argued that particular groups, such as rural people of Appalachia (Roberts, 1977) or African Americans (Kalish and Reynolds, 1976), supposedly exhibit less fear of death than other groups. However difficult it may be to generalize about the emotional life of different communities, it is important to recognize that emotions are part of larger cultural styles of life.

In response to the deaths of others, the emotions of loss and grief may certainly be personal psychological experiences, but the cultural forms of mourning are part of a larger social and ritual pattern of action. Andaman Islanders may respond to death with dramatic displays of emotion, as each "sits down and wails and howls and the tears stream down his or her face" (Radcliffe-Brown, 1964: 117). But Javanese Islanders avoid all open displays of grief, achieving a state of *iklas*—a "willed affectlessness"—that has been described as "a calm, undemonstrative, almost languid letting go" (Geertz, 1960: 72). Such contrasts reveal as much about social styles as they do about personal emotions (Huntington and Metcalf, 1979: 23–43). Psychological analysis must also be sensitive to the social contexts of human death and dying.

Sociological Death

Demography charts the statistical characteristics of a given population. The demography of death has varied dramatically in the history of human societies (Prior, 1997). Estimates of human life expectancies suggest that the average life span was eighteen years in prehistoric societies, twenty-two years in ancient Greece and Rome, thirty-three in medieval England, thirty-five in colonial America, and forty-seven in nineteenth-century America. In the 1980s, American life expectancy at birth reached seventy-eight years for females and seventy-one years for males. Of course, these statistics are deceptive. Prehistoric cave dwellers did not all live to age eighteen and then suddenly die. Low premodern life spans were largely the result of high infant mortality rates.

Nevertheless, the decline in the rate of infant and childhood deaths and the general expectation of a long life in modern, Western societies have considerably altered the social process of dying and social responses to death. Dying has become controlled and managed by medical institutions where predictable populations (usually elderly) die in predictable places (over 75 percent of American deaths occur in a hospital or nursing home).

Furthermore, death has become a relatively rare occurrence in the social experience of most people in modern, Western societies. When the death of a relative or friend takes place, it is managed by specialists in medical and funeral industries, little disruption of the society is evident, and people tend easily to resume their social roles.

In other societies, death has been more a part of life. The event of death has been more important in defining the different roles that make up a society and has been more disruptive of the social order, requiring greater ritual efforts to restore social relations disrupted by death. The disruptive social effects of death may be easier to observe in small-scale, local, or tribal societies than in large-scale modern societies. Groups that are woven together by the bonds and obligations of kinship may be more obviously disrupted by the death of any one of their members. Society, composed of these networks of interpersonal relations, dissolves in any death but can be effectively restored by means of ritualized social practices. As we will see, ritual may function to restore a relatively unified social order that is sundered by death. Small-scale societies may put more time and effort into funeral rituals in response to their obvious disruption by death, in contrast to the relatively brief and private funeral rituals in modern, Western, industrialized societies (Parsons and Lidz, 1967).

Whereas a society may represent a relatively unified order in the face of death, it is also an order that is divided by the collective, social classification of persons. Persons are distinguished in life by social roles—age roles, gender roles, status roles—that are reinforced in a group's social responses to death. Different degrees of social disruption may occur at the deaths of different persons. The deaths of high-ranking individuals, for example, may cause greater disruption, because of the importance of their social and economic ties within the community, than the deaths of individuals of lesser rank (Binford, 1971). The death of a child, however, particularly in communities where infant and childhood mortality rates are high, may cause less disruption. When they are less integrated in the predominant social order, the deaths of children cause less disruption than those of adults, those of women less than those of men, those of the poor less than those of the wealthy, and those of slaves less than those of free persons. A direct correlation has often been noticed between the degree of community disruption by death and the energy, effort, and expense that go into the funeral rituals for that person (Tainter, 1975, 1978). Although a society may be disrupted by any death, not all deaths are experienced as equally disruptive.

Social classifications of persons, therefore, are important in the sociology of death. A social order is not only a relatively unified whole, it is also made up of stratified parts. Some classes in a society may be more likely to die: infants in preindustrial communities, the poor in Third World countries, warriors in all societies. In modern America, women have a longer life expectancy than men, unmarried women longer than married women, married men longer than unmarried men, middle class longer than poor, and whites longer than blacks. All these features of the sociology of death may indicate important differences in the ways human beings die. They also contribute to different social responses to death even within a single society. We will return to some of these considerations when examining ritual and social practices in response to death.

One final consideration in the sociology of death needs to be noted: social death. Some classifications of persons operate as functional equivalents to death in the life of a society. It has been noted that slavery, for example, operates as a type of social death (Patterson, 1982). The slave is cut off from the ties of kinship, dishonored, and often treated as a form of property. The result is a socially sanctioned elimination of the person as a fully human social person. The death of a slave may not count as a human death in slave societies because the life of a slave was not regarded as a fully human life. The identity of the slave had already been circumscribed within a social death.

Other examples of social death include banishment, excommunication, and confinement in prison, asylum, or hospital. In all these cases, the person is excluded from society, effectively becoming "dead" in social terms. Significantly, most biological deaths in modern American society are preceded by a type of social death in the institutionalized confinement of the person in a hospital or nursing home (Sudnow, 1967). Cut off from society, modern Americans experience this type of social death even before they die.

DEATH AND RELIGIOUS TRANSCENDENCE

Religious discourse and practice transform the biological, psychological, and social forms of death into patterns of transcendence. Following the suggestion made by Robert Jay Lifton, we can recognize that religious symbols of transcendence provide ways of imagining a meaningful continuity between what has gone before an individual's personal life and what can be expected to follow after. The religious symbolism of death opens and connects the human person to larger, ongoing forms of life. Not merely the denial of death, religious patterns of transcendence integrate death into human experience in meaningful ways.

The ways in which death is imagined may allow human beings to die meaningful deaths, but they also may give a certain shape to life, organize priorities, and orient human beings toward issues of ultimate meaning, significance, and urgency. Therefore, these religious patterns of transcendence not only mediate the experience of dying but also represent possibilities for authentic ways of living. Since these patterns of transcendence will appear frequently throughout this book, we will outline them only briefly here as four characteristic religious ways of symbolizing the transcendence of death: ancestral, experiential, cultural, and mythic patterns of transcendence.

Ancestral Transcendence

In the history of religions, biological death is often transformed into what we will call *ancestral transcendence*—ways of connecting the individual with a continuous biological chain of parents and offspring. Biological death may be transcended by recognizing that any human person is an integral part of a network of kinship relations. That ongoing biological continuity of family may be only apparently broken by death. Parents may live on in and through children, while children may keep alive relations with parents through specific ritual and social practices.

Those practices have sometimes been called "ancestor worship." Fathers and mothers, grandfathers and grandmothers, great-grandfathers and great-grandmothers, and so on may remain alive in the lives of their offspring. The offspring may recognize these "living dead" through rituals that remember and venerate them. This ritual recognition of ancestors may be understood to fulfill ongoing obligations of children to their parents that are not canceled by biological death. But ancestor worship also indicates a mode of transcending death by affirming that human beings live on in and through their progeny. Ancestral transcendence signifies an unbroken connection between the living and the dead.

We will examine ancestral transcendence as it has operated in small-scale communities in Australia and Africa. In Australia, each family was part of a clan. Each clan had a *totem*—a symbolic animal, plant, or object—that signified the group's shared, communal identity. Each totemic group had an ancestor who lived at the beginning of time and who originally gave the group its totem. In the beginning, that totemic ancestor set out the laws for the community, introduced ritual practices, and marked out the land as a place for human beings to live. Although dying long ago, that ancestor continued to be a living force in the life of the community. The totemic ancestor continued to hold authority over the living—over the birth of children, the initiation of children into adulthood, marriages, and the food supply that sustained the community. The clan continued to look to the ancestor for guidance in all these matters.

Contact with the ancestor occurred through dreams, through ritual, and, finally, in death. Death was understood as a return to the ancestor. In this sense, human beings might transcend death by an ongoing connection with a primordial ancestor that lived on through them and with whom they were joined in death. Ancestral transcendence in Australian aboriginal religion, as we will see, signified a unity of the living among each other, a unity of the living and the dead, and an ultimate unity that was unbroken by biological death of the living, the dead, and the primordial ancestors.

The totemic ancestor worship of Australia may be contrasted with the reverence for ancestors that we will find in traditional African religions. In most traditional African communities, ancestors played a vital role in religion, society, and even daily life. The ancestor, however, was not a cultural hero from the beginning of time but a close relative, deceased but still alive in the experience of family relations. Fathers and mothers became ancestors on their biological deaths. Without children, a person could not become an ancestor. Therefore, the biological continuity of offspring was essential to maintaining this connection between the living and the dead.

Children performed ritual services for their parents, rituals that might be understood to display the same kind of respect, reverence, and obedience that should be shown to parents during their lives. Ongoing ritual attention to parents was felt to be appropriate because, although elders might have passed through biological death, they were not dead. Deceased parents became the "living dead." They were expected to continue to exert an influence on the lives of their descendants. Ancestors lived on as moral examples but also as influential forces in the procreation and well-being of descendants in their genealogical line. Religious respect for ancestors demonstrated a transcendence of biological death in the unbroken continuity of family relations.

We will also find examples of ancestral transcendence in the so-called world religions of East and West. Ritual veneration of ancestors may be found in the Hindu *śrāddha* rituals of India, in which sacred rice balls are offered to deceased fathers, grandfathers, great-grandfathers, and ancestors. This ritual might be performed as part of a funeral service or during an annual festival for the dead. Ancestor worship is also found in Chinese and Japanese religious practices that act out an ideal of filial piety that continued to be shown to deceased parents. Household shrines might include mortuary tablets dedicated to parents, affirming the continuing presence of parents in the lives of their children. Also, larger kinship or lineage groups might hold regular observances for ancestors that reinforced their authority over the extended family of the living.

Ancestral transcendence may also appear in Judaism, Christianity, and Islam. Often called "Abrahamic religions," these traditions trace their heritage to a common ancestor, Abraham (Peters, 1982). According to the Hebrew Bible, that patriarch was given a promise by God, not a promise of personal immortality but a promise that he would live on in and through his offspring and that the extended family of his descendants would become a great nation. In the Bible, God said to Abraham, "Look up into heaven and count the stars if you can. Such will your descendants be" (Gen. 15:5). Abraham lived on through his offspring, and those offspring lived as part of his family. Ancestral transcendence, therefore, appears in different traditions in the history of religions to transform biological death into symbolic forms of connection between the living and the dead.

Experiential Transcendence

Human beings have found different ways to transcend death by imaginatively incorporating it into their experience. In the history of religions, the psychological experience of death is frequently transformed into what we will call *experiential transcendence*—profound and often intense psychological experiences that embrace death in acceptance or ecstasy. Death may be embraced by accepting it as the end of life; perhaps such an acceptance results in an experience of psychological tranquility. Or death may be embraced through intense, dramatic experiences of dying and being reborn that may occur even in life. Religious ecstasy—the experience of being transported out of the body, or out of place, or out of the world—may represent one important form of the imaginative, experiential transcendence of death.

A type of transcendence may be achieved by accepting death as the extinction of the human person. This type of experiential transcendence was recommended by the Greek philosopher Epicurus (324–270 B.C.E.) as a way of rising above death anxiety. According to Epicurus, if death is the end of consciousness, a person after death will not be conscious of pain or suffering or other traumas that people usually fear. In fact, a person will not even be aware that he or she is not aware. Simply, the person will not be. Death will not even be experienced as a loss of consciousness because there will be no consciousness to experience the loss. Therefore, death is nothing to fear because death is nothing. In the experiential transcendence Epicurus proposed, death "is of no concern to us: for while we exist death is not present, and when death is present, we no longer exist" (Kupfer, 1978).

Following this lead, the Roman philosopher Lucretius (99–55 B.C.E.) also found a type of experiential transcendence by accepting death as an extinction of consciousness in which there is nothing to fear because one will no longer exist with any capability of experiencing fear (or anything else). Like Epicurus, Lucretius derived comfort from this kind of acceptance of death (Wallah, 1976).

Beginning with the publication of her influential book *On Death and Dying*, Elisabeth Kübler-Ross argued consistently and persuasively that attitudes toward the process of dying should move from denial to acceptance. Her work has suggested that a type of experiential transcendence may be achieved by consciously accepting one's own death in the process of dying.

According to Kübler-Ross, the process of dying moves through five characteristic stages. The first stage is denial. Among the 200 dying patients Kübler-Ross interviewed for her book, most reacted to the initial awareness of having a terminal illness with the statement "No, not me; it cannot be true." At the point that denial could no longer be sustained, the second stage emerges: anger. In rage and resentment, the dying person asks, "Why me?" The third stage is bargaining. The person tries to negotiate with doctors or with God to postpone death. In the fourth stage, anger gives way to depression. In pain and increasing weakness, the dying person experiences a sense of great loss. Finally, the fifth stage is acceptance. If the dying person has had sufficient time to work through denial, anger, bargaining, and depression, Kübler-Ross concluded, "he will contemplate his coming end with a certain degree of quiet expectation." In these five stages from denial to acceptance, Kübler-Ross outlined a new art of dying that promised an experiential transcendence of death (Kübler-Ross, 1969, 1974, 1975).

Calm acceptance of death may represent one type, but other forms of religious experience suggest more intense, dynamic, and dramatic types of experiential transcendence. In the religions of many small-scale hunting societies, a person may be distinguished through special powers and techniques as a master of death, a *shaman*. A shaman is often a healer, responsible for maintaining the health and well-being of a community. Frequently, the healing practices of a shaman will involve going into a trance in which he or she may journey to the world of the dead to discern the cause of some illness or to find a soul that may be lost there.

The experience of the shaman may incorporate death in a number of important ways. The shaman may be initiated into that special religious role through an extraordinary process in which he or she "dies" and is reborn; the shaman may journey to the world of the dead on different occasions, exploring and mapping that world for the benefit of the living; and the shaman may serve as a guide for deceased persons—as *psychopomp*—on their journeys to the other world. Found in the religions of Siberia, Asia, North and South America, Africa, and Australia, these claims by shamans suggest a remarkable experiential embrace of death.

Historian of religions Mircea Eliade has called the practices of shamans "techniques of ecstasy" (1964: 4). Through trance, dreams, or other ecstatic states, the shaman leaves the body to ascend to the sky or descend to the underworld. Frequently, a shaman becomes a master of these techniques as a result of passing through an initiation that takes the form of a symbolic death and rebirth. In Australia, the anthropologist A. W. Howitt reported that in one tribe a person could become a shaman by sleeping on a grave. The spirit of the deceased visited him, seized him by the throat, opened his stomach, took out his internal organs, replaced them (perhaps with magical rock crystals), and then closed the wound. As a result of this ordeal, the person emerged reborn as a shaman (1904: 404–5).

In Africa, the anthropologist S. F. Nadel reported that one Sudanese shaman gained his power after he was struck by lightning, and, "as he put it, 'he was dead for two days'" (1946: 28–29). In many Native American religions of North America, the initiation of a shaman involved some type of physical and spiritual ordeal. Frequently, shamans described being tortured, cut to pieces, put to death, and then restored to life. This entry into death signified the supernatural reservoir of a shaman's power. "It is only this initiatory death and resurrection," Eliade noted, "that consecrates a shaman" (1964: 76).

Having entered death while still alive, the shaman became an authority on the world of the dead. Shamans traveled to that world—whether it was beyond the ocean, above the skies, or beneath the earth—and reported what they saw. The geography of the world of the dead was mapped, and the supernatural beings living there were described. "In all probability," Eliade suggested, "many features of 'funerary geography,' as well as some themes of the mythology of death, are the result of the ecstatic experiences of shamans" (1964: 509).

We will return to Australian, African, and Native American shamans in the next chapter, but it is important to note that visionary journeys through the world of the dead have played a significant role in other religious traditions. We will be examining two visionary journeys in some detail—*The Tibetan Book of the Dead* (in Chapter 4) and Dante's *Divine Comedy* (in Chapter 6)—that both resemble shamanic journeys through the world of the dead. Although one travels through a Buddhist world and the other through a Christian world, these texts carry echoes of the experiential transcendence of the shaman—embracing death through dreams, trance, ecstasy, creative imagination, and symbolic death and rebirth—to signify a transcendence of death even in life.

Cultural Transcendence

In the history of religions, the social event of death tends to be transformed into what we will call *cultural transcendence*—forms of collective memory and commemoration that keep persons alive as social persons. We have already seen this type of religious transcendence operating in ancestor worship. But cultural transcendence expands the frame of reference for memory and commemoration outward from the family, the lineage, and the clan to encompass a larger society. In studying the death rituals of southeastern Africa, the anthropologist Max Gluckman (1937) distinguished between ancestor worship and the "cult of the dead." Whereas ancestor worship was directed toward deceased relatives, the cult of the dead recalled all those who had died in the society. Cultural transcendence depends on a society's ability to remember its dead. In this regard, a person does not die by undergoing biological death; a person dies only when he or she is forgotten.

In cultural transcendence, the dead live on in the hearts, minds, and memories of the living. A kind of immortality may be achieved by living on in the collective memory of a society. This transcendence of death may lie in the immortality of the arts, sciences, or other cultural achievements that a society values. Artists, for example, may achieve a type of immortality through their work. The novelist and critic André Malraux maintained that "human continuity" is revealed through the creative arts. "More than any other activity," he suggested, "art escapes death" (Lifton, 1979: 21). The arts and sciences provide avenues for transcending death by establishing forms of cultural continuity that rise above and go beyond the life span of any individual.

Cultural transcendence may also appear in heroic acts—often acts of self-sacrifice—on behalf of a society. Death in battle has almost universally been interpreted in transcendent terms. In the Gilgamesh epic of ancient Mesopotamia, an epic poem dating back as far as 2000 B.C.E., the hero Gilgamesh reconciled himself to the possibility of his own death in battle against a monster of the forest that was threatening his city by anticipating that his death would bring him the cultural immortality of fame. "Should I fall," Gilgamesh declared, "I shall have made me a name" (Pritchard, 1958: 51). Almost 4,000 years later, President Ronald Reagan promised a cultural transcendence of death for thirty-seven sailors on the USS *Stark* who had been killed accidentally by a misguided Iraqi missile in the Persian Gulf. "These men made themselves immortal," Reagan announced, "by dying for something immortal" (*Newsweek*, June 1, 1987). From Gilgamesh to Reagan, dying in battle has been interpreted as one way of achieving a cultural transcendence of death.

Cultural transcendence, however, does not consist only of a society's arts, sciences, and histories of heroic deeds. Ritual commemorations of the dead often keep alive the collective memory that cultural transcendence depends on. As the sociologist W. Lloyd Warner noted, death rituals signify a "visible symbol of the agreement among [human beings] that they will not let each other die" (1959: 285). Death breaks but ritual remakes that agreement. Funerals, cemeteries, shrines, memorials—all are part of this agreement a culture makes to transcend death. They celebrate an ongoing cultural connection between the living and the dead.

One vivid illustration of cultural transcendence through ritual celebration may be found in the annual Mexican festival for the dead, the *Dia de los Muertos* (Beimler and Greenleigh, 1991; Green, 1980; Hellbom, 1971; Kelly, 1975). The Day of the Dead has been the high point of a celebration of death that may last several days, combining elements of both Christian and pre-Christian Aztec religious symbolism.

Before the celebration, considerable time, energy, and expense went into the preparations. Each family baked special bread—the *panes de muertos*—in stylized shapes: a body with arms crossed at the chest, a skeleton, a femur bone, or a death's heart. Sugar skulls were made in different shapes and sizes, decorated with colorful paper, and labeled with the names of both the living and the dead. These skulls were displayed in shop windows, reminiscent of the displays of skulls from ancient Aztec human sacrifices, and were exchanged as gifts, often with the name of the recipient written on the skull. They were eaten during the festival.

Beginning on October 30, the bread, skulls, food, drink, and even tobacco were placed along with garlands of yellow flowers—the Aztec color of death— on a family altar in the home. Everything enjoyed by the dead while they were alive was offered. October 30 commemorated infants who died unbaptized, October 31 commemorated all who died as children, and November 1 was the Dia de los Muertos, the day of the adult dead. The dead were believed to visit the home and partake of the offerings. Although the food was later eaten by the living, they said that it had no flavor or fragrance because its essence had been consumed by the dead. Such meals, therefore, were communions between the living and the dead.

On the Dia de los Muertos, the living paid a ceremonial visit to the cemetery. Graves were swept clean and arranged with flowers, candles, incense, and offerings of food and drink. Often, a family spent the night at the graves of its ancestors. The night might be spent in mourning, in solemn communication with the souls of the dead, as the living called on the dead to be present with them on this one day of the year.

But that night might also be spent in celebration. Mourners were warned against shedding too many tears that might make the path for the dead wet and

slippery on their annual return to the world of the living. The living participated in a fiesta of death, a celebration that played with death, poked fun at it,
and broke through many of the ordinary restraints on social life. As the poet
and novelist Octavio Paz noted, the Day of the Dead was "an experiment in
disorder, reuniting contradictory elements and principles in order to bring
about a renascence of life" (1961: 51). Order and disorder, solemnity and celebration, life and death—all were united in this annual cult of the dead in Mexican culture.

The noted Spanish writer Miguel de Unamuno once remarked that this
"cult of death" should actually be called a "cult of immortality" (Brodman,
1976). As in ancestral transcendence, the dead were "living dead" because they
continued to play important roles in the social life that defined a human community. The Dia de los Muertos combined two cultural traditions—the Christian All Souls' Day and indigenous religious symbols of sacrifice, offerings, and
communion with the dead—to fashion an annual renewal of Mexican culture
and community. Granted a cultural transcendence of death, the dead were included in a revitalized community of which they formed a vital part.

Cultural transcendence, therefore, appears in beliefs and practices that symbolize the fact that a society outlives any individual. Those beliefs and practices
allow individuals to participate in ongoing cultural connections that sustain a
society and provide a way of rising above or going beyond death.

Mythic Transcendence

Perhaps the most obvious form of religious transcendence in the face of death
is found in the ways that human beings have imagined personal survival after
death in some type of afterlife. We will call these images of afterlife *mythic transcendence*. Myths—from the Greek *muthos* ("story")—are sacred narratives.
Religions have generated a wide variety of stories concerning the nature of
life after death. Mythic transcendence lies in those stories, visions, and expectations that imaginatively transform death into a transition to another realm of
experience.

Ancestral, experiential, and cultural transcendence certainly contain mythic
elements, but the ways of imagining personal survival after death are worked
out entirely in the medium of myth. Calling expectations of personal survival
"myths" does not mean they are false; it simply means they take the form of
stories that activate the imagination. Often, mythic transcendence allows for
ways of imagining death that give shape to life and may even signify the possibility of an authentically human death.

We will be examining a wide range of myths concerning death and afterlife. Many deal with the survival of the person in a new and different place.
That place may be imagined to be on this earth. Some Australian, African, and
Native American myths of afterlife located the survival of the dead in a different
part or dimension of the same world inhabited by the living. The dead may
journey to an unknown region—a hidden forest, a distant lake, a remote
mountain, or a faraway island—that is nevertheless located on this earth. Or
the dead may be transformed into birds, animals, stones, trees, or other human
bodies and remain part of the world of the living. Or, as in the case of African

ancestors, the dead may occupy a different dimension of the world of the living, perhaps lingering around the family home, animating rain and fertility, and entering into the process of human procreation as they continue to participate in the same world in which they lived. The ancient Celtic Land of Youth (Tir na nOg), the ancient Greek Isles of the Blest in the Western Ocean, and the Chinese earthly paradise in the East were all ways of imagining survival after death in a different place that was, nevertheless, still in this world.

Many myths, however, locate the place of the dead under the earth. A subterranean world of the dead seems to follow from the widespread practice of earth burial. Sometimes that underworld is imagined as a place in which life goes on much as it did aboveground, as we will find in some of the Australian, African, and Native American myths of afterlife. But often underworld survival has been imagined as a dark region of shadows, where humans survive as shadowy traces of their former selves. The underground land of no return known as Arulla in ancient Mesopotamia, She'ol in ancient Israel, Hades in ancient Greece, and the Yellow Springs in ancient China were all underground places where the dead were reduced to a semiconscious, dreamlike afterlife in a dark and desolate world. These were not places of punishment but simply underworlds in which all human beings were reduced to shadows after death.

A third location for the survival of the person in a different place is the sky. Dating back as far as 4000 B.C.E., ancient Egyptians imagined a celestial afterlife. They imagined that some of the dead lived on with the stars in the sky and assisted the sun god on his daily journey through the heavens. A celestial afterlife was also anticipated in ancient Rome, as we find in Cicero's *Dream of Scipio,* where the souls of the dead might ascend to the heavens to achieve the immortality of the stars. Another example of a celestial afterlife appears in the Taoism of traditional China. As the Chinese religious philosophy of Taoism developed, Taoists could aspire to becoming perfected immortals, ascending to the heavenly constellations after death and taking their places in a celestial government that ruled the skies.

Finally, many myths of afterlife specify different places for different persons. After-death survival may be determined by two types of religious practice: ritual or ethics. Proper ritual disposition of the body may be required for the person to survive in a good place or condition in the next world. In ancient Egypt, for example, ritual embalming, mummification, and other procedures became essential for survival after death. Without the necessary ritual preparations and magical instructions, a person could not expect to survive in the next world. In many religious traditions, survival may be dependent on and determined by the types of rituals that are performed in the disposition of the dead.

The location of personal survival may also be determined by ethical considerations. Perhaps dating as far back as 2000 B.C.E., the Zoroastrian tradition of ancient Persia based the afterlife destiny of a person on his or her thoughts, words, and deeds during life. Heavens awaited the good, hells were reserved for the wicked. This ethical polarization of afterlife was developed in the religious traditions of Judaism, Christianity, Islam, and Buddhism to produce often vivid images of heavens, purgatories, and hells where rewards and punishments were destined for human beings based on their past actions. In those traditions, the geography of the afterlife became very elaborate: 9 heavens and 103 hells in Zoroastrianism, 14 heavens and 136 hells in Buddhism, and 7 levels of paradise and 7 levels of hell in Islam. All these locations were imagined as places that were destined for persons according to their conduct during life.

Regardless of the location, mythic transcendence tends to be based on a commitment to the survival of the person after death. Whether on earth, underground, in the sky, or in places of reward and punishment, the person is imagined to survive the death of the body. What is involved in imagining that a person survives death? Some further considerations of the nature of a human person in mythic transcendence may be necessary to bring the notion of afterlife into clearer focus.

Continuity Earlier we noted that a person may be regarded as a human animal, a conscious agent, and a social person but also as a being that lives in a world made meaningful by religious symbolism. In the forms of mythic transcendence we will be encountering, two ways of symbolizing the continuity of a person from life into afterlife may appear: cognitive and forensic continuity.

In cognitive terms, a person may be said to be the same person in life as in afterlife on account of the survival of a continuous consciousness. Consciousness orients the person in time—with memory of the past, awareness of the present, and anticipations of the future. In life, memory may play the most important role in creating a sense of having a continuous personal identity. Although it may not be possible to remember every discrete event, memory is nevertheless capable of stringing events together into a relatively coherent narrative. That narrative, or life story, gives the impression that a person has been the *same* person from moment to moment, the *same* person in the past as in the present, having a continuous, uninterrupted identity.

When death interrupts that life story, mythic transcendence may find ways of imagining its continuity after death. A cognitive definition of that continuity will emphasize the survival of consciousness, particularly the survival of the faculty of memory that is able to bridge the transition of death. Consciousness may change, but it nevertheless continues. However, in order to say that personal identity continues after death, some kind of memory is important.

Religious myths of afterlife elaborate on the theme of memory—rivers of memory and forgetfulness, mirrors of self-recognition, reunions with remembered loved ones, recollections of past lives, and other modulations of memory frequently appear in stories of the personal survival of death. Loss of memory, on the other hand, may signify the loss of identity, perhaps absorbing personality into some corporate or cosmic whole. In all these cases, memory is important because it is that faculty of consciousness that gives the impression that a person has one continuous identity. Memory performs this function in life; it also performs this function in many myths of the transcendence of death.

Forensic continuity implies a definition of a person that is framed in legal terms. A forensic definition of a person is based on some notion of continuous personal responsibility for actions. Forensic continuity is personal responsibility for actions and their consequences. A person is the *same* person from moment to moment because of this personal responsibility. As a human actor, a person may experience consequences from past actions, may be held responsible for present actions, and may be rewarded or punished for those actions in the future.

Personal identity, in this sense, is based on a continuous responsibility for acts that are assumed to be performed by the same person. As the philosopher John Locke argued, personal identity can be seen as a "forensic term, appropriate to actions and their merit" (Flew, 1974). Whereas a cognitive definition of personal identity insists on a continuity of consciousness and memory, a forensic definition is concerned with continuous responsibility for conscience, will, and action.

Forensic concerns often appear in the mythic transcendence of death. Personal survival may be symbolized in terms of an afterlife judgment of the dead (Brandon, 1967). The postmortem ordeal, the weighing of a person's deeds or heart in the balance, the reading from the Book of Life, the appearance before the throne of a divine judge, the separation of the wicked from the righteous, the experience of consequences from past actions, and other forms of personal judgment figure prominently in many myths of the afterlife. They are based on a forensic definition of human continuity: Persons are the same persons after death as they were in life because they may be held responsible for their actions.

If human beings are regarded as individual conscious agents, we can expect both forms of continuity—cognitive and forensic—to appear in mythic transcendence. But we should be prepared for their appearance in many different forms. Some ways of imagining survival will emphasize disjuncture, rather than continuity, in the afterlife. Individuals may survive with radically diminished consciousness, faded memories, and only minimal responsibility for past actions and scope for future actions. Or they might survive with a higher consciousness, expanded memory, and greater scope for action. On the other hand, some forms of mythic transcendence dissolve personal identity entirely, eliminating any trace of personal consciousness or will.

But in those stories that develop the theme of personal survival, we will find some placing greater emphasis on cognitive continuity, while others depict the continuity of personal identity primarily in forensic terms. The Buddhist mythic transcendence of death found in *The Tibetan Book of the Dead,* for example, will symbolize the transition through dying as a series of changes in consciousness. Transcendence of death, in these terms, is based on both continuity and change in awareness as a person passes through the extraordinary challenges that a human consciousness can expect to face in the afterlife.

By contrast, the Christian mythic transcendence described in Dante's *Divine Comedy* maps out the world of the dead in forensic terms, charting the different degrees of punishment and reward for past actions that can be expected in hell, purgatory, and heaven. Conscience, rather than consciousness, appears as the most important factor in determining the fate of a person after death. Although both visionary journeys through the world of the dead treat human beings as conscious agents—imagining the continuity of the person in both cognitive and forensic terms—they differ in the degree to which they emphasize the importance of consciousness or conscience in the transcendence of death.

Survival Mythic transcendence, therefore, appears in the different ways human beings have found to imagine survival after biological death. After the death of the body, the person is nevertheless imagined to continue. That continuity, however, must be in some other form. Four forms of survival have been characteristic in the history of religions:

1. *Disembodied spirit.* The person survives with consciousness and will but without any bodily form. Personal survival may be symbolized as a shadow, a shade, a trace, an afterimage, an ether, or a spirit, but in all these cases the person is imagined to continue to exist independent of a body. In philosophical terms, the independence of mind, soul, or spirit from the body has been called Platonic–Cartesian dualism, because the philosophers Plato (427–347 B.C.E.) and René Descartes (1596–1650) argued that the immortal mind exists independently and, therefore, survives the death of the mortal body.

2. *Spiritual embodiment.* The person survives death in some form of spiritual, ethereal, astral, or subtle body. That spiritual body may be imagined as part of the ordinary embodiment of a person in life, but it is a body that is eventually separated from the physical body in death.

3. *Reincarnation.* The person survives by being born again in a different physical body. A person may have lived through a sequence of lifetimes, occupying different human bodies like moving through a series of different homes. Although there are significant differences, both Hindu and Buddhist forms of mythic transcendence imagine survival through a series of births. A special case of this form of survival, transmigration, may also recognize the possibility that human beings might be born again in animal, plant, or other life forms.

4. *Resurrection.* The person survives by being born again in the same physical body. The resurrection of the dead in Judaism, Christianity, and Islam is imagined as a return to life in the same physical body the person occupied during his or her lifetime. That body might be transformed or spiritualized, but it is restored as the same recognizable form.

These ways of imagining personal survival become more complex in living religious communities and traditions. In some cases they may be combined, and in others they may be provisional forms of personal survival to be overcome in an ultimate extinction of the personality. Nevertheless, disembodied spirit, spiritual embodiment, reincarnation, and resurrection are the basic possibilities that appear in mythic transcendence for symbolizing a personal survival of the death of the physical body.

Each of these modes of survival is imagined to be independent of the body that the deceased animated during life. The body dies, but the person lives on through some different form of survival. Important philosophical challenges to any expectation of surviving biological death have been offered. These challenges begin with the assumption that a human being is necessarily an embodied being. Even the mental activity of consciousness and will is necessarily embodied. Three ways of formulating this assumption that a person is an embodied person have been suggested.

First, philosophers have argued that mental activity depends on the functioning of a physical organism, the brain. The notion that the mental activities of consciousness and will are dependent on brain function has often been called *epiphenomenalism*. Mind is regarded as an epiphenomenon, or secondary effect, of the biological functions of the brain. The philosopher Bertrand Russell argued that "what we regard as our mental life is bound up with brain structure and organized bodily energy." In other words, mental activity depends on a living brain and neural system. The brain does not survive death. Its electrochemical energy ceases with the death of the body. "Therefore," Russell concluded, "it is rational to suppose that mental life ceases when bodily life ceases." Such a conclusion would eliminate any possibility of personal survival after death (Russell, 1925: 6–7).

Second, a stronger version of this argument is found in the philosophical position of *materialism*. Philosophers such as D. M. Armstrong (1968), J. J. C. Smart (1970), and Antony Flew (1976) have argued that mental activity is not only dependent on brain function, it *is* brain function. All mental activity, from thinking to dreaming, is simply electrochemical processes in the brain. Mind is physical, a result of neurological charges in the brain. It cannot be regarded as an immaterial or independent essence of the person. Therefore, according to the materialists, when the brain dies, mental activity must certainly cease. Nothing remains that might survive the death of the body.

A third argument that insists on the necessary relation between a person and a body is based on the analysis of the ordinary language that is used to talk about people. In ordinary language, all the terms used to discuss mental activity presuppose a physical body. Mental activities such as knowing ("seeing the point"), communicating ("speaking your mind"), loving ("heartwarming emotion"), and nervousness ("butterflies in the stomach") all presuppose a physical body that is the locus for these activities of consciousness and will. Even the most basic orientation of human consciousness in the world—the awareness of up and down, front and back, left and right, inside and outside—is based on the physical body. Therefore, a disembodied person is unimaginable. From this perspective, the phrase "person without a body" is a nonsense statement. It would be like saying "square circle." A person is necessarily an embodied person (Hobbes, 1909: 34–45; Wittgenstein, 1953: sec. 390).

These philosophical arguments drawn from epiphenomenalism, materialism, and language analysis challenge any belief in transcendence through a personal survival of the death of the body. From all three perspectives, the notion of a disembodied spirit is regarded as an impossible and incoherent idea. The idea of mental activity without a body is regarded as nonsense, so any mythic transcendence of death through a disembodied spirit, soul, or mind is ruled out of the question.

The notion of a spiritual embodiment fares little better. A spiritual body would be like a physical body—having size, shape, position, and dimensions that would perhaps allow for many of the human functions that depend on a body—but it would be unlike a physical body in that it would not be able to be easily detected through ordinary sense perception. If this spiritual body is not like the physical bodies that we recognize as bodies, what sense does it make to call it a body? How would a spiritual body that could not be seen, heard, or otherwise detected be different from an imaginary body, a fantasy body, or no body at all?

Beliefs in reincarnation and resurrection present a special problem. Not only do they require that the person survive the death of the body, they involve a reproduction of the person in another time and place—in another physical embodiment—that might make it difficult to conclude that the new person was the same as the old person who had lived before. Beliefs in reincarnation or resurrection may require the kinds of cognitive and forensic continuity that we discussed in the previous section in order to make sense as forms of personal survival. They may require a continuity of memory and responsibility in order to establish that the reincarnated or resurrected person is the same person as the one who lived before. But these beliefs are still vulnerable to the philosophical arguments that insist a person cannot survive the death of the body.

In response to those arguments, research in the field of parapsychology has sought evidence to prove that mental activity can occur independent of the body. Materialist philosophers may remain unconvinced by the alleged evidence (Flew, 1987a). But one materialist admitted that even if a single example of paranormal mental activity were found to be genuine, the conclusions of materialism would be shown to be false (Campbell, 1970: 91). In concluding this introduction to mythic transcendence, it may be useful to look briefly at some of the areas in which evidence has been alleged to prove the independence of mental activity from the body.

Evidence Throughout the history of religions, shamans, mystics, prophets, and other religious visionaries have claimed access to extraordinary experiences beyond the ordinary limits of the body. Extrasensory perceptions in trance states, ecstatic out-of-body transports, and mystical visions of alternative realities are among the many kinds of extraordinary experiences described in the myth and literature of religious traditions. With respect to death, these are examples of what we have been calling experiential transcendence—rising above or going beyond the limitations of the body. They suggest the possibility of a transcendence of death even in life.

Recently, evidence of similar extraordinary experience has been marshaled by the discipline of parapsychology. Attempts have been made to document the occurrence of mental activity independent of the body by means of methods that claim scientific validity. While skepticism may be justified, many investigators have been convinced that parapsychology provides new evidence for life after death. The philosopher C. D. Broad, for example, admitted that the relevant normal facts do not suggest a survival of mental activity after death. But on the other hand, Broad concluded, "There are many quite well attested *paranormal* phenomena which strongly suggest such persistence, and a few which strongly suggest the fullblown survival of a human personality" (1962: 430). Paranormal evidence has been collected in three basic areas: extrasensory perception, out-of-body experiences, and near-death experiences. Extraordinary experiences in these three areas have suggested to some investigators evidence of mental activity beyond the body and the likelihood of survival beyond death.

In response to the widespread nineteenth-century enthusiasm for spiritualism, societies for psychical research were established in Europe and America to investigate evidence of extrasensory perception (ESP). Trance mediums claiming clairvoyant powers were subjected to empirical tests. The object of this research was to study by the methods of science all mental phenomena—real or alleged—for which there was no available scientific explanation. At the very least, ESP seemed to suggest the possibility of mental activity independent of the ordinary sensory channels of the body.

In addition to extrasensory perceptions about the living, trance mediums claimed to have mental contact with the dead. Psychic sessions with acclaimed trance mediums such as Mrs. Piper and Mrs. Leonard included contacts with deceased people apparently unknown to the mediums. Although these sessions were explained by some investigators as examples of telepathy with the minds of living people who had known the deceased, or simply as cleverly staged hoaxes, other investigators were convinced that the ESP of the mediums indicated the possibility of contact with the disembodied minds of the dead (Brandon, 1983).

ESP research claiming scientific status continues to be conducted, gathering alleged evidence of spirit apparitions, electronic voice recordings, poltergeists, and mediumistic trance channeling that are all purported to demonstrate human survival of death (Berger, 1987). If such evidence is accepted, it may support two conclusions—that mental activity can operate independent of the body and that disembodied minds can survive death.

A second type of evidence examined by parapsychology has been out-of-body experience (OBE). An OBE is an experience in which a person seems to perceive the world from a position other than that occupied by the body. These experiences may be of two types: autoscopic (in which the person has out-of-body perceptions of this world) or transcendental (in which the person claims out-of-body perceptions of another reality). Certainly, this latter, transcendental type of experience has been characteristic of the reports of religious mystics who claim to have ascended out of their bodies into another reality. The second-century Hellenistic philosopher Plotinus, for example, claimed that many times he was lifted out of his body. Above and beyond the ordinary world, Plotinus experienced a sense of oneness with the divine before descending back again to the body (*Enneads* IV,8,1; Plotinus, 1964: 62). But parapsychology has tried to examine such mystical claims scientifically as evidence of mental activity outside the body and therefore as evidence for the survival of death.

In the 1960s, OBE researcher Robert Crookall collected accounts from people who claimed to have had an OBE, or "astral projection," recording 160 descriptions in one book (1961) and 222 in another (1964). Crookall argued that if "astral projection is true and soul is distinct from body, survival is to be expected" (1964: 12).

Descriptive accounts have been supplemented by tests that claim to scientifically validate the occurrence of OBEs. In his *Journeys out of the Body*

(1972), Robert Monroe described how he began his experiments in OBE with repeated intentional inhalations of the fumes of contact cement. He proceeded to self-hypnosis and finally developed techniques that he claimed would induce OBEs. Those experiences were subjected to an allegedly scientific testing that revealed that during an OBE the person's brain energy, measured in a narrow frequency span, unusual galvanic skin response registered, and other strange physiological features could be recorded. These measurable observations seemed to provide scientific confirmation of descriptive accounts of OBEs that would support the assumption that human beings can be expected to survive the death of the body.

Perhaps the most popular research claiming scientific status in this field has been the study of near-death experiences (NDEs). Interest in NDE was stimulated by the extraordinary reports collected by Raymond Moody (1975) from people who were declared clinically dead yet survived. Assembling a composite model of their experiences, Moody identified key elements in an NDE: hearing a loud buzzing or ringing noise; feeling transported through a long, dark tunnel; seeing deceased loved ones; meeting a "being of light"; reviewing the course of one's life; feeling forced to return; and coming back with feelings of joy, love, and peace.

Subsequent scientific research has confirmed the prevalence of extraordinary experience in near-death events. Cardiologist Michael Sabom (1981), for example, determined that about 40 percent of near-death survivors reported some kind of extraordinary experience. Sabom found a marked decrease in death anxiety and increase in afterlife belief among those who underwent an NDE.

Research and literature on NDE have proliferated (Berman, 1996; Ring, 1980, 1984; Gallup and Proctor, 1982). Some researchers have even argued that these NDEs provide conclusive evidence of life after death. Others, however, have raised the objection that NDE evidence is still obtained in life, no matter how near to death. Those extraordinary experiences, therefore, cannot be treated as if they were reports from people who have returned from the dead (Cherry, 1986).

What counts as evidence for survival after death? In religious traditions, the story of Jesus' resurrection might count as evidence for the possibility of resurrection for Christians; the story of the Buddha's recollection of all his past lives might count as evidence for the possibility of acquiring such memory for Buddhists. In other words, myths are used as evidence to support mythic transcendence. The research on ESP, OBE, and NDE, however, uses a new story—science—to validate and reinforce old myths of the transcendence of death. Scientific methods and standards are invoked to defend what in the past might have been regarded as claims to religious experience. No scientific consensus, however, has emerged on the subject. Many would probably still agree with Bertrand Russell that a proper scientific conclusion would be that mental activity ends with the cessation of brain function. Nevertheless, parapsychology continues to be a vital field of investigation because it seems to provide a bridge between old myths of transcendence and the newer mythic framework of science.

Mythic transcendence, however, has not operated in the history of religions under the scrutiny of scientific investigation. In other words, the survival of death has not traditionally been regarded as a proposition to be confirmed or refuted by evidence. Beliefs in life after death have flourished in living religious traditions as part of a context of religious beliefs and practices animating a human community. In order to understand mythic transcendence, it is necessary to locate it in the larger context of religious practices relating to death and dying in the history of religions.

DEATH AND RELIGIOUS PRACTICES

Religions cultivate specific practices relating to the process of dying and the event of death. Arts of dying have been developed in religious traditions as practical ways of making that transition. Involving more than attitudes, these arts of dying may include important ritual preparations for the experience of dying. Although death may stand outside human experience as its limit, the process of dying is experienced within life. We can begin considering religious practices of death and dying by looking briefly at the art of dying.

Arts of Dying

Religious arts of dying involve preparations for death. Since death is possible at any moment, a religious tradition may encourage people to be constantly prepared. More specifically, however, preparation for death may take the form of rituals to be performed during the process of dying. Two arts of dying may serve as illustrations of the ritual preparation for death, one Christian, the other Buddhist.

A Christian Art of Dying During the Middle Ages in Europe, the Roman Catholic tradition developed an art of dying—the *ars moriendi*—that assumed the character of a ceremony of death. Dying was a ritual orchestrated by the dying person. Lying on his or her back so as to face toward heaven, the dying person conducted this ritual in the presence of family, friends, and neighbors while being assisted by a priest or priests. Death was the last sacrament, the final sacred ritual act in a human life.

The *ars moriendi* involved certain characteristic elements that can be arranged in a composite picture of this ritual preparation for death. The dying person made a profession of faith, attesting to his or her allegiance to the Christian religion. Because that faith was something to be demonstrated in the social context of family and community, the dying person was expected to make peace with the living before making the transition into death. The dying person asked forgiveness from survivors and pardoned those who might have done some wrong. Often priest confessors, sometimes accompanied by lawyers and notaries, assisted the dying person in resolving more practical affairs—the inheritance of property, provisions for family, and gifts to the poor. Customarily, donations were made on behalf of survivors to the church. These acts were part of a public ceremony of reconciliation that would allow the dying person to leave the world of the living in peace.

As the end drew near, three final ritual practices were enacted. A priest heard the last confession of sins and gave absolution. In the last communion, or viaticum, a priest administered the eucharist of bread and wine to the dying person. After this preparation of the soul for its journey, the final ritual of extreme unction anointed the body with oil and commended the soul to God. At the end, the reciting of prayers and singing of hymns culminated in a final prayer for that soul in the hope of eternal life. After the final prayer, the dying person was prepared for death and could wait in silence for the end (Ariès, 1981: 14–18; McManners, 1985: 234–50; Paxton, 1990).

A Buddhist Art of Dying While Christians in Europe were practicing an art of dying that would allow them to depart life with a peaceful conscience, Buddhists in Tibet were developing a different art of dying. As we have already noted, emphasis in the Tibetan Buddhist approach to dying was on consciousness. The Buddhist art of dying developed in Tibet was designed to effect a transfer of consciousness from the body.

The dying person may have devoted a lifetime to meditation practices, training the consciousness to perceive other levels of reality. The art of dying was also a type of meditation practice. Images and sounds were used to focus the person's attention during the transition through death. The dying person was surrounded by sacred pictures of the Buddha and other divine beings. If the person had been guided in meditation practices in life by a teacher, a picture of that guru was also placed by the deathbed. More than pictures of religious exemplars, these images were considered to be powerful aids in raising the consciousness above the dying body. Focus on sacred images encouraged a calm and controlled consciousness in preparation for death.

As the person lay dying, priests chanted sacred sounds and prayers, called *mantras,* into the dying person's ear. The mantra *om muni muni maha muni ye svaha* assisted the dying person in maintaining self-control over the mind. The supreme mantra in Tibetan Buddhist meditation practice, *om mani padme hum,* was the last sound the dying person was to hear. The repetition of these sounds focused consciousness, controlling negative thoughts and desires, so that the person could pass freely through the dying process. Even after consciousness had left the body, a priest might still guide the person through death by reading instructions and reciting prayers that would aid the person in moving through the extraordinary experiences of the afterlife.

The Tibetan Buddhist art of dying placed great importance on a person's last thoughts before death. Those final thoughts indicated the state of mind in which the person died. Since afterlife was determined by consciousness, those last thoughts also indicated what kind of future life could be expected for the person after death. Every element of the ritual of dying, therefore, was designed to produce a calm, controlled, and focused consciousness. Although the prayers of priests and family might assist, the individual's focused consciousness was the essential ingredient in a successful passage through death. That consciousness may have been trained through years of meditation, but it was ultimately tested in the art of dying (Mullin, 1986: 78–79; Rinpoche, 1992).

Arts of dying, therefore, represent practical contexts within which religious beliefs about dying, death, and afterlife may be experienced. Both Christian and Buddhist practices assisted the dying in their confrontations with death, but they clearly emphasized different concerns. The Christian art of dying prepared a peaceful conscience, whereas the Buddhist art of dying cultivated a focused consciousness. Nevertheless, they both supported a process of dying that affirmed the integrity of the person within the context of a religious community and allowed a person to die a fully human death with the support of that community.

Rituals of Death

After a person dies, ritual practices mark the importance of that death in the life of a community. Many different ritual activities may enact a community's response to death: the treatment and disposal of the corpse, the funeral rituals, memorials, commemorations, and shrines for the dead. These practices demonstrate a commitment to the deceased person as a social person. They include the deceased in a society that encompasses both the living and the dead. Ritual practices of inclusion are essential to any cultural transcendence of death.

Any death may be ritually marked as representing simultaneously two kinds of events in a community: a passage and a crisis. Since death is both a personal passing and a social crisis, ritual practices that respond to death may be regarded as rites of passage and rites of crisis.

Rites of Passage Death rituals are rites of passages that symbolize a change from one state of existence to another, from life to death. In this regard, death rituals can be compared to other rites of passage—birth, adulthood, and marriage—that symbolically mark a change from an old status to a new status in the life cycle. Passage from unborn to born, from child to adult, or from single to married may also be symbolized as ritualized transitions involving death to the old and a rebirth to a new status. But death tends to be a particularly intense, highly charged transition in the life cycle. Death rites of passage, therefore, may require tremendous effort, energy, and expenditure to ensure that the deceased continues to be included as a social person in the community.

The basic pattern of all rites of passage was outlined by the anthropologist Arnold van Gennep, who argued in his *Rites of Passage* that "beneath a multiplicity of forms, either consciously expressed or merely implied, a typical pattern always recurs: *the pattern of the rites of passage*" (1960: 191). That pattern has three stages: separation, transition, and incorporation. In the rite of passage, the person is separated from his or her old status in the community in order to be reincorporated in a new status. In between, however, lies a period of transition, a crossing of a boundary, in which the person is neither in the old status or in the new. Death rituals bridge that transition period in which the person is not recognized as living yet not fully incorporated into the world of the dead.

The first stage in the rite of passage is marked by rituals of separation. These practices separate the deceased from the world of the living. Rituals of separation focus on the corpse, moving it outside the home, washing, anointing, embalming, or otherwise preparing it, and employing some method for its disposal, whether earth burial, cremation, or exposure. The body of the deceased is separated not only from the living but also from possessions, which may be burned or buried or distributed among survivors. Also during this first stage, the body is separated from whatever nonphysical, immaterial remnant of the person is believed to survive after death. But at this point in the rite of passage, that surviving soul may not be regarded as fully included in the world of the dead.

Beginning with the stage of separation, mourners may observe special restraints on conduct, and, particularly, close relatives and associates of the deceased may suspend ordinary social activities. The suspension of daily life characterizes the second stage in the rite of passage—the transition stage—in which both the mourners and the dead enter into what van Gennep called a "special world." For the mourners, this stage of transition involves a type of social death in which ordinary social life stops. This period of suspended animation links the mourners with the deceased in the social event of death. Mourners may wear special clothing, refrain from certain foods, and observe other regulations and prohibitions. While personal feelings of loss, grief, or bereavement may be expressed, the period of transition is determined by social practices that create this special world shared by the living with the dead on the boundary between life and death.

In this transition stage (or what van Gennep called the *liminal* stage), survivors observe ritual practices of mourning. Color symbolism may indicate this special world of death. The use of black to symbolize death has wide distribution, but some cultures may use white or red or yellow to indicate the transition period of mourning (Turner, 1967). Hair may be regarded as a symbol of life to be specially treated, either to be cut off or to remain uncut for the duration of the period of transition (Leach, 1958). Percussion, noise, and music may also be employed in rituals to symbolize movement through the transition of death (Needham, 1967). These and other practices are performed to mark out the crossing of the boundary between life and death, during a period in which the deceased is neither in one world or the other.

That transition period may last for varying lengths of time. Its duration tends to be determined by three factors. First, mourners may remain in this phase until the deceased is believed to be incorporated into the world of the dead. Mourning may last for as long as the soul is thought to take in reaching the world of the ancestors and in being accepted in that world. Second, the duration of the transition period may depend on the kinship or social ties to the deceased. Closer relatives may observe longer periods of mourning. Finally, the transition may last longer and have wider effect if the deceased has important social standing in the community. In response to the deaths of leaders, chiefs, or kings, the suspension of ordinary life may affect an entire society, and the period of mourning may be of longer duration (van Gennep, 1960: 147–48).

At the end of that period of transition, rites of passage are completed by rituals of incorporation. Frequently, a ritual of incorporation will take the form of a ceremonial meal after funerals and at commemorations for the dead. That meal reunites the survivors as a group but may also be understood to be shared by the deceased. Prayers, songs, and dances may be performed to anticipate and to celebrate the successful incorporation of the deceased into the afterlife. But the reincorporation of the deceased into the ongoing social life of the community may be symbolized by cemeteries, memorials, and commemorative celebrations that keep the memory of the person alive and thereby allow the person to live on as a social person in a cultural transcendence of death.

Rites of Crisis Practical efforts to reincorporate the deceased into an ongoing human society that includes both the living and the dead suggest that death rituals respond to the crisis of social disruption that occurs with any death. Because a community is made out of the social relations of its members, a community itself "dies" when any one of its members dies. Death rituals can be understood as rites of crisis, working to restore a community by reviving the social relations through which a community lives and by reconnecting social relations broken by death.

Robert Hertz observed the disruptive effect that the crisis of death has on human societies. "When a [person] dies," Hertz noted, "society loses . . . much more than a unit; it is stricken in the very principle of life, in the faith it has in itself" (1960: 78). Ritual practices that attend death are designed to renew the life of a society and reaffirm that faith in its ongoing, collective existence. Hertz focused on three basic elements in funeral ritual: the corpse, the soul, and the mourners. Although he drew his examples from one small-scale community, the Ngaju Dyak of Borneo, Hertz concluded that rituals of death may weave these three elements together to restore the fabric of any society torn by death.

After a death, the Ngaju Dyak did not immediately inter the corpse in its final place of burial. The body was kept during an extended wake, either in the home, in a miniature wooden house, or on a small platform covered by a roof. The corpse remained in that place until the flesh fell away from the skeleton and the bones became dry. The body was kept in isolation while the soul was believed to be making its journey to the world of the dead. The Dyak believed that the progress of the soul was indicated by the decomposition of the body. While the corpse was still decomposing, the soul was thought to linger around or return to its old home. During this period, the mourners had to show care for the body. They washed the body, kept watch over it, brought offerings of food, and beat gongs to drive away evil spirits. But the body was also perceived as a source of impurity and danger from which the mourners had to be protected by special ritual precautions. In fact, their ordinary social activities were restricted by ritual prohibitions on their behavior while the corpse of the deceased decomposed.

Finally, a great feast marked the burial of the bones in their final resting place and the end of the period of mourning. Performed months after the person died, this final ceremony also united the corpse, the soul, and the mourners: It provided the final burial for the deceased, it confirmed the soul's entrance into the land of the dead, and it set the living free from the obligations of mourning to resume their normal lives.

The great feast lasted for days or even weeks. Reduced to dried and cleaned bones, the body was no longer an object of danger to be feared. The bones were treated with pride as they were deposited with elaborate ceremony in their final place of rest. The crisis of the body was over. The body had been a defiling presence in the community. It had been regarded as impure not in terms of hygiene but in the terms that the anthropologist Mary Douglas has defined ritual impurity, as "matter out of place" (1966). At the great feast, the corpse was no longer impure because it was finally in its proper place. That site of final burial provided an appropriate place for the body because it was felt both to separate the survivors from that corpse and to provide a safe place for them to contact and commemorate the deceased.

With the final burial of the bones, the crisis of the soul was also over. The wandering soul was now felt to be firmly established in the village of the dead, reunited with the family ancestors. The celebrants enacted the triumph of the soul at the great feast. With prayers and songs, they called on the divine guide of the dead, the psychopomp Tempon Telon, to escort the soul to its new home. Dancing, sweating, and foaming at the mouth in ritual frenzy, a shaman described the journey to the world of the dead. As the bones were deposited in the family burial place, the soul of the deceased was imagined to rejoin the ancestors.

Finally, the feast itself ended the period of mourning and allowed relatives to return to the normal life of their society. The crisis of the mourners was over. Their association with the dead, which had set them apart from the rest of the community, came to an end with this final communal meal. Relatives bathed in a river and sacrificed animals to symbolize their new purity. During the funeral banquets, they were free to interact with other people, as the entire community joined in the celebration. Having passed successfully through the crisis of death, the mourners were able to return to their ordinary lives in a restored community.

Death rituals, therefore, respond to the crises posed by the corpse, by the soul, and by the mourners. Each is involved in different ways in the event of death, but the crises posed by each are resolved for the community as a whole through ritual practices. The practices of the Ngaju Dyak described and analyzed by Robert Hertz show the ritual resolution of death in a small-scale community. The crisis of death and its resolution may be easier to observe in a small society woven together by close ties of kinship than in large-scale, mass societies. Nevertheless, death rituals may also function in larger societies to respond to the crisis of death and to restore some sense of a human community that includes both the living and the dead.

Rites of Exclusion Among the Ngaju Dyak, Robert Hertz also noticed a kind of ritual practice that excluded certain persons from society. Some persons were not woven back into the fabric of society through the usual means of death rituals but were excluded in death. For reasons of low social status, or for violating the ethical order of the community, or because they may have died in ways considered unnatural—such as through suicide, drowning, being struck by lightning, or dying in childbirth—the deaths of some persons were attended by rituals of exclusion. In these cases, "death will be eternal," Hertz noted, "because society will always maintain towards these accursed individuals the attitude of exclusion that it adopted from the first" (1960: 86). Rather than restoring them to a renewed society that embraces the living and the dead, rituals of exclusion permanently separate some persons from that circle of humanity.

Exclusion requires practices that are contrary to the customary rituals of inclusion. Rites of exclusion often reverse the usual funeral practice. They cremate when they would otherwise bury; they bury when they would otherwise cremate. Some Central American groups, for example, were reported to dispose of their dead by earth burial, but the bodies of criminals were laid out exposed on the ground. Native Americans in Alaska practiced death rituals in which the corpse was broiled with oil, moss, and driftwood, but the bodies of criminals were exposed to rot. In these cases, whether the normal way of disposing of the body was burial or cremation, the rite of exclusion required that the body simply be left exposed on the ground (Frazer, 1913–24: I:399–400).

Exposure of the body, however, is not a necessary ingredient in every rite of exclusion. In the case of the Hidatasa Sioux of North America, exposure was the usual practice; they normally disposed of the dead by placing the corpse on a scaffold. Murderers, however, were excluded from the human community in death; their bodies were the only ones that were buried in the ground (Bendann, 1930: 219). Therefore, rites of exclusion do not merely show a neglect of the dead. They indicate specific practices performed on the corpses of certain persons to exclude them from the human society of the living and the dead.

Returning to the Ngaju Dyak of southern Borneo fifty years after Robert Hertz had examined their funeral rituals, another observer confirmed their practice of ritual exclusion. Hans Schärer reported that the community held slaves, who had no genealogy of ancestors and no hope of any afterlife in the village of the dead. Unable to trace a lineage of ancestors, these slaves were denied what we have called ancestral transcendence. They had no symbolic connection with a continuous biological line made up of parents and children that would remain unbroken by death. Furthermore, the slaves were denied what we have called mythic transcendence by the dominant belief in the community that slaves had no place in the afterlife world of the dead. Cut off from a fully human past, and cut off from a fully human future, these slaves were "buried without ceremony," Schärer observed, "far outside in the bush or the forest" (1963: 44). In this case, a rite of exclusion eliminated an entire class of persons—slaves—from the cultural transcendence of death provided by the normal ritual practices of the community. Denied a human status in life, these slaves were excluded from the circle of humanity in death.

Rites of exclusion underscore the importance of death rituals in reconstructing a human community in the face of death. They reinforce a dominant image of a community, defining it by what it excludes. Such practices have been found not just in remote, exotic, or so-called primitive societies. In medieval Europe, for example, criminals, heretics, and suicides were all denied burial in the sanctified space of a Christian church, churchyard, or cemetery. After death, their bodies were dragged through the streets, put on display, tortured, and burned rather than buried. As the historian Philippe Ariès noted, the corpses of these social outcasts "were left in the fields, or, as the place was later called, the dump" (1981: 42). These were not human dead to be reincorporated but garbage to be eliminated through a rite of exclusion.

In more recent history, the United States held slaves who were denied a fully human status. Visiting America in 1831–32, the French sociologist Alexis de Tocqueville observed American social institutions, including the practices of slavery. A slave's "inferiority is continued to the very confines of the other world," Tocqueville reported. "When the Negro dies, his bones are cast aside, and the distinction of condition prevails even in the equality of death" (1967: I:374).

Rituals of death, therefore, are practical experiments in creating human identity within a human community. They are rites of passage that allow for the transition of a person from an old status to a new status, while at the same time they are rites of crisis that restore a community threatened by dissolution at the death of any of its members. As both Arnold van Gennep and Robert Hertz suggested, religious beliefs about the personal survival of death make sense only within these practical, ritual, and social contexts. Beliefs in personal survival cannot be treated in isolation but must be appreciated within the context of practices that allow human beings to die human deaths within a human community.

RELIGION, DEATH, AND DYING

A human person is multidimensional: a human animal, a conscious agent, and a social person. These are the biological, psychological, and sociological dimensions of personal identity. In addition, those dimensions may be made meaningful by religious symbolism. Human beings are symbol-using, -owning, and -operating beings. By definition, religion is the context within which the most crucial symbolic activities of human life are conducted. Religion is not merely a matter of belief; it also involves more dynamic practices that act out what it means to be a human being in relation to other human beings. Through beliefs, actions, and interactions, religions conduct experiments in being human.

Since a human life is multidimensional, a human death must also be appreciated on several different levels. A human death is not merely the cessation of certain biological functions. It is also a psychological event for each individual and a social event for every community.

Sigmund Freud insisted that a healthy psychological approach to death depended on accepting death as the extinction of the person. Freud regarded any other attitude as an unhealthy denial or avoidance of reality. But the Freudian analyst Robert Jay Lifton countered Freud by observing that human beings required symbols of transcendence in order to die genuinely human deaths. Not merely symptoms of denial, avoidance, or numbing, symbols of transcendence allow a healthy affirmation of human connections to family, community, culture, nature, or perhaps the universe even when those connections seem to be broken by death. Symbolic connections allow human beings to die authentically human deaths and to acknowledge the humanity of others when they die.

Human deaths are not isolated events; they occur within specific social contexts. Societies are divided by social classifications—gender, age, status, wealth, ethnicity, and so on—that affect where, when, and how different people die within a single society. In addition, certain persons may be excluded from full participation in society, relegated to a condition of social death even while they are alive. For all these divisions, however, a society forms a relatively unified whole in the face of death. Since society is an abstraction for a network of interpersonal relations, every society is disrupted when a person dies. Social groups tend to affirm their unity through ritual and social practices that mend the fabric of society that is inevitably torn by death.

Religion transforms the process of dying and the event of death into patterns of transcendence. We will return frequently to four basic ways in which religious beliefs and practices rise above or go beyond death. These patterns of transcendence—ancestral, experiential, cultural, and mythic—are four ways in which human beings have attempted to make a human death meaningful. Because they have appeared often in the history of religions, we will encounter these patterns of transcendence many times in the course of this book.

First, ancestral transcendence connects the individual person with a continuous biological chain of parents and offspring. The death of a parent may seem to create an unbridgeable gap, but ancestral beliefs and practices attempt to bridge any separation created by death. Through ancestral transcendence, parents live on through their children. In a real sense, parents, grandparents, and even more distant ancestors may be kept alive by specific practices that show honor, respect, reverence, and service to the "living dead." Ancestral transcendence represents rising above and going beyond death to the extent that ancestors live on through their children and continue to have an effect on their descendants.

Second, experiential transcendence attempts to rise above or go beyond death by incorporating death in life. Experiential transcendence embraces death, either through acceptance or ecstasy, as part of the process of living. One type of experiential transcendence might be achieved through a calm, tranquil, perhaps philosophical acceptance of death. Epicurus, Lucretius, and, more recently, Elisabeth Kübler-Ross have advocated this type of transcendence of death through acceptance.

Another type of experiential transcendence of death appears in the more extraordinary experiences of symbolic death and rebirth described by shamans, mystics, and other specialists in ecstasy. As a technical term, *ecstasy* refers to the experience of being out of the body, out of place, or out of the world. In this sense, ecstasy is a kind of symbolic rehearsal for death. By symbolically dying and being reborn, a person might achieve an experiential transcendence of death even during the course of life.

Third, cultural transcendence appears in beliefs and practices that affirm the continuity of a social group. Individuals might die, but cultural transcendence celebrates the survival of a community. Social survival is sustained by a shared cultural memory of artistic, scientific, and heroic achievements that keeps the name and fame of the dead alive.

A society is also sustained by ritual. In cultural transcendence, ritual practices are of vital importance. As rites of passage, death rituals mark the transition of a dying person from the world of the living to the world of the dead. Death rituals also respond to the social crisis represented by death by affirming unbroken bonds within the community of the living and between the living and the dead. Funerals, cemeteries, memorials, and celebrations for the dead contribute to a cultural transcendence of death by affirming the continuity and survival of a living society that includes the dead among its members.

Fourth, mythic transcendence appears in meaningful, powerful, and often compelling stories about death and afterlife. Myths map the geographies of worlds beyond death. But they also set the conditions for imagining a successful passage through death. They define the continuity of personal consciousness and the continuity of personal responsibility for actions—cognitive and forensic continuity—that allow people to imagine that they will be the same persons before and after death. In addition, myths symbolize a person's relation to the physical body after death: Myths specify whether survival can be expected as a disembodied state, as a spiritual embodiment, as a resurrection of the same body, or as a reincarnation in a different body. All these elements have appeared in religious myths about the transcendence of death.

Although myths about the transcendence of death can be subjected to logical analysis, their power resides primarily in the context of ritual. Religious myths about death are part of practical contexts—arts of dying, rites of passage, rites of crisis, and rites of exclusion—that allow human beings to die human deaths and to acknowledge the deaths of others as human. Rituals act out a transcendence of death for individuals and for social groups. Supported by myths, ritual practices provide ways through the process of dying and provide ways of responding to the event of death in a human community.

Chapter One: References

Ariès, Philippe. (1981). *The Hour of Our Death*. Trans. Helen Weaver. New York: Random House.

Armstrong, D. M. (1968). *A Materialist Theory of Mind*. London: Routledge and Kegan Paul.

Badham, Paul, and Linda Badham (eds.). (1987). *Death and Immortality in the Religions of the World*. New York: Paragon House.

Bannister, D. (1966). "A New Theory of Personality." In Brian M. Foss (ed.), *New Horizons in Psychology*. Baltimore: Penguin, 361–80.

Beimler, Rosalind Rosoff, and John Greenleigh. (1991). *The Days of the Dead*. San Francisco: HarperCollins.

Bendann, Effie. (1930). *Death Customs: An Analytical Study of Burial Rites*. New York: Alfred A. Knopf.

Berger, Arthur S. (1987). "A Critical Outline of the Prima Facie Evidence for Survival." In Paul Badham and Linda Badham (eds.), *Death and Immortality in the Religions of the World*. New York: Paragon House, 188–213.

Berman, Phillip L. (1996). *The Journey Home: What Near-Death Experiences and Mysticism Teach Us About the Gift of Life*. New York: Simon & Schuster.

Binford, Lewis R. (1971). "Mortuary Practices: Their Study and Their Potential." In James A. Brown (ed.), *Approaches to the Social Dimensions of Mortuary Practices*. Washington, D.C.: Society for American Archaeology, 6–29.

Bloch, Maurice, and Jonathan Parry. (1982). *Death and the Regeneration of Life*. Cambridge: Cambridge University Press.

Brandon, Ruth. (1983). *The Spiritualists: The Passion for the Occult in the Nineteenth and Twentieth Centuries*. New York: Alfred A. Knopf.

Brandon, S. G. F. (1967). *The Judgment of the Dead: A Historical and Comparative Study of the Idea of a Post-Mortem Judgment in the Major Religions*. London: Weidenfeld and Nicolson.

Broad, C. D. (1962). *Lectures on Psychical Research*. London: Routledge and Kegan Paul.

Brodman, Barbara. (1976). *The Mexican Cult of Death in Myth and Literature*. Gainesville: University of Florida Press.

Brokaw, Cynthia J. (1991). *The Ledgers of Merit and Demerit: Social Change and Moral Order in Late Imperial China*. Princeton, N.J.: Princeton University Press.

Campbell, Keith. (1970). *Body and Mind*. London: Macmillan.

Carrithers, Michael, Steven Collins, and Steven Lukes (eds.). (1985). *The Category of the Person: Anthropology, Philosophy, History*. Cambridge: Cambridge University Press.

Cherry, Chris. (1986). "Near-Death Experiences and the Problem of Evidence for Survival After Death." *Religious Studies* 22: 397–406.

Crookall, Robert. (1961). *The Study and Practice of Astral Projection*. London: Aquarian Press.

———. (1964). *More Astral Projections*. London: Aquarian Press.

Douglas, Mary. (1966). *Purity and Danger: An Analysis of the Concepts of Pollution and Taboo*. London: Routledge and Kegan Paul.

Douglass, William. (1969). *Death in Murélaga*. Seattle: University of Washington Press.

Ducasse, C. J. (1961). *A Critical Examination of the Belief in a Life After Death*. Springfield, Ill.: Charles C Thomas.

Durkheim, Émile. (1965). *The Elementary Forms of the Religious Life*. Trans. Joseph Ward Swain. New York: Free Press (orig. ed. 1912).

Eliade, Mircea. (1961). *The Sacred and the Profane*. Trans. Willard R. Trask. New York: Harper & Row.

———. (1964). *Shamanism: Archaic Techniques of Ecstasy*. Trans. Willard R. Trask. Princeton, N.J.: Princeton University Press.

———. (1967). *Myths, Dreams, and Mysteries*. Trans. Philip Mairet. New York: Harper & Row.

———. (1978). *A History of Religious Ideas*. 3 vols. Trans. Willard R. Trask. Chicago: University of Chicago Press.

Evans-Wentz, W. Y. (1927). *The Tibetan Book of the Dead*. Oxford: Oxford University Press.

Flew, Antony. (1955). "Death." In Antony Flew and Alisdair MacIntyre (eds.), *New Essays in Philosophical Theology*. London: SCM Press, 267–72.

———. (1956). "Can a Man Witness His Own Funeral?" *Hibbert Journal* 54: 242–50.

———(ed.). (1964). *Body, Mind and Death*. New York: Macmillan.

———. (1974). "Locke and the Problem of Personal Survival." In Baruch A. Brody (ed.), *Readings in the Philosophy of Religion*. Englewood Cliffs, N.J.: Prentice Hall, 624–40.

———. (1976). *The Presumption of Atheism*. London: Pemberton/Elek. Reprinted (1984), *God, Freedom and Immortality*. Buffalo, N.Y.: Prometheus.

———. (1978). "Survival." In Hywel D. Lewis (ed.), *Persons and Life After Death*. London: Macmillan, 94–109.

———. (1987a). *The Logic of Mortality*. Oxford: Basil Blackwell.

———. (1987b). "The Logic of Mortality." In Paul Badham and Linda Badham (eds.), *Death and Immortality in the Religions of the World*. New York: Paragon House, 171–87.

Frazer, James (1911–15). *The Golden Bough*. 3rd ed. 12 vols. London: Macmillan.

———. (1913–24). *The Belief in Immortality and the Worship of the Dead*. 3 vols. London: Macmillan.

Freud, Sigmund. (1915). "Thoughts for the Times on War and Death." In Ernest Jones (ed.), *Collected Papers*. London: Hogarth Press, 1948, IV: 288–317.

Gallup, George, and William Proctor. (1982). *Adventures in Immortality*. New York: McGraw-Hill.

Geertz, Clifford. (1960). *The Religion of Java*. New York: Free Press.

Gervais, Karen Grandstrand. (1986). *Redefining Death*. New Haven, Conn.: Yale University Press.

Gluckman, Max. (1937). "Mortuary Customs and the Belief in Survival After Death Among the South-Eastern Bantu." *Bantu Studies* 11: 117–36.

Green, Judith Strupp. (1980). "The Days of the Dead in Oaxaca, Mexico: An Historical Inquiry." In Richard A. Kalish (ed.), *Death and Dying: Views from Many Cultures*. Farmingdale, N.Y.: Baywood, 56–71.

Hellbom, Anna-Britta. (1971). "The All Saints' Cult in Mexico." *Temenos* 7: 58–65.

Hertz, Robert. (1960). *Death and the Right Hand*. Trans. Rodney and Claudia Needham. London: Cohen and West (orig. ed. 1907).

Hobbes, Thomas. (1909). *Leviathan*. Oxford: Clarendon Press (orig. ed. 1651).

Howitt, A. W. (1904). *The Native Tribes of South-East Australia*. London: Macmillan.

Huntington, Richard, and Peter Metcalf. (1979). *Celebrations of Death: The Anthropology of Mortuary Ritual*. Cambridge: Cambridge University Press.

James, E. O. (1957). *Prehistoric Religion*. London: Thames & Hudson.

Kalish, Richard A. (ed.). (1980). *Death, Dying, Transcending*. Farmingdale, N.Y.: Baywood.

Kalish, Richard A., and David K. Reynolds. (1976). *Death and Ethnicity*. Los Angeles: University of Southern California Press.

Kelly, Patricia Fernandez. (1975). "Death in Mexican Folk Culture." In David E. Stannard (ed.), *Death in America*. Philadelphia: University of Pennsylvania Press, 92–111.

Kohler, Kaufmann. (1923). *Heaven and Hell in Comparative Religion, with Special Reference to Dante's Divine Comedy*. New York: Macmillan.

Kübler-Ross, Elisabeth. (1969). *On Death and Dying*. New York: Macmillan.

———. (1974). *Questions and Answers on Death and Dying*. New York: Collier Books.

———(ed.). (1975). *Death: The Final Stage of Growth*. Englewood Cliffs, N.J.: Prentice Hall.

———. (1981). *Living with Death and Dying*. New York: Macmillan.

Kupfer, Joseph. (1978). "What's So Bad About Death?: Epicurus' Catch." In Florence M. Hetzler and Austin H. Kutscher (eds.), *Philosophical Aspects of Thanatology*. 2 vols. New York: Arno Press, II: 115–21.

Lamb, David. (1996). *Death, Brain Death, and Ethics*. London: Avebury Press.

Leach, Edmund. (1958). "Magical Hair." *Journal of the Royal Anthropological Institute* 88: 149–64.

Lester, David. (1967). "Experimental and Correlational Studies of the Fear of Death." *Psychological Bulletin* 67: 27–36.

Lifton, Robert Jay. (1979). *Broken Connection*. New York: Simon & Schuster.

Lubbock, John. (1902). *The Origin of Civilisation and the Primitive Condition of Man*. 6th ed. London: Longmans, Green (1st ed. 1871).

Luckmann, Thomas. (1967). *The Invisible Religion: The Problem of Religion in Modern Society*. New York: Macmillan.

Malinowski, Bronislaw. (1954). *Magic, Science, and Religion*. New York: Doubleday.

Matsunami, Kodo. (1998). *International Handbook of Funeral Customs*. Westport, Conn.: Greenwood Press.

Mauss, Marcel. (1979). "A Category of the Human Mind: The Notion of Person, the Notion of 'Self.'" In Ben Brewster (trans.), *Sociology and Psychology*. London: Routledge and Kegan Paul, 57–94.

McManners, John. (1985). *Death and the Enlightenment: Changing Attitudes to Death Among Christians and Unbelievers in Eighteenth-Century France*. Oxford: Oxford University Press.

Middleton, John. (1982). "Lugbara Death." In Maurice Bloch and Jonathan Parry (eds.), *Death and the Regeneration of Life*. Cambridge: Cambridge University Press, 134–54.

Monroe, Robert. (1972). *Journeys out of the Body*. Garden City, N.Y.: Doubleday.

Moody, Raymond A. (1975). *Life After Life*. New York: Bantam Books.

Mullin, Glenn H. (1986). *Death and Dying: The Tibetan Tradition*. Boston: Arkana.

Nabes, Clyde. (1981). "Presenting Biological Data in a Course on Death and Dying." *Death Education* 5: 56.

Nadel, S. F. (1946). "A Study of Shamanism in the Nuba Mountains." *Journal of the Royal Anthropological Institute* 76: 25–37.

Needham, Rodney. (1967). "Percussion and Transition." *Man,* new series, 2: 606–14.

Parry, Jonathan. (1982). "Sacrificial Death and the Necrophagous Ascetic." In Maurice Bloch and Jonathan Parry (eds.), *Death and the Regeneration of Life*. Cambridge: Cambridge University Press, 74–110.

Parsons, Talcott, and Victor Lidz. (1967). "Death in American Society." In Edwin S. Shneidman (ed.), *Essays in Self-Destruction*. New York: Science House, 133–40.

Patterson, Orlando. (1982). *Slavery and Social Death: A Comparative Study*. Cambridge, Mass.: Harvard University Press.

Paxton, Frederick S. (1990). *Christianizing Death: The Creation of a Ritual Process in Early Medieval Europe*. Ithaca, N.Y.: Cornell University Press.

Paz, Octavio. (1961). *The Labyrinth of Solitude: Life and Thought in Mexico*. New York: Grove Press.

Pearson, Mike. (2001). *Archaeology of Death and Burial*. Austin: Texas A & M University Press.

Peters, F. E. (1982). *Children of Abraham: Judaism, Christianity, Islam*. Princeton, N.J.: Princeton University Press.

Plotinus. (1964). *The Essential Plotinus*. Trans. Elmer O'Brien. New York: New American Library.

Pressman, Peter, John S. Lyons, David B. Larson, and John Gartner. (1992). "Religion, Anxiety, and Fear of Death." In John F. Schumaker (ed.), *Religion and Mental Health*. Oxford: Oxford University Press, 98–109.

Prior, Lindsay. (1997). "Actuarial Visions of Death: Life, Death, and Chance in the Modern World." In Peter C. Jupp and Glennys Howarth (eds.), *The Changing Face of Death: Historical Accounts of Death and Disposal*. London: Macmillan, 177–93.

Pritchard, James B. (1958). *The Ancient Near East: An Anthology of Texts and Pictures*. Princeton, N.J.: Princeton University Press.

Radcliffe-Brown, A. R. (1964). *The Andaman Islanders*. New York: Free Press (orig. ed. 1922).

Reynolds, Vernon. (1980). *The Biology of Human Action*. 2nd ed. Oxford: W. H. Freeman.

Ring, Kenneth. (1980). *Life at Death: A Scientific Investigation of the Near-Death Experience*. New York: Coward, McCann & Geoghegan.

———. (1984). *Heading Toward Omega: In Search of the Meaning of the Near-Death Experience*. New York: W. W. Norton.

Rinpoche, Sogyal. (1992). *The Tibetan Book of Living and Dying*. San Francisco: HarperCollins.

Roberts, Cecilia M. (1977). *Doctor and Patient in a Teaching Hospital*. Lexington, Mass.: D. C. Heath.

Russell, Bertrand. (1925). *What I Believe*. London: Routledge and Kegan Paul.

Rzhevsky, Leonid. (1976). "Attitudes Toward Death." *Survey* 22: 38–56.

Sabom, Michael B. (1981). *Recollections of Death: A Medical Investigation*. New York: Harper & Row.

Schärer, Hans. (1963). *Ngaju Religion: The Conception of God Among a South Borneo People*. Trans. Rodney Needham. The Hague: Martinus Nijhoff.

Smart, J. J. C. (1970). "Sensations and Brain Processes." In C. V. Borst (ed.), *The Mind-Brain Identity Theory*. London: Macmillan, 52–66.

Sneath, Elias Hershey. (1922). *Religion and the Future Life: The Development of the Belief in Life After Death*. London: Allen & Unwin.

Spencer, Herbert. (1896). *Principles of Sociology*. 3rd rev. ed. New York: Appleton (orig. ed. 1875–76).

Spiro, Melford. (1966). "Religion: Problems of Definition and Explanation."

In Michael Banton (ed.), *Anthropological Approaches to the Study of Religion*. London: Tavistock, 85–126.

Sudnow, David. (1967). *Passing On: The Social Organization of Dying*. Englewood Cliffs, N.J.: Prentice Hall.

Tainter, Joseph A. (1975). "Social Inference and Mortuary Practices: An Experiment in Numerical Classification." *World Archaeology* 7: 1–15.

———. (1978). "Mortuary Practices and the Study of Prehistoric Social Systems." In Michael B. Schiffer (ed.), *Advances in Archaeological Method and Theory*. New York: Academic Press, I: 105–41.

Tarlow, Sarah. (1999). *Bereavement and Commemoration: An Archaeology of Mortality*. Oxford: Blackwell.

Templer, Donald I. (1970). "The Construction and Validation of a Death Anxiety Scale." *Journal of General Psychiatry* 82: 165–77.

———. (1972). "Death Anxiety in Religiously Very Involved Persons." *Psychological Reports* 31: 261–62.

Templer, Donald I., and Richard Lonetto. (1986). *Death Anxiety*. Washington, D.C.: Hemisphere.

Tocqueville, Alexis de. (1967). *Democracy in America*. 2 vols. Ed. Phillips Bradley. New York: Random House (orig. ed. 1835).

Turner, Victor. (1967). *The Forest of Symbols*. Ithaca, N.Y.: Cornell University Press.

Tylor, Edward Burnett. (1920). *Primitive Culture*. 2 vols. 6th ed. New York: G. P. Putnam's (orig. ed. 1871).

van Gennep, Arnold. (1960). *The Rites of Passage*. Trans. Monika B. Vizedom and Gabrielle L. Caffee. Chicago: University of Chicago Press (orig. ed. 1909).

Wallah, Barbara Price. (1976). *Lucretius and the Diatribe Against the Fear of Death: De rerum natura III 830–1094*. Leiden: E. J. Brill.

Warner, W. Lloyd. (1959). *The Living and the Dead: A Study of the Symbolic Life of Americans*. New Haven, Conn.: Yale University Press.

Wittgenstein, Ludwig. (1953). *Philosophical Investigations*. Trans. G. E. M. Anscombe. Oxford: Basil Blackwell.

Younger, Stuart J., Robert M. Arnold, and Renie Schapirs (eds.). (1999). *Definition of Death: Contemporary Controversies*. Baltimore: The Johns Hopkins University Press.

2

Indigenous Transcendence

An Australian man of the Warumeri clan was unconscious, lying on the ground, near death. His relatives gathered around him, singing sacred songs about the sea and the totems of the sea. The songs invoked the ancestors who were connected with those symbolic emblems, the ancestors who resided deep in the well of their clan but who were now felt to be present as the man lay dying.

As the relatives sang the song of the crayfish totem, the dying man moved one of his hands convulsively like a crayfish. When the relatives sang the song of the whale totem, the man began kicking his legs in imitation of the movements of a whale's tail. His family recognized those motions as signs of death. The dying man was calling on his ancestors to be present and to take him home to the ancestral well.

When the dying man became still, he was declared to be dead, even though his heart was beating. The dying had begun his journey back to the ancestors. "I see that go," one relative said, "and I knew he was dead." Confident that the ancestors were present, moving in the dying man's heart, and taking him back to the Warumeri well, the relatives began preparations for the funeral (Warner, 1937: 25).

A Zulu woman of southern Africa walked back to her home after her husband's funeral. The year before, she had buried one of her sons. Both were untimely deaths, before the men had finished the natural courses of their lives. Some evil force, therefore, must have been attacking the family.

"It is clear that somebody is working to kill us," she said. "Was it not shortly, only about a year ago, that we were doing this thing of burying? Now it is here again. Who is this person?"

Since these were bad deaths, a witch, or a sorcerer, or an evil spirit must have caused them. A good death, in the fullness of age, would require no explanation. It would be the result of the natural aging process, a welcome transition from the world of the living to the world of the ancestors.

A good death was not to be feared because the deceased was not really dead. Such a person became one of the "living dead," an ancestor to be served with reverence by children and grandchildren because that ancestor remained part of the family of the living.

But a bad death was fearful, cutting off the person from that family. As the widow mourned her loss, a sympathizer said, "This is a fearful thing, in truth. It is destroying them, today even killing the head of the homestead. Yesterday the bull-calf. Today the bull itself. No, this is fearful" (Berglund, 1976: 80).

In a pueblo community of the American Southwest, a Zuni girl was ill. One night she dreamed that she visited the world of the dead. In that underwater realm, she saw the spirits of the dead—the *kachinas*—living a happy afterlife existence in the sacred lake of the dead.

The kachinas lived much like they had in life. In the kachina village, they danced and sang and feasted, clothed in beautiful beads and feathers. They occasionally visited the world of the living, appearing in the form of flying ducks or in the rain-giving clouds.

During the course of each year, the dead participated in the kachina festivals of the Zuni community. Their spirits were believed to animate the masked dancers who played the dramatic roles of the kachinas in the ceremonies, celebrating the ongoing connection and communion between the living and the dead.

Recovering from her illness, the girl claimed to have seen her grandfather and other relatives in the world of the dead. She felt a new sense of calmness about death. "Since then I have never worried about dying," she said, "because I saw all these dead people and saw that they were still living the way we do" (Parsons, 1939: I:68).

Australia, Africa, and America—these continents have been home for centuries to small-scale local communities in which human beings have lived and died in religious contexts. Their religions were based on oral traditions, not written texts. Nevertheless, the oral transmission of religious myths and teachings cultivated a continuous cultural memory, a shared repository of knowledge about the ways of life and death. Their religions were highly ritualized, acted out in singing, chanting, praying, dancing, and sacrificing, during special times of ritual attention that marked out sacred events in each human life cycle and in the calendar of the community. Often supported by small-scale, local, subsistence-level economies, their religions were closely related to the activities of hunting or agriculture that sustained them.

When Europeans first encountered Australian, African, and Native American societies, they failed to appreciate those religions. More interested in conquering the people, taking their lands, and controlling the wealth of new territories, Europeans dismissed the traditional cultures and religions that had flourished for centuries, not recognizing the humanity of the people who lived and died within those cultures and religions. European invaders and colonizers called them savages, natural slaves, or subhuman creatures; European scholars called them primitives.

Recent scholarship has tried to move beyond labeling the indigenous people, cultures, and religions of Australia, Africa, and the Americas as "primitive" (Gill, 1982). A new recognition of the humanity of those people may be possible. Although their societies may have (or once may have had) relatively simple economies and technologies, they nevertheless developed deep, rich, and meaningful religions. Those religions were ways of life that perhaps revealed their depth, richness, and meaning most clearly in relation to death and dying.

AUSTRALIAN DREAMTIME

More than 500 distinct traditional, or aboriginal, peoples developed and practiced religions in Australia. Many still continue today. They can be divided into two basic groups: The inland desert communities practiced religions that were concerned mainly with fertility, reproduction, and life. Their primary religious focus was the ongoing reproduction of human beings in a land that could sustain life. The woodland and coastland communities practiced religions that were mainly concerned with death. They developed rituals that would safely conduct the spirits of the deceased back to the underground world from which they had originally come (Charlesworth et al., 1984: 7–8; Peterson, 1975: 5–6).

Although the different religions of Australia showed marked diversity, they nevertheless had much in common. Some of these common interests were important for the religious transcendence of death: the power of clan totems, the centrality of totemic ancestors, the role of spirit children in reproduction, the symbolic death and rebirth involved in initiating children into adulthood, the activities of shamans, the frequent identification of sorcery as a cause of death, and the crucial function of funerals in restoring human spirits to the world of the dead. All these elements appeared in the Australian transcendence of death.

Behind these beliefs and practices, however, was one basic feature of all Australian religions: the Dreamtime. This Dreamtime did not refer to the illusion of dreams. Rather, the Dream, or the Dreaming, or the Dreamtime was understood as the spiritual basis of reality, the origin and foundation of an aboriginal religious transcendence of death.

The Dreaming

In the beginning, the ancestors shaped the world as a place for human beings to live. The land was already there when the ancestors emerged, but it was flat, featureless, and lifeless. The ancestors roamed the land, exploring, camping, making love, and fighting, and through their activities they fashioned the world. Usually remaining within a fairly small geographical area, each group of ancestors shaped the features of that landscape—the rocks, caves, hills, trees, rivers, and water holes, the plants and animals of each region—as they wandered around. When finally they disappeared, the ancestors left their eternal traces in the landscape, merging into the things they had fashioned. The ancestors remained present in those sacred traces they left behind from that time of beginnings, from the time of the Dreaming.

Source of Life The Dreamtime was the basic reservoir of knowledge and power in Australian religions. The Dreaming meant four different things. First, it was the time of beginnings. In the Dreamtime, the immortal ancestor heroes shaped the entire world. Their adventures in that time laid out the landscape for their human descendants. Those adventures were remembered, told, and retold by human beings. The Dreamtime, therefore, was recalled in the mythic narratives about those first ancestors and their exploits in creating a world for human beings.

Second, the Dreamtime was the power of the ancestors that remained present in the land. Spiritual power of the ancestors was embodied in the landscape. It was alive in certain sites—in wells, water holes, rivers, caves, rock formations, and so on—that were associated with the ancestors. That power was also alive in certain animals, plants, or sacred objects that had been given by the ancestors. The Dreamtime, therefore, was not a lost time of origins stretching back on a horizontal line to the beginning. Rather, the Dreamtime was both then and now, a time of beginnings but also the time of the present in which people could contact the power of the ancestors through their traces in the world.

The main points of contact with the ancestors were the special emblems, or totems, that identified their clans. The dying man of the Warumeri clan, part of a larger tribal group on the northern coast of Australia, had lived with ancestral totems of the sea. The crayfish and whale were associated with the ancestor of his family, lineage, and clan. During his life, the Warumeri man had contacted the power of the Dreamtime through those totems. One other Warumeri totem symbolized birth and death: the wild duck that represented the well of his ancestors. From this well he had emerged at birth, and to that well he would return through death. As his family prepared his body for the burial ceremony, they painted the totemic symbol of the wild duck on his chest to signify his return to the ancestors and the Dreamtime.

Third, the Dreamtime introduced the ways of life and death to human beings. In the Dreamtime, the ancestors gave the laws for moral and social life. They established a path for human beings to follow. In addition, the ancestors gave human beings the ritual practices and ritual objects through which they could remain in contact with the Dreaming. During rituals, clan members could reenact the heroic adventures of their ancestors. But participants did not merely imitate their ancestors; they *became* those ancestors. By representing the totemic ancestors in ritual, through the totems of crayfish, or whale, or wild duck, or rock kangaroo, human beings could enter into and become absorbed by the presence of the Dreaming. In daily life, a person of the kangaroo clan might say, "I am a kangaroo." But in ritual, the person could become the essence of that totem as it continued to exist in the Dreaming.

Fourth, the Dreamtime was the ongoing source of human life. In most Australian religions, children were born animated by spirits that came from the Dreamtime. These spirit children lived with the ancestors and waited to be born in human form. In traditional Australian belief, a man would have a dream or a vision or notice some strange movement in the desert that would reveal to him a spirit child. When he contacted a spirit child, the man would point out the woman who was to be the child's mother. The spirit child entered the body of its mother in order to be born as a human being.

If a child died, it might go back to the Dreamtime, wait there for a while, and then return to the same family. In one Warumeri family, for example, a baby died and was believed to have returned to the ancestral water hole. One night its father dreamed that his own father came back from the dead to visit him, saying, "I will bring my son's son back to you." Soon another baby was born, bearing a resemblance to the child who had died. That similarity was recognized by the community, confirming the truth of the father's dream. The first child had not really died; it had only returned to the well of the ancestors in order to be born again (Warner, 1937: 22).

Besides giving the father credit for procreation, the concept of the spirit child affirmed Australian belief that all human beings came from the Dreamtime. Originally spiritual beings, they entered the world in the care of women and in the company of other children. Eventually, the male child would be separated from that world of women and children to be initiated into adulthood. As a fully initiated male adult, he could participate in the rituals and ceremonies that contacted the power of the Dreamtime. A man became identified with his totem in life, becoming a sacred being like the ancestors. In death, that man, as well as women and children, would return to the clan's sacred totem in the Dreamtime.

Life and death, therefore, formed a cycle that began and ended in the Dreamtime, but that cycle was also sustained throughout by the constant and powerful presence of the totems, the ancestors, and the Dreaming in both life and in death. Death was understood as an integral part of the cycle of life. It was not a final end but part of a series of movements animated by the Dreamtime.

Origin of Death Biological death was understood to have begun in the original Dreamtime. Myths of the origin of death related different versions of those events, but in most cases they were imagined as mistakes made in the Dreamtime that caused human beings to be mortal.

Some myths of the origin of death suggested that human beings could have died and immediately returned to life like the waning and the waxing of the moon. One representative myth related that in the Dreamtime the moon and the wallaby got into an argument about what human beings should drink. The moon wanted human beings to drink his urine so they could die and return to life like he did. The wallaby, however, insisted that human beings should drink *his* urine. The wives of the moon and the wallaby—the red-bellied water snake and the black-nosed python—resolved this disagreement by choosing the urine of the wallaby. Rather than aging, dying, and returning to life like the moon, human beings became mortal and had to undergo a death that removed them from the world (Maddock, 1972: 159).

Snakes, which figured in this myth of the origin of death, have often symbolized immortality—shedding their skins to die and be reborn—in myths about death. In this myth, however, the red-bellied water snake and black-nosed python made a choice that denied that type of immortality to human beings. Human beings would not be immortal like the moon or like snakes but would die like other forms of animal life.

Other Australian myths attributed the origin of death to mistakes made by human ancestors. One myth related that originally human beings died but were immediately called back to life by the moon. The moon simply told them to get up, and they were restored to life. One day, however, an old man said, "Let them remain dead." From that day, only the moon died and returned to life. Human beings became mortal, not to be restored to life again in the same body (Howitt, 1904: 429).

Although this myth ascribed the origin of death to a mistake by a male ancestor, Australian myths more frequently blamed death on mistakes made by women. One myth told of a certain tree in the Dreamtime that women were forbidden to go near, a hollow tree containing a beehive flowing with honey. Wanting to steal the honey, a woman one day approached the tree and chopped into it with an ax. Instead of honey, however, a huge black bat, "the spirit of death," suddenly flew out, bringing death into the world (Parker, 1905: 98).

Other myths of the origin of death explained its present nature as the result of some violation of ritual rules. Formerly, human beings were restored to life in their same but rejuvenated bodies by special rituals. But at some point someone broke the rules of those special rituals, and they lost their power to bring people back to life. In one myth, the special rituals lost their power because a man walked too closely to the women when coming out of the grave (Strehlow, 1947).

These myths of the origin of death, therefore, were not only imaginative efforts to make sense out of human mortality, they also reinforced certain social roles—such as the lower status of women—and the importance of following ritual rules in the cycle of life and death.

Initiation

The mysteries of the Dreamtime were introduced to human beings through initiation. Two important initiations in Australian religious life were the initiations of all male adults and the initiations of shamans. Both were based on symbolism of death and rebirth. In passing from childhood to adulthood, each male of the community confronted death. The initiation of a shaman, however, was an entry into a guild of specialists in death, practitioners of techniques of ecstasy that promised an experiential transcendence of death. In an important sense, initiation as an adult or as a shaman was a rehearsal for death, acting out a symbolic death and rebirth in the course of life.

Adults The most important social and ritual practices in the life cycle were the initiations of male children into adulthood, symbolized as dying to an old status and being reborn to a new. Some time between age six and thirteen, a boy was separated from the status of women and children to be initiated into the world of men. That initiation was usually marked by some type of mutilation—often the cutting of the boy's penis in circumcision or subincision—that indicated his emergence into manhood. Symbolism of death featured prominently in the drama of initiation.

A representative initiation ritual was observed by the anthropologist R. H. Mathews in the 1890s among the Wiradthuri people of central New South Wales. The ritual began when the boys were separated from their mothers, other women, and the children of the community. Women and children were told that the boys had been taken by a powerful giant named Dhuramoolan, a snakelike monster with a voice like thunder. The boys were removed to a secret place, where they were given instruction in the myths and laws of their people. During this time, each boy had a tooth removed. At night, the men hid outside the encampment, making a frightening, roaring noise with a bull-roarer, two leather thongs swung overhead that sounded like the voice of the monster Dhuramoolan.

On the last night, they told the boys that the monster was coming to burn them and eat them. With their heads covered, the boys felt fire approaching them and the thundering sound growing louder. Suddenly, their head covers were removed, and they were shown the secret source of that thundering sound, the bull-roarer. Returning to the rest of the community after this ordeal, the boys were received as if they had returned from the dead (Mathews, 1896: 307–12).

Similar initiation rituals were practiced in other Australian communities. In almost all cases, the ritual symbolized death. The Walbiri of central Australia, for example, explicitly identified initiation as ritual killing. Boys between the ages of eleven and thirteen were circumcised after a period of preparation and instruction in the sacred songs, designs, myths, and rituals of their kangaroo totem. They were treated like sacrificial victims, as the men sharpened the circumcision knife, relatives mourned their "deaths," and each boy's mother in the main camp held a burning fire stick representing her son's life, only to extinguish its flame at the moment of circumcision when the boy "died." After the ordeal, the child was reborn as a man in the community (Meggitt, 1962: 281–312).

A boy's initiation, therefore, was a type of rehearsal for death, enacting a transition from one status to another that would continue throughout the life cycle and culminate when a man died. At around age eighteen, if the young man had become a father, he was shown more powerful totems for the first time and was thereby initiated to a higher status. Finally, at about age thirty-five, he was shown secret totems and raised to the status of full adulthood as an elder in the community. These rituals marked changes in the male life cycle that progressively introduced the man into an essential, sacred role as representative of the totemic ancestors. He had emerged from the spirit world to be born as a human child with the same status as women and children, but gradually, through ritual initiations into the mysteries of the Dreamtime, he became increasingly spiritualized until, at death, he returned to the ancestral world of the spirits (Warner, 1937: 5).

Women also were believed to have emerged from the spirit world and to return there at death, but they were not acknowledged as making any spiritual progress during their lives that would invest them with authority in the community. Nevertheless, women also knew the stories of the Dreamtime and were familiar with the ways the totemic ancestors had shaped and sanctified the landscape.

When two visitors asked a group of Willowra women to explain the myths and the laws of the Dreamtime, the women explained the Dreamtime by showing its enduring presence in their country. The visitors reported that the women "began by singing of the travels of the ancestral heroes in the area; they took us into the country to display its bounty; while in the country they continued singing; they displayed to us their sacred boards and other ritual items which validate their ownership of the land and encode the myths of the Dreamtime" (Bell and Ditton, 1980: 52; Charlesworth et al., 1984: 12). Although they did not participate equally in life, both men and women were believed to have come from the Dreamtime and to return there at death.

Shamans Some men became shamans, specialists in the mysteries of the Dreamtime. They were also initiated through symbolic death and rebirth. In Chapter 1, we noted that a shaman could be initiated by sleeping on a grave. A spirit from the dead visited him, "killed" him by taking out his internal organs, replaced those organs with magical rock crystals, and gave him the power to be a shaman (Howitt, 1904: 404–5).

That death and rebirth was part of a ritual ceremony conducted by old, experienced shamans who had served their community as medicine men. Tired from a long day of hunting, the initiate was settled down at night by a grave, with small fires around him smoking from the forbidden animal fat that had been placed on them. He was told by an elder shaman that while he slept, the spirits would put white stones into his body through the back of his neck or the top of his shoulder.

On the following morning, the initiate discussed his dreams with the elder shamans. That next night he was taken to sleep in a remote place and was told that visiting spirits would remove his internal organs and replace them with new ones. Surviving this ordeal, he received a personal totem that would assist him in his work and protect him from danger. Under the guidance of the elder shamans, the initiate began assisting in the ritual and magical practices of his new profession (Elkin, 1977: 138–48).

The special totem the shaman received in his initiation—perhaps a snake, or the Rainbow Serpent—would guide him in his journeys out of the body through the Dreamtime. He might go down to the underworld, where he would meet other snakes that would give him magical powers by rubbing against him. Then he might ascend to the sky—to the place of a supreme god, sky god, or father god—in order to gain powers over illness and death. One shaman described such a heavenly journey: "We went through the clouds and on the other side was the sky. We went through the place where the Doctors go through, and it kept opening and shutting very quickly" (Howitt, 1887: 50). Passing through these obstacles, the shaman demonstrated and expanded his extraordinary powers.

Magical rock crystals, powerful snakes, and heavenly light symbolized the special powers of the shaman. Although healing abilities indicated a type of transcendence of death, the shaman had other abilities that were important in Australian religious approaches to death. The shaman became adept at going into trance states or dream states through which he could see things others could not. When someone died, a shaman or medicine man could see and identify the cause of death. If someone died from old age, the cause was fairly obvious. But the cause of almost every other death was identified as the evil influence of sorcery.

In Australian cultures, as anthropologist Kenneth Maddock noted, sorcery was "the art of inflicting death, injury or other misfortune by carrying out physical, and hence empirically observable, operations possessed of mystical efficacy" (1972: 161). In causing death, sorcerers were believed to perform observable acts—pointing a bone, announcing a curse, casting a spell—that could separate the spirit of a person from his or her body.

As an explanation for a particular death, sorcery answered two questions. First was the question of causation: Given the fact that all human beings die, how were the specific circumstances of any particular death to be explained? Why did some people die where they did, how they did, and, especially, before they should? Second was the question of retribution: Given the fact that a particular person had died, how could his or her family exact revenge on the cause of that death? Unless the cause was identified as another person, how could a balance of justice be restored through revenge?

As a person was dying, he or she might have had a dream that indicated the identity of the sorcerer who was responsible for separating the spirit from its body. The totem of another clan—a green ant, a honeybee, a spider—might have appeared to a dying person of the kangaroo clan that suggested evil influences from someone in another clan. If that dream was told to the surviving family, it was remembered and related to a shaman, who would then conduct an inquest to reveal the identity of the sorcerer who had caused that particular death.

Revenge was achieved by an act of countersorcery. A shaman could cast a spell on the enemy clan that had been revealed as causing the death. It was not considered necessary to cause the death of an enemy immediately. Usually it was sufficient for survivors to visit the enemy camp where the identified sorcerer lived and terrify that clan with incantations, curses, and spells. But when someone in an enemy group later died, the family could understand that death as having resulted from their act of revenge.

Observers of Australian communities have been interested in deaths that seemed to be caused by sorcery. Often called "voodoo deaths," these deaths seemed to result from the effectiveness of a shaman's curse. A shaman might point a bone at an enemy and utter a death curse, and the person would die shortly after. Voodoo death has been explained as the result of the psychosomatic effect of sorcery beliefs. Cursed by a sorcerer, an Australian believer in the power of sorcery might give up the will to live. Such a mental state could have a powerful effect on the body and actually cause death.

More recently, however, an observer has suggested that voodoo deaths result from a common physiological cause: dehydration. A person under a shaman's curse might be so convinced of its power that he or she would give up the will to live, refuse to drink water, and die three days later from dehydration. In some cases, other members of a clan might refuse to allow a cursed person to drink water, thereby causing that person's death (Eastwell, 1982).

However these deaths are explained, they show the power of sorcery in Australian religious practice as an explanation for the cause of any particular death and as a way of seeking revenge on that identified cause.

Death Rituals

Funeral rituals differed among the various groups of Australia. In all cases, however, the rituals of death accomplished three important functions: They separated the spirit of the deceased from its body, they separated the corpse from the community, and they ensured the return of the spirit to its ancestral place of origin. After a person died, the survivors devoted considerable time and energy to rituals that assisted the passage of the spirit back to its original home.

Rites of Passage The rituals that separated the spirit from its deceased body were important to an effective passage of the person through death. The corpse could be treated in several different ways. Some groups dried the body in the smoke of a fire made of acrid green leaves, hardening and preserving the corpse. In some cases, the corpse of a prominent member of the community might have been preserved in this way and then carried around with the group for as long as six months as it moved from place to place, perhaps stopping to perform special rituals at places that had been important to the deceased (Howitt, 1904: 467–69).

Earth burial was often practiced. Sometimes the legs of the body were broken, or the body was tied and bound, to prevent the spirit from reanimating it. One group was reported to take more dramatic action to prevent a reanimation of the corpse: Survivors beat the corpse with clubs; cut into it through the shoulders, stomach, and lungs; and filled the body with stones (Howitt, 1904: 474). Other groups reportedly treated the corpse by rubbing and scraping off the outside layer of skin to expose the white layer of underskin, symbolizing the whiteness and purity of the spirit separated from the body (Parker, 1905: 91).

In some cases, two burials were performed—one for the flesh, the second for the dried bones after the body had decomposed. When secondary burials were practiced, the corpse was usually exposed on a raised platform until the flesh rotted and the bones could be recovered and buried. In other cases, cremation was the preferred method for disposing of the corpse. Whether the corpse was buried, exposed, or cremated, the ritual practice signified a final separation of the spirit from the body that affirmed the spiritual survival of the person after death.

Rituals also separated that spirit from the community. Often, the community abandoned the camp in which a death had occurred, moving immediately to a new location. The survivors were forbidden to use the personal name of the deceased. The person was no longer part of the familiar world of the living, so he or she could be referred to only as an ancestral grandfather or grandmother of the clan. Although these practices separated the deceased from the community, the survivors continued to show care and concern for him or her, often keeping watch over the corpse before its final disposition, protecting it from evil influences and looking for signs that would reveal the identity of the sorcerer who had brought about that death (Mathews, 1905: 145).

Finally, funeral rituals conducted the spirit back to its ancestral home. Some groups believed the spirit world was located in the depths of a water hole, others saw it in the sky, while others imagined that it was found on a remote island off the coast. In any event, funeral rituals directed the surviving spirit toward that place. Frequently, the corpse was placed on the ground, and finally in its grave, so that its head faced the direction of its totemic emblem. By pointing the body toward the compass point associated with the deceased's totem, the spirit was directed on its journey back to the spirit world (Howitt, 1904: 453).

Rites of Crisis Funeral rituals, however, were not merely rites of passage that helped the deceased return to his or her ancestral home. Funerals were also rites of crisis. Because death probably had been caused by a sorcerer's curse, evil influences were understood to have attacked the entire community. Much of the drama of Australian funeral rituals can be seen as an attempt to re-store a community disrupted by evil influences, sorcery, and death. Those dangers were personified in dynamic funeral rituals that seemed to enact the crisis and conflict brought about by the death of one of the members of a community.

The anthropologists Baldwin Spencer and F. J. Gillen described a dramatic ritual of crisis in response to a death in one community they observed. As people of the Warramunga clan returned from a totemic ceremony, a piercing cry from the main camp was heard: Someone was dying. Immediately, people ran to the camp, howling and wailing. On the bank of a creek that ran past the camp, men sat down with their heads between their knees to weep and moan. In the camp, the shelters were already being torn down so that the community could abandon the place of death. Some of the women were lying on the body of the dying man, and others were standing nearby, wailing loudly and pierc-ing the tops of their heads with sharp digging sticks so that the blood ran down their faces.

When the men entered the camp, the women moved away from the dying man so that the men could throw themselves on the body. Soon the scene of death was a struggling mass of bodies. While men and women continued to wail, one man rushed in waving a stone knife. With a loud cry, he suddenly cut deeply into the muscles of his own legs. Unable to stand, he fell bleeding into the group of writhing bodies on the ground. After a while, he was carried off by female relatives, who laid him on the ground and sucked blood from his wounds.

When the dying man finally died later that evening, the wailing was re-sumed, but now louder and wilder. Men rushed around the body, cutting themselves with stone knives and sharp sticks. Women hit each other over the head with clubs, making no attempt to avoid the blows. The wailing and crying—but especially the violent injuries—seemed dramatically to act out the crisis brought about by a death in the community. It was a crisis that no one could avoid because everyone was affected. If nothing else, that ritual-ized frenzy demonstrated the vital solidarity of the community in the face of death. After about an hour, the frenzy subsided. Torches were lit to guide a procession in which the corpse was taken away from the camp to be left in branches of a tree (Durkheim, 1965: 435–36; Spencer and Gillen, 1899: II:506–45).

That dramatic rite of crisis certainly provided an opportunity to express personal emotions of grief at the loss of a relative, friend, or valued member of the community. Sorrow became intensified and perhaps released as it was shared with others. Pain also seemed to be mixed with anger, as survivors injured themselves and others in a ritual drama of combat. But whatever personal emotions may have been involved, the ritual response to the crisis of death reaffirmed a certain degree of social solidarity among the survivors. Like all rites of crisis, those rituals of mourning provided a social means for dramatizing both the disruption of the community by death and the community's cultural transcendence of death.

In Australian rituals of death, cultural transcendence—the affirmation that a society survives the death of any of its members—was identified with ancestral transcendence. The totems of the Dreamtime ancestors symbolized continuity and the survival of death. Songs and sacred designs of the totems were used in funeral rituals to invoke the power and presence of the mythic ancestors of the clan. They also guided the human spirit back to its ancestral source.

Many Australian religions assumed that human beings had two souls. The Murngin people of the northern coast, for example, believed that each person had two distinct spirits during life. One was a soul that was associated with the body, a shadow soul that was of little value in life but that left the body at death to linger in the world, perhaps in the bush or jungle, and return occasionally to harass the living. This shadow soul, or *mokoi,* was a kind of spiritual duplicate of the body. It was a trickster spirit that remained as an afterimage of the person after death.

But the mokoi was not the true identity of the person. The genuine essence of the person was the *warro,* or totemic well spirit. The warro was the soul that came from the ancestral well as a spirit child. It was the personal soul that grew and developed through a lifetime of initiations into the power of the totems, the mythic ancestors, and the Dreaming. Ultimately, this soul was assumed to return to the well of the ancestors. Murngin claimed to be able to see the reflections of their own warros whenever they looked into the water hole as well as to discern the warros of ancestors, perhaps appearing in the form of fish, when they gazed down into the depths of the well. For the Murngin, each person had a spiritual essence that came from and returned to the well of the ancestors. Mythic transcendence—the personal survival of death—was, therefore, also identified with ancestral transcendence, as every person was reabsorbed after death into the spiritual totem of the clan in the depths of their sacred well (Warner, 1937: 443–50).

As part of that sacred totem, the dead continued to participate with the living through frequent ceremonies that invoked the presence of the Dreamtime ancestors by means of the songs, designs, and objects associated with the totems. The dead were therefore not dead but continued to live on in the Dreamtime. In some Australian religions, a type of reincarnation was imagined that would cause the dead to come back to life in another body but usually within the same clan. Even without a belief in reincarnation, however, Australians understood that the dead came back to life constantly by living on in and through the clan. That living kinship group continued to remain in close relationship with the dead in the Dreamtime.

AFRICAN ANCESTORS

Those who are dead are never gone:
they are there in the thickening shadow.
The dead are not under the earth:
they are in the tree that rustles,
they are in the wood that groans,
they are in the water that runs,
they are in the water that sleeps,
they are in the hut, they are in the crowd,
the dead are not dead.
Those who are dead are never gone:
they are in the breast of the woman,
they are in the child who is wailing
and in the firebrand that flames.
The dead are not under the earth:
they are in the fire that is dying,
they are in the grasses that weep,
they are in the whimpering rocks,
they are in the forest, they are in the house,
the dead are not dead.

This poem by Birago Diop of Mali sings of the African ancestors, the "living dead" who constituted a vital part of any family or community (Mbiti, 1969: 149ff.; Taylor, 1963: 160). Although great diversity may be observed in the religious beliefs and practices that have flourished on the vast African continent, one common feature of African religions has been the importance of ancestors. The ancestors became the focal point of African beliefs and practices that created a religious transcendence of death by affirming an unbroken biological continuity of parents and children, of ancestors and their descendants who continued to serve them, communicate with them, and receive their guidance unhindered by death.

The Origin of Death

Many myths regarding the origin of death appeared in traditional African religions (Abrahamsson, 1951; Zahan, 1979: 36–52). Like Australian myths, these African stories of the origin of death were ways of symbolizing the meaning and significance of human mortality. Myths of death were meditations on the meaning of life. Two types of myths appeared frequently in different African traditions as explanations for the origin of death: One explained death as a problem of communication between the eternal world of God and the mortal world of human beings, the other explained death as necessary for the reproduction of the human species. Although ancestors may not have appeared explicitly in these myths, both myths presupposed the power of ancestors to resolve basic human dilemmas—whether dilemmas of communication or reproduction—in relation to the eternal, sacred world of God. As we will see, African ancestors were mediators in human communication with the spiritual world and in human reproduction of the family and community.

Communication The first myth, dealing with a problem of communication, has been called the "story of the message that failed." This myth was told and retold in different forms throughout Africa but was perhaps most common in the central and southern regions of the continent. In this story, death originated when God sent a message that promised immortality to human beings, but the message was inadvertently lost or changed by the animals entrusted with the task of delivering it to humans. The basic human dilemma out of which death arose, therefore, was the communication gap between God and the world.

In the Zulu tradition of southeastern Africa, after human beings came into the world, the Lord of the Sky, known as Unkulunkulu, called on two animals to convey messages to the people: the slow, lethargic chameleon to carry the message of immortality and the swift lizard to carry the message of death. Quicker than the chameleon, who took time out to eat berries and sleep along the way, the lizard raced to the world of human beings and delivered his message of death.

The lizard told the humans that they would die and not come back to life. The human beings accepted the message of death. When the chameleon finally arrived, no one believed his message. The people accused the chameleon of lying. "We have received the word of the lizard," they said. "What you now say is in vain." The people threw stones at the chameleon and drove him away. From that day, however, human beings had to live with the message of the lizard. They would die, and they would not come back to life (Callaway, 1970: 3–4).

Why did Unkulunkulu send the two messages? In one Zulu version of the myth, he actually intended humans to be immortal. Having entrusted that message with the slow chameleon, however, Unkulunkulu grew angry and impatient. So he sent the second message—the message of death—with the quick lizard because of the chameleon's delay. But in other versions, no reason for two messages is given. The failed messages simply indicated a communication gap between God and humans. Regardless of why they were sent, the messages were perverted through a communication breakdown between the two worlds. Traditionally, both chameleons and lizards were hated by the Zulu, often killed if they were found, because of their roles in bringing death to human beings.

In other versions of this myth, different animals may have played the roles of messengers in the message that failed. In the myths of the southern African Khoisan, for example, the messages of life and death were sent by the moon. The moon entrusted a message of life with an insect. That insect was told to give the moon's message to human beings: "As I die, and dying live, so ye shall also die, and dying live."

On his way to the human world, however, the insect was overtaken by a hare. The hare learned the message and hurried on ahead of the insect to tell it to the humans. But the hare got the message mixed up and related just the opposite promise as that given by the moon: "As I die, and dying perish," the hare reported, "in the same manner ye shall also die and come wholly to an end." The humans accepted this perverted message. From that day, they died but did not return to life like the moon. Learning of the failed message, the moon was so angry that he punched the hare in the nose, causing a cleft that remained in the noses of all the hare's descendants (Bleek, 1864: 69).

Again, the myth of the message that failed indicated a communication breakdown. Whether God or the moon intended immortality for humans, precisely the opposite of that message was actually received. Death originated from that gap between the immortal, spiritual world and the mortal world of human beings. What could bridge that gap? As we will see, one of the functions of ancestors was to provide a communication link between those two worlds.

Reproduction A second type of myth explaining the origin of death dealt with the human dilemma of reproduction. It has been called the myth of "begetting and death" and described how death originated in a human choice between personal immortality and biological reproduction. Originally, humans were immortal, but they did not reproduce children. They were deathless like stones but not reproductive like plants and animals. In order to produce children, human beings had to accept the consequences of death.

A Nupe myth of west Africa related how God, whom the Nupe called Soko, created stones, tortoises, and humans. Each species was created male and female, but they did not give birth to offspring. All three were immortal. The stones did not die. Tortoises and humans also did not die but became young again when they grew very old.

One day, the tortoises approached Soko with a special request. They wanted to produce offspring. Soko reminded them that he had made them immortal but forbidden them to reproduce. The tortoises, however, persisted in their request. Finally, the humans joined the tortoises in petitioning Soko to allow them to have children. Soko gave in and allowed them to reproduce, but they would have to pay the price of death. Because the stones did not want children, they would not have to die (Abrahamsson, 1951: 68; Frobenius, 1928: 227).

The deaths of fathers and mothers allowed the next generation to live. Death, therefore, was necessary to make room in the world for children. But the myth also suggested that death was a choice made by the first humans between personal immortality and biological reproduction. Human beings chose not to remain deathless like the stones but to live, produce offspring, and die like the tortoises.

This choice between the deathless life of a stone or a life-giving, death-requiring existence common to all plants and animals appeared frequently in myths about the origin of death. Human beings sacrificed personal immortality for the reproductive continuity of the species. Sometimes the myth posed the dilemma as a choice between dying like the moon or dying like a banana. This myth was particularly prevalent on the island of Madagascar, off the southeast coast of Africa. The banana represented reproduction, putting forth its shoots to create new life that would take its place. Instead of choosing to die and reappear like the moon, human beings chose life-giving reproduction that would require their own deaths. As a result of that choice, human beings died, but their children took their places in the world of the living (Abrahamsson, 1951: 120–21).

In a variation on the theme of reproduction, one widespread African myth related that human beings originally had children but were nevertheless immortal. When people grew old, they simply went into a secluded place, shed their skins like snakes, and returned to life rejuvenated. One day, however, as an elderly mother was about to shed her skin, her child discovered her and cried out in fright. In order to comfort her child, the mother stopped shedding her skin. As a result, the mother died in her old skin and did not come back to life. From that day, human beings lost the ability to rejuvenate themselves by shedding their skins like snakes (Abrahamsson, 1951: 58–59).

In some versions of this myth, death was chosen for the sake of a child. In other versions, a child interrupted its mother while she was shedding her skin, prevented her rejuvenation, and thereby brought death into the world. In either case, human beings could not restore themselves to life like snakes but had to suffer death. No longer immortal, human beings nevertheless lived on through their children.

Rather than remaining deathless like a stone, or dying and rising again like the moon, or shedding their skins like snakes to come back to life, human beings chose a life and death that would allow them to produce children but would require each person to die and not return to life. Personal immortality was sacrificed, but a type of immortality remained in the beliefs and practices of ancestral transcendence. As ancestors, human beings remained very much alive in the lives of their descendants. They remained the "living dead," in constant contact with the "living living" who succeeded them in the world. Reproduction may have caused death, but it also provided a way of transcending death through the unbroken, biological continuity of parents and children that formed the basis of an African ancestral transcendence of death.

Ancestors

In African religions, the ancestors resolved the two basic human dilemmas that appeared in the myths of the origin of death: communication and reproduction.

First, ancestors served as mediators between the spiritual world of God and the world of human beings. Death may have originated from a breakdown in communication between those two worlds, but the ancestors provided a bridge for communication. Rituals for ancestors, particularly rituals of animal sacrifice, were not only ways of remembering and serving the dead, they were ways of keeping that communication link open.

Second, the ancestors served as connecting links in the biological chain of human reproduction. Although the ancestors died to let their children live, the children lived conscious of their continuing presence. They may have been buried beneath the earth, but the ancestors continued to be present in the home of their family, in their circle of cattle, in their health and well-being, and even in the reproductive process itself that gave birth to new children. Because ancestors often were believed to enter into the semen, they were understood to live on in the birth of any child in their family line.

Ancestral transcendence, therefore, could be traced on both a vertical and a horizontal axis. Ancestors allowed human beings to transcend death by providing a vertical line of communication between the three levels of reality: the dead, the living, and supernatural spirits. The ancestors linked the underworld they inhabited after burial with the human world, and they linked the human world with the spiritual domain of God or other supernatural beings by serving as mediators for communication with that higher reality. On a horizontal axis, the ancestors represented the unbroken line of human reproduction that linked each generation to the next. They allowed human beings to go beyond death by living in that ongoing biological and reproductive continuity.

These forms of ancestral transcendence can be illustrated through the example of one traditional community, the Zulu of southeastern Africa, that developed religious beliefs and practices revolving around ancestors. Some elements of their religious life were unique to the Zulu, but their attention to ancestors was representative of a respect for the "living dead" widespread throughout traditional African religions. In Zulu tradition, as in most African traditions, religious transcendence was closely identified with an ancestral transcendence of death.

Zulu Ancestors The Zulu traditionally lived in small villages, called *kraals,* arranged in a circle around a central enclosure for cattle. Huts stood around that circle of cattle, the most important being the hut of the headman of the village, with the homes of his wives and sons located on either side. In that family village, the headman was father, ruler, and priest. His home was the center of kinship relations and also the center of political and religious power in the village.

At the back wall of the headman's hut were placed special ritual objects — spears, knives, shields, and other objects — that were invested with sacred power because of their association with the ancestors. The ancestors regularly visited that part of the hut, partaking of food offerings of meat and beer that were placed there. Although every home had such a special place at its back wall, called an *umsamo,* where the ancestors came to visit, the umsamo of the headman was a place of special power because of his importance in the life of the village.

In Zulu religion, the Lord of the Sky, Unkulunkulu, might have been worshiped occasionally on the hillsides surrounding the village, but the ancestors were worshiped daily within the kraal. Perhaps *worshiped* is the wrong term because the Zulu communicated with and interacted with the ancestors in a spirit of familiarity based on kinship relations. Services performed for the dead were understood to be basically similar to the acts of respect and reverence that ought to be shown to living elders. As in other African communities, elders were often regarded as if they were already ancestors, and ancestors were treated as respected senior members of the community (Brain, 1973; Kopytoff, 1971). Nevertheless, the ancestors, or *amadlozi,* were powerful beings to be praised, thanked, and served through specific ritual practices that placed the living in direct contact with their power and protection.

While alive, each human being was believed to be animated by a spirit called the *isithunzi.* The Zulu term *isithunzi* might refer to a person's shadow or to a person's moral worth and social prestige, but it also referred to a person's soul. If a person lived to old age, not dying prematurely as a result of sorcery, witchcraft, evil spirits, lightning, suicide, or leprosy, the body was committed to the ground, but the spirit remained alive in the form of an ancestor, as one of the amadlozi, or "living dead."

The amadlozi were important actors in the life of the kraal. Although buried beneath the earth, the ancestors also lingered around the home. They appeared often in dreams, sometimes in the form of snakes, and regularly through their effects on the lives of their descendants. The ancestors made their power felt by bringing illness and misfortune on the living if they should neglect the dead. When ancestors were not served, harmony between the world of the living and the dead was disrupted. Zulu commonly explained illness, misfortune, and often death as resulting from a failure to maintain harmonious relations with the ancestors.

Services for Ancestors In order to preserve harmony, descendants conscientiously served their ancestors. Ancestors brought peace and prosperity to their children and grandchildren who honored them by setting aside a special cow in the cattle enclosure, by placing beer and food in the umsamo of the hut, by leaving unwashed cooking pots on the hearth for them to lick, and by being conscious of their constant presence. As a Zulu woman remarked, "They are in me. When they are in me, I know that they are there. I feel them. They are happy with me and I am happy with them. I think of them always. They know that I am thinking of them" (Berglund, 1976: 197). In this way, the ancestors lived on in the thoughts and actions of their descendants.

Communication with the ancestors was maintained through ritual. The amadlozi were present whenever the family sang its special clan song, whenever men gathered for the ritual drinking of beer, and especially whenever a ritual killing of an animal was performed. Any animal slaughter could be regarded as a sacred ritual, performed with prayers and offerings to the ancestors. In this sense, every meal of meat could be a communal meal shared with the ancestors. But sacrifices were also performed on special occasions to open lines of communication with the ancestors and during times of trouble when those communication links had been broken by neglecting or offending the ancestors. Animal sacrifices for the ancestors maintained or restored the vital connection between the human world and the world of the spirits.

When the cow or goat was killed, its gallbladder was offered to the ancestors. Bitter to the living, the gallbladder was thought to be sweet to the dead. Because the gallbladder was round like a hut, that part of the animal was saved during the ritual of sacrifice as a home for the ancestors. Through that ritual home, the ancestors could enter into the place where their descendants lived and remain with them in close contact and communion.

The gallbladder of the sacrificed animal was likened not only to a hut but also to a womb. Ritual killing, therefore, also symbolized the fertility of reproduction. Just as the ancestors entered the hut, they also entered a mother's womb through the father's semen whenever a child was conceived. The ancestors remained alive because their spirits lingered around the homes of the living and because they acted as vital ingredients in the process of reproduction. Ancestral transcendence in Zulu traditional religion, therefore, was based on the recognition of ongoing processes of communication and reproduction that continued after death.

Death Rituals

African death rituals were instrumental in the transition of the deceased into the world of the ancestors. The Zulu saw the dimension occupied by the ancestors as a reversed world in which black was white, up was down, and bitter was sweet. The LoDagaa of west Africa saw that other dimension as a place of individual and collective judgment of the dead for their deeds during life. Nevertheless, the world of the ancestors was felt to remain in close contact with the living world through the links of communication in ritual and the birth of offspring. Death rituals, particularly the rituals that marked the deceased's change into an ancestor, were essential for maintaining those connections between the living and the living dead.

The Reversed World If a person died at home, the Zulu made a special exit at the back of the hut opposite the door for the body to be taken out. The body was elevated to a sitting position, the face was washed, and hair was cut before the corpse was covered with an ox hide or blanket. The bearers of the corpse often entered the hut walking backward and left by the special opening facing backward so that their footprints always led away from the home. A grave was dug near the hut. While the body was being prepared, the mourners wailed and cried, but they maintained silence once the funeral began and the body was taken out of the hut to be laid in the grave with its head facing back toward the home.

Zulu death rituals involved many reversals of ordinary behavior. Leaving a hut backward, for example, was regarded in everyday life as rude and unacceptable behavior. But precisely the opposite of normal behavior was required at a funeral. Besides the custom of walking backward while carrying the corpse, women often wore their dresses inside out. In conversations after the funeral, mourners would say "yes" when they meant "no" and "no" when they meant "yes." Instead of using the preferred right hand, they used the left hand. Before the burial, the deceased's eyes were closed with the left hand, and women washed the body with their left hands. After the burial, men placed logs over the grave with their left hands. Traditionally, the entire death ritual was conducted at night.

What did these reversals mean? They were important parts of a death ritual that removed the deceased from the ordinary world of the living and directed him or her toward the world of the ancestors. That world was under the ground, an exact reversal of the human world. Although the world of the dead had trees, mountains, pastures, and hunting grounds, everything was reversed, upside down, and backward. Underground, the ancestors survived on the other side of a flat world, where they lived a mirror-image existence.

Even the color of the ancestors was reversed. The living were black, but ancestors were white. The cattle they tended there were also white. As white shadows, the ancestors could be easily seen at night. They could be seen clearly by shamanic diviners who specialized in knowing their ways and wishes. No wonder the diviners frequently prescribed animal sacrifices for the ancestors, offering them the bitter gall as a special delicacy because in the ancestors' reversed world, the bitterest taste was the sweetest. Funerals directed the deceased to that reversed world of the dead.

But the deceased did not settle in that world and become an ancestor until a year after burial. Particularly if the deceased was the headman of the village, a long process of mourning was required. For the first month after a burial, the villagers abstained from work and sex. They took special medicines to protect themselves from the danger of evil spirits that might attack the community after a death, particularly after the death of someone as important as the headman. At the end of that month, men returned to hunting and women to farming through a ceremony called "washing the spears," involving prayers, praises for the deceased, and a final sacrifice. The widow, however, did not return to work. She remained in mourning for the rest of the year following the death of her husband.

When that year was over, the village performed a ritual called "bringing home the ancestor." The deceased had been lingering all year in an in-between state but was now settled into the world of the ancestors through that final ceremony. In this joyous and festive occasion, the village sacrificed a special ox along with other animals as a ritual offering to the deceased. For the first time, the deceased was addressed and praised as an ancestor. Offerings were placed at the umsamo of the hut for the new ancestor, who from that time forward would be regarded as one of the "living dead" so important in the daily life and ritual practice of the Zulu community.

Afterlife Judgment Other African communities practiced similar rites of passage to conduct a person to the world of the dead and to confirm the deceased as an ancestor. The LoDagaa of west Africa, for example, developed elaborate rituals of death that also extended over several months from the initial rites of burial to the final ceremony that incorporated the deceased into the world of the ancestors.

Among the LoDagaa, the ideal way to die was sitting up, held in the arms of a close kinswoman. Earth priests carried the body out of the home on two ebony poles while the death was announced by messengers, the wailing of women, and the rhythmic beating of xylophones. The corpse was prepared for burial by procedures of purification: Water cleansed the body, a fresh egg was broken symbolizing life, whitewash dug from the earth was used to paint the corpse, and the body was swept clean with the feathers of birds that were later sacrificed. Widows were also purified with washings and whitewashings. Immediately after the burial, close relatives met in private to share a meal, reaffirm their solidarity, and perform rites that would prepare for the redistribution of the deceased's property.

Like the Zulu, the LoDagaa observed an interim period between burial and a final ceremony that acknowledged the deceased as an ancestor. During this period, the spirit of the deceased hovered around the treetops, unable to return home but also unable to proceed to the world of the ancestors. The final ceremony, which the LoDagaa called Cool Funeral Beer, was performed at least three months after burial, usually after the corn harvest, when the village had accumulated enough provisions for the food and beer necessary for the great feast.

Although this final ceremony might be performed for anyone, it was felt to be most crucial for male heads of households. The Cool Funeral Beer ceremony began when a special branch from a tree was cut so that it would fall into the arms of the deceased's eldest son. As the branch fell into his arms, the father's authority fell on his heir. A shrine was carved from this branch and placed by the grave. The wooden shrine stood as a symbol of the deceased's soul and as a sacred place for the survivors to communicate with the deceased. After setting up the shrine, women bathed to signify the end of mourning, the children of the deceased shared a meal to indicate that they were assuming the social roles of their father, and the property of the deceased was divided according to ritual rules among his survivors. The deceased was finally released from the human world to undertake his journey to the world of the dead.

On that journey, the deceased was thought to travel west toward the setting sun on his way to the country of the Great God. Before entering that world of the ancestors, however, the soul had to cross the River of Death. Arriving at the river, the soul was required to pay the ferryman's fare out of the ritual offerings that had been provided by surviving relatives during the funeral ceremonies. If those offerings had been generous and the person had lived a good life, that soul would easily cross the River of Death. A bad person, however, would fall through the bottom of the boat and be forced to swim for three years to get to shore.

If the person had died of witchcraft, he or she would be met by the One-Breasted Woman before crossing the river. If the soul became angry on learning that witchcraft had been the cause of death, the Woman made the soul laugh in order to forget any wrathful thoughts of revenge. Instead of returning to the world of the living to seek revenge, that soul remained on the riverbank until the witch died and the two souls could continue the journey together. The witch, however, was forced to eat his or her own arm and leg before swimming across the river to the Land of the Dead.

In the Land of the Dead, souls were subjected to ordeals that were determined by how they had lived their lives. First, souls were made to sit on the tops of trees, exposed under a burning sun. The duration of exposure depended on the person: three months for those with good hearts, four months for liars, five months for thieves, six months for souls with evil dispositions, three years for witches, and three years for the rich because the rich made others suffer so that they could be wealthy. When that allotted time elapsed, souls were then made to work hard as farmers in the Land of the Dead for a period of time that depended on how hard they had worked during their lives.

A person's fate in the Land of the Dead, however, was not determined just by individual deeds during life. The LoDagaa imagined a collective judgment of the dead in which the fate of entire families and kinship groups would be bound together. Bad family groups that contained many witches, liars, and thieves could expect to be punished as a group. They suffered pain, worked hard for their food, and had only salt water to drink in the Land of the Dead. Good family groups enjoyed the afterlife as a time of rest and a place of plenty. If they merely thought of what they wanted, they would get it without any labor.

Even in the personal survival of death, therefore, the LoDagaa understood the identity of a person to be part of a collective family group. Because their fate in the Land of the Dead was determined by the moral character of their families, ancestors naturally took an interest in surviving relatives, kept in contact with them through the ancestral shrines, and rebuked them by bringing illness or misfortune when they went astray. The LoDagaa Land of the Dead reinforced the corporate character of ancestral transcendence in the ongoing kinship ties that connected the living and the dead.

Because traditional African societies were based on kinship, cultural transcendence was identified with ancestral transcendence. As the anthropologist Jack Goody noted, "The ancestor cult [was] a projection of social relationships in a perfectly concrete and meaningful way" (1962: 228). The continuing social relations of the living were determined by the power and position of parents in kinship-based societies.

Because the Zulu and LoDagaa were farming and herding societies, the ancestors' bequests played a crucial role in the distribution of the land and cattle through which those societies were supported. By contrast, social position based on land and cattle was less important in African hunting societies, where the role of ancestors did not appear to be as fully developed in religious beliefs and practices concerning death (Woodburn, 1982). But most African societies did base a transcendence of death on myths and rituals of ancestral transcendence. As the anthropologist A. R. Radcliffe-Brown observed with regard to the importance of ancestors in African religion, "The belief in the world of the spirits rests on the actual fact that a dead person continues to affect society" (1964: 304). In African traditional religions, therefore, a person was a person because he or she participated in a larger kinship group. The permanent reality of that group was affirmed through religious attention to ancestors, through beliefs and rituals that continued to recognize a person as a person within kinship groups even after he or she had died.

In ancestral transcendence, a person may also have been regarded as an individual soul. The Akan-speaking people of west Africa, for example, understood that each person had an immortal soul, or *kra,* that was a part of God inside every human being. A human had a kra, but an animal did not. Human beings were also composed of blood from the mother's line and a personality from the father's line, but the kra was a divine spiritual essence.

When sent by God into the world, the soul was given a destiny, its particular *nkrabea.* After death, that soul was thought to return to God to give an account of its life on earth. If the kra had not fulfilled its destiny, it would have to return to earth in order to complete its nkrabea. That soul would reincarnate in the same family in which it had lived before.

When its destiny was completed, the soul would return to God and remain in the world of the spirits as an immortal ancestor. Although each person had an immortal soul and a unique destiny, the highest destiny was to become an ancestor remaining in contact with one's kinship group as a mediator between God and the world (Brookman-Amissah, 1986; Danquah, 1968; Opoku, 1978: 94–96). Akan belief, therefore, affirmed the possibility of a type of reincarnation for souls who had not fulfilled their destinies. Other African traditions imagined what has been called "partial reincarnation," in which certain qualities of the deceased may be reborn in children and grandchildren, while the soul of the deceased remains incorporated in the world of the ancestors (Idowu, 1962: 159). In both cases, reincarnation beliefs supported ancestral transcendence by affirming the continuity of family or clan. As an ancestor, the deceased remained in communication with that kinship group, while full or partial reincarnation affirmed the importance of the deceased in the ongoing reproduction of the group.

Again, ancestors resolved the two dilemmas of the human condition reflected in African myths of the origin of death: the problem of communicating between the human and spirit worlds and the problem of reproducing a human family that would live on as an eternal reality in spite of death. In ancestral transcendence, death was not death because the dead continued to live by communicating with their family and participating in its reproduction.

AMERICAN SPIRITS

Whether they flourished in the forests of the eastern seaboard and the Pacific Northwest, or in the deserts of the Southwest, or on the plains of the Midwest, Native American religions were based on a close relationship with nature. Religious beliefs and practices showed respect and reverence for the earth and for the plant and animal life the earth sustained.

Identification with the natural environment, however, did not merely imply respect for Mother Earth. It also meant that those religions were closely related to the ecologies in which they developed (Hultkrantz, 1961). Some Native American religions developed in hunting ecologies, while others developed in the different ecology of settled agriculture.

In societies primarily based on hunting, fishing, and food gathering, religion revolved around animal ceremonies. Often directed toward a Supreme Being who was a master of the game, these ceremonies empowered hunters and paid homage to animals and animal spirits that gave their lives so that human beings might live. Because hunting societies were fairly mobile, no permanent places of worship were built. Communion with the masters of the game and animal spirits might occur anywhere. Shamans were particularly important in gaining access to the spiritual world, including the world of the dead, which tended to be located beyond the horizon or in the sky.

In hunting societies, the dead were often contacted as guardian spirits. A hunter might contact a personal guardian spirit through a vision or with the aid of a shaman who would assist him in the hunt. Guardian spirits provided both help and power. Those spirit helpers were sometimes identified with the masters of the game or thought to work closely with them, as supernatural forces that would make animals available for the hunter.

Among the Algonkian of eastern North America, prayers were directed to the dead during funeral rituals. At an Ojibway funeral, the deceased was addressed with prayers and praises and then was requested to intervene with the animal spirits on behalf of his relatives and bring game to them in abundance (Jones, 1861: 99).

A neighboring Algonkian group, the Ottawa, also used the funeral to enlist the aid of the dead in the hunt. The headman of a village conducted the funeral ceremony, calling on all the dead of the family group for whom the funeral was being performed to accept their offerings of food and to assist them in their hunting (Henry, 1969: 131).

The agricultural ecology of planting, cultivating, and harvesting involved different natural concerns. Those concerns were evident in religions that revolved around rain and fertility ceremonies. Rituals were integrated into the cycles of the seasons, often devoted to invoking supernatural beings associated with rain clouds, thunderstorms, and the fertility of the earth. In those religions, shamanism appeared in organized healing societies dedicated to maintaining the harmony and well-being of the community as a whole. When they contacted the spirits of the dead, who lived underground, or in a sacred lake, or in the rain clouds, these agricultural communities often sought their aid in bringing rain that would make the crops grow in abundance.

Such a cult of the dead was clearly developed among the Pueblo Indians of the American Southwest. Among the settled agricultural communities of the Pueblo area, the dead were closely identified with the cloud and rain spirits known as kachinas. On many occasions, Pueblo communities called on the kachinas to intervene with the sky gods and goddesses on their behalf. Depicted in vivid masks and ceremonial costumes, the kachinas were invoked to bring life, old age, health, power, fertility, and much-needed rain in that desert region. After death, a person might become a kachina or might live on in the world of the kachinas and assist them in bringing rain to the earth. In those Pueblo communities—whether Zuni, Hopi, Tewa, or Navaho—the recently dead, as well as more distant ancestors, were worshiped along with the kachinas in regular and elaborate ceremonies of fertility and prosperity.

Large-scale rituals of death, involving the entire community in prayers, offerings, songs, and dances for the dead, were practiced among the Algonkian of the northeastern forests and the Pueblo Indians of the southwestern deserts (Hultkrantz, 1978: 125). The forest and desert environments were felt to be animated, in different ways, by the spirits of the dead, and those spirits were celebrated by different types of rituals for the dead.

Forests

Algonkian Indians formed hunting and fishing societies that lived in the northeastern woodland regions of North America. The Ojibway, the Huron, and the Iroquois were part of this larger Algonkian-language group that extended from what is now the northern United States into central Canada. For much of the year, people hunted in small family groups, moving through the forests in search of food. Death by starvation was a constant possibility, so human life depended on the hunter's skill. Only during summer, when sufficient food was available, did the hunting families gather together with the larger group. Otherwise, the life of hunting required mobility, isolation, and self-sufficiency to ensure survival.

Other-Than-Human Persons Algonkian groups developed religious beliefs and practices suited to their ecological situation. In the isolation of the hunter's life, dreams became an important source of spiritual power. Hunters paid close attention to dreams, particularly to those in which they contacted a spirit helper who would assist them in the hunt. That spirit helper conveyed spiritual power—a power the Ojibway called *manitou*—that would aid the hunter in the difficult, dangerous, and ceaseless quest for food.

Among the Ojibway, the dead left the human world to enter the realm of what A. I. Hallowell called "other-than-human persons" (1976: 455). The spirits of these supernatural beings—the Sun, the Thunderbirds, the owners or masters of certain species of animals—contacted humans and conveyed their power through the medium of dream imagery. Those images assumed a variety of forms, but they always appeared as spirit persons in relation to the human persons they visited and assisted. Shamans and skilled hunters became adept in such contacts, but relations with other-than-human persons were possible for anyone.

However, the Ojibway seemed somewhat ambivalent about the dead. On the one hand, their myths and rituals insisted on a radical separation of the dead from the human world. The dead were to travel on to the Land of the Dead, never to return. But on the other hand, the Ojibway invoked the dead and the master of the dead as spiritual helpers and guardians in the hunt. They developed ritual practices to enlist the help of the dead in their quest for power and animals.

One Ojibway myth of the afterlife captured their concern for separating the dead from the world of the living. According to that myth, the deceased was assumed to be just as conscious after death as he or she was while alive. The soul still had all the thoughts and desires of a human being, but after death it was unable to communicate with the living in ways they could easily recognize. As the soul traveled along the road to the Land of the Dead, it found a giant strawberry. If the soul ate that strawberry, it would forever be unable to return to the world alive. If the soul refused to eat it, return in some other form might still be possible.

Continuing on its journey, the soul was suddenly grabbed from behind by the Skeleton-Woman of the Land of the Dead. The Skeleton-Woman cracked open its skull, took out its brains, and replaced them with moss. After that shocking experience, the soul was no longer a conscious, thinking being. Losing all interest in the human world, the unconscious soul had no reason to return to the living. This myth, therefore, described a final detachment of the dead from the living human community (Radin, 1937: 28–29).

Although this Ojibway myth reassured the community that it would not be visited by dangerous and frightening dead, it was told with a marked sympathy for the fate of the dead person. Nevertheless, that myth of separation was reinforced by certain ritual practices designed to guarantee that the dead would not return to disturb the living. For example, after her husband's funeral, an Ojibway widow apparently jumped over the grave and then ran a zigzag course around the trees, as if fleeing some danger and dodging the ghost of the deceased so that he could not find her (Jones, 1861: 99). Such a ritual may have been intended to prevent the deceased from haunting the living, perhaps motivated by a fear of the dead and their dangerous nonhuman power. But it certainly contrasted with other practices that called on the presence, attention, and power of the dead.

In calling on the dead as spiritual helpers, the Ojibway frequently threw food and tobacco on the fire as offerings to them. After the introduction of whiskey, the Ojibway always poured a few drops on the ground for the Great Spirit and the spirits of the dead before drinking. Responding to these signs of respect, the dead were thought to report to the Master of the Dead, who would reward the living with success in the hunt, prosperity, and long life. Periodically, the Ojibway performed the Dream Dance, a ritual of power believed to have been introduced by an ancient ancestor in which drums were rhythmically beaten to communicate with the spirits of the dead. All these practices attempted to maintain a close communion between the living and the dead (Hallowell, 1940: 37–48).

That connection was perhaps most important when a spirit of the dead became a personal guardian spirit, giving the hunter power and skill in the hunt. The dead revealed themselves to the hunters in dreams in order to assume the role of guardian spirit. Frequently, the Master of the Dead himself was understood to become that guardian spirit. Most often, however, a guardian spirit was a supernatural animal spirit that represented an entire species of animal life. But since the dead had also become other-than-human persons, they were sometimes included in the supernatural powers that assisted the Ojibway hunters.

Although the spirits of the dead were not central to Ojibway religious beliefs and practices, they nevertheless played important roles as spiritual intermediaries. They were often asked to carry the prayers of the living to higher powers, such as the Master of the Dead or the Master of the Animals. In this sense, they were part of a larger system of powers felt to impinge on human life and particularly to affect the success or failure of hunting.

The Feast of the Dead Every eight to twelve years, Algonkian groups participated in a great Feast of the Dead. That ceremony was an example of what Robert Hertz called "secondary burial," death rituals that required an interim period between preliminary and final dispositions of the corpse. In Algonkian ritual, the interim period between an initial burial and the second burial was very long, and that second burial was communal, performed for all who had died since the last Feast of the Dead.

Hertz was particularly interested in the ceremonies performed by the Huron and the Iroquois, calling those rituals "the most brilliant and solemn of all [their] observances." The Feast of the Dead illustrated two important themes in Hertz's analysis of death rituals: First, it showed that death could be understood as a gradual process in which the journey of the soul to the world of the dead was synchronized with the decomposition of the body. During the interim period, the soul was neither in the world of the living nor yet integrated into the world of the dead. Second, the Feast of the Dead reaffirmed social ties by burying all the bones of the community's dead in one place. "As the bones of the deceased relatives and friends were united in one place," Hertz concluded, "so [the living] would live together in the same unity and harmony" (1960: 71).

Immediately after death, the soul was believed to remain near the body. Covered in a beaver robe, the body was taken to the grave by mourning relatives and friends. The soul of the deceased was believed to walk on ahead of the mourners in the funeral procession. Once the corpse was buried, the soul remained at the grave, periodically visiting the village to eat food left over from evening meals and to participate in ceremonial feasts (Tooker, 1964: 128–34).

The soul lingered around the corpse until the great Feast of the Dead. At that time, each family dug up the bones of their relatives, cleaned the bones of any remaining flesh, and dressed them in new clothes, beads, and flowers. The clean, dry bones were referred to as the souls of the deceased. For two or three days, the bones were kept in the lodges and homes of the village, while feasts were held and gifts were distributed.

After ceremonies in each village, the relatives gathered up all the bones, crying "Hai, hai" in imitation of the cries of the souls, and they proceeded to a remote meeting place where people from all the villages gathered for the final ceremony. In that central place, all the bones were reburied in a common grave. That final burial marked the release of the souls from their bodies so they might continue their journeys to the world of the dead. But that final Feast of the Dead also affirmed the unity of all the villages, brought together at the common burial site of all their dead (Lafitau, 1977: 245–52).

One class of the dead, however, was excluded from this celebration of unity: those who had met violent death in war. Among the Iroquois, for example, warriors who died in battle were believed to have no contact with other souls in the afterlife, so their bones were left in their graves and not included in the great communal Feast of the Dead.

Because the death of a warrior left a breach in the community—in this life and the afterlife—that place had to be filled by capturing an enemy. The Iroquois avenged the death of a kinsman in battle by taking a captive, who may have been allowed to live as a substitute for the dead warrior. Often, however, that captive was tortured and killed in a ritual of revenge. The chief gave a feast for the victim and invited people of other villages to join in the torture ritual and burial of the captive.

The torture and killing of the captive was carried out according to ritualized formulas. Respect was shown to the victim because he was offered as a ritual sacrifice to the spirits. If the ritual was carried out with dignity, it was thought to bring power in war to the people who participated. In fact, the victim was exalted if he showed courage under torture. If the victim showed bravery, parts of his body might even have been eaten by those who killed him.

According to one account of a man taken captive by the Iroquois, the victim said, "Ah! You will kill me, you will burn me. But also you must know that I have killed and burned many of your people. If you eat me, I have the consolation of having also eaten several of your nation. Do then what you will: I have uncles, I have nephews, brothers and cousins, who will well avenge my death and who will make you suffer more torments than you know how to invent against me" (LeClercq, 1910: 272–73; Sanday, 1986: 49).

Grief over the loss of a valued warrior may have been eased through this ritual of torture and revenge. A family might have felt that the death of an enemy compensated for the loss of one of its sons in battle. However, those rituals of torture and human sacrifice showed how death not only provided occasions for social cohesion but also was a cause for social conflict. The principle of revenge required continuous conflict. No matter how respected the enemy, revenge required his death. Whereas the Feast of the Dead demonstrated social unity, the death rituals of war, torture, and revenge showed the social conflict between opposing groups in those Native American societies of the forests.

Deserts

The Pueblo Indians who lived in what became Arizona and New Mexico developed stable societies based on settled agriculture and complex ceremonies. Rituals were synchronized with the seasons, acting out the natural and social harmony of the Pueblo world. Since successful farming in a desert depended on rain, many ceremonies were devoted to the spirits that controlled the rain, clouds, thunderstorms, and lightning. The Sun Father and Moon Mother may have looked over the world from the beginning, but the rain spirits were responsible for its continuing survival as a place for human beings to live.

Emergence and Return In Pueblo myth, human beings emerged into the world from under the ground. A Zuni emergence myth, for example, related how the first humans were trapped in a dark underworld. The Sun Father sent his twin starlike sons down to bring the humans up to the empty world above. Carrying sacred bundles for making rain fall and seed grow, the humans climbed up through the soot world, through the sulfur-smell world, through the fog world, and through the feather-wing world, until they finally emerged into the bright, sunlit world. After many trials, the human beings found the center of that world and settled there to grow corn and to live in peace.

On the journey there, however, death had entered the world. Two witches came up from the underworld to kill some of the human beings so that the world would not become overcrowded. When those people died, they were taken back under the ground. Some time later, the people were crossing a river. Many of the women could not hold on to their small children and lost them in the water. Soon after that, however, the people heard the drowned children singing and dancing from the depths of a lake. The dead children called out that they wanted to remain in that lake rather than return to the distant underworld where the witches were taking the people they killed. For the Zuni, that sacred lake became the underwater world of the dead (Parsons, 1923).

Like most Pueblo places of the dead, the Zuni underwater world of the dead was a village in which people lived after death much as they had lived during life. The deceased joined the same clan group they had belonged to in the world. Life went on as usual, with the dead planting, hunting, and celebrating the ceremonies of the seasons in the depths of their sacred lake.

Only the Hopi anticipated ordeals and punishments after death. The Hopi place of emergence was located at a precise spot on one of the walls of the Grand Canyon. There the dead—or some of them—journeyed in their breath bodies back to the place of their origin. They were met by the spirit guard Tokonaka, who allowed only the good to proceed.

The guard forced all others to take a forked trail to the purifying fire pits. If the breath body emerged from the first fire pit purified, it was allowed to go back to the main trail and proceed to the underground village of the dead. Otherwise, it was sent to the second fire pit. If it came out of that pit purified, the breath body was turned into a beetle. If not, it had to go on to the third fire pit, where a purified breath body would be transformed into an ant. If after these ordeals the breath body remained so evil that it could not be purified, it was sent to the fourth pit, where it was consumed by fire and remained there as ashes and soot (Parsons, 1939: I:216).

Whether underground or underwater, the Pueblo Indians imagined a continuity in human life after death. While the dead continued in the ordinary pursuits of the living, however, they also assumed a new role as rain spirits, becoming part of the complex spirit world associated with the life-giving clouds and thunderstorms. They became part of the world of the kachinas.

Rain Spirits *Kachina* was the Hopi word for the rain spirits. Among the Hopi, the rain spirits included animal deities, the stars, and other supernatural beings. Even the Divine Sun participated with the rain spirits in bringing life, fertility, and health to the human world. But the dead were also included in the world of the kachinas. As anthropologist J. Walter Fewkes noted, "Ancestral worship plays a not inconspicuous part in the Hopi conception of a Kachina" (1897: 251).

After death, a Hopi could expect to become a rain spirit. When a person died, the Hopi asked the deceased to bring rain and to intervene on behalf of the living with the gods and goddesses who fertilized the fields. The deceased was addressed in prayers and songs as a kachina. No longer spoken of as individuals, however, the Hopi dead were invoked through the spiritual collectivity made up of ancestors and kachinas (Fewkes, 1901).

In elaborate ceremonies, masked, costumed impersonators of the kachinas danced in their honor and invoked their power to bring the rains. The dancers were members of kachina societies that specialized in the rituals of the rain spirits. Kachina worship was an essential component of Hopi religion and society, involving entire villages in ritual communion with those life-supporting spirits that included the spirits of the dead (Dockstader, 1954).

The Zuni called these rain spirits *koko*. They distinguished between the koko and their deceased ancestors by using different prayer sticks in their ceremonies, but the ancestors and the koko were closely related. The recently deceased were able to bring rain after their deaths. When a person died, the spirit was thought to linger around the body and the village for a period of four days. During that time, the survivors mourned their loss. On the fourth day, the spirit of the deceased was transformed into a koko and departed for the sacred lake. The family burned the deceased's personal property, severing that connection with the world of the living. But the deceased still might visit the human world, returning occasionally from the happy underwater world of the dead in the rain-giving clouds.

As a group, all the ancestors became identified with the clouds and the rain to whom the Zuni prayed for life and power. The dead, therefore, were closely associated with the koko. The original koko were the spirits of children who had died during the emergence of human beings into the world. By imitating the koko in regular ceremonies, the masked koko dancers brought the whole village into communion with the spirits.

In Zuni myth and ritual, the dead, the ancestors, and the rain-spirit koko were intertwined as powers to be called on in support of agricultural fertility and human well-being. Invoking the koko, therefore, was also a way of remaining in communion with the dead. As the anthropologist Ruth Bunzel noted, "The worship of the dead is the foundation of all Zuni ritual. The dead form part of the great spiritual essence of the universe, but they are the part which is nearest and most intimate" (1932: 483).

INDIGENOUS TRANSCENDENCE

The small-scale, indigenous societies of Australia, Africa, and America developed complex ways of life and death. Like any religious way of life, the religions of Australia, Africa, and America were experiments in being human. A human life's most profound and enduring significance was revealed in religious beliefs and practices relating to death. In summary, it might be useful to review the patterns of transcendence that appeared in the traditional religions of those three continents.

Ancestral transcendence was probably the most important way of rising above or going beyond death in the primal religions we have considered. In different ways, primal religions affirmed continuing ties of kinship that were regarded as unbroken by death.

Australian totemic ancestors lived on in the Dreamtime, remaining involved in the lives of their descendants. The ancestor's presence was felt to unify and empower his or her surviving kinship group. Contacted through dreams and ritual, the ancestor was a living presence to which Australians expected to return after death.

Bonds of kinship also transcended death in traditional African religions. Zulu and LoDagaa ancestors, for example, were close relatives who continued to be shown the honor and respect due to elders even after their deaths. In fact, ancestors were not thought of as being dead. They were the "living dead" because they remained alive to their families and continued to have an effect on the well-being of their descendants.

Perhaps to a lesser extent, ancestral transcendence was also important in Native American religions. Deceased relatives might become spirit guides for the hunters of the forests or rain spirits for the farmers of the deserts. But ancestral transcendence was most clearly celebrated in festivals—such as the Feast of the

Dead and the kachina ceremonies—that celebrated the bonds between the living and the dead.

More than simply remembering departed relatives, ancestral transcendence affirmed their living presence in the lives of their children, families, and extended kinship groups. In ancestral transcendence, the dead did not die but lived on through their descendants.

Experiential transcendence of death appeared in rituals of initiation. In Australia, Africa, and America, the initiation of males and the initiation of shamans were both rituals that enacted a symbolic death and rebirth. In this sense, initiations were symbolic rehearsals for death. They ritually incorporated death into life in order to gain a type of transcendent power over both life and death.

The shaman in particular became a specialist in the experiential transcendence of death. Having passed through a ritual dying and rebirth, the shaman became a specialist in techniques of ecstasy. Leaving the body, exploring the world of the dead, and communicating with the spirits, the shaman was a powerful figure in the religions of Australia, Africa, and America.

Cultural transcendence in these religions was identified with ancestral transcendence. Whereas a cult of the dead commemorates the dead of an entire society, ancestral rituals are directed to departed family. Because indigenous Australian, African, and American societies were organized along the lines of kinship, the continuity of society as well as family was symbolized by the survival of ancestors. In this sense, ancestral transcendence was equivalent to cultural transcendence. The ancestors who survived death represented the ongoing continuity of a family and, at the same time, the continuity of a society based on family and kinship relations.

Death rituals, therefore, were supervised and performed by the surviving family. As social practices, death rituals restored the social order disrupted by death by affirming the importance of the family and kinship relations. Taking direct responsibility for conducting the necessary rituals, the family reorganized and restored itself in response to the crisis of death.

Mythic transcendence was worked out in stories about the origins of death and the nature of life after death. Traditional African myths of the origin of death were representative of themes that appeared frequently in indigenous religions. Death may have been introduced by mistake, by a choice, or by some other change in the original design of the world, but death became the basic fact of the human condition. Myths of the origin of death provided ways of thinking about and coming to terms with the meaning of death. As we saw, African myths raised two dilemmas—the communication gap between human and divine worlds and the reproduction of the human species—that were regarded as fundamental to human life. In this way, myths of the origin of death reflected basic concerns about the meaning and purpose of life.

Myths of afterlife presented vivid pictures of the places occupied by the dead: the Warumeri ancestral well, the Zulu reversed world, the LoDagaa collective judgment across the river, the Pueblo underwater realms, and the Ojibway road on which the dead encountered a giant strawberry and had their brains replaced with moss by the Skeleton-Woman on their way to the village of the dead. Each myth represented an imaginative possibility for the transcendence of death. But these myths were also related to the other types of transcendence in these religions: Myths of afterlife supported the ancestral, experiential, and cultural transcendence of death that was achieved by the living.

Whether or not the dead actually ended up in the places described by the myths can remain an open question. That question can also remain open in relation to the myths we will encounter in subsequent chapters. If nothing else, these myths demonstrated the power of the human imagination to invest death with meaning. In mythic transcendence, human beings did not merely die but died meaningful deaths. Mythic transcendence was already achieved to the extent that those stories gave meaning and significance to the process of dying and the event of death in human communities. In each case, myths of death both reflected and shaped a way of life—from beginning to end—in the religions of Australia, Africa, and America.

Chapter Two: References

Abrahamsson, Hans. (1951). *The Origin of Death: Studies in African Mythology.* Uppsala: Almqvist.

Bell, Diane, and Pam Ditton. (1980). *Law—The Old and the New: Aboriginal Women in Central Australia Speak Out.* Canberra: Central Australian Legal Aid Service.

Berglund, Axel-Ivar. (1976). *Zulu Thought-Patterns and Symbolism.* London: C. Hurst.

Bleek, Wilhelm. (1864). *Reynard the Fox in South Africa.* London: Trübner.

Boas, Franz. (1917). "The Origin of Death." *Journal of American Folklore* 30: 486–91.

Brain, James L. (1973). "Ancestors as Elders in Africa: Further Thoughts." *Africa* 43: 122–33.

Brookman-Amissah, Joseph. (1986). "Akan Proverbs About Death." *Anthropos* 81: 75–85.

Bunzel, Ruth. (1932). *Introduction to Zuni Ceremonialism.* Washington, D.C.: Bureau of American Ethnology.

Callaway, Henry. (1970). *The Religious System of the Amazulu.* Cape Town: C. Struik (orig. ed. 1868–70).

Charlesworth, Max, Howard Morphy, Diane Bell, and Kenneth Maddock (eds.). (1984). *Religion in Aboriginal Australia: An Anthology.* St. Lucia: University of Queensland Press.

Danquah, J. B. (1968). *The Akan Doctrine of God.* 2nd ed. London: Frank Cass (orig. ed. 1944).

Dockstader, Frederick J. (1954). *The Kachina and the White Man: A Study of the Influence of White Culture on the Hopi Kachina Cult.* Bloomfield Hills, Mich.: Cranbrook Institute of Science.

Durkheim, Émile. (1965). *The Elementary Forms of the Religious Life.* Trans. Joseph Ward Swain. New York: Free Press (orig. ed. 1912).

Eastwell, Harry D. (1982). "Voodoo Death and the Mechanism for Dispatch of the Dying in East Arnhem, Australia." *American Anthropologist* 84: 5–18.

Eliade, Mircea. (1973). *Australian Religions: An Introduction.* Ithaca, N.Y.: Cornell University Press.

Elkin, A. P. (1977). *Aboriginal Men of High Degree.* 2nd ed. St. Lucia: University of Queensland Press.

Fabian, Johannes. (1973). "How Others Die: Reflections on the Anthropology of Death." In Arien Mack (ed.), *Death in American Experience.* New York: Schocken, 177–201.

Fewkes, J. Walter. (1897). *Tusayan Katcinas.* Washington, D.C.: Bureau of American Ethnology.

Fewkes, J. Walter. (1901). "An Interpretation of Katcina Worship." *Journal of American Folklore* 14: 81–94.

Firth, Raymond. (1955). *The Fate of the Soul: An Interpretation of Some Primitive Concepts.* Cambridge: Cambridge University Press.

Fortes, Meyer. (1961). "Pietas in Ancestor Worship." *Journal of the Royal Anthropological Society* 91: 166–91.

———. (1965). "Some Reflections on Ancestor Worship in Africa." In M. Fortes and G. Dieterlen (eds.), *African Systems of Thought.* Oxford: Oxford University Press, 122–44.

Frobenius, Leo. (1928). *Atlantis.* Jena: E. Diedrichs.

Gill, Sam D. (1982). *Beyond "The Primitive": The Religions of Nonliterate Peoples.* Englewood Cliffs, N.J.: Prentice Hall.

Gluckman, Max. (1937). "Mortuary Customs and the Belief in Survival After Death Among the South-Eastern Bantu." *Bantu Studies* 11: 117–36.

Goody, Jack. (1962). *Death, Property, and the Ancestors: A Study of the Mortuary Customs of the LoDagaa of West Africa.* London: Tavistock.

Hallowell, A. Irving. (1940). "The Spirits of the Dead in Saultreaux Life and Thought." *Journal of the Royal Anthropological Institute* 70: 29–51.

———. (1976). *Contributions to Anthropology: Selected Papers of A. Irving Hallowell.* Chicago: University of Chicago Press.

Henry, Alexander. (1969). *Travels and Adventures in Canada and the Indian Territories, Between the Years 1760 and 1766.* Ed. James Bain. New York: B. Franklin (orig. ed. 1809).

Hertz, Robert. (1960). *Death and the Right Hand.* Trans. Rodney Needham and Claudia Needham. London: Cohen and West.

Hiatt, L. R. (1975). "Swallowing and Regurgitation in Australian Myth and Rite." In L. R. Hiatt (ed.), *Australian Aboriginal Mythology.* Canberra: Australian Institute of Aboriginal Studies, 143–62.

Howitt, A. W. (1887). "On Australian Medicine Men." *Journal of the Royal Anthropological Institute* 16: 23–58.

———. (1904). *The Native Tribes of South-East Australia.* London: Macmillan.

Hultkrantz, Äke. (1953). *Conceptions of the Soul Among North American Indians.* Stockholm: Ethnographical Museum of Sweden.

———. (1961). "An Ecological Approach to Religion." *Ethnos* 31: 131–50.

———. (1978). "The Cult of the Dead Among North American Indians." *Temenos* 14: 97–126.

———. (1983). "The Concept of the Supernatural in Primal Religion." *History of Religions* 22: 231–53.

Idowu, E. Bolaji. (1962). *Oldumare: God in Yoruba Belief.* London: Longman.

Jones, Peter. (1861). *History of the Ojebway Indians.* London: W. Bennett.

Kopytoff, Igor. (1971). "Ancestors as Elders in Africa." *Africa* 41: 129–42.

Kuckertz, H. (1983–84). "Symbol and Authority in Mpondo Ancestor Religion." *African Studies* 42: 113–33; 43: 1–18.

Lafitau, Joseph François. (1977). *Customs of the American Indians Compared with the Customs of Primitive Times.* Trans. and ed. William N. Fenton and Elizabeth L. Moore. Toronto: Champlain Society (orig. ed. 1724).

LeClercq, Christian. (1910). *New Relations of Gaspesia.* Trans. and ed. W. F. Ganong. Toronto: Champlain Society (orig. ed. 1686).

Maddock, Kenneth. (1972). *The Australian Aborigines: A Portrait of Their Society.* London: Allen Lane/Penguin Press.

Mathews, R. H. (1896). "The Burbung of the Wiradthuri Tribes." *Royal Anthropological Institute Journal* 25: 35–38.

———. (1905). *Ethnological Notes on the Aboriginal Tribes of South Wales and Victoria.* Sydney: F. W. White.

Mbiti, John S. (1969). *African Religions and Philosophy.* London: Heinemann.

Meggitt, Mervyn J. (1962). *Desert People: A Study of the Walbiri Aborigines of*

Central Australia. Sydney: Angus and Robertson.

Opoku, Kosi Asare. (1978). *West African Traditional Religion.* Accra, Ghana: F.E.P. International.

Parker, K. Langloh. (1905). *The Euahlayi Tribe: A Study of Aboriginal Life in Australia.* London: A. Constable.

———. (1953). *Australian Legendary Tales.* Sydney: Angus and Robertson (orig. ed. 1896).

Parsons, Elsie Clews. (1923). "The Origin Myth of the Zuni." *Journal of American Folk-Lore* 36: 135–62.

———. (1939). *Pueblo Indian Religion.* 2 vols. Chicago: University of Chicago Press.

Peterson, Nicolas. (1975). *Change and the Aboriginal.* Canberra: Department of Aboriginal Affairs, Australian Government Publishing Service.

Radcliffe-Brown, A. R. (1964). *The Andaman Islanders.* New York: Free Press (orig. ed. 1922).

Radin, Paul. (1937). *Primitive Religion: Its Nature and Origin.* New York: Viking Press.

Rivers, W. H. R. (1926). "The Primitive Conception of Death." In *Psychology and Ethnology.* London: Kegan Paul, 36–50.

Sanday, Peggy Reeves. (1986). *Divine Hunger: Cannibalism as a Cultural System.* Cambridge: Cambridge University Press.

Schwarzbaum, Haim. (1957). "The Overcrowded Earth." *Numen* 4: 59–71.

Spencer, Baldwin, and F. J. Gillen. (1899). *The Native Tribes of Central Australia.* 2 vols. London: Macmillan.

———. (1927). *The Arunta: A Study of a Stone Age People.* 2 vols. London: Macmillan.

Strehlow, T. G. H. (1947). *Aranda Traditions.* Melbourne: Melbourne University Press.

Taylor, John V. (1963). *The Primal Vision.* London: SCM Press.

Tooker, Elisabeth. (1964). *An Ethnography of the Huron Indians, 1615–1649.* Washington, D.C.: Smithsonian Institution.

Warner, W. Lloyd. (1937). *A Black Civilization: A Social Study of an Australian Tribe.* New York: Harper.

Woodburn, James. (1982). "Social Dimensions of Death in Four African Hunting and Gathering Societies." In Maurice Bloch and Jonathan Parry (eds.), *Death and the Regeneration of Life.* Cambridge: Cambridge University Press, 187–210.

Zahan, Dominique. (1979). *The Religion, Spirituality, and Thought of Traditional Africa.* Trans. Kate Ezra Martin and Lawrence M. Martin. Chicago: University of Chicago Press.

3

Asian Transcendence

A woman's infant son had died. Taking his body in her arms, the anguished mother went from house to house, saying, "Give me medicine for my child." The people she met replied, "Where have you ever seen medicine for the dead?" One person, however, advised her to go to the Buddha, who was staying in a nearby monastery. Perhaps he would have medicine for her son.

So the woman went to the Buddha. Standing in the congregation, she said, "O Exalted One, give me medicine for my son." The Buddha replied, "You did well coming to me for medicine. Go back to your village and find tiny grains of mustard seed from a house in which no one has died."

The woman returned to the village. Going from house to house, she requested mustard seeds. But at every house someone had died. Realizing that every family in the village had known death, the woman held her child and said, "Dear little son, I thought that you alone had been overtaken by this thing which men call death. But you are not the only one death has overtaken. Death is a law common to all mankind."

The woman returned to the Buddha. "Did you find the tiny grains of mustard seed?" he asked. "I am done with that," the woman answered. "I only want to learn your teachings" (adapted from Burtt, 1955: 43–46).

India, China, and Japan have all known the teachings of the Buddha and have adapted them at one time or another into forms of religious transcendence of death. Other traditions as well have flourished in those areas, producing distinctive religious approaches to life and death. Death and dying may be common to all humanity, but human beings have found remarkably diverse ways to work out a transcendence of that common fact. An exploration of religious approaches to death in the traditions of India, China, and Japan gives some idea of the diversity that has appeared in Asian ways of transcending death.

HINDU LIBERATION

More than 3,500 years ago, people who called themselves Aryas left their homelands in northwest Asia and eastern Europe in search of new territories. One group of Aryas migrated into the Indian subcontinent. There they encountered an indigenous population that they forced south and eventually conquered. Out of that struggle emerged a pastoral culture based on cattle breeding but supplemented by settled agriculture. It was a culture that prized the exploits of warriors in fighting enemies, conquering territories, and raiding neighboring groups for cattle (Lincoln, 1981b). But the Aryas also developed a rich religious life, reflected in the sacred scriptures, the Vedas, that were composed at that time.

Ancient Indian society developed a system of social classes in which political power was controlled by a warrior class and religious power was exercised by a priestly class. The concentration of social power in warriors and priests evolved into the traditional Indian caste system in which priests, warriors, merchants, and laborers formed a stratified hierarchy of social classes (Dumont, 1970).

In the hierarchical society of ancient India, priests officiated at the rituals—particularly rituals of sacrifice—for the gods who upheld the cosmic order. Warriors controlled the cattle and lands that formed the basis of their political power. The merchant class included farmers, traders, and entrepreneurs who kept the economy going. The laborers at the bottom of this social hierarchy were regarded as the natural servants of the three higher classes, excluded from social privileges and from full participation in Vedic religion.

The sacred texts, the Vedas, supported that social hierarchy. Understood as revealed texts, the Vedas assumed that the social order was built into the creation of the world. In one creation myth, the world was described as the result of a primordial death. The divine person, Puruṣa, was sacrificed by the gods to create the world. From the body of Puruṣa came the four classes of traditional Indian society: From his mouth came the priests, from his arms came the warriors, from his thighs came the merchants, and from his feet were produced the lowest social class, the laborers (*Ṛg Veda* X.90; O'Flaherty, 1981: 29–32).

Creation, therefore, originated in a ritual killing, in the sacrifice, death, and dispersion of the cosmic person, Puruṣa. The sacred order of that world could be maintained only by further sacrificial rituals performed by priests. That Vedic myth of origins also reinforced a commitment to maintaining the hierarchical social order. Because the social hierarchy was understood to have been part of the original design of creation, it was considered necessary to maintain.

Throughout the history of traditional Hindu religions, two seemingly contrary but interwoven religious motives have been evident: to maintain the cosmic and social order and to achieve liberation from it.

In the interest of maintaining order, Hindus were required to observe the ritual and ethical duties that were specific to their social classes. Those class duties were called *dharma*. Sometimes translated as righteousness, dharma implied a whole set of duties, obligations, and responsibilities incumbent on people because of their position in society. Simply, a priest's dharma was performed in sacrifice, a warrior's dharma on the battlefield, and a merchant's dharma in trade, agriculture, or the accumulation of wealth. Their duties were determined by their positions in the larger social order.

The most important religious duties, however, were fulfilled in performing or paying for ritual sacrifices. Although the lowest class was excluded from the rights and responsibilities associated with sacrifice, the householders, rulers, and priests performed various duties in that ritual. By doing those duties, they not only upheld the order of society but also gained merit that would be important in determining their fates after death (Hocart, 1950: 1–23).

Other forms of Hindu religion, however, sought liberation from a cosmic order that was experienced as oppressive. The term for that liberation was *mokṣa.* In those forms of Hindu religion that developed the idea of reincarnation, a person's social position was determined by actions in a previous life. According to the principle of *karma,* good actions produced good results, bad actions produced bad results. Those results were realized in a person's next life, as each life was part of a chain of cause and effect, actions and reactions.

While doing one's dharma might result in a good rebirth, the objective of many forms of Hindu religious beliefs and practices was to avoid being born again at all. Mokṣa implied liberation from the entire cycle of birth, death, and rebirth. As we will see, that freedom from rebirth might have been sought through a liberating knowledge or through a liberating devotion, but in either case mokṣa was understood as an ultimate freedom—perhaps achieved in this life but finalized in death—from a world order that was perceived not as a system to maintain but as a prison to escape.

The historian of religions Wendy O'Flaherty once noted that "much—some might even say all—of Indian religion is dedicated to the attempt to achieve immortality in one form or another" (1976: 214). Immortality might be achieved through rituals that conducted human beings along the paths of the gods and the ancestors. In traditional Hindu funeral rituals, for example, the immortality of the dead was a type of ancestral transcendence, ensuring the deceased's incorporation in the world of the ancestors. The rituals were efforts to assure rebirth in another place. However, immortality might also be achieved through forms of liberating knowledge and liberating devotion that released the human soul from the cycle of rebirth. In those cases, efforts were made to prevent rebirth through a radical freedom from the world, often taking the form of an experiential transcendence of death even in life.

Vedic Ritual

From the fourteenth century B.C.E. to the present, Hindu death rituals followed a consistent and common format throughout most of India. The formula for those rituals was set out in the Vedas, elaborated in commentaries, and practiced in almost all forms of Hindu religion. It specified cremation of the corpse, followed by a sequence of funeral ceremonies to be performed by surviving relatives. The ceremonies, or *śrāddhas,* ensured the entry of the deceased into the world of the ancestors and affirmed the ongoing connections that held families together, bridging whatever gaps in the generations death might have created.

Śrāddha In traditional Hindu practice, the bodies of people who died from leprous diseases, or of children, or of ascetics who had already performed their own funeral rites might be buried, but cremation was the preferred form for the disposition of the body. The corpse was regarded as a sacrificial offering to the fire. The Vedic god of the sacrificial fire, Agni, received the body and dispersed its elements. The body was reduced to ashes, the eyes directed to the sun, the breath scattered to the winds. The deceased was consumed by the cremation but might be reborn from the fires. If the rituals were performed correctly, a new body would be formed in which that person might live in the next world.

The formation of that new body was regarded as a long, gradual process. It began with the sacrificial offering of the old body to the flames and continued through a series of ceremonies in which surviving relatives played an essential role.

On the day after the cremation, the son of the deceased formed a ball out of cooked white rice. That rice ball, about the size of a tennis ball, was called a *piṇḍa*. It represented the temporary body of the deceased, a body that would be nourished by surviving relatives while that person made the transition to the world of the ancestors. Because the rice ball represented an ancestor in the making, it was treated with respect and reverence. It was placed on a small altar about half an inch high made out of dirt and was honored with incense, flowers, and white threads symbolizing clothing. A small lamp was set next to it.

While offering prayers for the deceased, the son poured a mixture of water and sesame seeds from a clay cup over the rice ball, signifying the nourishment and strengthening of a new body for the deceased. For ten days this piṇḍa service, the *sapiṇḍīkaraṇa,* was repeated. Each day, however, the number of cups of sesame seed water was increased, until on the final day ten cups were poured out over the rice ball.

The entire ritual process was meant to create and sustain a spiritual body for the deceased. The head was created the first day, the neck and shoulders the second day, then the heart and chest, the back, the stomach, the thighs and bowels, the lower legs and skin, the knees and hair, the genitals, and finally on the tenth day the power of digestion. The power of digestion signified that the spiritual body of the deceased would experience hunger, which could be satisfied only if surviving relatives continued to perform sacrifices and to present offerings of food for the dead. Śrāddha services, therefore, were death rituals that continued to be performed long after the death of a relative in order to keep providing nourishment for the spiritual body that had been created.

During the ten days after death, the deceased lingered in an interim state as a ghost. The ghost, or *preta,* was not yet integrated into the world of the ancestors. Its transformation depended on the ritual observances of surviving relatives. The incorporation of the ghost into the world of the ancestors—transforming a preta into a *pitṛ* or ancestor—did not occur until the eleventh day of the services after death. On that day, mourners were released from the impurity that resulted from their association with death. After ritual bathing, they returned to their homes purified. There a final ceremony was performed that acted out the introduction of the deceased into the company of the ancestors.

The ceremony on the final day lasted as long as ten hours, involving many different ritual observances. Eleven priests were invited to represent the ancestors. They were fed and honored as if they were the *pitarah,* the ancestors in heaven. One priest served as a stand-in for the ghost as it became an ancestor. Saying and doing nothing, that priest received worship and offerings from the surviving relatives. Offerings, gifts, and food for those priests were regarded as essential to the support of the deceased in the world of the ancestors.

In that final ceremony, the ghost was symbolically assimilated into its ancestors. A longer mass of cooked rice for the ghost was laid out on the ground next to three rice balls representing the lineage of the deceased's generations: father, grandfather, and great-grandfather. Reciting prayers from the Vedas, the son performing the ritual cut the cooked rice representing the ghost into three portions and blended each into the rice balls of the ancestors. Calling on each ancestor by name, the son blended the rice of the recently deceased into the rice balls of its father, grandfather, and great-grandfather. The son bid the deceased, "Go to your father, go to your grandfather, go to your great-grandfather." Finally, all three rice balls were blended into one, signifying the acceptance of the deceased into the company of the ancestors. From that moment, the ghost was now a revered ancestor in heaven (Bayly, 1981; Knipe, 1977).

Śrāddha rites, therefore, involved relatives in the survival of a deceased person after death. Priests served as mediators, but the relatives were ultimately responsible for meeting the needs of the deceased. In an important sense, the śrāddha rite was a ritual of rebirth. Fathers and mothers may have given birth to their children, but in the śrāddhas children gave birth to their parents. Surviving children provided the bodies and the nourishment that would allow their parents to be reborn in another world. The ten days of piṇḍa offerings echoed the ten-month gestation period according to the Hindu lunar calendar necessary for a human birth. The Vedic Hindu prayed, "May I be immortal through my children" (Griffith, 1963: I:471). This prayer could be answered in two ways: by living on through offspring and by being reborn in heaven through their ritual work in the śrāddha rites.

The Vedic funeral ceremony was a long, elaborate ritual process for marking the transition from ghost to ancestor. On the twelfth day, the transformation was complete. But that ritual process also marked the beginning of an ongoing commitment to nourishing and sustaining the ancestor through sacrifices and services that would continue to be performed by the survivors. In their homes, at temples, or on special pilgrimages to sacred shrines, the living continued to practice śrāddha rites that honored and supported their dead in the world of the ancestors.

Sacrifice The Hindu religion of the ancient Vedic texts was based on rituals of sacrifice. The sacred texts and commentaries gave detailed instructions for the ritual killing of animals and their offering to the sacrificial fire. As we noted, creation originally resulted from the sacrifice of the cosmic person, Puruṣa.

The gods sacrificed that primordial human to produce the order of nature and society. Not only the sun, moon, stars, earth, and water but also the four social classes were born from the killing and dismemberment of Puruṣa. That creative act was performed as a ritual sacrifice by the gods. It was reenacted through the ritual sacrifices performed by priests that were understood to give and sustain life for those who participated.

In other texts of the Vedas, Puruṣa was identified with the Lord of Creatures, Prajāpati. The divine Prajāpati gave birth to all beings through sacrifice. New life continued to be produced through sacrificial rituals. In the ritual killing of animals, Prajāpati was the sacrificer, the sacrificial victim, the recipient of the sacrifice, and the entire sacrificial ritual. Every part of the sacrifice was identified with the creative, life-giving power of the god. Although priests performed those rituals, Prajāpati animated the sacrifices by being present in all its aspects, bringing life out of death.

The gods themselves, however, were thought to be kept alive by the food offerings placed by priests in the sacrificial fires. And because the gods upheld the order of dharma, feeding the gods was a ritual means of supporting that order. The gods were preserved from death (*mṛytu*) and achieved a state of "nondying" (*amṛtam*) by means of continuous offerings provided for them on the altars of sacrifice. In Vedic religion, death was always regarded as evil (O'Flaherty, 1976: 213–14). But death—for both gods and humans—could be controlled and to a certain extent transcended through ritual sacrifice.

By performing sacrifices, people could achieve freedom from death in this life and the afterlife. Achieving nondying during the course of life simply meant living a long, full life. A long life span was considered to last 100 years. Givers of sacrifices lengthened their life spans. Those who paid fees to the priests officiating at sacrifices also shared in nondying by lengthening their lives and benefiting from the blessings in wealth, cattle, and children that were hoped to accompany a long life.

This power over death was reserved for the three higher classes of traditional Hindu society. Priests, rulers, and householders were among the "twice-born." In the ritual logic of sacrifice, the sacrificer was identified with the sacrificial victim. Instead of living the course of a life only to die at its end, the sacrificer died and was reborn every time the ritual was performed. Through successive deaths and rebirths, a certain power over death was attained.

When they entered the ritual space of the sacrifice, the sacrificers were thought to enter a sacred place, a *loka,* which was identified as heaven on earth. In that place, they gained the power of heaven. That power was not absolute because death still ended every human life. But the power of nondying generated by ritual sacrifice was thought to extend the length of a life.

After death, the food offerings made during a lifetime of ritual would be important for the survival of the deceased, as if that person had saved up a stockpile of food in the other world to consume after death. The ritual supply of food was supplemented by the offerings of surviving relatives, but each person could ensure sufficient provisions by conscientiously performing or providing for sacrifices while alive. In addition to laying in sacrificial food for the other world, the person worked at acquiring merit. Through a long lifetime of ritual observance, a person could transfer merit acquired during life into an afterlife existence. Rituals of sacrifice, therefore, not only were symbolic encounters with death and rebirth that generated the power of nondying in this life but were believed to provide the food and merit necessary to support a successful afterlife.

Cremation was also a sacrifice, the "third birth" of a person who had devoted a religious lifetime to the performance or support of ritual sacrifices. Vedic funeral hymns described the cremation as an offering to Agni, the god of the sacrificial fire. The survivors petitioned Agni to consume the body but to set the person free to journey on to the world of the ancestors. The living addressed the spirit of the deceased: "Go forth on those ancient paths on which our ancient fathers passed beyond." Finally, the survivors celebrated their own power of nondying generated by the sacrificial ritual of cremation. "We have gone forward to dance and laugh," the survivors declared in one funeral hymn, "stretching farther our own lengthening span of life" (*Ṛg Veda* X.14–18; O'Flaherty, 1981: 43–54).

Desiring a long and happy life, the living anticipated and prepared for a long life after death. Those who had prepared by participating in sacrificial rituals expected to live on in another place. Two places, or lokas, were possible: the loka of the ancestors and the loka of the gods (Gonda, 1966).

The loka of the ancestors (*pitṛ-loka*) was at the end of the path along which the deceased traveled after the funeral rituals. There the ancestors were sustained by the sacrifices of their children, but they were often called from that place to intercede on behalf of their descendants on earth.

Closely associated with the loka of the ancestors, the loka of the gods (*deva-loka*), located at the top of the sky, was ruled by Yama, the Lord of the Dead (Lincoln, 1981a). The Vedas described Yama as "the first of men that died." It was Yama "who first reached the river, spying out a path for many."

As the first to discover that path to the world of the gods, Yama ruled over the humans who came after him, accompanied by his two four-eyed dogs that acted as guides to those who were welcomed there but also as dangerous guards preventing entrance to others. Across the river of death, Yama ruled over a heavenly paradise where the dead drank the beverage of the gods, *Soma,* which increased their power of nondying. Restored to health and reunited with their families, survivors in Yama's world were saved from the danger of going through another death.

In the Vedic vision of the afterlife, images of hells or places of punishment were not developed in much detail. The sacred texts mentioned a "house of clay" or an "abyss" that seem to have been places of afterlife punishment in a gloomy underworld. There people were out of place, described as wandering about "like women without brothers, like wicked females hostile to their husbands." Places of punishment were reserved for enemies and for particularly evil people. But they were also destined for people who violated ritual standards and practices. Those who ignored the sacrifices could expect an afterlife of being devoured by the animals they had eaten in this world. People who showed so little respect for the ritual order that they went so far as to spit on a priest could expect to live after death in a pool of blood, where they sat chewing hair. This punishment was also specified for rulers who demanded taxes or tribute from priests. Afterlife punishments, therefore, were expected to result from violations of the ritual order (Keith, 1925: 409–10).

In most cases, ignoring or violating ritual resulted in afterlife punishment for the simple reason that the afterlife depended on ritual sacrifices. A successful afterlife was based primarily on the effectiveness of sacrificial rituals in transferring food and merit to the world of the gods and ancestors. In this regard, one Vedic text promised that a person after death would be born into a world that had already been prepared by ritual: "He is born in the world made by him" (Śatapatha-Brāhmaṇa VI.2.2.27; Müller, 1879–1900: XLI:181). Good deeds, therefore, were ritual actions that would establish a person's merit, nourishment, and support, which were believed necessary for any personal survival after death among the gods and ancestors.

Certain terms appeared in the practice of Vedic sacrificial ritual that became important in later Hindu thought about death. The first was *karma*. Literally meaning "action," karma (or *karman*) referred to the power of the sacrificial ritual, particularly the power of ritual actions to cause good effects. As the notion of karma developed in Hindu thought, it was extended from ritual to all action. Karma assumed an ethical character in the analysis of human conduct. All action came to be understood as governed by a karmic process of cause and effect.

A second term in Vedic ritual that assumed later importance was *brahman*. Originally meaning "sacred word," brahman was understood in Vedic ritual as the sacred power present in the gods, the priests, and the ritual actions, objects, and prayers used in the sacrifice. Brahman was described as an unlimited power, symbolized by the expanse of the sky or the diffusion of the atmosphere. Although brahman was an impersonal power, it was thought to be possible for individuals to identify with it. According to one Vedic text, "Man, through his participation in *brahman,* is coextensive with the universe." By knowing and experiencing this universal power, human beings could transcend the fear of death and perhaps even death itself.

A third term appeared in Vedic funeral hymns recited during a cremation. As the corpse burned on the funeral pyre, a priest petitioned the fire god Agni not to destroy the person entirely but to disperse the physical elements that had formed the living body. One of those elements was the breath, or *ātman*. Although the more ancient Vedic hymn commended the ātman to the wind, subsequent Vedic texts identified the ātman as the spiritual body produced by performing sacrificial rituals during life and to be occupied after death. A Vedic text on ritual instructions stressed the importance of that process: "Whatever oblation he sacrifices here, that becomes his *ātman* in the other world. When he leaves who knows thus leaves this world, that offering that follows him calls out to him, 'Come here. Here I am, your [divine] *ātman*'" (Śatapatha-Brāhmaṇa XI.2.2.5; Müller, 1879–1900: XLIV:26–27). Having paid for the performance of sacrifices during life, a person could expect to arrive in a heavenly realm to find a body already purchased and prepared. That spiritual body was a divine ātman.

Later Hindu thought used this term to signify an eternal, essential core of each human being that was unaffected by death. The ātman was understood as the immortal self, beyond life and death, that existed independent of embodiment. Although it resided at the core of each person's identity, the ātman was ultimately identified with the universal power of brahman. Realizing that equation, a person attained a liberating knowledge through which freedom from death could be achieved. Transcendence of death through liberating knowledge was cultivated by sages and their disciples who produced a body of sacred Hindu texts called the Upaniṣads. Composed around 600 B.C.E., those texts promised a knowledge that would liberate from death those who realized that ātman is brahman, that the self is one with the eternal divine power animating the universe.

Liberating Knowledge

The Upaniṣads (Upanishads) were written by small groups of sages and disciples who had dedicated their lives to pursuing a wisdom that would distinguish reality from illusion. By knowing reality, the sages of the Upaniṣads were convinced, human beings could achieve liberation from illusion. A passage from one of the Upaniṣads captures the spirit of the liberating knowledge to which those sages were devoted: "From the unreal lead me to the real, from darkness lead me to light, from death lead me to immortality" (*Bṛhad Āraṇyaka Upaniṣad* I.3.28; Radhakrishnan, 1953: 162). Because the ultimate reality was the eternal self (ātman), knowledge of that reality was a liberation from death.

More than merely useful information, that knowledge was understood as a transformative self-realization. To know oneself was to realize that the self was one with the deathless, transcendent brahman. The self was real, luminous, and deathless because it was identical to the divine power diffused throughout the universe. Although the 108 texts of the Upaniṣads (13 of which have traditionally been considered essential) were written by and for small groups of renunciates, they nevertheless influenced subsequent Hindu religion, spirituality, and transcendence of death (Deussen, 1906).

The philosophy of the Upaniṣads has been called Vedanta, meaning "after the Vedas," not only because it developed subsequent to the Vedas but because its philosophical perspectives seemed to depart from a Vedic commitment to ritual sacrifice in the transcendence of death. Nevertheless, the Upaniṣads were produced in a religious and social context that presupposed the ritual practices of the Vedic priests.

The innovation of Vedantic philosophy was the insistence that the proper religious sacrifice was a person's life. Not only the ritual offerings on the altar but the whole of a person's life could be sacrificed to gain liberation from death. The self beyond death was not constructed through rituals; it was discovered through knowledge, discipline, and renunciation of the world. Through self-sacrifice, the ātman was found to be already present as the eternal essence of a person.

Modifications on the theme of Vedic sacrifice were played out in a story told in the Katha Upaniṣad (Radhakrishnan, 1953: 593–648). In order to participate in a ritual sacrifice, a man provided a cow to be offered by the priests

on the altar. Instead of providing a good cow, the man selected a worthless animal for the sacrifice. His son, Naciketas, was so ashamed of his father that he
offered himself for the sacrifice in place of the unacceptable cow. Angry with
Naciketas, his father said, "Unto Death shall I give thee." Although his father
may have intended his outburst as an angry expletive—the equivalent of "Go
to hell"—his obedient son dutifully followed his father's instructions and went
off to the world of Yama. When Naciketas arrived in the realm of the dead,
however, Yama was away on a journey. The boy had to wait three days for
Yama's return. The Lord of the Dead was embarrassed by the lack of customary hospitality on the boy's visit, so he offered to give Naciketas three boons to
make up for the inconvenience.

First, Naciketas requested that he be allowed to return from the Land of the
Dead to his father. This first request was consistent with the boy's attitude toward death. Whereas his father saw death as a gateway to an afterlife in heaven
prepared by sacrificial rituals, Naciketas described death as an event within the
cycle of life. Death was part of the natural process found in all plant life. Birth,
growth, decay, death, and new life were movements in a self-contained cycle
that human beings also endured. Rather than immortality in heaven, Naciketas
requested a return to the human world. Yama agreed to guarantee the boy's safe
return to the living.

Second, Naciketas requested instruction in the way to achieve heavenly immortality through the fire sacrifice. Yama granted the second request by giving
a detailed explanation of the Vedic ritual methods for achieving nondying. Describing the stages of the fire sacrifice, Yama summarized the ancient ritual
techniques for avoiding a second death after death by establishing a spiritual
body in the heavenly worlds of the gods or the ancestors.

For his third boon, however, Naciketas requested a different and more
difficult wisdom. The boy asked Yama to reveal the secret of the self. "There
is this doubt in regard to a man who has departed, some [saying] that he is and
some that he is not," Naciketas observed. "I would be instructed in this knowledge." At first, Yama did not want to respond to this last request. The Lord of
the Dead offered Naciketas children, wealth, and long life as alternatives to his
third request. But the boy was not tempted by what he saw as transitory rewards in a life that must eventually end in death, so he persisted in questioning
Yama about the nature of the self. Observing that the boy had transcended all
desires for the goods of life, Yama agreed to reveal to Naciketas the secret
knowledge of the immortal self that transcended death.

In speaking of the self, Yama assumed the role of the Upaniṣadic teacher,
the guru giving secret and difficult instruction in liberating knowledge to
a disciple. Although knowledge of the self was hidden, the reality of that self
was present inside every human being. At the core of every person was the
ātman, an unchanging, eternal self that "constitutes the inner reality of each
individual."

The inner self remained hidden because it could not be discerned by the
ordinary senses. The ātman was a reality that could not be seen, heard, smelled,
tasted, or touched but nevertheless could be known. Knowledge of that self en-
tailed the realization of deathlessness. "The knowing self is never born; nor

does he die at any time," Yama explained. "He is unborn, eternal, abiding, and primeval." Since the secret self of each person was beyond death, the ultimate reality of every human being was deathlessness. "By discerning that," Yama advised, "one is freed from the face of death." By knowing the self beyond birth, life, and death, a person achieved a self-realization that had the power to transcend death.

In the liberating knowledge of the Upaniṣads, every person was revealed as an immortal self. The problem, of course, was that not everyone had that liberating knowledge. In fact, the ātman was a hidden reality penetrated by only a few. The inner self was veiled by layers of embodiment. It was hidden by the gross physical body (sthūla-śarīra) that was deceived by the senses, by a subtle body (suksma-śarīra) that was governed by thoughts and feelings, and by a causal body (kāraṇa-śarīra) that contained the karmic seeds produced by past actions. These three bodies wrapped around the eternal self like layers of an onion, hiding the ātman from view. Knowledge of the ātman therefore depended on peeling away the layers of embodiment that obscured the self, sacrificing senses, thoughts, feelings, and all attachments to action in order to discover the immortal self beyond the world.

The vast majority of human beings lived in ignorance of the eternal self, caught in an endless cycle of action in the world. Every action was determined by the law of karma. As the principles of ritual were applied to all action, every act was thought to produce effects. Good actions produced good effects, bad actions produced bad effects, and those effects determined the character of a person's life situation in this life as well as in the next. The principle of karma, therefore, extended over a series of lifetimes, trapping human beings in an endless cycle of bondage to the effects of their past actions. That cycle of birth, death, and rebirth—saṃsāra—was symbolized as a trap, a web, or a wheel that bound human beings. Rather than desiring a good rebirth, the sages of the Upaniṣads deplored the entire process of saṃsāra. Instead of performing the dharma of good deeds and ritual work in hope of attaining a better life after death, those sages sought liberation—mokṣa—from the cycle of life and death.

The Upaniṣadic analysis of the human condition came to be shared by many schools of Hindu religious thought. Agreement on four principles became widespread.

First, there was general agreement on the principle of rebirth. Human beings were born, lived, and died through a series of lifetimes. Reincarnation set the pattern for human life and death. Rebirth actually was understood as "re-death" because a series of lifetimes implied many deaths, a series of deaths causing the person to be reborn in another physical body. When attempts were made to reconcile the concept of reincarnation with ancestor worship, the sages concluded that the heavenly lokas were only temporary places of reward. Even the ancestors living in those worlds had to die again in order to be reborn as humans.

Second, the ritual principle of cause and effect was applied to all action. Karma became a generally accepted principle for understanding the good and bad consequences of actions. Although other factors also entered in, such as fate, destiny, time, place, and astrology, karma was the essential ingredient in determining the conditions of a person's life. As an ethical principle of action, karma became the basis for a forensic definition of human continuity. The person was the same from lifetime to lifetime because that person was responsible for and experienced the consequences of past actions. The subtle or causal bodies surrounding the eternal self also accounted for the continuity of the person from lifetime to lifetime. Those spiritual bodies contained the seeds that were sown in previous lives by good or bad actions. The quality of those past actions largely determined the conditions within which a person lived in the present.

Third, the entire process of rebirth was negatively evaluated. The cycle of birth, life, and death—the continuous round of redeaths—was experienced as a prison. From this negative analysis of the human condition followed a fourth principle: liberation. The Upaniṣads promised liberation from death and redeath through self-realization. When the self was known, it was realized as the sacred power diffused throughout the universe. The liberating knowledge of the Upaniṣads was an equation: ātman is brahman. Knowing the self as that divine power, liberation from the cycle of life and death was achieved. "Knowing that immortal *brahman*," declared the Upaniṣadic sage, "I am immortal" (*Bṛhad Āraṇyaka Upaniṣad* IV.4.17; Radhakrishnan, 1953: 277). Beyond saṃsāra, this liberating knowledge was a self-realization that promised immortality.

Liberating Devotion

The quest for liberation from the cycle of birth, life, and death was not found just among the renunciates who produced the Upaniṣads. Liberation was sought in the philosophical school of Sāṅkhya (Larson, 1979), in the disciplines of Yoga (Eliade, 1959), in the asceticism of Jain monks (Jaini, 1979), and, as we shall see, in the meditation practices of the Buddhists. From all these perspectives, the ultimate task of life was to achieve freedom from death and redeath. In most cases, freedom was attained through a liberating knowledge.

The quest for liberation from the prison of saṃsāra also appeared in the great Hindu epics, the *Mahābhārata* and the *Rāmāyaṇa,* which wove together myths, legends, and ethical precepts in stories about the adventures of gods and heroes. In some cases, liberation was also described in the epics as a type of knowledge.

The *Mahābhārata,* for example, told of the discourse of the sage Sanatsujata to a blind king on the subject of death. Death was not merely caused by ignorance, the sage argued, "ignorance *is* death." People who are ignorant and governed by their passions "cast off their bodies and repeatedly fall into hell. They are always followed by their senses. It is for this that ignorance receives the name of death." In desire, lust, and anger, human beings were chained to the cycle of rebirth and redeath. Sages who conquered ignorance, however, were freed from death. Just as ignorance was death, knowledge was immortality. "Ignorance, assuming the form of Yama, cannot devour that learned man who controlled his desires," Sanatsujata advised. "Indeed, as the body is destroyed when brought under the influence of death, so death itself is destroyed when it comes under the influence of knowledge" (Roy, 1884–94: IV:95ff.). Restraining the senses, desires, and attachments, the sage acquired a deathless knowledge of the immortal self.

While the quest for that liberating knowledge continued, other moments in the epics and popular Hindu literature promised a different path to liberation. The best illustration of alternative ways of achieving liberation was the *Bhagavad Gītā,* the "Song of the Lord" (Mascaro, 1963). Produced in its present form during the second or third centuries of the common era, the *Bhagavad Gītā* assumed an important place in the development of Hindu spirituality. Although incorporated as part of the *Mahābhārata,* the text of the *Bhagavad Gītā* stood out as a powerful testimony to the quest for liberation through a devotional love of God.

The *Gītā* related a conversation between the warrior Arjuna and his chariot driver, Kṛṣṇa (Krishna). In the midst of battle, wanting to avoid the senseless killing of warfare, Arjuna refused to fight. His chariot driver, however, told him to take up his arms and perform his duty as a warrior. Kṛṣṇa insisted that Arjuna had to carry out the responsibilities of his social class but perform them without attachment. In this way, he would be free of the karmic consequences of his actions. Even if Arjuna died while performing his duty as a warrior, he would die well because, as Kṛṣṇa suggested, "to die in one's duty is life." Faithfully carrying out one's class duties led to freedom from death.

In addition to Arjuna's dharma, however, Kṛṣṇa urged a second reason for the warrior to fight: knowledge of the eternal self. If Arjuna understood that each person was ultimately an immortal self, he would realize his enemies would not really die if they were killed in battle. In any event, the death of the physical body was certain and should not be grieved. "For the death of all that is born is certain, as also is certain the birth of all that dies; so in a matter that no one can prevent, you should not grieve" (II.27–28). The ātman, however, was indestructible, beyond birth and death.

The supreme liberation promised by the *Gītā,* however, was disclosed when Kṛṣṇa revealed himself as the incarnation of God. As a manifestation of the god Viṣṇu (Vishnu), Kṛṣṇa was a divine being in human form. Revealing his divinity to Arjuna, Kṛṣṇa appeared as the supreme god of life and death. "I am life immortal and death," Kṛṣṇa declared (IX.19). Through Kṛṣṇa appeared the god Viṣṇu, while through Viṣṇu appeared the eternal brahman of the universe. Kṛṣṇa was a personalized form of that formless, immortal power. Liberation might be achieved through ritual, or it might be achieved by knowledge, but in the *Gītā,* Kṛṣṇa promised a liberation through devotion to his personal human and divine form. "Take refuge in devotion to me," Kṛṣṇa advised (XII.11). Through love of God, liberation from the cycle of rebirth could be achieved. "Having come to this world of sorrow," Kṛṣṇa said, "love thou me." In devotion to that personal form of God, Kṛṣṇa promised that "he who loves me shall not perish" (IX.33). The warrior Arjuna responded to this offer of salvation through love by crying out to Kṛṣṇa, "O god supreme: be gracious unto me" (XI.31).

The liberating devotion of the *Bhagavad Gītā,* therefore, represented an alternative to Vedic ritual and Upaniṣadic knowledge. By loving God, devotees could expect liberation in the form of saving grace. If at the moment of death a person concentrated all thoughts on Kṛṣṇa, salvation would be achieved. "If you fix your mind and soul on me," Kṛṣṇa promised, "you will no doubt come to me" (VIII.2−13). That devotional salvation bypassed the heavenly realms of Yama, the gods, and the ancestors. Directing the love of the heart toward Kṛṣṇa, devotees could avoid the normal process of dying and rebirth and join Kṛṣṇa in paradise.

Liberation through devotional beliefs and devotional practices—such as praying, singing, dancing, and chanting the names and praises of the god—featured prominently in popular Hindu religious approaches to death. Liberation became salvation, resulting from the grace given by a god to whom the devotee was bound in love. The religious path of devotion, or *bhakti,* was essential for the transcendence of death in the two major traditions of Hindu devotional religion, Vaiṣṇavite and Śaivite. Both traditions cultivated a devotion that would break the bonds of karma by means of a stronger bond, divine love, which transcended death.

In Vaiṣṇavite tradition, the personal god Viṣṇu manifested in the human forms of avatars such as Kṛṣṇa and Rama to offer saving grace to human beings. One devotional text asserted, "Only the one, unchangeable Viṣṇu is capable of granting emancipation" (Sanyal, 1929−39: IV:215). Devotees of Viṣṇu who died with their last thoughts on the forms of that god could expect to be saved from the cycle of birth and death in Viṣṇu's heavenly realm, Vaikuṇṭha. Likewise, the Śaivite tradition was devoted to the worship of the god Śiva (Shiva). A Śaivite devotional text claimed that Śiva worship was more important than the Vedas. "A master of the four Vedas," Śiva assured his devotees, "is not dearer to me than a [slave] devoted to me" (Shastri and Kunst, 1970: IV:1946). At death, the devotee could anticipate salvation in Śiva's heaven, Kailāsa. In both traditions, the heavenly realms of those gracious gods were reached through a devotion that enabled the devotee to bypass the kingdom of Yama and to achieve liberation from rebirth.

All the forms of Hindu transcendence we have considered attempted to achieve liberation from death—liberation from a "second death" in the Vedic worlds of the gods and ancestors, liberation from rebirth and redeath through the transformative self-realization that ātman is brahman, and liberation from the cycle of rebirth through devotional connection to a saving god. Although these were paths through death, they were also ways of life. Each path encouraged an incorporation of death within the course of life. The recurring theme of redemptive sacrifice appeared in each path, whether in the Vedic rituals that sacrificed animals and other forms of personal wealth to purchase a spiritual body in the next life or in the forms of self-sacrifice found in the renunciation of personal life for the sake of a higher self or a higher divine being. Particularly in the paths of liberating knowledge and devotion, self-sacrifice was regarded as necessary both for life and for life after death. In sacred knowledge or devotion, a person could die to the world while still alive (Kinsley, 1977).

BUDDHIST MEDITATION

The Buddhist path was one of several non-Vedic movements that originated in India during the sixth century B.C.E. Founded by Siddhartha Gautama, of the warrior class and the Śakya clan, the Buddhist religion gradually spread throughout Asia in many diverse forms. Rejecting Vedic rituals, the Buddha taught a path to liberation that was based on an analysis of the human condition similar in many respects to the basic Hindu principles of rebirth, karma, saṃsāra, and liberation. A crucial difference, however, appeared in the Buddhist doctrine of nonself, *anatta* (Sanskrit, *anātman*), which denied the existence of any permanent, abiding, eternal essence within a person. Liberation could be achieved not by discovering the eternal self but by extinguishing all the desires that created attachments to the world of saṃsāra, including any desire to have a permanent self-identity. The Buddhist term for that liberation, literally signifying the blowing out of the flame of desire, was *nirvāṇa*. A crucial technique in achieving that liberated state, in life as well as in death, was meditation. As we will see, meditation on death itself became an important technique on the path to nirvāṇa.

Nirvāṇa

According to Buddhist legend, Buddha Siddhartha Gautama had lived into his late twenties in wealth and luxury, sheltered from any contact with human suffering by his protective father. In spite of his father's precautions, however, the young Gautama one day saw a sick man, the next day an old man, and the next day a dead man, and seeing them made him aware for the first time in his life of suffering and death. Leaving home, wife, and children, Siddhartha Gautama renounced the world to become a wandering ascetic in search of a way to eliminate human suffering. For several years he practiced austerities, denying the desires of the body. Gautama went to such extremes of self-denial that he became so thin he could grasp his spine by reaching in through his stomach. He abandoned thoughts of suicide because he realized he would only be reborn in a worse condition. Unless a person was liberated in this life, death held no hope of liberation.

Enlightenment One evening, Siddhartha Gautama sat down beneath a tree, determined not to move until he had achieved liberating enlightenment. While he sat in silent meditation, the evil demon of death, Mara, appeared to him. Mara challenged Gautama by arguing that he was unworthy of enlightenment and by tempting him with worldly pleasures and rewards. All through that night, Siddhartha Gautama struggled with the demon of death (Boyd, 1975). In achieving enlightenment that night, Gautama ultimately conquered death.

In Buddhist tradition, that night of enlightenment was divided into three stages. During the first stage, Gautama acquired memory of all his past lives, in which he had gained the spiritual merits that had prepared him for enlightenment. The past lives appeared as a continuous stream, moving from the past to the present. But once he acquired that memory, Gautama realized the personal continuity of that series of lives was only apparent. His personal life stream flowed into the streams of all humanity.

During the second stage of that night, Gautama saw all human beings living through a series of lifetimes, suffering over and over again through birth, illness, aging, and death, only to be reborn again. Seeing the suffering inherent in all those lives, Gautama experienced a profound compassion for all of humanity. All were bound up together in an endless cycle of suffering. The awareness of human suffering became the central focus of the Buddha's teachings. He insisted that a therapeutic concern for human suffering was the heart of his doctrine: "There is only one thing that I teach: suffering and the end of suffering."

In the first sermon after his enlightenment, the Buddha proposed an analysis of the human condition in terms of four truths. First, the truth of suffering revealed the cycle of human life to be pervaded by pain, loss, sorrow, grief, unhappiness, frustration, and all the many forms of human suffering (*dukkha*). People do not get what they want, so they suffer; or they do get what they want, but in the natural course of things it is lost to decay or death, so they still suffer.

Second, the truth of the cause of suffering was revealed to be desire. People suffer on account of their desires, cravings, or grasping for things they either do not get, or, if they do get them, they lose in the natural process of decay. Desire was the primary cause of suffering.

Third, the truth of the elimination of suffering revealed the Buddhist therapeutic logic: Suffering was eliminated not by satisfying desires but by extinguishing desires. Freedom from suffering—and, ultimately, liberation from the cycle of birth, illness, aging, and death—began with the control of desire.

The fourth truth specified the Buddhist path that led to a liberating elimination of desire. That Eightfold Path outlined levels of wisdom, morality, and meditation practice that would lead to freedom from suffering. According to Buddhist legend, that concern and compassion for human suffering was born out of Gautama's vision of the interconnected mass of humanity during the second stage of his night of enlightenment.

Finally, the third stage of that night revealed to Gautama the interconnections of the entire universe. The whole universe appeared in a state of flux. Nothing was permanent, everything was changing. The only permanence in the universe was change. Realizing the transitory nature of the universe, Siddhartha Gautama attained enlightenment.

Moving through the three stages of the night of enlightenment—attaining conscious memory of past lives, acquiring compassion for suffering humanity, and realizing the impermanence of existence—the Buddha conquered death. Significantly, he did not have to die to overcome death. Rather, the victory over death occurred through a radical change of consciousness, through the extinction of the flames of desire, grasping, and attachment, through a passage from saṃsāra to nirvāṇa.

Life, Death, and Deathlessness In the last stage of enlightenment, Gautama saw that everything came into existence as the result of a complex series of causes. In other words, everything was dependent for its origin on some prior cause, which itself was dependent on a prior cause, and so on. A human being was such a constellation of interdependent causes. A human life of suffering, old age, and death had an obvious prior cause in birth. But birth was caused by a series of prior conditions, the most important of which was the consciousness that carried the karmic seeds from previous lives. The prior causes of that karma-bearing consciousness could be traced to the ignorance that perpetuated the cycle of birth, death, and rebirth. A person, therefore, was nothing permanent but was the product of a series of causes. Dependent on those causes, any person came into existence and passed out of existence only to perpetuate the cyclical series of causes by being reborn again.

In Buddhist analysis, a person was a complex aggregation of elements—body, feelings, thoughts, karma, and consciousness—that came together when there was life but fell apart in decay. Like everything else, those elements were in constant flux. Unenlightened people mistakenly assumed that those elements (*khandas*) made up a permanent self. But while it was possible to speak conventionally about a person and a person's thoughts, feelings, and actions, in reality the Buddhist analysis denied the existence of any abiding "self" that unified those different elements. Behind the play of appearances, no eternal self waited to be discovered. Rather, the reality of a person was a moving, changing constellation of causes and elements behind which there was no self (*anatta*).

A person was regarded not as a thing but as a process of constant change. In one sense, the doctrine of anatta had a therapeutic intention. By giving up the illusion of being a permanent ego, the Buddhist could relinquish the attachments that bound human beings to the cycle of birth, death, and rebirth. Because that entire cycle of saṃsāra only produced suffering, release from ego attachments—and the desire, anger, and ignorance behind them—promised a therapeutic release from the suffering that was symptomatic of the human condition. As one of the Buddha's disciples explained the ultimately therapeutic goal of the Buddhist path, "the destruction of lust, hatred, and delusion is what is called *nirvāṇa*" (*Samyuta Nikāya* IV.251; Davids and Woodward, 1950: IV:171).

That awareness of the changing, fleeting, or transitory character of human life relativized death. Every moment could be understood as a type of death and rebirth. Because the elements that made up a person were constantly in flux, the person "died" every moment only to be reconstituted in the next. As a process of constant change, life was understood as a series of momentary death equivalents. Biological death was merely one more change in the sequence of changes that perpetuated life.

Death was also relativized by understanding nirvāṇa as the genuine break in the stream of life rather than the biological death of the physical body. Because physical death was part of the causal sequence leading to rebirth, it did not represent the end of the life stream. That stream continued to carry the karma-laden consciousness into another embodiment. But nirvāṇa was the radical breakthrough in the conditioned cycle of rebirth. In that breakthrough, the enlightened person was described as "going out like a lamp." The fires of desire, anger, and ignorance were extinguished. The illusion of a permanent ego identity was dissolved. In that symbolic death, the enlightened Buddhist achieved deathlessness. That state was attainable during the course of a lifetime. As the Buddha observed, "Nirvāṇa is visible in life." Achieving the deathless state of nirvāṇa while all the elements of body, feelings, thoughts, karma, and consciousness remained intact, an enlightened Buddhist could expect to remain deathless when those elements fell apart in death.

Steering a middle path between affirming or denying the survival of an immortal soul after death, the Buddha suggested that the causal series continued to combine and recombine the elements of body, feelings, thoughts, karma, and consciousness, but no permanent self continued after death. The Buddhist understanding of rebirth implied neither the eternalism of an immortal soul nor the nihilism of personal extinction after death. Like a flame passed from the wick of one candle to another, the elements were reproduced in the next lifetime. In that transition, there was continuity but no absolute identity.

The object of Buddhist religious practice was to extinguish that flame. Failing that extinction, however, people passed from lifetime to lifetime, carried along on the currents of their karma: "Some persons are reborn on earth, while evil-doers go to hell and good-doers go to heaven." The enlightened Buddhist, however, in extinguishing all attachments, was beyond the causation and conditioning of karma. "Those who are free from the causes of rebirth," concluded Buddhist teaching, "achieve *nirvāṇa*" (*Dhammapada* 126; Müller, 1879–1900: X:35).

In Buddhist reflection on rebirth, people still bound to the wheel of saṃsāra were expected to be reborn in one of six places that were called the "worlds of desire." These places, or lokas, were states of consciousness, but they were also worlds in which people were reembodied for another round of birth, suffering, and death. As worlds of desire, these lokas were places to which a transiting consciousness was directed after death because it still remained attached through lust, anger, and delusion to embodiment.

A new body might be found in the human world or the animal world, or it might take shape as a spiritual body in the ghost world (*preta-loka*) or the demon world (*asura-loka*), or that new body might endure punishments in the hell world or might be rewarded with a happy existence in the heaven world. Because all those worlds remained within saṃsāra, they were places of temporary embodiment. Living in those places, people were still subject to death and rebirth. Punishment in hell was a temporary purgation, but rewards in the heavenly realm were also of limited duration. Even in the six divine places of reward in heaven, the life span ranged from 16,000 celestial years at best down to 500 celestial years at worst (Kloetzli, 1983).

Free from desire, however, an enlightened consciousness was unattached to embodiment. Having achieved nirvāṇa during life, that consciousness was free to move through death and not become reestablished in another body and another place. Such a person would not be found by Mara, the god of death (*Dhammapada* 170; Müller, 1879–1900: X:47).

An enlightened person at the death of the physical body passed into *parinirvāṇa,* the final nirvāṇa, described as an everlasting state of deathlessness. That final nirvāṇa could not adequately be described because it was outside time and space, birth and death, and all the conditioned qualities of existence familiar to ordinary awareness. In one Buddhist text, parinirvāṇa was described simply as a state unlike anything known: "There is that sphere wherein is neither earth nor water nor fire nor air; . . . where there is neither this world nor the world beyond nor both together." That final state, therefore, was radically different from anything else that could be experienced. However, nirvāṇa was not merely the negation of ordinary experience; it was also liberation, "free from coming and going, from duration and decay; there is no beginning and no establishment, no result and no cause; this indeed is the end of suffering" (*Samyuta Nikāya* I.157–59; Davids and Woodward, 1950: I:196–98).

The Buddhist path was devoted to achieving that end of suffering in the supreme deathlessness of nirvāṇa. Practical techniques of meditation were developed toward that end. Meditation disciplined the body, emotions, and mind in order to bring all attachments to the life stream under control. Through the rigorous discipline of the senses, desires, and consciousness in meditation practice, the meditator gained a new freedom that might result in the radical liberation of nirvāṇa.

The Buddha discouraged any mental speculations that might distract the meditator from this practical path, including speculations about the nature of its goal. When asked about nirvāṇa, the Buddha described it only as deathlessness, beyond rebirth, in which all the ordinary qualities and characteristics of human existence have ceased. A student, however, persisted in asking about what happened to an enlightened person after death. In his response, the Buddha implied that the question about the afterlife of an enlightened person— called here a *Tathāgata*—could not be answered in terms of ordinary logic. Enigmatically, the Buddha said,

> A Tathāgata *is* after death.
> A Tathāgata *is not* after death.
> A Tathāgata *both is* and *is not* after death.
> A Tathāgata *neither is nor is not* after death.

To take any of these positions, the Buddha concluded, would be mental speculation (*Majjhima Nikāya,* I.485–86; Horner, 1959: II:163–64). The object of the Buddhist path was not to form some idea about nirvāṇa but to experience it. The path to deathlessness required practical techniques, not mental speculation. Through the discipline of meditation, nirvāṇa could be attained in this life and finally entered as a supreme deathlessness after death.

Death Meditations

The Buddha noted that every person was caught up in the life-and-death stream of existence, but not everyone was aware of that basic fact. Each person would die, but most people went about their lives as if they would never end, ignoring or denying the inevitability of their own deaths. From the Buddhist perspective, this pretense that death was not inevitable was an important part of the ignorance that blocked human beings from achieving liberating enlightenment. In one sermon, the Buddha remarked that the denial of death was similar to the attitude of a man who walked around all day unaware that his turban was on fire. The body was like a burning building, being slowly consumed by the flames that led inevitably to death. Freedom from destruction could be achieved not by ignoring that danger but by consciously facing it. Similarly, a transcendence of death could be achieved only by a conscious confrontation. An important part of Buddhist meditation practice was devoted to practicing precisely that conscious confrontation with death.

Buddhist meditations on death were systematized by the scholar Buddhaghosa. Although writing in the fifth century C.E., Buddhaghosa organized formulas for meditation that had been handed down and practiced within every
Buddhist monastic community (saṅgha). Supported by dedicated lay Buddhists,
monks devoted their lives to meditation. They practiced meditation techniques
of silent concentration on the breath coming in and the breath going out in order to still the mind. But they also practiced types of meditation in which they
focused on certain sounds, images, or themes that were felt to produce powerful psychological effects.

The death meditations were of this second variety. Although they were designed for the spiritual specialists in the monasteries, they cultivated an awareness of death that was encouraged for all Buddhists. In the text of his *Visuddhimagga*—"The Path of Purity"—Buddhaghosa classified death meditations
into two types: meditations on the inevitability of death and meditations on the
foulness of corpses (Buddhaghosa, 1923). These meditation practices did not
result from a morbid obsession with death; rather, they were practical techniques for consciously confronting death in order to achieve an experiential
transcendence.

The Inevitability of Death In keeping with the Buddhist analysis of saṃsāra, Buddhaghosa observed that human beings bound to the cycle of birth
and death were like oxen yoked to a machine. Like animals, people were unaware of the reality of their situation. By being mindful of death, a person could
see the true nature of reality: impermanence (*anicca*), suffering (*dukkha*), and
no-self (*anatta*). Meditation on death, therefore, reinforced the basic Buddhist
analysis of the human condition. By appreciating the instability of that condition, the meditator was encouraged to strive for deathlessness along the Buddhist path. Meditation on death was an important element in realizing the goal
of deathlessness.

Meditation on death could be practiced quite simply. The meditator could
sit quietly with his or her mind focused on the thought that "death will occur,
the life faculty will be interrupted." Or the meditator could mentally repeat the
word "death, death, death" over and over again as a focus for meditation. Even
such simple meditation practices began to overcome the ignorance that denied
death. But Buddhaghosa formulated a more detailed sequence of eight meditations designed to lead the meditator into a more profound confrontation with
death.

The first meditation visualized death in the guise of an executioner. The
meditator imagined the executioner's ax poised over the head of every human
being, ready to fall. In commenting on this meditation, Buddhaghosa observed
it assisted the meditator in remembering that death was inevitable because it
was an integral part of life. All human beings succumbed to death, even the executioner, eventually. As the sun inevitably sets, as mountain streams inevitably
flow downhill, human beings rushed toward death without any possibility of
reprieve. By being born, they were condemned to die. "Whatever is born,
brought into being and conditioned," Buddhaghosa concluded, "must necessarily decay and dissolve." This first meditation, therefore, encouraged a rec-

ognition that birth was the crime for which human beings were inevitably sentenced to death.

The second meditation focused on death as the ruin of all success. The meditator imagined all the accomplishments destroyed by death, all the happiness brought to its sudden end. In this second meditation, death was imagined as part of the impermanence and suffering of the human condition. Death transformed whatever success might have been achieved during the course of a life into tragic failure. In death, happiness became sorrow, wealth became poverty, power became weakness, and every victory was lost in one final defeat. Even the great Buddhist king Aśoka, who conquered and ruled vast territories, was in the end defeated by death.

In the third meditation, reflection on death became more personal. Whereas the earlier meditations focused on the fact that death came to all, the third practice instructed the meditator to concentrate on his or her own death. The meditator imagined the lives of great people, recognizing that even the great ended in death. People of great political power, great ethical character, great physical strength, great magical powers, and great knowledge, and even those great ones who achieved enlightenment, including the Buddha himself, all ended in death. In imagining those great lives, the meditator was instructed to conclude that his or her life would also end. "If this death inevitably befell those of great fame and great following," the meditator should realize, "then how shall it not befall me?"

The next three meditations continued to personalize death by concentrating on the vulnerability of a person's life. The fourth meditation focused on fatal forces attacking the body. Internal agents of death, such as germs, parasites, and diseases, shared the body of the meditator and could cause death at any moment. External agents such as snakes, scorpions, wild animals, and other causes of accidental death presented constant dangers.

In a similar way, the fifth meditation concentrated on how tenuous were the vital forces that sustained life. Bodily life depended on a delicate balance of breath, nutrition, water, temperature, and other factors. If any of these factors was absent, disrupted, or out of balance, life ceased. Whereas the previous meditation focused on the forces attacking the body, this fifth meditation concentrated on how precarious the life of the body was and how vulnerable it was to those fatal attacks.

The sixth meditation further intensified the meditator's confrontation with death by focusing on the idea that death waited in secret. Although death was certain, the precise moment of its coming could not be known. The time of death, the cause of death, and the condition of a person after death were all unknown. Since death could be hiding anywhere, the meditator was encouraged to be prepared at all times for its approach.

The last two meditations concentrated on the momentariness of life. In the seventh meditation, the meditator contemplated the brevity of the human life span. At best, it lasted only 100 years. Compared to the endless eons of time stretching out before and after, the duration of even the longest human life was very short. The meditator was encouraged to picture his or her life span as a tiny dew drop on a blade of grass, evaporating quickly, or as a line drawn by a stick on water, vanishing instantly. Through these images, the duration of a human life was revealed to be merely a brief moment.

Finally, the eighth meditation completed the sequence by contemplating the way in which death occurred in every moment. Life existed only in the present moment, but that moment was fleeting. The life stream consisted of moments that were constantly dying. Ultimately, this final meditation relativized death by recognizing the fact that a person "died" in the passing of each fleeting moment. By practicing this sequence of meditations, the Buddhist became free of all attachments to life and therefore free of any fear of death. Rather than avoiding any thought of death, the meditator intensified his or her imaginative confrontation with death in order to conquer it and achieve deathlessness.

The Foulness of Corpses A second set of death meditations concentrated on vivid images of human corpses. Foul, rotting, and repulsive corpses, in various states of decay and decomposition, became focal points for meditative concentration. Buddhaghosa outlined ten types of corpses to be contemplated. Since his text was called "The Path of Purity," it is perhaps ironic that part of that path led through the impurity of confronting corpses. But just as deathlessness could be achieved by focusing on death, purity could be gained by meditating on the foulness of corpses. In both types of death meditation, the meditator concentrated and intensified his or her encounter with the process of dying and the event of death in human existence in order to achieve the radical freedom of nonattachment that was a prelude to nirvāṇa.

Buddhist meditations on the foulness of corpses required the meditator to contemplate a human corpse lying abandoned on a cremation ground. Significantly, that decomposing corpse was not incorporated in any funeral ritual; rather, it was left lying exposed in its naked, repulsive decomposition. The meditator was to compare the rotting corpse with his or her own body: "As this is, so that is; as that is, so this is."

Again, this death meditation intensified the awareness of the meditator. Buddhaghosa suggested that the corpse meditations should be valued by the meditator as a vile medicine would be valued by the sick. In this case, the sickness was the attachment to the body, the assumption that the body provided the basis for a permanent self-identity. In breaking that attachment, Buddhist meditation provided a program of what, in one sense, could be called "shock therapy," which revealed the true nature of the body to be foulness. Although the images of rotting corpses were repulsive, Buddhaghosa promised that the meditations would bring joy and happiness to meditators who used them to get free from bondage to the life and death of the body.

Meditation on the foulness of corpses could be practiced in solitude, using the imagination. But it could also be performed in front of actual decaying corpses. The meditator could sit by a corpse (downwind, Buddhaghosa suggested) in order to contemplate the foulness of the human body directly.

Meditating on the different decaying conditions of corpses encouraged detachment from various aspects of human embodiment. If the corpse was bloated, swollen, or distorted, the meditator overcame lust for the enjoyment of any bodily form. The corpse's discoloration overcame attachments to complexion, its stench broke attachments to fragrance, its rigidity dissolved attachments to the graceful movements of bodies. If the corpse had been cut open, broken, or mangled in death, the meditator intensely contemplated the fact that a human body was not a stable thing. By meditating on corpses, the Buddhist was reminded that the body was not a substantial basis for any permanent self–identity. Not only eliminating physical desires for other bodies, meditation on the foulness of corpses dissolved the meditator's attachment to his or her own body.

The last two meditations on the foulness of corpses focused on the flesh and the bones. The meditator was to concentrate on a worm–eaten corpse, imagining the flesh as a home for worms, maggots, and other foul creatures. Ultimately, the flesh did not belong to a person but was shared in death by the worms. This meditation on the flesh overcame any tendency the meditator might have had to call his or her body "mine."

The final meditation contemplated the human skeleton. The meditator concentrated on the horrible condition of the human bones after death. A human skeleton represented the final state of foulness in the decomposition of the body. By way of contrast, the Ngaju Dyak analyzed by Robert Hertz saw the bones of the skeleton as symbols of purity. After the decomposition of the flesh, the bones were equated with the soul of the deceased. As that soul entered the land of the dead, the bones were entered with honor and celebration in a final burial. Similarly, the Iroquois had referred to the bones as the "soul" of the deceased. Denying the notion of an immortal soul, the Buddhists who practiced these meditations on corpses saw the skeleton as the final symbol of decay, decomposition, and the foulness of the body. Beneath the surface of all living flesh, the skeleton waited to emerge in death. By meditating on the foulness of corpses, Buddhists brought the skeleton to the surface of awareness in order to attain freedom from life and death.

These death meditations might be explained as psychotherapeutic strategies for overcoming death anxiety. In some ways, they were similar to the therapeutic techniques developed by the psychologist Victor Frankl for overcoming any anxiety. Frankl had considerable success with patients suffering from anticipatory anxiety. Fears were overcome not by avoiding them but by intensifying the very feelings of anxiety that made the patient uncomfortable. Through a psychological process Frankl called "implosion," the anxiety was intensified in order to be released (Frankl, 1962).

In Buddhist death meditations, however, that "implosion" was not merely the release of death anxiety. The purpose of the meditation practices was detachment from the desire and ignorance that bound a person to the cycle of life and death. In this regard, the meditations were ritual techniques in which the meditator symbolically died to the world. They may have functioned like the symbolic deaths in the initiation rituals of young boys and shamans that we considered in Australian religion. By confronting death in a highly charged ritual context, those practices allowed meditators, like initiates, to achieve an experiential transcendence of death even in the course of life (Bond, 1980).

All these Buddhist beliefs and practices that we have considered were developed in India in a Buddhist tradition called Theravāda. Subsequent developments altered and elaborated the strict logic of that Theravādan tradition.

First, the increasing importance of lay community involvement in the Buddhist religion led to popular emphasis on acquiring merit during a lifetime that would ensure a good rebirth. While the monks sought liberation from the cycle of rebirth, lay Buddhists could aspire to a better future life as a result of their good deeds in the present. Perhaps in the next life, householders might be reborn in life situations where they could become monks with the opportunity to achieve nirvāṇa. For lay Buddhists living an ordinary life outside the monastery, a popular text advised that "merit is pleasant at the time of death" (*Dhammapada* 331; Müller, 1879–1900: X:79).

Second, the Buddha was elevated to a semidivine status, to be shown worship and reverence at the various shrines, or *stupas,* that contained relics from his body or celebrated his memory. Along with Siddhartha Gautama, other enlightened beings began to receive popular devotion. Bodhisattvas, enlightened beings who postponed their final entry into nirvāṇa out of compassion for suffering humanity, were invoked and worshiped in popular Buddhist practice. Those gracious Buddhas were thought to share the merit they had gained with human beings, to extend a saving grace to people struggling in the cycle of life and death. Although Siddhartha Gautama's last words were recorded as "All things die, work out your own salvation with diligence," a popular Buddhist tradition began to invoke the saving grace of divine Buddhas.

The Bodhisattva Avalokiteśvara (the "Lord who looks down") was thought to extend grace to human beings out of his infinite compassion. The Bodhisattva Amitābha, the enlightened being of "boundless light," was believed to preside over a heavenly paradise. From that Pure Land, Amitābha extended saving grace to Buddhists who called on him in devotion. Like the Hindu movements devoted to the personal deities Viṣṇu and Śiva, forms of Buddhist worship emerged in the liberating devotion to Bodhisattvas. After death, a devotee could expect to be rescued from the cycle of rebirth by the saving grace of a divine Buddha.

These two developments—reliance on merit and dependence on saving grace—were important to the formation of the Buddhist tradition known as *Mahāyāna* (Suzuki, 1963). In that form, Buddhist beliefs and practices were transmitted throughout Asia. Although monastic and meditative disciplines also were adopted, they were combined with these popular religious developments. As we will see, varieties of Buddhist thought and practice became important in the religious life and the transcendence of death in China, Japan, and Tibet as well as other regions of the Far East.

CHINESE HARMONY

Archaeologists have discovered traces of religious life in China dating as far back as the Shang dynasty (c. 1523–1027 B.C.E.). At burial sites, bones were found inscribed with characters indicating the spiritual part of a person believed to return to the earth after death (*kuei*), a deceased ancestor (*tsu*), and spiritual beings (*shen*). Those inscriptions may have referred to practices of burial and beliefs about afterlife that persisted in China for centuries (Smith, 1958: 168).

In elaborate state funerals, the ruling class of the Shang dynasty was buried along with great displays of wealth, sometimes including dogs, horses, elephants, and even human beings in the same grave. Although usually less elaborate, earth burial was the common custom for the disposition of the body after death. Evidence has been found to suggest that efforts were made to keep the kuei spirit in the buried corpse by stopping up all its orifices, perhaps to protect the living. Nevertheless, ancestors were petitioned to intercede with the spiritual beings that ruled the universe on behalf of their descendants (Chang, 1968; Treistman, 1972).

Ancestor worship continued to develop as an important part of ancient Chinese religious practice during the Chou dynasty (c. 1027−256 B.C.E.). Originally reserved for the dynastic nobility, regular sacrificial offerings at ancestral temples kept alive the contact between the living and the spirits of their deceased ancestors.

In the context of ancestor worship, the aristocracy of the Chou dynasty was understood to have two spirits: *hun* and *p'o*. The hun spirit was the conscious personality during life; the p'o spirit was the vital, animating force of the body. After death, those spirits separated. The hun spirit remained conscious, retaining its faculties of intellect and will. Following the performance of a funeral ritual called "summoning back of the hun spirit," that spiritual personality joined the celestial court of the Emperor of Heaven (*T'ien*). Residing in that empire among the stars, the deceased became a spiritual being—a shen—served with sacrifices and invoked by surviving relatives for aid.

The p'o spirit, however, remained with the body after death, transforming into a dangerous ghost, or kuei spirit. That kuei might remain in the grave or it might descend to the shadowy world of the ghosts called the Yellow Springs that was located just beneath the surface of the earth. Originally, common people were thought to lack a hun spirit. At death, they were assumed to remain as ghosts in the ground or beneath the earth. Perhaps they were thought to contribute to the fertility of the fields, but they ceased to exist as conscious agents after death.

Gradually, however, these ancient Chinese concepts of life and death were generalized to apply to all human beings. Each person was composed of consciousness (hun) and vitality (p'o) during life, but those two spirits were separated at death. The hun spirit might become an immortal being in the celestial empire or in the blessed island of the spirits located somewhere to the east. The p'o spirit, however, would descend to the dark, gloomy underworld of the Yellow Springs to endure a sleeplike existence (Lai, 1983; Loewe, 1982: 25−37; Needham, 1954−74: II:71−126).

Contributing to the systematization of Chinese beliefs about death and afterlife were two traditions that emerged during the Chou dynasty, the Confucian and Taoist traditions. They had a profound impact on the development of subsequent Chinese religious history.

Tracing its origin to the philosopher Confucius (*Kung fu-tze,* 551−479 B.C.E.), the Confucian tradition cultivated a philosophical, ritual, and ethical way of life devoted to harmony. One aspect of that harmony was found in the analysis of life in terms of positive forces (*yang*) and negative forces (*yin*). Life revealed itself as a harmonious balance between yang and yin, in the corresponding positive and negative qualities that came together in life and dispersed in death.

Drawing its original inspiration from the text of the *Tao-te Ching,* a composite work attributed to the sage Lao-tzu (a contemporary of Confucius), the Taoist tradition also developed a way of life based on harmony. In addition to the balance of yang and yin, Taoists perceived a basic, underlying harmony in the natural way, or *tao,* of the universe. Attuned to the natural rhythms of the tao, some Taoists achieved a transcendent acceptance of death, a supreme calmness in returning to nature. Other Taoists, however, understood the way of nature to hold secrets of immortality that could be learned and used to live a long life and even to avoid death. Transcendence of death, therefore, was sought in acceptance as well as in a rejection of death through efforts to become immortal.

A third religious tradition, Buddhism, was introduced into China from India during the first century of the common era. The Mahāyāna Buddhist schools were disseminated throughout China and became well established by the T'ang dynasty (618–907 c.e.). Merging with local traditions, the Buddhist path assumed a distinctively Chinese character. All three traditions coexisted in close cooperation.

Confucian Balance

The teachings of the sage Confucius were oriented primarily toward living a balanced life in this world. Life was harmonized around the principle of *li,* usually translated as "propriety," which orchestrated both ritual and ethical action. In ethics, the principle of li took the form of reciprocity in human relations. Confucius recommended that people not do to others what they would not want done to themselves. The reciprocal principle of li led to balanced, harmonious relations among individuals, within families, within communities, and ultimately in the state. Living a humane life, therefore, was the primary concern of the original Confucian teachings.

In that humanistic spirit, Confucius did not encourage speculation about life after death. When one of his students questioned him about the existence of spiritual beings, Confucius responded, "If we are not yet able to serve man, how can we serve spiritual beings?" Before entering into speculations about other worlds, Confucius insisted that the human world must first be made a better place through mutual relations of service among people. Nevertheless, that student persisted in asking about what happened to the human spirit after death. But Confucius replied, "If we do not yet know about life, how can we know about death?" (Chan, 1963: 36).

Confucius supported ancestor worship because it contributed to harmonious human relationships among the living. The piety demonstrated in ancestor worship was a humane quality to be nurtured. Ancestor rituals were considered valuable because they provided a context within which humane virtues might be developed. In particular, the virtue of filial piety that was demonstrated in reverence to ancestors was a quality of character to be developed and demonstrated in all family relations.

If family relationships were harmonious, Confucius assumed that harmony would eventually permeate the entire political order. Sacrifices to ancestors might not bring blessings from the departed spirits, but they could cultivate the virtues of filial respect, loyalty, and love that would bring greater harmony to personal and social relations. The later Confucian philosopher Hsün Tzu (c. 298–238 B.C.E.) captured this attitude toward death rituals: "We should treat the dead like the living, the absent like the present; their end and their previous life should be alike" (Dubs, 1928: 227). Not only should the dead be respected, the living should be treated with the same service, reverence, and respect shown to the dead in ancestor rituals.

Confucian cosmology symbolized harmony in terms of the alternating balance of positive and negative forces. Everything in the universe was composed of yang and yin. These alternating forces accounted for all oppositions—male and female, light and dark, right and left, hot and cold, dry and wet, up and down, and so on. Not conflict but creative contrast was found in those oppositions. Nothing could exist without such contrasts. All living things were constituted by an alternating balance between those positive and negative forces. Therefore, any human being was composed of yang and yin. In Confucian thought, the conscious spirit—with intellect and will—was identified as a yang force; the vital, animating spirit was identified as yin. When they came together, there was a human life, but when they dispersed, there was death. Life and death were rhythmic alternations of those cosmic forces.

In human life, the alternation of positive and negative forces was thought to be coordinated by a refined material energy, ch'i, which integrated the contrasting forces. Because it held the positive and negative forces together, the ch'i was responsible for a person's life. When the ch'i ran out of energy, yang and yin forces separated, and the person died.

The neo-Confucian philosopher Chu Hsi summarized the developed Confucian analysis of life and death when he noted that a person was "born as a result of integration of refined material force [ch'i]. He possesses this material force only in a certain amount, which in time necessarily becomes exhausted." Circulating around the body and integrating its positive and negative forces, the limited energy supply of ch'i inevitably ran out.

When a person's ch'i was exhausted, the yang spirit and the yin spirit separated and proceeded along their different paths after death. "When exhaustion takes place," Chu Hsi observed, "the heavenly aspect of the soul [hun] and the vital force [ch'i] return to Heaven, and the earthly aspect of the soul [p'o] and body return to earth, and the man dies." In Confucian thought, therefore, a person was not a soul in a body; rather, a person was a balance of positive and negative forces, a harmony of heavenly and earthly spirits that were held together during life but separated at death.

Chu Hsi's summary of neo-Confucian doctrine was consistent with the general appreciation in Chinese religion for the natural balance of life and death. "Thus," Chu Hsi concluded, "as there is life, there is necessarily death, and as there is a beginning, there is necessarily an end" (Chan, 1963: 644–45). Life and death, like yang and yin, alternated in a necessary balance. A Confucian attitude toward death was cultivated in the calm acceptance of that balance.

Taoist Immortality

While Confucians aspired to a calm acceptance of death, the early Taoists embraced death and the symbolism of death through an ecstatic acceptance. In the early Taoist texts of the *Tao-te Ching* (fourth century B.C.E.) and *Chuang Tzu*

(c. 290 B.C.E.), death was imagined as a return to the original, powerful, chaotic unity that was the beginning and the end of all things. Chaos could also be embraced during life. The early Taoist ideal of action through nonaction, *wu-wei,* implied a way of life in which human intentions were not imposed on nature, but the natural, harmonious way, the tao, was followed wherever it might lead. Since that way led back to an original chaos, death was welcomed as part of the natural rhythm of the tao.

Later Taoists, however, drew on that natural way and its power for secrets of nature—meditations, breathing exercises, magical elixirs, and even immortality pills—through which they hoped to escape death. In the later Taoist immortality cults, a lengthened life and immortality were seen as the culmination of the way and the power of the tao (Creel, 1970: 1–24).

Early Taoists In moving from Confucian to Taoist approaches to death, a comparison with India may be apt. There we found two religious motives: One tried to maintain the order of the cosmos (through sacrificial ritual), the other attempted to break free from an order that was experienced as oppressive (through liberating knowledge or devotion). Similarly, Confucians understood the cosmic order as benevolent, leading to stability and good government. Life was devoted to maintaining that order; in death, a person remained within that order. The early Taoists, however, understood the cultural, social, and political orders—all the structures that organized human life—as oppressive, a great confusion that had been imposed on nature. Taoist beliefs and practices followed a trajectory back to a natural condition that was prior to all created order. Death was a return to that condition, but so was a life lived in harmony with the spontaneous, creative, and chaotic rhythms of the tao (Girardot, 1983: 129–33).

The *Tao-te Ching* advocated an attitude toward the human body very different from that of the Buddhist death meditations. For the Taoist, the body was treasured not only as a natural medium for human expression but also as a transcendent emblem for the entire world. By accepting the body—including its suffering, illness, aging, and death—the Taoist embraced the world. One passage of the *Tao-te Ching* stated, "Therefore treasure the body as the world, as if it can be trusted to the world. Love the body as the world, as if it can be trusted to the world" (Chen, 1973: 237). By loving and valuing the body, the Taoist aspired to be at peace with the world, in harmony with the natural rhythms of the world that were experienced through the body. When the world was identified with the body, the body was no longer a locus of self-centered ego identity but was as eternal as heaven and earth.

Death was viewed not as an end but as a way of disappearing in order to reappear. In that sense, even the tao died. The natural rhythm of the tao was an alternation of disappearing and reappearing, moving away and returning, dying in order to be renewed. In keeping with that natural rhythm, the physical death of the human body was a disappearance, but it was a phase that was understood to be a necessary part of the rhythm of life. If people separated themselves from the tao, then they suffered a real death with no possibility of renewal. In that spiritual death, the person was cut off from the creative, regenerative power of nature. Alienated from that life force, the person was re-garded as spiritually dead, even while the body was alive, because he or she had turned away from the renewing energy of nature.

By identifying with the tao, however, the Taoist did not suffer a self-centered spiritual death. Rather, the person in selfless surrender to the natural, living and dying rhythms of nature was said to be "long-lasting." The *Tao-te Ching* stated, "To be *tao* is to last long. This is to lose the body without com-ing to an end" (Chen, 1973: 238). The physical body may have been lost be-cause it was perishable. But the Taoist did not come to an end because the body had been identified with the universal tao. That union was described as simple and effortless: "When work is done the body retires. Such is the Tao of heaven" (Chen, 1973: 243).

After death, such a person was renewed by returning to the origin of life. The *Tao-te Ching* symbolized that regenerating return as a reunion with the original mother of life. "The world has an origin, which is the Mother of the world," one passage observed. "Return and abide by the Mother. This is to lose one's body without coming to an end" (Chen, 1973: 239). In this sense, death was understood as a return to life's origin. The tao was the root, the egg, the womb, and the mother of life. As an infant does not desire an identity separate from its mother, the Taoist gave up egotistical self-identity in life as well as in death. Letting go of individual life, the person lived on in the everlasting and universal mother of all life.

The Taoist text of the *Chuang Tzu* pursued this ecstatic acceptance of the natural rhythms of life and death. The text was traditionally ascribed to the poet Chuang Tzu (c. 399–295 B.C.E.), who understood life and death as arbi-trary distinctions made by people who did not perceive the underlying unity of all things that was the tao. In fact, he playfully resisted all such distinctions. In one story, Chuang Tzu related that he had dreamed on the previous night he was a butterfly. On waking, however, he was no longer sure whether he was a man who had dreamed he was a butterfly or a butterfly that was now dream-ing he was a man. Like the distinctions between sleeping and waking, dreams and reality, the common assumption that life and death were in opposition was questioned.

> Life is the companion of death, death is the beginning of life. Who un-derstands their workings? Man's life is a coming together of breath. If it comes together, there is life; if it scatters, there is death. And if life and death are companions to each other, then what is there for us to be anx-ious about? (Watson, 1968: 235)

Because the Taoist sage perceived the underlying unity of "all the ten thousand things," life and death were also one. In harmony with the tao, Chuang Tzu noted, "the sage wanders in a realm where things cannot get away from him. All are preserved. He delights in early death; he delights in old age; he delights in the beginning; he delights in the end" (Watson, 1968: 81).

According to Taoist legends about Chuang Tzu, the sage demonstrated that perception of underlying unity in his own life. After his wife died, Chuang Tzu was discovered by a visitor to be relaxing, sitting on the ground, singing a tune,

while beating out the rhythm on the back of a wooden bowl. The visitor re-
proached Chuang Tzu for not observing the customs of mourning. Chuang
Tzu replied that he was a normal man and had grieved when his wife died.
"But then I remembered," he explained, "that she had existed before this
birth."

> At that time she was without a body. Eventually, substance was added to
> that spirit, and taking form, was born. It is clear to me that the same pro-
> cess of change which brought my wife to birth eventually brought her to
> death, in a way as natural as the progression of the seasons. Winter follows
> autumn. Summer follows spring. To wail and groan while my wife is
> sleeping peacefully in eternity would be to deny these natural laws of
> which I cannot claim ignorance. So I refrain. (Kapleau, 1971: 13)

In the matter of his own death as well, Chuang Tzu demonstrated a Taoist embrace of nature and natural process. His disciples wanted to provide for him an
elaborate burial, with an expensive coffin and generous funeral gifts. Arguing
that he would have heaven and earth for his coffin, Chuang Tzu insisted that
his body simply be laid out on the ground. When his disciples protested that
the birds would eat his corpse, Chuang Tzu playfully replied, in effect, "Why
should we rob the birds to feed the worms?" (Watson, 1968: 361). From
Chuang Tzu's perspective, the body, nature, and the tao were unified in life and
death. The Taoist sage recognized death as a return to the origin of life. In that
ultimate harmony, death was an event that could be enthusiastically accepted
as a spiritual journey home.

Later Taoists As the Taoist tradition developed, a different concern for the
body became more prominent. Rather than accepting the natural changes of
the body in aging, death, and decay, Taoists developed a variety of techniques
to lengthen life and even to make the body immortal. Taoists practiced forms
of meditation, yoga, and other spiritual exercises to achieve longevity and immortality. They developed breathing exercises, called "embryonic breathing,"
in which the Taoist sat quietly, breathing rhythmically and holding the breath
as long as possible. The breath could be visualized as light circulating around
the body. Through this exercise, the rhythmic, luminous respiration was believed to produce a "Sea of Breath" within the physical body. Located in the
abdomen, that center of vital energy (ch'i) was expected to gradually form into
a living, spiritual replica of the person. That embryo of vital energy was thought
not only to lengthen a person's life but also to fly out of the body in death as a
new spiritual body (Wilhelm and Jung, 1931).

   Meditation techniques were often combined with medications, including
an immortality pill, that were thought to extend life. In Chinese alchemy, the
transformation of base matter into gold was identified with the process of spir-
itualizing the physical body. Elixirs were produced from various concoctions,
but gold often figured in the immortality potions. Other ingredients included
purple flowers, grasshoppers, snake blood, and wine made from rainwater, cin-
namon, and licorice. Since immortality elixirs also contained arsenic and mercury, they sometimes proved to be fatal. At least eight emperors died from ar-

senic or mercury poisoning as a result of taking immortality mixtures (Śivan, 1968: 41). Nevertheless, immortality potions and pills were considered important ingredients in the formation of a new and deathless body within the old body that would allow the person to survive death.

Significantly, these techniques all focused on the physical body. But Taoist longevity techniques were also believed to be effective in forming a new body within the old that would be released at death like a butterfly emerging from a cocoon. One sign these Taoists looked for to indicate that the techniques had been effective was the resistance of the corpse to decomposition. If the body left behind did not decay like ordinary corpses, then the techniques had worked. Unlike Chuang Tzu's ideal of merging into nature with the natural decay of the body, these later Taoists sought personal immortality through the transformation of the physical body into a permanent spiritual body (Robinet, 1979; Schipper, 1993).

Through those special techniques, the Taoist hoped to be transformed into an immortal being. As early as the fourth century B.C.E., Taoists imagined that some people after death did not descend to the Yellow Springs or merge into the universal tao but lived on in a spiritual body that had been formed and perfected during life. Transcending the world, those *immortals* traveled freely after death through worlds of light. In their spiritual forms, the immortals lived on the tops of sacred mountains or in a distant paradise in the east. Enjoying complete freedom after death, the immortals might still take an interest in the human world. But their spiritual existence transcended the world because they had achieved a personal immortality.

Buddhist Rebirth

The heavenly immortals—particularly the Eight Immortals—continued to play an important role in the development of popular Chinese religion. The immortals resided in 108 paradises, the most important of which was the blessed island of the Eight Immortals, who ruled over what was imagined as an elaborate bureaucracy of the afterlife. Characteristically, life and afterlife were both understood to be under an organized, bureaucratic administration.

In popular Chinese religion, human conduct traditionally had been thought to be under the jurisdiction of heaven. One text stated, "Heaven beholds the people on earth, and weighs their righteousness. After this examination, Heaven gives to each long life or short, according to his merits" (Brokaw, 1991; Weiger, 1969: 22). As the immortals developed as celestial administrators, an Arbiter of Human Destiny was believed to hold jurisdiction over human lives. That administrator of life spans shortened human lives on account of demerits that accrued from their actions. The immortal judge deducted days, weeks, months, and years from a human life on a sliding scale, depending on the seriousness of a person's misdeeds.

The Mahāyāna Buddhist movements that migrated from India to China merged with these indigenous Chinese religious concerns. First, the divine Buddhas—Bodhisattvas—became understood as something like the immortals, important celestial administrators in the cosmic bureaucracy. They ruled over paradises of heavenly reward, but they also served as tribunals who administered places of punishment. Second, the principles of karma and rebirth were introduced to explain the accounting system of merits and demerits, as good actions produced karmic merit, bad actions karmic demerit. In Buddhist analysis, however, the karmic consequences of action did not simply affect a life span but extended over a series of lifetimes. Even the places of afterlife punishment were merely temporary places of purgation, preparing a person after death for another birth.

By the tenth century C.E., these Chinese and Buddhist concerns for the administration of rewards and punishments had coalesced in a systematic picture of ten divine kings of hell, acting as ten Chinese magistrates, in ten underworld courts of justice. During the interim between death and rebirth, the transiting consciousness still bound to the cycle of saṃsāra could anticipate punishment in one or more of those hells. Past deeds were judged by tribunals presided over by divine Buddhas, who supervised the administration of appropriate punishments. The entire system was imagined as a vast underworld bureaucracy where people were judged and punished by divine magistrates before being sent on to their next lives.

The first tribunal of the underworld weighed people's past deeds. If good and bad deeds balanced equally, they were immediately sent back to be reborn. No further punishment was thought necessary. If bad deeds outweighed the good, however, they were taken to the "Terrace of the Mirror of Sinners." In that karmic mirror, they were forced to watch images of all the harm they had caused and the sufferings of all the people they had hurt. After that confrontation with the consequences of their past actions, they were directed to one of the other tribunals to receive punishments that corresponded to their sins.

If they had been dishonest, or inefficient doctors, or fraudulent marriage brokers, they were sent to the second tribunal. Under the direction of the divine magistrate, they were punished by being subjected to torture. Some were cut to pieces, some were devoured by animals, some were bound to red-hot pillars. In pain and torment, they were punished for their past deeds.

Many of the torments endured by the dead were punishments that were actually applied within the Chinese criminal justice system. Other punishments were more imaginative. People might be punished, for example, by having their brains removed and replaced by a hedgehog. Perhaps exchanging the brain for a hedgehog symbolized a loss of consciousness (like the Ojibway myth of the Skeleton-Woman replacing the deceased's brain with moss). On the other hand, that punishment might have signified a more remedial, educational change in consciousness since the hedgehog was valued as a symbol of wisdom throughout most of Asia. In either case, all the punishments were regarded as remedial because they purged and purified the consciousness before it could be reborn.

Each level of this Chinese Buddhist hell was reserved for the punishment of different kinds of sin. The consciousness was like a criminal, paying for crimes committed during a lifetime. Payments were demanded by the punishments administered at each level by a different divine king. Indicating the long cultural migration of these images of afterlife punishment, the king of the fifth tribunal was Yen-Wang—Chinese for the Vedic Lord of the Dead, Yama—who had become a divine Buddha in the administration of the Chinese Buddhist hell. In Chinese tradition, Yen-Wang had originally been responsible for the first level of hell but had been demoted because his punishments were too lenient.

After sinners had been sufficiently punished, they were all taken to the tenth tribunal. This last tribunal was not a place of punishment but a place of preparation for rebirth. Those who arrived at the tenth tribunal were forced to drink a "broth of oblivion" that would make them forget their past lives, as well as the interim period of punishment. Finally, they were thrown off the "Bridge of Pain" into the crimson river leading to rebirth (Brandon, 1967: 183–87; Goodrich, 1981).

Buddhist movements also migrated into Japan. One important movement originated in Chinese schools of meditation, called *Ch'an,* that had little use for the elaborate system of rewards and punishments described in the ten levels of hell. Ch'an meditation practice in China developed in Japan into the Buddhist discipline of Zen. Devoted to meditation, Zen Buddhists achieved states of mind that were considered beyond heaven and hell. A conversation between the Zen master Hakuin (1686–1769) and a warrior illustrates the transcendent quality of this alternative Buddhist position found in Chinese Ch'an and Japanese Zen approaches to death:

> A samurai warrior approached Hakuin, asking, "Do heaven and hell really exist?"
>
> "Who are you?" Hakuin asked in return.
>
> "I am a samurai," the warrior replied.
>
> "What kind of a samurai are you?" Hakuin exclaimed. "No ruler would have you as his guard. Your face is too stupid and ugly."
>
> Enraged, the warrior reached for his sword. But Hakuin calmly continued, "So, you have a sword. It's probably too dull to cut my head off."
>
> In a fury of anger, the warrior drew out his sword. At that moment, Hakuin looked directly at him and said, "*That* is hell!"
>
> Profoundly impressed by this, the warrior sheathed his sword and bowed before the Zen master with a new sense of humility and respect.
>
> "And *this*," Hakuin concluded, "is heaven." (adapted from Kapleau, 1971: 54)

JAPANESE DISCIPLINES

As in China, evidence of Japanese burial practices has been discovered in very ancient prehistoric sites. Skeletons have been found that had been buried with carefully folded arms, curled in a fetal position. Two interpretations of this practice have been offered: It may have been based on a belief that a dead person bound in such a position would not be able to return to haunt the living. Or it may have signified the hope that the person in that embryonic position would be reborn as a spirit (Kitagawa, 1987: 32). Perhaps both interpretations are correct. From ancient times, the dead were believed to be separated from their families only to be transformed into spirits that could be recontacted through ancestral rituals.

The world of spirits was important to ancient Japanese religion. Malevolent and benevolent spirits were felt to affect human life but also to exist in the form of human beings. The term *kami* was used for spiritual power. The kami were beings who held great spiritual power, the gods and goddesses, the sun, moon, and stars, and all the many beings of the spirit world. However, the term *kami* was also used for the spirits or souls of human beings. Impersonal spiritual power as well as those beings—both divine and human—who were endowed with power were kami.

Since no strict division between human beings and kami existed, the deceased easily moved into this realm of the divine spirits. In that state—as ancestors—the dead continued to be regarded as part of their family but also as part of the world of the spirits. With the appropriate funeral services and proper ritual attention, ancestors were understood to become kami. Clan ancestors were regularly worshiped in the home and at special shrines. Altars, memorial tablets, and ceremonial commemorations for ancestors became an important part of Japanese religion. Ancestor worship not only kept alive the memory of parents but also maintained contact between human beings and the world of the kami (Newell, 1974).

From ancient times, Japanese religious beliefs and practices included these three elements: contact with the world of the spirits, deification of human beings after death, and the ideal of filial piety (*ko*) directed toward elders during their lives as well as after their deaths (Hori, 1967: 214). Those elements of Japanese religion came together in the tradition of ancestor worship that continued throughout Japanese history to the present (Smith, 1974).

After the introduction of Buddhism from China in 538 C.E., Japanese religion developed into a complex syncretism of ancient and imported beliefs and practices (Kamstra, 1967). Only after the introduction of Buddhism did the Japanese require a name for their traditional religion. Those beliefs and practices were called *Shinto*. The term was derived by translating *kami* into a variation of the Chinese word for "spirit" (*shen*) and by adapting a word for "way" from the Chinese term, *tao*. Shinto, therefore, was the way of the spirits, to be distinguished from the way of the Buddha. Nevertheless, the traditions coexisted in harmony through much of Japanese history.

One strategy of reconciliation identified the ancient kami as Buddhas, as divine spirits acting for the benefit of human beings (Matsunaga, 1969). In that syncretism, the gods and goddesses of ancient Japan were equated with the enlightened beings and Bodhisattvas of India and China. With the equation of kami and Buddhas in Japanese Buddhist thought, it was generally assumed that human beings could become Buddhas after death. Annual Buddhist ceremonies for the dead, therefore, not only invoked the ancestors but also celebrated the dead that had become Buddhas (Ashikaga, 1950; Duyvendak, 1926).

In one important devotional tradition, Jōdo Shinshū founded by Honen (1133–1212) and his disciple Shinran (1173–1263), the dead were thought to enter the paradise of the Pure Land through the grace of the Bodhisattva Amida. But in many forms of popular and devotional Buddhist thought, death was seen as entry into Buddhahood. Japanese Buddhist beliefs and practices, therefore, involved a unique combination of indigenous and imported religious concerns for the dead, weaving together the powerful kami and the enlightened Buddhas.

While popular, devotional, and ceremonial forms of Japanese religion perpetuated ancestor worship, two more specialized spiritual disciplines cultivated distinctive ways of transcending death. Those disciplines were the way of meditation and the way of the warrior. Buddhist meditative discipline was practiced in Japanese schools of Zen. The meditation practice of Zen resulted not only in tranquility of mind but also in an experiential transcendence of death. By meditating on the impermanence of all things, the Zen Buddhist realized that every moment was a type of dying. In that realization, physical death could be faced with the same transcendent calm that was achieved through meditation practice during life.

Zen discipline had a profound impact on the class of warriors, or samurai, that served powerful warlords in the traditional Japanese political order. In that feudal order, a close relation between Zen monasteries and samurai developed. Out of that relationship emerged the way of the warrior, *Bushidō*. That rigorous warrior discipline adapted many Zen techniques. Martial arts, swordsmanship, archery, and combat itself were regarded as forms of meditation. Most important, however, Bushidō demanded a Zen-like resolution toward death on the part of warriors. A seventeenth-century manual for warriors, *Hagakure Bushidō*, instructed the samurai to embrace death as a friend: "When all things in life are false, there is only one thing true, death" (Iwadō, 1937). The Japanese disciplines of Zen and Bushidō, therefore, both cultivated an experiential transcendence of death. In similar ways, the monk and the warrior both embraced death in life.

Zen Masters

During the thirteenth century, two Buddhist schools of meditative discipline were established in Japan: Rinzai Zen, founded by Eisai (1141–1215), and Sōtō Zen, founded by Dōgen (1200–1253). Eisai and his student Dōgen had learned Ch'an meditation techniques through their travels in China. They modified and adapted those practices in the Japanese context to form two schools of Zen that have continued to flourish up to the present. The Rinzai and Sōtō schools both practiced techniques to achieve Buddhist enlightenment (*satori*). They differed, however, in their approach: The Rinzai school sought sudden illumination, while the Sōtō school advocated a more gentle, gradual approach to the experience of satori. Nevertheless, both schools of Zen developed an experiential transcendence that became important to the Japanese religious encounter with death.

In an essay on death, Dōgen summarized some of the basic insights into the human condition that were realized in Zen practice. His essay was titled *Shōji*—"Birth/Death." *Shōji* was the Japanese term for saṃsāra, the cycle of birth, death, and rebirth. Although Theravādan Buddhists in India had understood nirvāṇa to be radically different from saṃsāra, later Mahāyāna schools—including Zen—were convinced that the breakthrough of enlightenment came only by realizing that nirvāṇa was already present in saṃsāra. Zen Buddhists, therefore, might enter enlightenment by realizing that nirvāṇa was immediately available, precisely in the midst of life, and not some distant goal to be achieved. Dōgen advised,

> Only when one comes to understand that birth/death [saṃsāra] is the same as nirvāṇa does [the process] of being born and of dying become something which is not loathed and only then does "nirvāṇa" come to be something which one does not seek after. Then for the first time a [real] release from birth/death comes into being. (LaFleur, 1974: 237)

Ironically, Dōgen suggested that people could find nirvāṇa only when they stopped looking for it. Finding it everywhere, they did not have to search for it because it was already present. The quest for release from life and death was understood as an obstacle to any genuine liberation. The very struggle to get free turned life and death into a prison. By accepting life and death, however, the liberating release of nirvāṇa could be discovered in their midst. The eighteenth-century Zen master Hakuin also supported this perspective: "Not knowing how near the Truth is, people seek it far away: what a pity! This very earth is the Lotus Land of Purity, and this body is the body of the Buddha" (Suzuki, 1935: 151–52).

Zen meditation practice cultivated a tranquil attitude of mind. The practice of *zazen*—sitting quietly, regulating the breathing, and stilling the mind—contributed to a calm disposition toward life. Meditation was also the path to the radical breakthrough of enlightenment, satori (Suzuki, 1962: 153–247). In that experience, ordinary consciousness, thoughts, and feelings ceased to operate, so that a state something like death was achieved. But that meditative "death" was described as a state of great joy, an experience of illumination and freedom. Although that ecstatic experience was temporary, its effects continued to be manifested in a transcendent disposition toward life and death.

Confrontation with death—similar in some respects to the death meditations of Buddhaghosa—was also an essential part of Zen practice. Hakuin stressed the importance of a mindfulness of death. He advocated an experiential transcendence that did not avoid or deny death but confronted it directly. Imaginative entry into death, Hakuin advised, was crucial for the practice of Zen. "If you should have the desire to study Zen under a teacher and see into your own nature," he said, "you should first investigate the word *shi* [death]."

In order to investigate death, Hakuin recommended that a person contemplate one enigmatic question: "After you are dead and cremated, where has the main character gone?" The person should repeat that question throughout the day, while working, walking, standing, sitting, or lying down, so that the question might reveal its significance in the midst of life. Because it was an enigma, the question could not be resolved with any answer. Rather, the question intensified awareness of the basic existential dilemmas of the self (or no-self), impermanence, and death. After a few days of contemplating this question, Hakuin promised, the person would break through into a "decisive and ultimate great joy." By penetrating the enigmatic question, the person will have discovered "the key to the realm in which birth and death are transcended" (Yampolsky, 1971: 219).

Zen practice cultivated an experiential transcendence in meditation, in the activities of life, and finally in death. The process of dying could be accepted as an integral part of life but also as an opportunity for demonstrating a transcendence of the entire cycle of life and death that had been realized through meditation.

The most prominent exponent of Rinzai Zen to the Western world, D. T. Suzuki, identified this transcendent attitude toward the process of dying as an ideal in Zen as well as in Japanese culture more widely. That ideal was to die *isagi-yoku*—a conscious, graceful letting go of life. "To die *isagi-yoku* is one of the thoughts very dear to the Japanese heart," Suzuki observed. He explained,

> *Isagi-yoku* means "leaving no regrets," "with a clear conscience," "like a brave man," "with no reluctance," "in full possession of mind," and so on. The Japanese hate to see death met irresolutely and lingeringly; they desire to be blown away like the cherry blossoms before the wind.
> (Suzuki, 1959: 84–85)

In Zen, isagi-yoku was demonstrated not only through a conscious acceptance of death but also through the clarity, grace, and often even humor a person might show in the process of dying. Stories of the deaths of Zen masters served as ideal illustrations of a Zen art of dying. Their deaths became emblems of transcendence, symbolizing a freedom beyond life and death.

Some of these death stories related the way in which masters of Chinese Ch'an meditation practices had died. The process of dying was shown to be an opportunity for teaching Buddhist transcendence by example. When the master T'ien-huang was dying, he called the monk who was in charge of food and clothing in the temple to come to his room. As the monk sat on his bed, T'ien-huang asked, "Do you understand?" "No," the monk replied. Without a word, T'ien-huang picked up his pillow, threw it out the window, and fell back dead. The story of the master's death became a focal point for meditation, an incident to be contemplated for what it might reveal about the transcendence of life and death. It also became an example to be emulated by the Japanese Zen masters.

The deaths of many Zen masters demonstrated conscious control over the process of dying. The master Etsugen (1616–1681) called his monks together and told them that he had decided to die in one week, on the day of the Buddha's enlightenment. "If you have any questions left about the Teaching," Etsugen told his students, "you'd better ask them before then." During that week, Etsugen continued with his regular duties. But on the last night, he gave a sermon on the Buddha's enlightenment before the assembly of monks. The next morning, Etsugen bathed, put on ceremonial robes, and sat in the meditation position. He composed his death poem:

> [The Buddha] descended the mountain.
> I went up.
> In my teaching, I guess I've always been
> something of a maverick.
> And now I'm off to hell—yo-ho!
> The inquisitiveness of men is pure folly.

Writing a death poem was a common practice of Zen masters. The poem condensed a lifetime of teaching into a single, final gesture—like throwing a pillow through a window—that could be contemplated and meditated on by the master's students. Often enigmatic, playful, or even irreverent, Zen death poems captured a distinctive transcendence of death (Hoffman, 1986). Finishing his poem, Etsugen closed his eyes and died.

Other stories related a supreme control over the process of dying. The Zen master Fugai (1779–1847) felt one day that death was approaching. He asked one of his disciples to dig a grave for him. With great calmness and dignity, Fugai climbed into the grave and instructed his disciple to cover him with dirt. More recently, the Rōshi Yamamoto (1865–1961) decided that at age ninety-six it was time for him to die. Welcoming death, the master stopped eating. When his disciples asked him why he was not eating, Yamamoto told them that he did not want to be a burden to the community in his old age, so he was ready to die. Since it was midwinter, his disciples complained to him that everyone would be cold and uncomfortable at his funeral. If he died then, he would be an even greater nuisance than if he lived. Yamamoto resumed eating. But when the weather turned warm, he stopped eating again and died (adapted from Kapleau, 1971: 65–69).

Bushidō Warriors

In most religious traditions, warriors have played a special role. Killing and dying in battle, warriors have evoked religious symbolism in their confrontations with the power, violence, and tragedy of death (Aho, 1981). Complex religious symbols of redemptive sacrifice have worked in many different ways to absolve the warrior of any blame or guilt for killing and to assure the warrior of redemption should he die in battle. Redemptive sacrifice featured prominently in the religious disciplines of the warrior in India, China, and Japan (Dumezil, 1970).

In Hindu tradition, the ruling class was instructed in the "blameless, primeval law for warriors" (Müller, 1879–1900: XXV:230–32). By Kṛṣṇa's divine counsel in the *Bhagavad Gītā* the warrior Arjuna was exhorted to go into battle, recognizing that the eternal souls of his enemies could not really die and he could not really be killed. If he were killed, however, he would be redeemed because he had done his duty honorably.

A passage in the Hindu epic the *Mahābhārata* confirmed the religious and ethical duty of a warrior. He should not die in bed of old age; rather, "surrounded by kinsmen and slaughtering his foes in battle, a [warrior] should die at the edge of keen weapons" (Roy, 1884–94: VIII:222).

Traditional China also glorified the warrior within the symbolism of redemptive sacrifice. The sacrifice of men on the battlefield was equated with the sacrifice of animals on the altars to the gods: "The Great Affairs of the state are sacrifice and war. At sacrifices [in the ancestral temple] the officers receive the roasted flesh; in war they receive that offered at the altar of the land; these are the great ceremonies in worshipping the Spirits" (Legge, 1895: V:382).

While being offered to the spirits on the altar of the battlefield, human lives sacrificed in war were also sacrificed for political interests. The symbolism of redemptive sacrifice on the battlefield clearly served the interests of ruling classes, feudal warlords, and states. In those interests, religion and politics merged in the powerful religious legitimation for the violence, killing, and death in warfare (Chidester, 1987: 270–79). In the religious symbolism of redemptive sacrifice, a type of cultural transcendence was achieved. Warriors might die in battle, but they would live on through their heroic and sacrificial deeds in the culture, society, or state for which they died. Death in battle has been a powerful form of cultural transcendence in the history of religions.

The discipline of the warrior, Bushidō, in traditional Japan provided more than religious legitimation for involvement in warfare. Bushidō developed into a spiritual way of life in which the warrior realized a transcendence of death that was similar in many respects to that achieved by the Zen master. In fact, the master Hakuin observed that the battlefield was the supreme test for a Zen transcendence of the cycle of life and death:

> Mounted on a sturdy horse, the warrior can ride forth to face an uncountable horde of enemies as though he were riding into a place empty of people. The valiant, undaunted expression on his face reflects his practice of the peerless, true, uninterrupted meditation sitting. Meditating in this way, the warrior can accomplish in one month what it takes the monk a year to do; in three days he can open up for himself benefits that would take the monk a hundred years. (Yampolsky, 1971: 68)

Not only had the warrior benefited from Zen meditation, but the entrance into battle itself had the qualities of a meditation in motion. In quiet meditation, a Zen monk might experience the quality of "emptiness." But the warrior could experience that same transcendent quality on a battlefield full of raging enemies. Confronting death so directly, the warrior could gain the transcendent insights that Hakuin felt were essential to the Zen Buddhist path. Like the monk, the warrior had to be consciously mindful of death. The samurai, however, had to confront and come to terms with death in contexts that were immediately dangerous. "The word *death*," Hakuin concluded, "is the vital essential that the warrior must first determine for himself" (Yampolsky, 1971: 219).

Although the term *Bushidō* did not come into use until the Tokugawa period (1600–1867), the idea that warriors could follow the Buddhist path dated back at least to the time of Minamoto Yoritomo (1148–1199), the first shōgun at Kamakura (Anesaki, 1930: 210–14; Nukariya, 1913). The shōgun enlisted warriors into his service and into the Buddhist path at the same time. Over a long history of almost constant conflict among rival warlords, the discipline of the warrior developed into a religious way of life in the face of death. In that discipline, the first demand was absolute loyalty to the warlord. That loyalty spanned heaven and earth: "Wherever we may be, deep in mountain recesses or buried underground, anytime or anywhere our duty is to guard the interest of our Lord." The Buddhist doctrine of nonself was translated into a selfless service of the shōgun and the interests of that warlord. "This is the backbone of our faith," warriors were to affirm, "unchanging and eternally true."

After surrendering self to the warlord, the warrior was to enter into the rituals of warfare in a state of mind that abandoned rationality. Just as Zen meditation transcended ordinary reason, the discipline of the warrior required an attitude that was beyond reason. Whereas self-preservation might be rational, self-sacrifice consciously defied reason. More than that, however, Bushidō aspired to a nonrational power that would emerge when reason was sacrificed. "When you are on the field of battle," the warrior was advised, "close your mind to reasoning: for once you begin to reason, you are lost. Reasoning robs you of that force with which alone you can carve your goal." All the martial arts cultivated a power beyond reason—the *ki* (Chinese *ch'i*)—that directed the hands, or the sword, or the arrow in ways that rationality could not determine.

Finally, the discipline of Bushidō required the warrior to be dedicated to death. The way of the warrior was the way of death. The "Great Death" of the Zen master—conscious, graceful, and in the fullness of life—was the ideal of the samurai warrior. Like a cherry blossom falling from a tree, the warrior should be prepared to fall in battle. Prepared for death, the warrior achieved a transcendent state of mind. Instructions for warriors insisted that they prepare themselves for death:

> Every morning make up your mind how to die. Every evening freshen your mind with the thought of death. And let this be done without end. Thus will your mind be prepared.

These instructions in Bushidō were given in a text called *Hagakure* ("Hidden Behind Leaves") of the seventeenth century (Iwadō, 1937). But the ideals of redemptive sacrifice—loyalty, power beyond reason, and preparation for death—were essential for the samurai warrior class in Japan over preceding centuries of military and political conflict. Warriors prepared to participate in those conflicts by sacrificing any sense of self before they sacrificed their bodies. The warrior enacted the ideal Zen death on the battlefield.

The warrior was prepared not only to die in battle but by suicide when that act was considered necessary. *Seppuku,* or *hara-kiri,* was a self-inflicted death that became one of the warrior's arts of dying. In some cases, seppuku was considered an honor granted to warriors when they had been convicted of crimes. Instead of submitting to execution, they were allowed to take their own lives. But seppuku might also be performed voluntarily for other reasons. In order to avoid the disgrace of falling into enemy hands, to follow the warlord into death, or to protest some injustice, an act of intentional self-sacrifice might be performed. The warrior followed a strict formula in that suicide, cutting into the center of spiritual power—ki—represented by the abdomen, revealing that center to be pure, undefiled by any guilt or shame. In seppuku, the warrior was not only prepared for death but brought about death intentionally by a controlled, transcendent act of self-sacrifice (Seward, 1968).

ASIAN TRANSCENDENCE

The religions of India, China, and Japan developed many different ways of transcending death. In some cases, such as the Vedic rituals of ancient India and the Taoist immortality rituals of ancient China, death was an evil to be avoided. Techniques of ritual sacrifice, funeral rites, yoga, alchemy, and even immortality pills were used to gain the blessing of a long life and to make a body to live in after death. The goal of these practices was to transcend death by not dying.

In other instances, death was incorporated within life. Forms of self-sacrifice supported a transcendence of death by making death a part of life. Buddhists in particular found ways of transcending death by recognizing that every moment of life was dying and rebirth. In that realization, Buddhists could regard themselves as being just as dead in each moment as they ever would be in the future. In other words, death was merely another name for the process of change that made life impermanent. The goal of the Buddhist path was to transcend death by confronting, accepting, and embracing death in the extinction of desires. By dying well, however, a person might also achieve deathlessness—freedom from the cycle of rebirth and redeath in the unconditional state of nirvāṇa.

Patterns of transcendence in the religions of India, China, and Japan were complex and varied. It might be useful to briefly recollect some of the beliefs and practices that supported a transcendence of death in those religious traditions.

Ancestral transcendence was important in the popular religious practices of India. The traditional Hindu śrāddha ritual acted out an ancestral transcendence. The ritual was a long, detailed, and careful process that marked the transition of the deceased from a ghost to an ancestor. Established in the world of the ancestors by the efforts of descendants, the ancestor continued to receive their support through rituals that celebrated family ties between the living and the dead. On pilgrimages to holy places, for example, families often performed śrāddha rituals in honor and in support of their deceased ancestors. These rituals celebrated the living reality of family and kinship relations that lived on after death.

Likewise, ancestral transcendence was a vital part of the religions of China and Japan. In China, all three religious traditions—Confucian, Taoist, and Buddhist—integrated ancestral rituals into their worship. All three religions supported the popular practice of offering "spirit money" to ancestors at their temples. Paper money was burned in special furnaces as an offering to the dead. Spirit money came in different denominations—for gods, spirits, ancestors, hungry ghosts, and the living—but they were all offered as a form of spiritual payment. When offered to ancestors, spirit money represented a transfer of credit to pay the living's debts to the dead and to ensure good fortune for both the living and the dead (Seidel, 1977). The religions of India, China, and Japan, therefore, supported ancestral transcendence through ritual practices in the home, in the temple, at sacred shrines, and during special festivals that honored and supported the dead.

Experiential transcendence appeared in various forms of self-sacrifice. In different ways, the self—as a personal ego identity—was given up in life in order to overcome death. If a person had no separate, personal identity, that person could not really die. By sacrificing attachments to the ego, body, and personal desires, Naciketas found the ātman, Gautama found nirvāṇa, Arjuna found bhakti, Chuang Tzu found the tao, and Hakuin found satori. Whatever these discoveries were, they had one thing in common: They were beyond death. In different ways, they represented a liberation from death that was accomplished in the midst of life.

When it came to dying, the Buddhist path in particular supported a calm acceptance. The Zen Buddhist ideal of a tranquil, effortless letting go—isagi yoku—was held by both Zen masters in meditation and Bushidō warriors in the heat of battle. But Zen also encouraged an open, honest, and even playful encounter with death. A Zen encounter with death was perhaps most clearly revealed in the practice of writing death poems. Sometimes those poems showed a disarming honesty in approaching death.

A Zen master was about to die. Asked to write his death poem for his disciples, the master lay on his deathbed and thoughtfully wrote out his last words. In the assembly hall, the disciples gathered to listen to a reading of their master's death poem. With reverence, the chief disciple opened the paper and read, "I do not want to die."

Fearing some mistake, the disciple returned to the master and asked once again for a death poem that would be a fitting last testament to the master's teachings. Slowly and carefully, the master wrote another death poem. When the chief disciple returned to the assembly hall, opened the paper, and read the poem, the gathering of monks heard the last words of the master: "Truly, I do not want to die!"

Cultural transcendence symbolized the continuity of the social order. In India, the system of four classes idealized a social order that outlived any individual. Living and dying while performing the duty (dharma) of one's class symbolized a type of cultural transcendence of death. The class system lived on as the human social world in which people were born and reborn over a series of lifetimes. In a sense, reincarnation represented the continuity of individuals as well as the social order in which individuals were reborn.

Another aspect of cultural transcendence appeared in the continuity of the political order ensured by the sacrifices of warriors on the field of battle. As Confucius suggested, animal sacrifices to the gods were made on the altar of the temple; human sacrifices to the state were made on the altar of the battlefield. By sacrificing their lives, warriors participated in a cultural transcendence of death. Most clearly illustrated in Japanese Bushidō, the way of the warrior was often glorified as a form of redemptive self-sacrifice: The warrior gave himself to death in order that the political order of a society might live.

The ideology of redemptive sacrifice in battle has been a persistent form of cultural transcendence in the history of religions. In the modern world, redemptive sacrifice became the central doctrine of religious nationalism. As the dominant religion of the modern world, nationalism promised a cultural transcendence of death that could be achieved by those who died for their country.

Mythic transcendence in the religions of India, China, and Japan sometimes promised life after death in an otherworldly place. The Vedic worlds of gods and ancestors, the paradises of devotional deities, the underworld hells of afterlife punishment—these were all places that were mapped out in religious myths.

However, some religious approaches to death promised an afterlife in no place. Beyond all considerations of place, death represented an entry into a supreme transcendence of time and space. Entry into brahman, or nirvāṇa, or the tao after death transcended all considerations of place. Life after death promised to be every place and no place at the same time. From this perspective, Hakuin advocated a mythic transcendence of myth itself: Heaven and hell were nothing more (or less) than states of mind. In the liberation of consciousness, both heaven and hell could be transcended in an unconditional state beyond death.

Transcendence of death through the radical liberation of consciousness during life was an important theme that appeared frequently in the religions of India, China, and Japan. We will also encounter this approach to death among the Tibetan Buddhists we will consider in the next chapter. As we will see, *The Tibetan Book of the Dead* was a visionary journey through myth toward a transcendence of myth in the liberation of consciousness.

Chapter Three: References

Aho, James A. (1981). *Religious Mythology and the Art of War: Comparative Religious Symbolisms of Military Violence.* Westport, Conn.: Greenwood Press.

Anesaki, Masaharu. (1930). *History of Japanese Religion.* London: Routledge and Kegan Paul.

Ashikaga, Ensho. (1950). "The Festival of the Spirits of the Dead in Japan." *Western Folklore* 9: 217–28.

Bayly, C. A. (1981). "From Ritual to Ceremony: Death Ritual and Society in Hindu North India since 1600." In Joachim Whaley (ed.), *Mirrors of Mortality: Studies in the Social History of Death.* London: Europa Publications, 154–86.

Becker, Carl B. (1993). *Breaking the Circle: Death and Afterlife in Buddhism.* Carbondale: Southern Illinois University Press.

Bond, George D. (1980). "Theravāda Buddhism's Meditations on Death and the Symbolism of Initiatory Death." *History of Religions* 19: 237–58.

Boyd, James W. (1975). *Satan and Mara.* Leiden: E. J. Brill.

Brandon, S. G. F. (1967). *The Judgment of the Dead: An Historical and Comparative Study of the Idea of a Post-Mortem Judgment in the Major Religions.* London: Weidenfeld and Nicolson.

Brokaw, Cynthia J. (1991). *The Ledgers of Merit and Demerit: Social Change and Moral Order in Late Imperial China.* Princeton, N.J.: Princeton University Press.

Buddhaghosa. (1923). *The Path of Purity.* Trans. Pe Maung Tin. London: Luzac.

Burtt, Edwin A. (ed.). (1955). *The Teachings of the Compassionate Buddha.* New York: New American Library.

Chalmers, Lord (ed.). (1932). *Buddha's Teachings: Being the Sutta-Nipata or Discourse Collection*. Cambridge, Mass.: Harvard University Press.

Chan, Wing-tsit. (1963). *A Sourcebook in Chinese Philosophy*. Princeton, N.J.: Princeton University Press.

Chang, Kwang-chih. (1968). *Archaeology of Ancient China*. 2nd ed. New Haven, Conn.: Yale University Press.

Chen, Ellen Marie. (1973). "Is There a Doctrine of Physical Immortality in the *Tao-te Ching?*" *History of Religions* 12: 231–49.

Ch'en, Kenneth K. S. (1973). *The Chinese Transformation of Buddhism*. Princeton, N.J.: Princeton University Press.

Chidester, David. (1987). *Patterns of Action: Religion and Ethics in a Comparative Perspective*. Belmont, Calif.: Wadsworth.

Collins, Steven. (1982). *Selfless Persons: Imagery and Thought in Theravāda Buddhism*. Cambridge: Cambridge University Press.

Creel, Herrlee G. (1970). *What Is Taoism? And Other Studies in Chinese Cultural History*. Chicago: University of Chicago Press.

Davids, C. A. F., and F. L. Woodward. (1950). *The Book of Kindred Sayings*. London: Oxford University Press (orig. ed. 1917–30).

Deussen, Paul. (1906). *The Philosophy of the Upanishads*. Trans. A. S. Geden. Edinburgh: T & T Clark.

Domoulin, Heinrich. (1963). *A History of Zen Buddhism*. Trans. Paul Peachey. Boston: Beacon Press.

Dubs, Homer H. (1928). *The Works of Hsüntze*. London: Arthur Probsthain.

Dumezil, Georges. (1970). *The Destiny of the Warrior*. Trans. Alf Hitebeitel. Chicago: University of Chicago Press.

Dumont, Louis. (1970). *Homo Hierarchicus: An Essay on the Caste System of India*. Trans. Mark Sainsbury. Chicago: University of Chicago Press.

Duyvendak, J. J. L. (1926). "The Buddhist Festival of All-Souls in China and Japan." *Acta Orientalia* 5: 39–48.

Edgerton, Franklin. (1926–27). "The Hour of Death." *Annals of the Bhandarkar Oriental Institute* 8: 219–49.

Eliade, Mircea. (1959). *Yoga: Immortality and Freedom*. Trans. Willard R. Trask. New York: Pantheon Books.

Frankl, Viktor E. (1962). *Man's Search for Meaning: An Introduction to Logotherapy*. Trans. Ilse Lasch. Boston: Beacon Press.

Fürer-Haimendorf, Christoph von. (1953). "The After-Life in Indian Tribal Belief." *Journal of the Royal Anthropological Society* 83: 37–49.

Girardot, N. J. (1983). *Myth and Meaning in Early Taoism: The Theme of Chaos (hun-tun)*. Berkeley and Los Angeles: University of California Press.

Gonda, Jan. (1966). *Loka: World and Heaven in the Veda*. Amsterdam: North Holland Publishing.

———. (1975). *Vedic Literature*. Wiesbaden: Harrassowitz.

Goodrich, Anne Swann. (1981). *Chinese Hells: The Peking Temple of Eighteen Hells and Chinese Conceptions of Hell*. St. Augustin: Monumenta Serica.

Griffith, Ralph T. H. (1963). *Hymns of the Rig-veda*. 2 vols. Varnasi: Chowkhamba Sanskrit Series Office (orig. ed. 1889–92).

———. (1968). *Hymns of the Atharvaveda*. 2 vols. Varnasi: Chowkhamba Sanskrit Series Office (orig. ed. 1895–96).

Hocart, A. M. (1950). *Caste*. London: Methuen.

Hoffman, Y. (1986). *Japanese Death Poems Written by Zen Monks and Haiku Poets on the Verge of Death*. Rutland, Vt.: Charles E. Tuttle.

Holck, Frederick H. (ed.). (1974). *Death and Eastern Thought: Understanding Death in Eastern Religions and Philosophies*. Nashville: Abingdon Press.

Holt, John. (1981). "Assisting the Dead by Venerating the Living." *Numen* 28: 1–28.

Hori, Ichirō. (1966). "Mountains and Their Importance for the Idea of the Other World in Japanese Folk Religion." *History of Religions* 6: 1–23.

———. (1967). "The Appearance of Individual Self-Consciousness in Japanese Religion: Its Historical Transformations." In Charles A. Moore (ed.), *The Japanese Mind: Essentials of Japanese Philosophy and Culture*. Honolulu: University of Hawaii Press, 201–27.

Horner, I. B. (1959). *The Collection of the Middle-Length Sayings*. London: Oxford University Press.

Iwadō, Z. Tamotsu (trans.). (1937). "'Hagakure Bushidō' or the Book of the Warrior." *Cultural Nippon* 7: 33–55; 7: 57–78.

Jaini, Padmanabh S. (1979). *The Jaina Path of Purification*. Berkeley and Los Angeles: University of California Press.

Johansson, Rune. (1969). *The Psychology of Nirvāna*. London: George Allen and Unwin.

Kaelber, Walter O. (1978). "The 'Dramatic' Element in Brahmanic Initiation: Symbols of Death, Danger, and Difficult Passage." *History of Religions* 18: 54–76.

Kaltenmark, Max. (1969). *Lao Tzu and Taoism*. Trans. Roger Greaves. Stanford, Calif.: Stanford University Press.

Kamstra, J. H. (1967). *Encounter or Syncretism: The Initial Growth of Japanese Buddhism*. Leiden: E. J. Brill.

Kapleau, Philip (ed.). (1971). *The Wheel of Death: A Collection of Writings from Zen Buddhist and Other Sources on Death, Rebirth, Dying*. New York: Harper & Row.

Kaushik, Meena. (1976). "The Symbolic Representation of Death." *Contributions to Indian Sociology* 10: 265–92.

Keith, Arthur Berriedale. (1925). *The Religion and Philosophy of the Vedas and Upanishads*. Cambridge, Mass.: Harvard University Press.

Kinsley, David R. (1977). "'The Death That Conquers Death': Dying to the World in Medieval Hinduism." In Frank E. Reynolds and Earle H. Waugh (eds.), *Religious Encounters with Death: Insights from the History and Anthropology of Religions*. University Park: Pennsylvania State University Press, 97–108.

Kitagawa, Joseph M. (1966). *Religion in Japanese History*. New York: Columbia University Press.

———. (1987). *On Understanding Japanese Religion*. Princeton, N.J.: Princeton University Press.

Kloetzli, Randy. (1983). *Buddhist Cosmology*. Delhi: Motilal Banarsidass.

Knipe, David M. (1977). "*Sapiṇḍīkaraṇa:* The Hindu Rite of Entry into Heaven." In Frank E. Reynolds and Earle H. Waugh (eds.), *Religious Encounters with Death: Insights from the History and Anthropology of Religions*. University Park: Pennsylvania State University Press, 111–24.

LaFleur, W. R. (1974). "Japan." In Frederick H. Holck (ed.), *Death and Eastern Thought: Understanding Death in Eastern Religions and Philosophies*. Nashville: Abingdon Press, 226–56.

Lai, T. C. (1983). *To the Yellow Springs: The Chinese View of Death*. Hong Kong: Kelly and Walsh.

Larson, Gerald. (1979). *Sāṅkhya: An Interpretation of Its History and Meaning*. Rev. ed. Berkeley and Los Angeles: University of California Press.

Lay, Arthur Hyde. (1891). "Japanese Funeral Rites." *Transactions of the Asiatic Society of Japan* 19: 507–44.

Legge, James (trans.). (1895). *The Chinese Classics*. 5 vols. Oxford: Clarendon Press.

Lincoln, Bruce. (1981a). "The Lord of the Dead." *History of Religions* 20: 224–41.

———. (1981b). *Priests, Warriors, and Cattle: A Study in the Ecology of Religions*. Berkeley and Los Angeles: University of California Press.

Loewe, Michael. (1982). *Chinese Ideas of Life and Death: Faith, Myth and Reason in the Han Period (202 BC–AD 220)*. London: George Allen and Unwin.

Long, J. Bruce. (1975). "The Death That Ends Death in Hinduism and Buddhism." In Elisabeth Kübler-Ross (ed.), *Death: The Final Stage of Growth*. Englewood Cliffs, N.J.: Prentice Hall, 52–72.

———. (1977). "Death as a Necessity and a Gift in Hindu Mythology." In Frank E. Reynolds and Earle H. Waugh (eds.), *Religious Encounters with Death: Insights from the History and Anthropol-*

ogy of Religions. University Park: Pennsylvania State University Press, 73–96.

Mascaro, Juan. (1963). The Bhagavad Gītā. Baltimore: Penguin.

Matsunaga, Alicia. (1969). The Buddhist Philosophy of Assimilation: The Historical Development of the Honji-Suijaku Theory. Tokyo: Sophia University.

Matsunaga, Daigan, and Alicia Matsunaga. (1972). The Buddhist Concept of Hell. New York: Philosophical Library.

McDermott, James P. (1976). "Is There Group Karma in Theravāda Buddhism?" Numen 23: 67–80.

———. (1980). "Karma and Rebirth in Early Buddhism." In Wendy D. O'Flaherty (ed.), Karma and Rebirth in Classical Indian Traditions. Berkeley and Los Angeles: University of California Press, 165–92.

Müller, F. Max. (1879–1900). The Sacred Books of the East. 50 vols. Oxford: Clarendon Press.

Munro, Donald J. (1969). The Concept of Man in Early China. Stanford, Calif.: Stanford University Press.

Needham, Joseph. (1954–74). Science and Civilisation in China. 5 vols. Cambridge: Cambridge University Press.

———. (1975). "The Cosmology of Early China." In Carmen Blacker and Michael Loewe (eds.), Ancient Cosmologies. London: George Allen and Unwin, 87–109.

Newell, William H. (ed.). (1974). Ancestors. The Hague: Mouton.

Nukariya, Kaiten. (1913). The Religion of the Samurai: A Study of Zen Philosophy and Discipline in China and Japan. London: Luzac.

O'Flaherty, Wendy D. (1976). The Origins of Evil in Hindu Mythology. Berkeley and Los Angeles: University of California Press.

——— (ed.). (1980). Karma and Rebirth in Classical Indian Traditions. Berkeley and Los Angeles: University of California Press.

——— (ed. and trans.). (1981). The Rig Veda: An Anthology. Harmondsworth: Penguin.

Orenstein, Henry. (1970). "Death and Kinship in Hinduism: Structural and Functional Interpretations." American Anthropologist 72: 1357–77.

Plath, David W. (1964). "Where the Family of God Is the Family: The Role of the Dead in Japanese Households." American Anthropologist 66: 300–17.

Radhakrishnan, S. (ed. and trans.). (1950). Dhammapada. London: Oxford University Press.

——— (ed. and trans.). (1953). The Principal Upaniṣads. London: George Allen and Unwin.

Reynolds, Frank E. (1979). "Death: Eastern Thought." In Warren T. Reich (ed.), The Encyclopedia of Bioethics. 4 vols. New York: Free Press, I: 229–35.

Reynolds, Frank E., and Earle H. Waugh (eds.). (1977). Religious Encounters with Death: Insights from the History and Anthropology of Religions. University Park: Pennsylvania State University Press.

Robinet, Isabelle. (1979). "Metamorphosis and Deliverance from the Corpse in Taoism." History of Religions 19: 37–70.

Roy, Pratap Chandra (trans.). (1884–94). The Mahābhārata. 10 vols. Calcutta: D. Bose.

Sanyal, J. M. (trans.). (1929–39). Srimad-Bhagavatam. 5 vols. London: Luzac.

Saso, Michael. (1977). "Buddhist and Taoist Ideas of Transcendence: A Study in Philosophical Contrast." In Michael Saso and David Chappell (eds.), Buddhist and Taoist Studies I. Honolulu: University of Hawaii Press, 3–22.

Schipper, Kristopher M. (1978). "The Taoist Body." History of Religions 17: 355–86.

———. (1993). The Taoist Body. Stanford, Calif.: Stanford University Press.

Schopen, Gregory. (1987). "Burial 'ad sanctos' and the Physical Presence of the Buddha in Early Indian Buddhism: A Study in the Archaeology of Religions." Religion 17: 193–225.

Seidel, Anna. (1970). "A Taoist Immortal of the Ming Dynasty: Chang San-Feng." In William Theodore de Bary (ed.), Self and Society in Ming Thought. New York: Columbia University Press.

Seidel, Anna. (1977). "Buying One's Way to Heaven: The Celestial Treasury in Chinese Religion." *History of Religions* 17: 419–31.

———. (1987). "*Post-Mortem* Immortality; Or: The Taoist Resurrection of the Body." In S. Shaked, D. Shulman, and G. G. Stroumsa (eds.), *Gilgul: Essays on Transformation, Revolution, and Permanence in the History of Religions.* Leiden: E. J. Brill, 223–37.

Seward, Jack. (1968). *Hara Kiri: Japanese Ritual Suicide.* Tokyo: Charles Tuttle.

Shastri, Dakshinaranjan. (1963). *Origin and Development of the Rituals of Ancestor Worship in India.* Calcutta: Bookland.

Shastri, J. L., and Arnold Kunst (eds.). (1970). *The Śiva Purāna.* 4 vols. Delhi: Motilal Banarsidass.

Śivan, Nathan. (1968). *Chinese Alchemy: Preliminary Studies.* Cambridge, Mass.: Harvard University Press.

Smith, D. Howard. (1958). "Chinese Concepts of the Soul." *Numen* 5: 165–79.

———. (1968). *Chinese Religions.* London: Weidenfeld and Nicolson.

———. (1973). *Confucius.* London: Temple Smith.

Smith, Robert J. (1974). *Ancestor Worship in Contemporary Japan.* Stanford, Calif.: Stanford University Press.

Suzuki, Daisetz T. (1935). *Manual of Zen Buddhism.* London: Rider & Co.

———. (1956). *Zen Buddhism.* Ed. William Barrett. Garden City, N.Y.: Doubleday.

———. (1959). *Zen and Japanese Culture.* Princeton: Princeton University Press.

———. (1962). *The Essentials of Zen Buddhism.* Ed. Bernard Phillips. New York: E. P. Dutton.

———. (1963). *Outlines of Mahāyāna Buddhism.* New York: Schocken Books.

Swearer, Donald. (1971). *Secrets of the Lotus.* New York: Macmillan.

———. (1973). "Control and Freedom: The Structure of Buddhist Meditation in the Pāli Suttas." *Philosophy East and West* 23: 435–55.

Teiser, Stephen F. (1986). "Ghosts and Ancestors in Medieval Chinese Religion: The Yü-lan-p'en Festival as Mortuary Ritual." *History of Religions* 26: 47–67.

Treistman, Judith M. (1972). *The Prehistory of China.* New York: Doubleday.

Ware, James R. (trans.). (1966). *Alchemy, Medicine, and Religion in China of A.D. 320: The Nei P'ien of Ko Hung.* Cambridge, Mass.: MIT Press.

Warren, Henry Clarke (ed.). (1950). *Visuddhimagga of Buddhaghosacariya.* Revised by Dharmananda Kosambi. Cambridge, Mass.: Harvard University Press.

Watson, Burton (trans.). (1968). *The Complete Works of Chuang Tzu.* New York: Columbia University Press.

Weiger, Leo. (1969). *A History of the Religious Beliefs and Philosophical Opinions in China.* Trans. Edward Chalmers. New York: Paragon (orig. ed. 1927).

Welbon, Guy Richard. (1968). *The Buddhist Nirvāna and Its Western Interpreters.* Chicago: University of Chicago Press.

Welch, Holmes, and Anna Seidel (eds.). (1979). *Facets of Taoism.* New Haven, Conn.: Yale University Press.

Wilhelm, Richard, and C. G. Jung. (1931). *The Secret of the Golden Flower.* Trans. Cary F. Baynes. London: Routledge and Kegan Paul.

Williams, David M. (1974). "The Translation and Interpretations of the Twelve Terms in the Paṭiccasamuppāda." *Numen* 21: 35–63.

Wimberly, Howard. (1969). "Self-Realization and the Ancestors: An Analysis of Two Japanese Ritual Procedures for Achieving Domestic Harmony." *Anthropological Quarterly* 42: 37–51.

Yampolsky, Philip B. (trans.). (1971). *The Zen Master Hakuin: Selected Writings.* New York: Columbia University Press.

Yü, Ying-shih. (1964–65). "Life and Immortality in the Mind of Han China." *Harvard Journal of Asiatic Studies* 25: 80–122.

4

The Tibetan Book
of the Dead

The separation of the consciousness from the body at death was thought by Tibetan Buddhists to take as long as four days to complete. That process could be assisted, however, by a specialized Buddhist teacher known as the "extractor of consciousness." Sitting on a mat at the head of the body, the teacher guided the consciousness out of the body. Like a shaman, that Buddhist specialist was a psychopomp, a guide for the dead. He chanted, prayed, and went into a trance to be with the consciousness as it began its journey to another world. Surrounded by the fragrance of incense, the flickering of candles, and the deep resonance of chanting by the monks, the teacher whispered instructions that would aid the consciousness in its encounter with the world of death.

Instructions given to the dying and whispered into the ear of the deceased were taken from a text that has been called *The Tibetan Book of the Dead*. The Tibetan Buddhists called that text the *Bardo Thödol,* which could be translated "Liberation by Hearing in the Other World" (Evans-Wentz, 1927; Rinpoche, 1992; Thurman, 1994). The text, which was prepared and used by schools of Tibetan Buddhists from around the eighth century, served as a map and guidebook to the world that followed death. The extraordinary territories of that other world had been explored in meditation, but they were expected to be encountered in their full splendor, as well as terror, by the consciousness during its passage through death.

Funeral rites and observances lasted about two lunar months. An astrologer was called in to cast a horoscope that showed the arrangement of the heavens at the time of death. The horoscope would influence the types of rites performed as well as the precise time and place for the funeral. While the corpse was placed in a fetal position within a death chamber, a carved image of the deceased was kept in the home or monastery for forty-nine days. During that interim time in the death ritual, survivors made offerings of food and drink to that effigy. Priests performed magical rites to assist the dead (Beyer, 1973). After the interim period, the body was disposed of by means of cremation, burial, or exposure in a final funeral ceremony.

As Robert Hertz observed in many death rituals, the Tibetan Buddhists treated the corpse in a way that reflected the progress of whatever remnant of the person was thought to survive death. The Ngaju Dyak, for example, had buried the bones at the exact time that they thought the soul entered the world of the dead. The bones were identified with the soul. For the Tibetan Buddhists, the surviving remnant of the person was not an immortal soul but a moving consciousness that passed out of the body on a trajectory toward rebirth. The funeral rites took forty-nine days; the entire process from death to rebirth was thought also to take forty-nine days to complete. In this way, ritual mirrored a mythic transcendence that imagined the transition of consciousness into another embodiment.

As there was an interim period in the ritual disposition of the body, so Tibetan Buddhists imagined an interim in the transition of consciousness from death to rebirth. During that period, the consciousness was expected to travel through an extraordinary realm of lights and sounds, dazzling visions, and terrifying horrors. Riding the karmic waves that had been set in motion during life, the consciousness was overwhelmed by attractive but also by repulsive and frightening visions in the other world. The consciousness was battered about by the winds of karma until it finally dissolved into unconsciousness in the womb of a new embodiment.

Primarily, the *Bardo Thödol* was a ritual text used in the ceremonies in which Tibetan Buddhist priests helped the deceased achieve liberation—nirvāṇa—during that passage through death (Brauen and Kvaerne, 1978). But this book may also have been used as a visionary text for meditation. It gave detailed descriptions of everything a consciousness could expect to encounter in the strange world after death. A person could prepare for those encounters by meditating on the visionary imagery of the *Bardo Thödol* during life. The temple, the monastery, and even the home could be decorated with pictures of the other world that would familiarize the consciousness with it. By being prepared, a person would be less likely to be overwhelmed by the powerful sights and sounds experienced in the passage through death.

During the first centuries of the common era, Buddhist missionaries had followed the trade routes from India into China. By the year 500, some had moved into the Himalayan country of Tibet. Different Tibetan Buddhist schools were formed, some gaining considerable power and political influence. They combined Buddhist meditation disciplines with shamanic practices that had developed in the indigenous Tibetan Bon religion (Powers, 1995; Samuel, 1993; Snellgrove, 1967). The Tibetan Buddhists also developed the unique institution of the *lāma,* or reincarnated Bodhisattva, who stood as the religious and political leader of the community. In established monasteries under the centralized authority of the lāma, Tibetan Buddhist monks practiced meditation techniques that would liberate them from the cycle of rebirth. The text of the *Bardo Thödol* contained much of the dramatic and intense imagery that was the focus of those meditations.

The *Bardo Thödol,* however, was also a visionary journey through death. As an imaginative text of mythic transcendence, it related everything that could be expected to occur to a consciousness after it was separated or extracted from the body. That journey was imagined to take place in three stages: the moment of dying, an interim stage of illusions, and the process of rebirth. Each of these stages after death was an alternative reality, a *bardo,* through which consciousness passed. The term *bardo* was used by the Tibetan Buddhists for any state of consciousness that was other than the reality experienced by ordinary waking consciousness. Three bardos were experienced in the course of an embodied life: in the womb, in dreams, and in meditation. Disembodied, the consciousness traveled through three alternative realities in the moment of dying, in the interim stage of illusions, and in the process leading to rebirth.

After death, the consciousness passed through each of those three stages. At every stage, however, it was exhorted to recognize everything it saw or heard as a projection of itself. When consciousness encountered the light and sound of the Buddha nature at the moment of dying, it was told, "Know that as you." When consciousness met the merciful and wrathful Buddhas in the interim stage of illusions, it was told, "Know them as you." Even when it was being judged, punished, and finally forced back into a body, the consciousness was instructed to recognize the whole process as a projection of itself. "Know it as you," the consciousness was told. Failing those tests of recognition, the consciousness remained locked in the cycle of rebirth. At every moment the person was bound, but at every moment there was an opportunity to get free. The *Bardo Thödol* was not only a road map to the other world, it was an instruction manual for liberation.

DYING

When breathing stopped, the energy that had served as a breathlike, vital force in the body was imagined to contract. That energy (*rlung* in Tibetan; *prāna* in Sanskrit) moved down the psychic nerves on the left and right sides of the body, draining vitality from the spinal column and the entire nervous system. The process of dying was described as a sensation of pressure, like the body sinking into the earth; it was a clammy coldness, like "earth sinking into water"; it was feverish heat, like "water sinking into fire"; and finally it felt as if the body were being smashed to atoms, "like fire sinking into air." Moving through the four elements, the body seemed to dissolve in the experience of dying. Although the body was beginning to be dispersed back to its elements, the consciousness passed out of the body into a strange new level of experience.

Chikhai Bardo

At the moment of dying, the consciousness entered the first bardo after death, the Chikhai Bardo. As consciousness left the body, it encountered a powerful, radiant, and reverberating void. That pure void was alive with light and sound. The text described this encounter as a vision of the "Clear Light of Reality." A lāma or a spiritual teacher stood by to remind the deceased that this was the light and sound of infinite Buddha nature. Since the transcendent Buddha essence was without any qualifying characteristics, it appeared as pure, undifferentiated light and sound.

Although that reverberating radiance was overwhelming, the consciousness was instructed to recognize the light and sound as its own nature. In the void entered at the moment of dying, the person could recognize that his or her own consciousness was the same as that Buddha essence. "Thine own consciousness," the deceased was reminded, "shining, void, and inseparable from the Great Body of Radiance, hath no birth, nor death, and is the Immutable Light." By recognizing that light and sound as its own, the consciousness could achieve liberation from rebirth in that first bardo at the moment of dying.

The pure light and sound of Buddha nature dispelled all past karma. According to the principle of karma, consequences of past actions would have bound the consciousness to rebirth. But the object of the Buddhist path was to be liberated from the entire cycle of cause and effect. That liberation was possible in the moment of dying and did not depend on merit gained from past actions. Rather, liberation was a radical change of consciousness that allowed the person to abandon the body and merge into the pure light and sound of the Buddha nature. Like the sun driving away darkness, the pure light of reality broke the bonds of karma that would have led to rebirth.

Recognition was all that was required. In an instant of recognition, an enlightenment was achieved that guaranteed freedom from rebirth. By recognizing the pure light and sound as a manifestation of consciousness, the person remained in that state of Buddhahood. Summarizing the moment of dying, the *Bardo Thödol* stated,

> When thy body and mind were separating, thou must have experienced a glimpse of the Pure Truth, subtle, sparkling, bright, dazzling, glorious, and radiantly awesome. . . . Be not daunted thereby, nor terrified, nor awed. That is the radiance of thine own true nature. Recognize it. From the midst of that radiance, the natural sound of Reality, reverberating like a thousand thunders simultaneously sounding, will come. That is the natural sound of thine own real self. (Evans-Wentz, 1927: 104)

When a person died, he or she was instructed not to cling to life but to recognize that luminous, thundering essence of Reality. Emerging from the body, the consciousness could merge into its own true nature as Buddha. That Buddha nature may have been recognized in life during meditation, but it was realized as the ultimate reality in the moment of dying. That moment, therefore, provided a supreme opportunity for liberation.

As the first stage in the journey after death, the Chikhai Bardo was thought to last as long as three and a half days. The consciousness was suspended in a swoon, lost in the void of the pure light and sound of Buddha nature. If the light and sound were recognized, liberation was achieved; however, most people were too bound by a sense of ego, by desire, and by illusion to recognize the Buddha nature as their own. They remained attached to a personal identity. Awed by the light and sound, they passed that first stage after the moment of dying in a hazy dream. Unable to recognize the void as themselves, they were carried along on the currents of their karma out of the first bardo and into the second, where they would be given further opportunities for liberation if they could recognize the Buddha forms.

The Hour of Death

The hour of death has been regarded in many different religious traditions as a moment of crucial importance for the fate of the dying person. In some cases, the disposition of the dying person's mind or heart in that last moment has been thought to determine the direction that person could be expected to take after death (Edgerton, 1926–27). Ritual arts of dying, therefore, have been important religious practices for preparing a person's consciousness or conscience. Besides allowing the dying to depart the world freely, they have been regarded as crucial techniques for directing the deceased on the right path to the next world.

The art of dying developed in the *Bardo Thödol* was almost exclusively concerned with the person's consciousness. Death was understood as the transition, release, or extraction of the consciousness from a body that was undergoing a reduction to its elements. As the body became earth, water, fire, and air, the consciousness emerged. Immediately, the consciousness was freed from the body to encounter its own nature.

Since Tibetan Buddhists were convinced that the consciousness continued after the cessation of all vital signs in the body, they remained by the body to direct instructions to the deceased as the consciousness passed into the first bardo. The art of dying developed in Tibetan Buddhism did not end with biological death but continued in the exhortations given to the consciousness by the priests and attendants. In this respect, dying was understood to occur not in a single moment but in an extended process of transition as the consciousness was given opportunities to establish itself in another reality and to liberate itself from rebirth.

The first opportunity for liberation was presented in the Chikhai Bardo. In the encounter with the pure, undifferentiated light and sound of the Buddha nature, the consciousness could merge into its own Buddhahood and achieve liberation. The Buddha nature encountered in that first bardo was understood by the Tibetan Buddhists to be the boundless, spiritual body of the Buddha. The spiritual body of the Buddha was one of three bodies of the Buddha as they came to be conceived in Mahāyāna Buddhist thought (Reynolds, 1977). In fact, each stage in the consciousness' passage through the world of death was identified with one of those three bodies of the Buddha: the formless spiritual body, the formed spiritual body, and the formed physical body.

The formless spiritual body of the Buddha, the Dharmakāya, was the body of ultimate truth, or ultimate reality. That body was without form, without limit, without any of the conditions that applied to things in time and space. This eternal, formless, spiritual body of the Buddha was symbolized by the pure light and sound of the first bardo. The formless spiritual body of the Buddha— also called the Buddha nature or the Buddha essence—was to be recognized as one's own. Because the consciousness was also formless in the first stage of death, it had the opportunity to merge into the formless spiritual body of the Buddha.

Significantly, the Dharmakāya was symbolized as an extraordinary transsensory experience of light and sound. In normal perception, lights are seen and sounds heard; the visual and the auditory are separate. But in the encounter with the Buddha nature, the consciousness was imagined to experience an extraordinary light that resonated like a thousand thunders, a sound that was radiant. In perceptual psychology, the experience of seeing sounds or hearing lights has been called *synesthesia* (Chidester, 1992; Marks, 1978). Such experiences are unusual, but so may be the experience of dying. In symbolizing that experience, the text described it as an extraordinary synesthetic fusion of light and sound.

In recent research on near-death experiences (NDEs), some investigators have argued that the reports of people who have regained consciousness after being declared clinically dead bear a marked resemblance to the account of the *Bardo Thödol*. The experience of sound and light in particular has received much attention. Many survivors of NDEs have reported that at the moment of clinical death they heard a loud ringing or buzzing sound. Often feeling like they were moving through a void or down a long, dark tunnel, many have also reported extraordinary experiences of light. A survivor reported to Raymond Moody, for example, that he had seen "a pure crystal clear light." Insisting that the light was not like any seen on earth, the person concluded that it was "a light of perfect understanding and perfect love" (Moody, 1975).

Using somewhat more controlled scientific procedures, cardiologist Michael Sabom found that more than 50 percent of NDEs involved some experience of light. A fifty-six-year-old executive from Florida described floating toward a source of light, "going through this shaft of light. . . . It was so bright, and the closer we got, the brighter it got, and it was blinding." A forty-five-year-old pharmaceutical salesman during a cardiac arrest experienced a light that he compared to sun shining on clouds as seen from an airplane. A fifty-four-year-old mechanic described the radiance not as light coming from a source but as the total absence of darkness. "This light was so total and complete," he reported, "that you didn't look at the light, you were *in* the light" (Sabom, 1981: 43–44).

Were these experiences of light the same as the experience described in the *Bardo Thödol?* Did the executive, the salesman, and the mechanic have the same encounter at the moment of dying that was anticipated by the Tibetan Buddhists? One difference certainly lies in the context within which the experience was reported to occur. Rather than a spontaneous, unexpected near-death event, the encounter with the light and sound of the Buddha nature was an experience that a Tibetan Buddhist prepared for through meditation and was guided through by priests and attendants. In other words, the experience was part of an entire ritual cycle that included a lifetime of meditation and the ritual procedures of the art of dying.

A second difference is found in the symbolism of the *Bardo Thödol*, which may have described the encounter with the formless spiritual body of the Buddha as light and sound because it was an experience that could not in fact be described. Calling that experience light and sound—particularly, a light that was heard and a sound that was seen—may have been a way of saying that it was so extraordinary that it was beyond description. Nevertheless, research on NDEs has suggested the intriguing possibility that scientific investigations could confirm the expectations of the Tibetan Buddhists that the moment of dying involved a powerful experience of light and sound (Epstein, 1990).

ILLUSIONS

After passing through the first bardo, the consciousness was thought to enter into a longer interim period of illusions, the Chönyid Bardo. This second stage was identified with the formed spiritual body of the Buddha, or Sambhoga-kaya, which was actually understood to be manifested in the many personalized forms of spiritual Buddhas that would be met in the interim stage after death. Assuming splendid, beautiful, but sometimes horrible forms, those Bodhisattvas were the formed spiritual body of the Buddha. In the second stage, the consciousness itself assumed a form, a thought body, which was its vehicle on its journey through the other world after death.

Experiences in that middle period assumed the quality of an extended dream, with vivid and dramatic images projected from the consciousness appearing as if they were real. Since the consciousness was traveling in a thought body, it did not need to fear those apparitions. They could not kill it because it was already dead. The consciousness had only to recognize them to get free.

Nevertheless, the consciousness still might not recognize the illusions of the second bardo as projections. It might be awed, overwhelmed, or even terrified by what it saw there. Therefore, the text of the *Bardo Thödol* advised the person to recognize everything encountered during that interim stage of illusions as a projection from consciousness. "Whatever may come—sounds, lights, or rays—are, all three, unable to harm thee: thou art incapable of dying," the text assured. "It is quite sufficient for thee to know that these apparitions are thine own thought-forms" (Evans-Wentz, 1927: 104). Recognizing all those appearances as projections from itself, the consciousness might achieve liberation from rebirth in the Chönyid Bardo. Failing that recognition, however, the consciousness continued on its trajectory toward rebirth, back into another body in another world.

Chönyid Bardo

On the fourth day after it had separated from the body, the consciousness, awakening from its swoon and wondering, "What has happened?," entered the second stage of its journey through the afterlife. The Chönyid Bardo was revolving, spinning around the thought body in which the consciousness was now clothed. Before the person could gain any sense of orientation, divine Buddha forms began to appear from all the directions of the compass. From east, south, west, north, and the center, the magnificent, merciful Buddhas appeared. In every appearance, the person was given a chance to achieve liberation. By merging into the forms that appeared, the person would be freed from rebirth.

But at the same time that the Buddha forms appeared, dull colored lights symbolizing the six worlds of desire where a person might be reborn also appeared, distracting and tempting the consciousness to turn back toward another birth. The white light of the heavens; the gray, smoky light of the hells; the red light of the ghosts; the green light of the demons; the blue light of the animal kingdom; and the yellow light of the human world—these six colored lights came from and led back to the lokas of rebirth.

If attracted to those lights, the consciousness would continue to whirl around on the cycle of human suffering. The text of the *Bardo Thödol*, therefore, exhorted the person to ignore those alluring, multicolored lights of the lokas. The consciousness was to resist any attraction to them by focusing on the rainbow splendor of the Buddha forms that appeared in the second bardo.

In this second stage after death, a new element was introduced: faith. The moment of dying had required a pure, conscious recognition of Buddha nature. The second stage offered opportunities for liberation through the quality of faith. In loving devotion to the divine Buddha forms that appeared, the consciousness could still attain Buddhahood by their grace. Merciful Buddhas came forward one after another to offer salvation in the second bardo. Beholding the "hook-rays of the light of grace," the consciousness could merge into those Buddhas through faith.

Although they awakened a liberating sense of devotion in the consciousness, those divine Buddha forms were nevertheless explained as spiritual forms projected from the person's own consciousness. The merciful Buddhas that appeared were all projections from the person's heart, manifestations of loving grace that could be recognized and embraced. But in all their splendor and magnificence, the Buddha forms were illusions, projections from consciousness. Repeatedly, the *Bardo Thödol* advised, "Recognize them as you." Like the Buddha nature beheld in the moment of dying, the spiritual Buddha forms were also identical to the genuine nature of the consciousness. Recognizing itself in the Buddha forms, the consciousness achieved liberation from rebirth.

The second bardo provided many opportunities to achieve liberation through faith, devotion, or love directed toward the Buddha forms. Unfortunately, most people failed to recognize the Buddha forms as themselves. At each appearance of a merciful Buddha, the consciousness recoiled from its splendor. Still attached to a personal ego identity, the consciousness failed to see that it was itself a gracious Buddha form, offering salvation for itself from the cycle of rebirth.

The symptoms of attachment to a personal ego identity were emotions—anger, pride, greed, jealousy, and so on—that separated the consciousness from the Buddha forms. They were like walls that protected the personal interests of the consciousness but at the same time blocked it from its ultimate liberation. At each appearance of a merciful Buddha, a selfish, egotistical, personal emotion blocked the consciousness, keeping it from merging into the rainbow lights of the Buddha forms.

As the entire bardo glowed a deep blue, the divine Buddha form of Vairochana suddenly appeared from its center, radiating a pure bluish-white light. In his splendor, that divine Buddha sat on a lion, holding the eight-spoked wheel of Buddhist wisdom. Each divine Buddha had a consort; the Buddha Vairochana was accompanied by his wife, the Mother of the Space of

Heaven. "From the heart of Vairochana as Father-Mother," the text said, that wisdom "will shoot forth and strike against thee with a light so radiant that thou wilt scarcely be able to look at it" (Evans-Wentz, 1927: 106). Although that light of wisdom was overwhelming in its intensity, the person was exhorted to look at it in deep faith, praying earnestly for saving grace from Vairochana. In humble prayer, the consciousness could merge in a halo of rainbow light into the heart of Vairochana and attain Buddhahood.

Off to the side, however, pulsated the dull white light of the heavens, which distracted and tempted the consciousness. "Do not look over there," the text warned. That way led to rebirth. At this stage, the light of the heavenly loka was a distraction from the saving grace of the divine, merciful Buddha. Later, it would lead the consciousness back into another embodiment.

By focusing in love on the divine Buddha, the consciousness could achieve liberation. But it probably would not do that. The emotions of fear, terror, and anger could block the person from recognizing the Buddha form and merging into it. In order to protect a sense of personal ego identity, the consciousness might try to run away from the divine Buddha. In this case, anger arose from the person's past karma. Unable to get free from that karmic influence, the consciousness was propelled forward on its journey through the afterlife world.

Having been blocked from liberation by the personal emotion of anger, the consciousness was confronted on the next day by the divine Buddha Vajra-Sattva, riding from the east on an elephant throne. He held the lightning bolt of illumination in his hand, glowing with the pure white light of Mirror-like Wisdom. Surrounded by his wife and family like a constellation of divine Buddhas, Vajra-Sattva offered saving grace for those who recognized and took refuge in him. The text exhorted the consciousness not to flee but to place its faith in the light of the divine Buddha form. Recognizing that merciful Buddha as a projection from itself, the consciousness could achieve liberation by merging into its gracious form. However, it would probably be distracted by the dull, gray, smoky light pulsating off to the side, which came from the hell loka. Once again, the consciousness would probably also try to defend its separate, personal identity. Trying to run away, anger turned into pride as the consciousness was carried along on the currents of its karma.

The next day, the consciousness encountered the magnificent Buddha form of Ratna-Sambhava coming from the south, riding a horse and holding aloft the jewel of wisdom. Again, the merciful Buddha was accompanied by his wife and family, offering salvation for any consciousness that merged into him in loving devotion. But once again, a loka light—this time the dull blue-yellow light of the human world—appeared off to the side to distract the consciousness. That loka represented the personal emotion of egotistical pride that tempted the consciousness back into rebirth. Instead of merging into the divine Buddha by recognition and faith, the consciousness would probably hold on to its separate ego identity. As it tried to run away from the merciful Buddha, the consciousness was locked into egotistical emotions that blocked faith and prevented liberation.

With the dawning of the following day, the emotion of greed arose. On that day, the divine Buddha Amitābha appeared on a peacock throne, holding a lotus in his hand, and accompanied by his divine family to offer his liberating grace. Off to the side, the dull red light of the ghost world—the loka of the preta, or hungry ghosts—radiated its dim but alluring glow. In the preta-loka, ghosts were consumed by desires but had no means to achieve their satisfaction. It was a world of all-consuming greed. If that emotion blocked the consciousness, it was prevented from merging into the Buddha form of Amitābha and receiving that merciful Buddha's saving grace. In fear, terror, and egotistical greed, the consciousness tried to run away. But it remained trapped in the bardo by its own karma and egotism.

As greed became jealousy, the consciousness moved on to the fifth and final confrontation with a divine Buddha form. On that day, the Buddha Amogha-Siddhi appeared. Riding a mythological bird, holding the thunderbolt, and surrounded by his family, that divine Buddha also offered grace. But the dull green light of the demon loka—the world of the *asuras*—distracted and attracted the consciousness that was wrapped up in jealousy, envy, and egotistical desires. As on the previous days, the consciousness was not to look over there but to focus in recognition and faith on the luminous, divine Buddha. In love, the consciousness could merge into its radiant form and attain liberation.

Since it probably would fail to do that, the consciousness was propelled on by its own evil, egotistical inclinations. On the next day, the consciousness was given one final chance. Appearing all at once in their magnificent rainbow light, the five Buddha forms presented one more opportunity for the person to receive their grace. At the same time, however, the lights of the lokas—now including the dull blue light of the animal world, along with the lights of the demon, ghost, human, hell, and heaven worlds—glowed off to the side. "Do not look over there," the text exhorted. In the purity of prayer, devotion, and love, the person was instructed to merge into the rainbow light of the merciful Buddhas and achieve liberating Buddhahood in the Chönyid Bardo.

The *Bardo Thödol* described the merciful Buddhas as projections from a person's heart. They were manifestations of divine love that promised salvation from rebirth. Failing to recognize them, the consciousness was forced to continue on its journey to rebirth. Suddenly, the experience of the consciousness shifted from mercy to a violent, shocking encounter with fifty-eight flame-enhaloed, ax-swinging, blood-drinking, wrathful deities. For twelve days, these terrifying Buddha forms attacked the consciousness. If the awesome majesty of the merciful Buddhas had been frightening, those wrathful Buddhas were terrifying beyond description. Consumed by terror, the consciousness was chased all over the bardo by them.

Those horrible Buddhas were only the merciful Buddhas appearing in different forms, however, shocking and terrifying the consciousness into a ruder awakening. Like the merciful Buddhas, these wrathful, vengeful Buddha forms were also projections from consciousness, but now they were projections from the intellect rather than the heart. Still, liberation was possible. If even these frightening Buddhas could be recognized as projections from consciousness, a person could achieve liberating enlightenment.

"When the fifty-eight Blood-Drinking Deities emanating from thine own brain come to shine upon thee," the text said, "if thou knowst them to be the radiances of thine own intellect, thou wilt . . . obtain Buddhahood" (Evans-Wentz, 1927: 146). Recognition may have been more difficult, as the Buddhas pursued, tortured, and terrified the fleeing consciousness. Nevertheless, it was still possible to recognize the mercy behind the vengeance and to achieve liberation through that recognition.

Since that liberating recognition had become so difficult by that point, most people were carried on to the next bardo that would prepare them for rebirth. After being chased all over the Chönyid Bardo by the terrifying Buddhas, the consciousness probably found the idea of rebirth attractive. Even if life in a body had been suffering, at least it was familiar.

Mental Life After Death

In the second stage after dying, everything was illusion. The Buddha forms appeared because they were projected from the consciousness. Merciful Buddhas emanated from the heart; wrathful Buddhas came from the mind. No matter how attractive or repulsive, they were to be recognized as projections. By recognizing the Buddhas as projections, the consciousness dissolved any separation between itself and its own Buddha nature. In recognition and faith, it merged into its own Buddhahood by merging into the rainbow lights of the Buddha forms. Although they were illusions, the Buddha forms nevertheless offered a saving grace to the person after death. They provided opportunities for giving up any sense of permanent personal identity, the egotistical attachment that bound consciousness to the cycle of rebirth.

Salvation was achieved, therefore, by a radical change of consciousness. In the bardo of illusions, the consciousness had to abandon any sense of separate personal identity in order to be liberated; it had to lose itself to be saved. If liberation from the cycle of rebirth was a type of salvation, it was a salvation from the ultimate illusion—the illusion of having a personal identity. The illusion of being a separate person was supported by the egotistical emotions of pride, anger, greed, and jealousy. Those were the sins from which consciousness had to be saved by a radical transformation into its enlightened Buddha nature. When a separate identity dissolved, all that remained was an enlightened freedom from the cycle of rebirth, a liberated Buddha.

If the illusions that appeared in the second bardo were all projections from consciousness, how did they get into the consciousness in order to be projected out after death? One answer to this question may be that after death a person projected what he or she had dwelled on during life. Consciousness may have been understood something like a movie projector running film that had been shot during life. In other words, the illusions that a person met after death were the images, sights, sounds, hopes, and fears that had preoccupied consciousness during life. The pattern of afterlife experience—from the moment of dying through the interim period of illusions to preparation for rebirth—might have been understood to be the same for everyone. But the precise content of the sights and sounds was determined by the consciousness that projected the illusions it encountered.

Tibetan Buddhists dwelled on the images of the five merciful Buddhas, meditating on their forms, their symbols, and everything associated with them, during a lifetime of spiritual discipline. Colorful statues of the five merciful Buddhas stood in an alcove in the monastery. Vivid designs depicting the Buddha forms were used to focus meditation. In this way, the consciousness was prepared to recognize what it encountered after death. More than that, however, the consciousness was prepared to recognize what it saw as projection. By recognizing projection as projection, the consciousness was freed from the web of illusion that tied it to the process of rebirth.

Taking this consideration of afterlife projections a step further, perhaps the content of the projected illusions was determined by the kind of training a consciousness had received during life. If the consciousness were trained in disciplined meditation, perhaps its afterlife illusions would appear in greater focus. But this also suggests the possibility that different trainings could produce different projections from consciousness after death. A Tibetan Buddhist might have been expected to see Buddhist imagery, but a Christian could be expected to encounter Christian imagery; a Hindu, Hindu imagery; a Muslim, Muslim imagery; and so on. In other words, each religious tradition would prepare a consciousness to project different content after death.

The *Bardo Thödol* seemed to imply that afterlife experiences would be specific to the religion and culture in which a consciousness had been trained. As a twentieth-century Tibetan Buddhist noted, "The illusory *Bardo* visions vary, in keeping with the religious or cultural tradition in which the percipient has grown up, but their underlying motive-power is the same in all human beings" (Evans-Wentz, 1927: lxii). The pattern might be the same, but the precise content would vary from religious tradition to tradition.

Obviously, some religious traditions would find it difficult to recognize that their God, or gods, or saviors, or saints were simply illusions projected by the human consciousness. Insisting on the ultimate reality of their divine beings, many religious traditions would find it hard to accept the Tibetan Buddhist claim that those divine beings were only projections. Nevertheless, that claim was central to the Tibetan Buddhist mythic transcendence outlined in the *Bardo Thödol*. By recognizing the divine forms as projections, the consciousness gained freedom from the imprisoning illusion that it was a separate, personal ego identity. In that change of consciousness, the person after death gained a deathless liberation, penetrating the illusions of self and gods to achieve the reality of a transcendent freedom from rebirth.

As an intriguing footnote to the afterlife illusions described in the *Bardo Thödol,* we might consider the theory of a purely mental afterlife proposed by the philosopher H. H. Price. In 1953, Price published an article, "Survival and the Idea of 'Another World,'" in which he suggested that dreams might provide a model for experience in the world after death.

Drawing his analogies from dream experience, Price suggested that a coherent picture of life after death could be imagined. If afterlife experience were similar to mental experience in dreams, it would consist of illusions projected by consciousness. Like a dream world, the afterlife would be a world of mental images. Experience would consist of a stream of consciousness. The person might still have the feeling of being alive if the consciousness continued to project mental images as in a dream after death. Experiencing those images as real, the person might not even realize that he or she was dead. Mental images would continue to provide the basis for an experiential sense of being alive even after death.

Price argued that such an image world would be just as "real" as the present world. Sights, sounds, and experiences would be familiar because they were projected from the person's own consciousness. But the projections would be based on the memories of the person before death. Since death was the end of life experience, no new images could be encountered. Memory provided the raw material of imagery with which a surviving consciousness could project its experience after death. In other words, the consciousness continued to experience the imagery that it had dwelled on during life.

Experience in that image world after death, however, would not have to consist merely of reruns of past experience. The imagery might be changed, arranged, and rearranged by a person's desires. In this way, afterlife experience might be an ongoing process of wish fulfillment, in which images were projected to satisfy desires. The raw material of the image world might come from memory, but the forms those images would take could be determined by the person's hopes, expectations, and wishes. Perhaps images might also be arranged according to a person's fears. Like the stuff of dreams, mental experience in such an afterlife image world would be derived from memory but shaped by desire. Survival in that image world would consist in the continuity of a self-contained consciousness that projected its own experience after death.

Survival in a projected mental world, of course, would make communication with other minds problematic. If all experiences were merely projections from consciousness only to be seen and heard by the same consciousness, how could two minds occupying such independent afterlife worlds communicate? Perhaps they could not. Or perhaps some type of extrasensory perception would bridge the gap between mental worlds, providing a means of telepathic communication. H. H. Price argued for the possibility of such a telepathy that would enable impressions to be shared among the different, independent image worlds occupied after death. Price even imagined that a variety of shared worlds might be constructed by like-minded individuals whose memories and desires might be similar enough to form image worlds that they could live in after death.

In some respects, the purely mental afterlife imagined by H. H. Price was similar to the afterlife experience anticipated by the *Bardo Thödol*. First, all experience was projected from the person's consciousness. Everything seen or heard could be (but probably would not be) recognized as projection. Second, the raw materials for those projections were derived from memory, particularly from the imagery that a person had dwelled on during life. A memory that had been trained within the Tibetan Buddhist religious and cultural tradition could be expected to project the vivid imagery of the merciful and wrathful Buddhas that had served as focuses for meditation. Other trainings might fill the memory with different content. Third, the raw material was shaped by desire. In the *Bardo Thödol*, however, the mental life of the other world was not an extended process of wish fulfillment. In fact, personal wishes, emotions, and desires blocked fulfillment. Only by giving up those personal desires could liberation be achieved. Unlike Price's image worlds, the *Bardo Thödol* saw the afterlife as a series of opportunities for achieving a Buddhist liberation from desire.

The Buddhist logic of desire, therefore, distinguished the afterlife of the bardos from the image worlds imagined by the philosopher H. H. Price. In the Chönyid Bardo, the interim stage of illusions, the emotions of anger, pride, greed, jealousy, and all other ego-centered desires, blocked the consciousness from merging into Buddhahood. Those desires, therefore, shaped an afterlife experience that was increasingly terrifying, as the consciousness tried to retreat from its real nature into a familiar sense of personal identity. By trying to hold on to what was familiar, the consciousness perceived the Buddha forms as unfamiliar, awesome, and finally as horrible monsters that threatened its sense of separate personal identity.

Ultimately, survival of death—in the sense of achieving a liberating deathlessness—was not shaped by desires but only made possible by eliminating personal desires. Failing to eliminate egotistical desires, the consciousness could not see through the illusions of the second bardo. In that failure, the consciousness was carried along on the currents of karma into the third and final stage of the afterlife in which it was made ready to be reborn in another body.

REBIRTH

If it failed to achieve liberation during the interim stage of illusions, the consciousness moved into the last bardo, the Sidpa Bardo, where it began preparations for rebirth. The six colored lights of the lokas appeared as possible destinations. Before rebirth, however, the consciousness was subjected to a process of judgment and punishment for its past actions. Battered by the winds of karma, the consciousness suffered its final purgation before it entered another body.

Like the punishments in the Chinese Buddhist hells, those punishments were remedial rather than permanent retribution for past deeds. They were part of the increasingly violent shock therapy after death designed to awaken the consciousness to its true nature. Even when judged and punished by the Lord of Death, the consciousness could still achieve liberation if it recognized the entire process as projection.

The pain and suffering were experienced as real, but the Lord of Death, the judgment, and the punishment were explained in the *Bardo Thödol* as projected hallucinations from a consciousness that did not know its true Buddha nature. If that ignorance persisted, the consciousness would end up in another body in one of the six worlds of desire to perpetuate the cycle of birth, suffering, and death.

Sidpa Bardo

After fourteen days in the bardo of illusions, the consciousness shifted into the grayish twilight of the last stage before rebirth. No longer surrounded by the dramatic rainbow splendor of the Buddha forms, the deceased proceeded into a dimmer state of consciousness. For the first time, the person became aware that he or she was in fact dead. Before that point the unenlightened consciousness had not had time to reflect on its condition. It had been too preoccupied with the overwhelming encounters with Buddha forms to realize that those experiences were not dreams but death. In the final bardo, however, the consciousness experienced the anguish of loss and separation. In misery, the person cried out, "I am dead! What shall I do?"

Lost and alone, the person looked back to the personal attachments he or she had formed during life. The consciousness saw dreamlike visions of friends and relatives left behind. To weeping friends and relatives, the person called out, "Here I am, weep not." But the survivors did not hear the anguished cries of the dead. In misery, the consciousness was blown about like a feather on the winds of karma.

Propelled by the powerful gusts of karmic wind, the consciousness was terrified by hallucinations. Demons struck terror with their war cries, fierce faces, and dangerous weapons. Terrible beasts of prey attacked. Under pursuit, the consciousness was swept through snow, rain, and darkness while all around it crashed the sounds of mountains crumbling down, seas overflowing, fires roaring, and fierce winds rushing. Trying to run away, the person was blocked by three cliffs, representing anger, lust, and ignorance. Like everything else in the bardo, these cliffs were illusory, but nevertheless these obstacles of anger, lust, and ignorance prevented the consciousness from getting free of the terrors it experienced as real.

In the midst of all this terrifying chaos, the *Bardo Thödol* promised, liberation was still possible. If the consciousness could remain undistracted by these hallucinations, it might still take refuge in the compassionate mercy of the Buddha. Dissolving the barriers of anger, lust, and ignorance, the consciousness might still achieve liberation from rebirth.

But liberation by that point had become very difficult. Instead of achieving a tranquil indifference that might set it free, the consciousness tended to be consumed by panic. Trying to escape the terrors of the bardo, the consciousness became obsessed with the desire to retreat into the safe familiarity of a body. "O what would I not give to possess a body!" the consciousness cried out. Unfortunately, its former body was no longer available. The old body had been frozen if death had occurred in winter, decomposed if in summer, and relatives may have already had it cremated, buried, thrown into water, or exposed on the ground for the birds. Although the text advised giving up any desire for a body, the consciousness heading toward rebirth started looking for a new body that would replace the old.

Before acquiring a new body, however, the consciousness had to go through a final judgment. The person's good deeds were counted out with white pebbles, bad deeds with black. In awe and fear, the consciousness appeared before the Lord of Death. Questioned about its previous life, the consciousness might lie and say, "I have not committed any evil deed." The Lord of Death, however, simply consulted the Mirror of Karma, in which the truth about all good and evil past deeds was reflected. The mirror revealed a judgment that could not be avoided. Disclosing the character of the person's past actions, the Mirror of Karma exposed the person to judgment.

Following that disclosure, the consciousness was punished in its thought body by the agents of the Lord of Death. The punishments were particularly horrible. Dragging the person along by the neck, an angel of death might "cut off thy head, extract thy heart, pull out thy intestines, lick up thy brain, drink thy blood, eat thy flesh, and gnaw thy bones" (Evans-Wentz, 1927: 166). Though under terrible torture, the person could not die because he or she was already dead. The thought body revived, only to be punished again.

Perhaps the punishment was intended as a violent form of shock therapy, a remedial punishment that might break attachments to having a body. Liberation might still be achieved at this point. The *Bardo Thödol* exhorted the consciousness to recognize that its thought body, its torturer, and even the Lord of Death were all hallucinations. Although the pain was experienced as real, the entire process of judgment and punishment was a projection from consciousness. Like everything else in the bardos, experience was determined by consciousness. If that experience was recognized as projection, liberation could be achieved. If not, the consciousness would continue to be carried along by the impetus of its past karma into another body.

The duration and intensity of punishment depended on a person's past deeds. After punishment was completed, the consciousness moved into the final stages of preparation for rebirth. As the colored lights of the worlds of desire appeared, the thought body began to glow with the light of the loka into which it would be reborn: white for the heaven world, smoky gray for the hell world, red for the ghost world, green for the demon world, blue for the animal world, or yellow for the human world. Even at this stage, liberation could still be achieved. Ignorance could be overcome by recognizing that even the process leading to rebirth was determined by consciousness.

For most, however, it was too late. By this point, the consciousness was probably consumed with desire for the safety, security, and familiarity associated with having a body. After all the intensity of the bardos, a body might seem like a safe haven. So the consciousness had one final vision of a mating couple in the world in which it would be reborn. If about to be reborn as a male, the consciousness would be attracted to the female; if about to be female, it would be attracted to the male. In that Tibetan Buddhist variation on the Freudian Oedipus-Electra complex, the consciousness began to reenter the worlds of desire.

In a moment of bliss in the union of sperm and ovum, the consciousness dissolved into unconsciousness in the womb. While that unconsciousness was probably a welcome rest from the splendors and terrors of the afterlife bardos, it signified a return to the cycle of suffering. Occupying another body in one of the six worlds of desire, the person would once again endure birth, life, and death, only to once again go through the entire process of afterlife experience outlined in the *Bardo Thödol*. That cycle would continue until the radical change in consciousness that led to liberation was finally achieved.

Reincarnation

In the Tibetan Buddhist visionary journey through the moment of dying, the interim stage of illusions, and the final return to embodiment, mythic transcendence of death was imagined within a theory of rebirth. Being born again in a different body provided a kind of transcendence; a genuine transcendence, however, was expected to be achieved only in liberation from the entire cycle of rebirth. Nevertheless, rebirth accounted for a certain degree of continuity from lifetime to lifetime. Although Buddhist thought in general emphasized the discontinuity that made every moment, let alone every lifetime, part of a process of constant change, the theory of rebirth involved the continuity of personal attributes over a series of lifetimes.

In Upaniṣadic Hindu thought, personal continuity over lifetimes was explained as a result of the existence of an eternal self, the ātman. In one sense, the ātman was incarnated in each lifetime, as the spiritual core of the person. Each embodied, living person was a *jīvātman,* a living eternal self. In another sense, however, the ātman was above and beyond the entire process of life, death, and rebirth, like a bird sitting on a branch, looking down on the person who was going through a series of lifetimes. Ultimately, as the eternal power diffused through the universe, the self in its supreme transcendence was unaffected by the whole process. The self merely waited for the person to awaken and to get free from the cycle of rebirth.

In Buddhist thought, however, the permanent, abiding, eternal self was denied. What continued after death was a set of influences in motion. A bundle of dispositions and inclinations persisted, but they did not add up to any eternal self. Instead, the very notion of a permanent, personal self was part of the ignorance that kept the bundle of dispositions and inclinations together and propelled it along in the process of rebirth. Seeing through that illusion, the consciousness radically changed and enabled the person to attain the liberating deathlessness of enlightenment. In that liberation, Buddhists imagined no eternal self. Although Buddhists were clear that nirvāṇa did not imply an immortal soul, they refused to specify precisely what that state would be like.

Regarding rebirth, Hindu thought emphasized continuity, whereas Buddhist thought stressed change. Both perspectives, however, evaluated the whole process of rebirth negatively. The reason for their negative assessment could be found in their understanding of karma. In karmic theory, actions were regarded as having good or bad consequences depending on their ethical merit. Good actions produced good effects, bad actions produced bad effects, but, as we have seen, the object was to gain liberation from the entire karmic process of cause and effect.

Failing to achieve liberation—whether it was called mokṣa, nirvāṇa, or satori—the person remained in the cycle of rebirth. In that case, the next best thing that could be expected would be a better rebirth. In order to be born again in better situations and circumstances, a person had to gain merit through good actions that would produce positive karmic results in the next life. Gaining merit and avoiding demerit became a secondary goal in the transcendence of death within forms of popular Hindu and Buddhist religion.

Not every religious tradition that has supported belief in reincarnation has evaluated that process negatively. In some Australian religions, after returning to the ancestral world at death a person might be transformed into a spirit child to come back again for another lifetime. That rebirth was imagined to occur within the same clan. Reincarnation, therefore, was regarded positively because it supported the ancestral and cultural transcendence of the clan. By being reborn in the same clan, a reincarnated person reinforced the continuity of that kinship group.

Similarly, the Trobriand Islanders of Melanesia studied by the anthropologist Bronislaw Malinowski imagined that after death a person's soul (*balōma*) descended to an underworld paradise called Tuma, where life went on much as it did on earth. When souls grew old, however, they were rejuvenated to become young again. They continued to live in Tuma until they became bored or were weakened by the evil effects of sorcery. Souls then reverted back to spirit infants in order to be reborn in the human world. Every birth, therefore, was regarded as a reincarnation of a spirit, a person born again in a different body but in the same clan and family lineage in which it lived before (Malinowski, 1927: 32). From the perspective of the Trobriand Islanders, the birth of every child was to be celebrated as the return of an ancestral spirit. Reincarnation was regarded not as resulting from an ancestor's failure to achieve liberation but as a welcome return to human life.

Among the Igbo of Nigeria, reincarnation was viewed positively because it gave people additional opportunities to achieve their goals and realize their destinies. Each person was assumed to have been given certain objectives in life by God. If a person did not achieve those goals, he or she would survive death in the world of the dead. The dead lived there much as they had during life: Spirits were organized by their clans, they continued in their occupations, and they thought and felt as if they were still alive. After spending time in the world of the dead, however, spirits were reborn on earth for another chance to achieve their personal goals in another lifetime. Reincarnation gave people numerous opportunities to improve their status, skills, and accomplishments. In that respect, reincarnation was regarded positively by the Igbo (Stevenson, 1985).

Tribal religions of India also seem to have held beliefs in reincarnation as a positive process (Fürer-Haimendorf, 1953). But in Hindu, Buddhist, Jain, and other Indian traditions, reincarnation came to be regarded as a cycle of bondage. The cycle of rebirth was understood as a trap to get out of, a wheel to get off of, or a prison to escape. The visionary journey through the world after death presented in the *Bardo Thödol* illustrated this negative evaluation of the entire process of rebirth.

This negative evaluation resulted from the development of the idea of karma. No concept similar to the Hindu or Buddhist notion of karma appeared in the reincarnation beliefs of the Trobriand Islanders or the Igbo of Nigeria. The principle of karma was central to the Hindu and Buddhist "ethicization" of life and death (Obeyesekere, 1980). All actions during life were given ethical significance that would carry consequences after death. A person was not reborn in the same family, clan, or kinship group but was reincarnated in a situation determined by the ethical quality of his or her past actions. Reincarnation, therefore, did not support the ancestral transcendence of a kinship group; rather, it reduced each person to an individual who was held accountable for the merits and demerits of past actions.

Over a series of lifetimes, cognitive continuity was broken by the loss of any memory of past lives. Only in rare cases, such as the Buddha's enlightenment, did a living person recover a detailed memory of past lives that would provide a sense of cognitive continuity. In the Buddha's case, of course, those memories were not worth remembering because they recalled a continuity that was ultimately seen as illusory. But many cases have been documented of claims to recollections and other circumstantial evidence for reincarnation (Stevenson, 1974, 1975, 1976). Memory of past lives is important for any theory of reincarnation because memory is the only basis for establishing a cognitive continuity that would guarantee that the person living now is the same as the person who lived before.

Although memory of past lives may be rare during life, a person might recall past lives during the interim period after death and before rebirth. After death, a person might recover a sense of cognitive continuity over lifetimes. As we have seen, memory was important in the *Bardo Thödol,* particularly in the recollection of personal attachments to relatives and friends that had been formed in the previous life or perhaps in a series of lifetimes. But the text instructed the consciousness to break free of all selfish, egotistical attachments that only contributed to its continuing suffering. In that respect, memory reinforced personal identity and personal relationships that needed to be broken in order for the person to achieve liberation from the cycle of karma.

A more binding forensic continuity, therefore, was determined by karma. A person remained the same person on account of ongoing karmic responsibility for actions. Even if unconscious of past deeds, a person nevertheless experienced their consequences. To a large extent, past actions determined present situations and circumstances; present actions determined the future. The cycle of rebirth was kept in motion by karma, resulting in a mechanical, automatic, and basically unconscious process of cause and effect over a series of lifetimes. A person's forensic identity was tied to that karmic cycle of consequences for action.

Transcendence of death could not be achieved within the cycle of rebirth. Even a good, moral life led to another life and another death in that mechanical cycle. Ultimately, in order to transcend death, a person had to get out of the mechanical cycle of cause and effect. Therefore, a genuine transcendence of death—a permanent deathlessness—required breaking out of the forensic identity that had been formed by karma. That breakthrough was a radical transformation of personal identity that dissolved karma and achieved the supreme freedom from the cycle of life and death.

THE TIBETAN BOOK OF THE DEAD

After it was translated into English in 1927, the *Bardo Thödol* had considerable impact on the Western imagination. The psychologist Carl Jung saw the text as a summary of his theory of personal individuation. Reading the text backward, Jung argued that it represented a progression from the oedipal phase of infancy and early childhood through the acceptance of one's own dark side—what Jung called "the shadow"—toward a conscious confrontation with the basic patterns (archetypes) of personality development. For Jung, *The Tibetan Book of the Dead* was a manual for an archetypal psychology of the human consciousness moving toward integration (Jung, 1927, 1999).

During the 1960s, the *Bardo Thödol* was read not as a manual for "normal" psychological development but as a guide to altered states of consciousness. Timothy Leary and his associates referred to the text in experiments with LSD and other hallucinogenic chemicals. Because of its central concern with consciousness, the *Bardo Thödol* provided a useful pattern of imagery for experiments with altered states (Leary et al., 1964). Finally, as we noted, the text of the *Bardo Thödol* was attractive to those who saw similarities between the experiences it described and the reports of near-death experiences.

In its original setting, however, the *Bardo Thödol* was not a guide for psychological development, a manual for using psychedelic drugs, or a scientific investigation of death. For Tibetan Buddhists, the *Bardo Thödol* was a ritual text to be used in the context of an art of dying and in the death rituals performed to mark the transition to rebirth. It focused basic Tibetan Buddhist religious concerns about death. In exhorting the transiting consciousness toward liberation, the text promised an ultimate transcendence of death. In conclusion, we can summarize the basic concerns of a Tibetan Buddhist transcendence of death.

1. The primary emphasis was on consciousness. As in most forms of Asian transcendence, the *Bardo Thödol* focused on changes in consciousness. Those changes occurred in the transition through death but, more important, in the radical change of consciousness that signified a transcendence of death. In moving through death, the consciousness was exhorted to recognize everything—light, sound, merciful and wrathful Buddhas, even its own judgment and punishment—as projections from itself. In reality, everything was a projection from consciousness. Consciousness was all-important. Liberation from rebirth and redeath—the ultimate transcendence of death—required the dramatic change of consciousness that Buddhists called nirvāṇa. Both death and its transcendence, therefore, were symbolized primarily as alterations in consciousness.

2. The physical body was devalued. If reincarnation (or rebirth) meant to be born again in a different body, each physical body a person occupied was merely one more address in a series of temporary homes. In the last bardo, the text advised the consciousness to abandon any desire for having a physical body. The body was understood as the center of a network of personal attachments that bound the person to rebirth, an anchor that held the person down to the worlds of desire. Embodiment in any physical form had to be avoided in order to transcend death.

3. Emotions blocked the ultimate transcendence of death. Personal emotions reinforced the personal ego identity that prevented liberation. Emotions were understood as the "deadly sins" that alienated consciousness from its Buddha nature and Buddha form. The emotions of pride, anger, greed, envy, lust, and so on kept the person being reborn in the worlds of desire. The goal in the Buddhist logic of desire was not to satisfy those desires

but to eliminate them. Transcendence of death depended on dissolving those personal emotions.

4. The moral dimension in the symbolism of death was understood as the principle of karma. In the continuous process of cause and effect, a person's actions were thought to have moral consequences. Transcendence of death, however, did not depend on living a moral life. Even a moral life still tied the person into the cycle of birth and death. The Buddhist path did insist on a moral foundation. The Buddhist was expected to abstain from killing, lying, stealing, sexual misconduct, and intoxicating beverages that tended to cloud the mind. A moral life may have been a foundation, but transcendence required a change of consciousness that went beyond the requirements of a moral life. Transcendence resulted from an enlightened, liberated consciousness above and beyond the moral consequences of actions determined by karma.

5. Punishment for past deeds was always remedial, in the sense that it was temporary and designed to purge, shock, and perhaps awaken the consciousness to its true nature. If judgment was determined by karma, punishment also followed from the mechanical, automatic consequences of past actions. Those consequences were experienced in the next life. But, as we have seen, punishment was also enacted after death in the final bardo before rebirth. Horrible tortures were exacted on the person's thought body, but they were projections of self-judgment and self-punishment by an unenlightened consciousness. They were a type of remedial shock therapy designed to awaken the sleeping consciousness. Afterlife punishment, therefore, was a temporary stage in the transition toward rebirth rather than permanent retribution.

6. Afterlife places were temporary. The six lokas for rebirth were temporary places of rewards and punishments for past actions. In a sense, every place of rebirth was a place of punishment because the person remained tied to the karmic cycle in one of the worlds of desire. Whether that punishment was located in the cold or fiery hells, in the world of the hungry ghosts or the aggressive warrior demons, or in the animal or human worlds, life in the lokas was necessarily of temporary duration. Even the heavenly loka was only a temporary abode. A person born into that place would also die and go through the entire process of rebirth again. The only permanent "place" that was imagined in the Buddhist world was no place. Deathlessness was beyond time, space, or any condition. Resulting from a dramatic change of consciousness, nirvāṇa was a permanent liberation from death that was beyond any conception of place.

7. The symbolism of death gave shape to life. The way in which death was imagined provided a basic orientation toward life. If death challenged the consciousness to recognize Buddha nature and Buddha forms, the priority of life was to prepare for that recognition. The most important preparation for death was meditation, concentrating on the Buddha nature and Buddha forms in ways that promised to transform the consciousness even while still alive in a physical body.

But the symbolism of death gave shape to life in a more profound sense: Life was impermanent, fleeting, momentary, in constant flux; it was dying and being reborn in every moment. Death was relativized, therefore, as part of the constant process of change within life. Realizing that impermanence, a Buddhist could recognize that the forms of life he or she beheld were also projections from consciousness. Sights and sounds in life could be recognized as similar to those encountered after death. Not real or permanent, they could be seen through as projections of consciousness. In that breakthrough of consciousness, a transcendence of death could be achieved even in the course of life.

Chapter Four: References

Beyer, Stephan. (1973). *The Cult of Tārām: Magic and Ritual in Tibet*. Berkeley and Los Angeles: University of California Press.

Brauen, Martin, and Per Kvaerne. (1978). "A Tibetan Death Ceremony." *Temenos* 14: 9–24.

Chidester, David. (1992). *Word and Light: Seeing, Hearing, and Religious Discourse*. Urbana: University of Illinois Press.

Edgerton, Franklin. (1926–27). "The Hour of Death." *Annals of the Bhandarkar Oriental Institute* 8: 219–49.

Epstein, Lawrence. (1990). "A Comparative View of Tibetan and Western Near-Death Experiences." In Lawrence Epstein and Richard F. Sherburn (eds.), *Reflections on Tibetan Culture*. Lampeter: Edwin Mellen, 315–28.

Evans-Wentz, W. Y. (ed.). (1927). *The Tibetan Book of the Dead*. Oxford: Oxford University Press.

———. (1928). *Tibet's Great Yogi Milarepa*. Oxford: Oxford University Press.

———. (1935). *Tibetan Yoga and Secret Doctrines*. Oxford: Oxford University Press.

Freemantle, Francesca, and Chögyam Trungpa. (1975). *The Tibetan Book of the Dead*. Berkeley, Calif.: Shambhala.

Fürer-Haimendorf, Christoph von. (1953). "The After-Life in Indian Tribal Belief." *Journal of the Royal Anthropological Society* 83: 37–49.

Getty, Alice. (1914). *The Gods of Northern Buddhism*. Oxford: Clarendon Press.

Hopkins, Jeffrey, and Lati Rinbochay. (1979). *Death, Intermediate State and Rebirth in Tibetan Buddhism*. London: Rider & Co.

Jung, C. G. (1927). "Psychological Commentary." Trans. R. F. C. Hull. In W. Y. Evans-Wentz (ed.), *The Tibetan Book of the Dead*. Oxford: Oxford University Press, xxxv–lii.

———. (1999). *Jung on Death and Immortality*. Ed. Jenny Young. Princeton, N.J.: Princeton University Press.

Karmay, Samten G. (1972). *The Treasury of Good Sayings: A Tibetan History of Bon*. London: Oxford University Press.

Kvaerne, Per. (1972). "Aspects of the Origin of the Buddhist Tradition in Tibet." *Numen* 19: 22–40.

Leary, Timothy, Ralph Metzner, and Richard Alpert. (1964). *The Psychedelic Experience: A Manual Based on the Tibetan Book of the Dead*. New York: University Books.

Lee, Jung Young. (1974). *Death and Beyond in the Eastern Perspective: A Study Based on the Bardo Thödol and the I Ching*. New York: Gordon and Breach.

MacHovec, Frank J. (1972). *The Tibetan Book of the Dead*. Mount Vernon, N.Y.: Peter Pauper Press.

Malinowski, Bronislaw. (1927). *The Father in Primitive Psychology*. New York: W. W. Norton.

Marks, Lawrence E. (1978). *The Unity of the Senses: Interrelations Among the Modalities*. New York: Academic Press.

Moody, Raymond. (1975). *Life After Life*. New York: Bantam Books.

Mullin, Glenn H. (1986). *Death and Dying: The Tibetan Tradition*. Boston: Arkana.

Obeyesekere, Gananath. (1980). "The Rebirth Eschatology and Its Transformations." In Wendy D. O'Flaherty (ed.), *Karma and Rebirth in Classical Indian Traditions*. Berkeley and Los Angeles: University of California Press, 137–64.

Paul, Robert A. (1982). *The Tibetan Symbolic World*. Chicago: University of Chicago Press.

Powers, J. (1995). *An Introduction to Tibetan Buddhism*. Ithaca, N.Y.: Snow Lion.

Price, H. H. (1953). "Survival and the Idea of 'Another World.'" *Proceedings of the Society for Psychical Research* 50: 1–25. Reprinted in John Donnelly (ed.) (1978), *Language, Metaphysics, and Death*. New York: Fordham University Press, 176–95.

Reynolds, Frank. (1977). "The Several Bodies of the Buddha: Reflections on a Neglected Aspect of Theravāda Tradition." *History of Religions* 16: 374–89.

Rinpoche, Sogyal. (1992). *The Tibetan Book of Living and Dying*. San Francisco: HarperCollins.

Sabom, Michael D. (1981). *Recollections of Death: A Medical Investigation*. New York: Harper & Row.

Samuel, G. (1993). *Civilized Shamans: Buddhism in Tibetan Societies*. Washington: Smithsonian Institution Press.

Snellgrove, David L. (1957). *Buddhist Himalaya*. London: Oxford University Press.

———. (1967). *The Nine Ways of Bon*. London: Oxford University Press.

Stevenson, Ian. (1974). *Twenty Cases Suggestive of Reincarnation*. 2nd ed. Charlottesville: University Press of Virginia.

———. (1975). *Cases of the Reincarnation Type, Vol. I: 10 Cases in India*. Charlottesville: University Press of Virginia.

———. (1976). *Cases of the Reincarnation Type, Vol. II: 10 Cases in Sri Lanka*. Charlottesville: University Press of Virginia.

———. (1985). "The Belief in Reincarnation Among the Igbo of Nigeria." *Journal of Asian and African Studies* 20: 13–30.

Thondup, Tulku. (1987). *Buddhist Civilisation in Tibet*. London: Routledge and Kegan Paul.

Thurman, Robert. (1994). *The Tibetan Book of the Dead*. New York: Bantam.

Tucci, Giuseppe. (1980). *The Religions of Tibet*. Trans. Geoffrey Samuel. London: Routledge and Kegan Paul.

Waddell, L. A. (1934). *The Buddhism of Tibet or Lāmaism*. 2nd ed. Cambridge: W. Heffer. Reprinted as *Tibetan Buddhism, with Its Mystic Cults, Symbolism and Mythology*. New York: Dover Publications (orig. ed. 1895).

Zaleski, Carol. (1987). *Otherworld Journeys: Accounts of Near-Death Experience in Medieval and Modern Times*. New York: Oxford University Press.

5

Abrahamic Transcendence

Long after Abraham and his wife Sarah had passed the age of childbearing, they unexpectedly had a son. Celebrating the long-awaited birth, Abraham and Sarah received the child as a miraculous gift from God. In the patriarchal society of ancient Israel, a son was regarded as necessary for the continuation of the family line. With the birth of his son Isaac, Abraham's line could continue after his death.

The Hebrew Bible recounted that God guaranteed Abraham a type of immortality through his descendants and their promised land. God said to Abraham, "The land on which you lie I will give to you and to your descendants" (Gen. 28:13). Abraham was promised an ancestral transcendence through his descendants and a cultural transcendence through the nation that would establish itself in the promised land.

One day, however, God demanded that Abraham take his son, his only hope of living on after death, up into the hills and kill him. In complete obedience to the will of God, Abraham prepared to do as he had been commanded. But as Abraham raised the knife to kill his son, God stopped the sacrifice.

Revealing that the order had been a test of Abraham's obedience, God instructed Abraham to substitute a ram for his son. Instead of killing Isaac, Abraham sacrificed the animal as an act of worship for God. According to the account in the Hebrew Bible, God commended Abraham's obedience and renewed the divine promise that Abraham would live on after death in his people and his land (Gen. 22).

Judaism, Christianity, and Islam all traced their lineages back to Abraham. Although they have often been referred to as Western religions, these three traditions were children of Abraham born out of the ancient Near East. Eventually spreading throughout the world, Judaism, Christianity, and Islam kept the memory of their common father Abraham alive. But each tradition recalled Abraham in a different way.

Jews revered the memory of Abraham as their first patriarchal ancestor. He was the first to receive revelations from the God of ancient Israel, Yahweh. Traveling all over the ancient Near East, from upper Mesopotamia down to Egypt, Abraham was finally buried in the land that would later be known as Israel. As long as his descendants continued to worship Yahweh, Abraham lived on through the people and their land.

Early Christians revered the memory of Abraham for his supreme demonstration of faith in God. In particular, Abraham's willingness to sacrifice his son proved the extent of his faith (Rom. 4; Heb. 11:8–19). Later Christians saw Abraham's sacrifice of Isaac as a symbol of the sacrificial death of Jesus on the cross: As Abraham sacrificed his son Isaac, Christians believed that God sacrificed his son Jesus so they might gain eternal life.

Muslims revered the memory of Abraham—or Ibrahim—as the first prophet and the father of their ancestor Ishmael, who was born to Abraham and Hagar. The prophet Abraham was regarded as the first Muslim because he practiced *islam*—submission in absolute obedience to the will of God—when he was commanded to sacrifice his son. Abraham and Ishmael founded the Ka'bah in Mecca, the most sacred place in the world of Islam, and received the Islamic faith directly from Allah.

In the seventh century, the prophet Muḥammad understood his mission as the restoration of that original religion of Abraham. In a vision of the paradise promised to Muslims after death, Muḥammad saw Jesus of the Christians in the second heaven and Moses of the Jews in the sixth heaven. But Abraham was seated on a throne in the seventh heaven, enjoying the eternal rewards of the highest level of paradise for his obedience to Allah (ibn Hishām, 1955: 181–87).

In all three traditions—Judaism, Christianity, and Islam—Abraham symbolized perfect obedience to the will of God. In obedience to the divine will, Abraham set the model for a good human life. But Abraham also symbolized the ancestral and cultural transcendence of death achieved by the continuity of a people in their promised land. Eventually, Abraham came to represent a mythic transcendence through such symbols as the bosom of Abraham and the throne of Abraham that promised an afterlife of rest or reward for those who had been faithful like Abraham to the will of God.

Because the children of Abraham emerged from the ancient Near East, we will begin by exploring ancient Near Eastern myths about life, death, and afterlife. Many of the themes in those ancient myths persisted in Jewish, Christian, and Islamic approaches to death. Human mortality, divine immortality, and the judgment of the dead on the basis of past thoughts, words, and deeds in a single lifetime were themes that Judaism, Christianity, and Islam inherited from the ancient myths of the Near East.

ANCIENT MYTHS

The ancient Near East encompassed a region that has been called the fertile crescent. Geography was dominated by rivers, from the Tigris and Euphrates Rivers of Mesopotamia in the north down to the Nile of Egypt in the south. In the center, the Jordan River of Canaan was an important geographical marker in an area that became known as Israel. The ancient Near Eastern societies of Egypt, Mesopotamia, Israel, and Persia were organized around institutions of sacred kingship and royal priesthoods. Society tended to be hierarchical. At the top, the king held ultimate political power. Political power, however, tended to be given a religious aura. The king not only supervised the royal priesthood and religious sacrifices but was often assumed to be divine or a representative of divinity on earth. These ancient religions were dedicated to maintaining a divine order, both in the universe and in human society.

Religious transcendence of death depended for the most part on human beings' finding and keeping their places in the larger cosmic order. In the order of the cosmos, gods were immortal, but human beings were mortal. With a few rare exceptions, all humans were expected to pass through death. Nevertheless, types of immortality were possible. One type was available to human beings through ancestral transcendence—living on through offspring. Another type was available in cultural transcendence—living on through heroic accomplishments in the cultural memory of a society. These forms of immortality were in keeping with a human's place in the cosmic order, mortal but capable of a type of immortality through children and achievements.

Religions of the ancient Near East also developed forms of mythic transcendence. The possibility of a successful passage through death was imagined in myths of afterlife. In some cases, the afterlife was imagined as a shadowy underworld in which a vague, semiconscious trace of the person continued after death. But in other myths, the afterlife was symbolized in terms of the judgment of the dead. Detailed expectations of judgment, rewards, and punishments were developed. Where myths of judgment appeared, they emphasized the moral conscience of the person that had been shaped in life. Death was not so much a change of consciousness as a testing ground for the moral worth of the person. In some myths, survival depended on the purity of conscience in the passage through death.

For purposes of comparison, we will briefly examine myths about death in three ancient religions—the religions of Egypt, Mesopotamia, and Persia. Ancient Egyptian religion developed detailed expectations about an afterlife judgment. In the judgment hall of the god Osiris, the moral worth of a person was weighed in the balance of truth. Ancient Mesopotamian religion, however, did not develop the symbolism of personal judgment. Everyone was expected to be reduced to the same shadowy existence after death in the underworld. Nevertheless, ancestral and cultural transcendence of death remained important. Finally, ancient Persian religion under the influence of the prophet Zoroaster developed an elaborate mythic transcendence of death. Zoroastrian myths combined symbolism of a judgment after death for each person with the anticipation of a final, collective judgment at the end of time. Although they revolved around different myths, the religions of ancient Egypt, Mesopotamia, and Persia all developed concerns about death, afterlife, and the judgment of the dead that continued to be important for the transcendence of death in later religious developments.

Ancient Egypt

Death rituals in ancient Egypt concentrated on the body. Techniques for treating, dying, preserving, and wrapping the body turned a decomposing corpse into a permanent mummy. The process of mummification required skilled work by ritual technicians of death that took as long as seventy days to complete. They extracted the internal organs, dried and preserved the corpse with a mixture of salts, then wrapped it in layers of specially treated linen. When preservation was complete, priests performed the ritual called "the opening of the mouth," which signified that the mummified corpse was a permanent home for the deceased's soul.

The surviving soul, however, was imagined not as a single entity but as several different spiritual functions that might live on after death. Each person had a *ka* that was a vital, life-giving force. The ka was symbolized as two arms, signifying the creative power and ability that animated the human person. An extension of divine energy, the ka was the same vital force that animated the gods. Because that vital force shared the essence of the gods, it did not cease to exist after the death of a person's body.

In addition to the ka, each person also had an independent, individual soul consisting of consciousness and will. That individual soul, or *ba,* was symbolized as a human-headed bird. If the corpse had been properly preserved, the ba was able to travel from the body and return to it. It remained an individual soul after death, perhaps glorified in the afterlife as an *akh*—a transfigured spirit— that was free to journey between the human world and the world of the dead. Closely associated with that independent, conscious soul was its moral conscience. Symbolized as a human heart, the conscience, or *ab,* became the focus for an afterlife judgment of the dead.

The Judgment of the Dead During the Old Kingdom (2425–2300 B.C.E.), mummification was reserved for kings, the divine pharaohs who were assumed to ascend after death to the sun god Rē and accompany him on his daily rounds across the sky. Gradually, however, mummification was included in the death rituals of anyone who could afford the expensive operations. The extension of the practice of mummification reflected the gradual "democratization" of mythic transcendence in the history of ancient Egyptian religion.

In the solar afterlife of the pharaoh, he was simply assumed to return to his father in the heavens. No judgment of the pharaoh after death was expected. The pharaoh was a god on earth. After death, he became a heavenly deity in the celestial company of the sun god. With the extension of mythic transcendence to ordinary people, however, an expectation of an afterlife judgment of the dead was developed. That judgment was expected to occur after death in the great halls of the Egyptian Lord of the Dead, the god Osiris.

According to Egyptian myth, Osiris had been a king of Egypt. Descended from the gods, he too was divine. While ruling the kingdom with his wife-sister Isis, Osiris was attacked and killed by his evil brother, Seth, who cut his body into thirteen pieces and scattered them all over Egypt. In grief, Isis searched for the dismembered parts of Osiris until she had found them all and put them back together. By restoring the dead body, Isis was able to conceive a child with Osiris, a son named Horus, who eventually defeated Seth in battle and avenged the death of Osiris. Although his body had been restored, Osiris descended to the underworld to rule there as Lord of the Dead.

The story of Osiris had two lasting implications for Egyptian beliefs and practices relating to death. First, the example of Osiris supported the ritual practice of mummification. By preserving the body from decomposition, ancient Egyptian funeral practices reenacted the restoration of the body of Osiris. Second, the example of Osiris suggested that the afterlife would be in that kingdom of the other world he had gone to rule. Before entering the great halls of Osiris, however, the soul would have to pass through the judgment of the dead.

The earliest *Pyramid Texts* (2425–2300 B.C.E.), inscribed on the inner walls of the burial places of pharaohs, referred to a divine standard of ethical judgment that was upheld by the gods. That ethical standard was called *Ma'āt*. Representing truth, justice, and righteousness, Ma'āt was the ultimate standard of cosmic order. Pharaohs were praised in the pyramid inscriptions as going forth to meet Ma'āt after death, bearing their own ethical righteousness before them to face the ultimate standard of truth. Since it was assumed that pharaohs did not have to face judgment, the inscriptions simply proclaimed the pharaoh as a servant of Ma'āt being welcomed into the afterlife with the gods.

By the time of the *Coffin Texts* (2160–1580 B.C.E.), references to an afterlife judgment of the dead by the ethical standard of Ma'āt became more explicit. The judgment of the dead was symbolized as a weighing of the person in the scales of a great balance. Inscriptions inside coffins that housed the mummies declared, "This is the balance of Rē, in which he weighs the Truth [Ma'āt]." Often the texts proclaimed the innocence or purity of the person who was entering the judgment of the dead. One text announced, "The offense of which thou art accused is eliminated, thy fault is wiped out, by the weighing of the balance . . . in the day of the evaluation of qualities."

But the wicked had much to fear in that judgment. They would not be able to avoid the inevitable and automatic weighing on the scale of Ma'āt. One text declared a fearful judgment on the wicked: "[You cannot] be protected from this god of mysterious form, whose two eye-brows are the two arms of the balance, who casts his rope over the wicked . . . who annihilates the souls in that day when evil is assessed." A person might be prepared by a variety of ritual practices, magical formulas, and secret incantations, but ultimately there was no escape from the judgment of the dead.

The Egyptian Book of the Dead In the New Kingdom period (1580–1090 B.C.E.), the judgment of the dead was developed in elaborate detail. Texts were written on papyrus scrolls and placed in tombs. Those papyrus texts, which have been called *The Egyptian Book of the Dead,* were designed to assist the deceased in his or her journey to the next world. *The Egyptian Book of the Dead* outlined the process of judgment that a person could expect in the great hall of Ma'āt. That judgment determined whether the person could enter the throne room of Osiris as a glorified spirit (akh) in the court of the Lord of the Dead. A representative example of the process of afterlife judgment in *The Egyptian Book of the Dead* is found in the *Papyrus of Ani,* a scroll that was made for a scribe named Ani, who had held an important religious office in the royal priesthood of Thebes around 1300 B.C.E. The *Papyrus of Ani* described and illustrated a successful passage through the Egyptian afterlife judgment of the dead.

Ani was depicted approaching the great hall of judgment in apprehension. At the center of the hall stood a large black balance, with two scales suspended from its beam. In the pan of one of the scales was placed the heart of Ani. That heart represented the moral conscience that had been shaped over the course of a life. Thoughts, words, and deeds had determined its character. A clear conscience would be one that was pure of any crimes against the gods or against human society. The heart was either pure or impure, light or heavy, good or wicked. In the judgment, the conscience of the person was placed in one scale of the balance.

In the other scale of the balance stood a feather, representing Ma'āt. Ani's heart was weighed against the feather of Truth. If his heart was free of guilt, shame, and impurity, it would be light. The heart would be in balance with Ma'āt. If, however, his heart was weighted down with wickedness, its heaviness would be revealed on the balance. The moment of judgment, therefore, placed the human conscience in the balance against truth. The character of the heart would reveal itself automatically. No divine judge would have to decide the person's fate after death. The heart would reveal itself in the balance against the impersonal, universal standard of Ma'āt.

The gods of the dead gathered around the balance. The jackal-headed god Anubis adjusted the scales. To his right stood the ibis-headed god Thoth, the god of wisdom and the divine scribe. Thoth prepared to write down the result from the weighing of the heart in the balance. Off to the side lurked a horrible creature with the jaws of a crocodile, the body of a lion, and the hindquarters of a hippopotamus. That creature was Am-mut, the eater of the dead. Am-mut also waited with interest for the results from the balance. If the scale holding the conscience dipped, the heart was immediately fed to Am-mut. Only if the heart balanced with the feather of Ma'āt could the person avoid becoming food for the eater of the dead (Zandee, 1960: 125–60).

In the *Papyrus of Ani,* Ani was expected to be vindicated by the balance. When his heart balanced against Ma'āt, Ani was proclaimed as Osiris-Ani. The divine scribe Thoth announced, "Just and righteous is the scribe Osiris-Ani. He is vindicated. He has not sinned, nor done evil before us. Am-mut shall have no power over him." Ani would not be annihilated by being fed to Am-mut; he would live forever in the court of Osiris as a godlike being. He had successfully passed the test.

Instead of becoming food, Ani was fed the sacrificial food of the gods and admitted into the presence of the Lord of the Dead, Osiris. His entrance was announced by Horus: "I come to you, bringing Osiris-Ani. His heart is just, coming forth from the balance. He has not sinned against any god or goddess. . . . Let there be given to him bread and beer which passes before Osiris; let him be as the followers of [Osiris] forever." In response, the transfigured Ani declared his innocence. The balance had proved that he was pure and righteous. Ani requested admittance to the divine court of Osiris. "Grant that I may be like the favored ones who are in thy following," Ani asked, "and that I may be an Osiris, greatly favored of the good God."

The myth of the death and resurrection of Osiris provided a divine pattern within which human beings might understand their own destinies. They would die, but if their bodies were embalmed, mummified, and ritually prepared, they might also be restored to life in the world of the dead. Survival in the world of Osiris, however, required a successful passage through the judgment of the dead. Balanced in the scales, the human conscience had to be vindicated against the ethical standard of Ma'āt.

The Egyptian Book of the Dead depicted the judgment of the dead as automatic, impersonal, and absolute. Judgment was automatic because everyone had to pass through it after death. There was no way around it, only through it. Judgment was impersonal because it was based on an objective ethical standard rather than the personal will, wishes, or whims of a divine judge. The impersonal ethical standard of Ma'āt, rather than the personal will of Osiris, provided the basis for the judgment of the dead. Finally, judgment was absolute since it was a final, once and for always separation of the good from the wicked. Based on the quality of a person's heart, that person either survived as a godlike being in the halls of Osiris or was annihilated by Am-mut, the eater of the dead. The dead were either in or out, based on the character of the conscience that was submitted for judgment.

The theme of the judgment of the dead was subsequently developed in Jewish, Christian, and Muslim traditions in ways that adapted and modified many of the concerns reflected in the ancient Egyptian myths. Perhaps most significantly, mythic transcendence in these religious traditions continued to emphasize the crucial importance of the conscience in a successful passage through death. In different ways, the heart was believed to be judged, rewarded, and punished after death.

Ancient Mesopotamia

The religions of ancient Mesopotamia did not develop the symbolism of judgment in their expectations about death and afterlife. Rather than an afterlife separation of the good from the wicked, they imagined that death reduced everyone to the same level. All human beings descended after death to a shadowy underworld, where they existed as traces of their former selves. That dark underworld, Arulla, was the common fate for all humanity. The good and the wicked, the rich and the poor, the mighty and the weak—all ended up reduced to shadows there. Immortality was strictly reserved for the gods; mortals were destined to die, only to linger on as semiconscious afterimages in the underworld (Jonker, 1995).

Human Mortality According to Mesopotamian myths, human beings had originally been created from the blood of a primordial sea god mixed with earth. Thus, they might have been regarded as having some aspect of divinity within them. But that sea god, Kingu, was regarded as a cosmic criminal. He had been the second husband of the great goddess of the salt waters, Tiamat, who had been killed in battle by the heroic champion representing the interests of all the other gods, the warrior Marduk. In the Babylonian epic *Enuma El-ish,* Marduk sacrificed the body of Tiamat, cutting it in half to make the skies and the earth. Kingu was held responsible for the warfare among the gods. After the gods executed him, they mixed his blood with clay to form human beings. In Mesopotamian myth, therefore, a barrier was maintained between immortal gods and mortal human beings.

Another myth related how the gap between gods and humans was almost bridged. A human by the name of Adapa—like the Hebrew Adam, representing the human race—had offended the god Anu. Calling Adapa to visit him, Anu intended to give Adapa the food of death. Another god, Ea, warned Adapa that he should not trust Anu. Ea instructed Adapa in what he should say and do in the court of the god. In addition, Ea advised him to refuse any food or drink that Anu might offer him for fear that he would be poisoned. On his visit to Anu, Adapa spoke and acted as he had been instructed. Anu was so impressed with Adapa that he decided to offer him the food of life instead of the food of death. That food would have made Adapa immortal, but he followed Ea's advice and refused to eat. Losing his chance for immortality, Adapa and the human race remained mortal and were denied the eternal life of the gods.

In some respects, the Adapa myth was similar to African myths of "the message that failed." The difference between heaven and earth was symbolized as a communication gap in which immortality was lost. In African myths immortality was lost when the animal messengers confused the messages; in the myth of Adapa immortality was lost by an ironic misunderstanding. Consistently, Mesopotamian religion insisted on an unbridgeable distance between the immortality of the gods and the mortality of humans. Human beings by nature had to die. Nevertheless, Mesopotamian myth also reflected ongoing struggles to come to terms with human mortality and the quest for a divine immortality. That quest was most clearly depicted in the Gilgamesh epic.

The Quest for Immortality The heroic tale of Gilgamesh probably dates to around 2000 B.C.E. In the somewhat later Babylonian version preserved in cuneiform on clay tablets, some of the story has been lost. Enough remains, however, to provide the outlines of the hero's ultimately futile quest for personal immortality. The Gilgamesh epic wrestled with the unavoidable fact of human mortality and explored possibilities for the transcendence of death. Although human beings inevitably had to die, they could discover forms of ancestral and cultural transcendence in the face of death. The hero Gilgamesh, however, was not content with transcending death through producing offspring and making a name for himself. His quest for personal immortality led him in search of the secret that would make him deathless like the gods. In the end, that secret was withheld from Gilgamesh.

Most of the Gilgamesh epic explored the themes of culture and nature. The hero was a shepherd, described as brave, strong, and arrogant, who rose to power as king of the city of Uruk. To challenge Gilgamesh, the gods created a hairy wild man by the name of Enkidu, who lived among the wild animals in the forest. As a herder of domestic animals and ruler of a community, Gilgamesh represented human culture. Living with wild animals, Enkidu represented a state of nature.

When hunters of Uruk complained that Enkidu was disturbing the animals, Gilgamesh proposed a plan. He hired a prostitute to seduce Enkidu. After his experience with the prostitute, Enkidu was no longer accepted by the wild animals. "Enkidu," the prostitute said, "you have become like a god!" Of course, the wild man had not become immortal like the gods, but he had been introduced into human sexuality, which provided one avenue for a symbolic transcendence of death.

Rejected by the wild animals, Enkidu set off to the city of Uruk. There Enkidu and Gilgamesh fought a tremendous battle. After fighting for a long time, Enkidu surrendered and praised Gilgamesh as king. Acknowledging the power and authority of society, Enkidu finally entered into human culture. Gilgamesh and Enkidu became close friends.

Participating in an ongoing culture also provided an avenue for a type of transcendence of death. The two friends set off to battle the monster of the forest, Huwawa. Before going into battle, Gilgamesh thought about death, dwelling on the great division between gods and humans. "Who can scale heaven?" Gilgamesh asked. "Only the gods live forever. As for mankind," Gilgamesh recognized, "numbered are their days."

Fighting the monster of the forest was dangerous and might lead to death. In that death, however, a cultural transcendence was still possible. Gilgamesh anticipated a type of immortality in which he would live on through the reputation he gained from his heroic deeds. "Should I fall," Gilgamesh concluded, "I shall have made me a name."

After defeating the forest monster, Gilgamesh drew the wrath of the goddess Ishtar. To exact her revenge, Ishtar convinced the gods to place a fatal illness upon Enkidu. Approaching death, Enkidu had a vision of the underworld. He saw "the House of Darkness . . . the house which none leave who have entered it, on the road from which there is no way back." In that place, all were reduced to the same level of semiconscious existence. It was the place "where the dwellers are bereft of light, where dust . . . and clay are their food."

As he was dying, Enkidu saw the shadowy underground city of Arulla, enclosed by seven walls and gates, engulfed in darkness, the common, final destination for all human beings. The miserable inhabitants of the underworld existed as shadows, traces, or afterimages on a diet of dirt. Enkidu saw where he would be going after death: *kur-nu-gi-a,* the place of no return. When Enkidu died, Gilgamesh realized that he would one day suffer the same fate. In terror at the thought, Gilgamesh set off on a quest for immortality.

Gilgamesh had heard of a human being by the name of Utnapishtim who had been given the gift of immortality by the gods. Setting off to find the immortal Utnapishtim, Gilgamesh encountered the sun god Shamash, who warned Gilgamesh, "The life you pursue you shall not find." But Gilgamesh would not abandon his quest. In response to the sun god, Gilgamesh compared death to sleep. "Must I lay my head in the heart of the earth, that I may sleep through all the years?" Discontented with that fate, the hero pursued his quest for immortality.

Next Gilgamesh met the ale wife Siduri. Gilgamesh told her of his grief at Enkidu's death and his search for immortality. In response, Siduri echoed the words of the sun god Shamash: "The life you pursue you shall not find." Siduri reminded Gilgamesh of the vast difference between the immortality of the gods and the mortal condition of human beings. "When the gods created mankind," she said, "death for mankind they set aside, life in their own hands retaining."

In place of personal immortality, Siduri exhorted Gilgamesh to take pleasure in work, play, and family. By producing children, Gilgamesh could achieve a type of biological immortality. In addition to the cultural immortality of fame, that was the only type of immortality to which Gilgamesh could aspire.

Not satisfied with Siduri's advice, Gilgamesh continued his quest until he finally found the immortal Utnapishtim. Known as Utnapishtim the Faraway, the old man agreed to reveal to Gilgamesh the secret of his immortality. As a favorite of one of the gods, Utnapishtim had survived a great flood that had destroyed all other life on earth. As a reward for his service, the god Enlil had given Utnapishtim and his wife the unique gift of immortality. "Hitherto Utnapishtim has been but human," the god declared. "Henceforth Utnapishtim and his wife shall be like unto us gods." That gift was never to be repeated.

Utnapishtim advised Gilgamesh to accept his fate. Since nothing lasted forever, Gilgamesh should come to terms with the fact that his life would end. But Gilgamesh persisted in his quest, so Utnapishtim agreed to tell him about a secret plant of immortality that grew at the bottom of a distant sea. Enduring great hardships, Gilgamesh finally found that plant of immortality. He dived to the bottom of the sea to pluck it up. But just as Gilgamesh was coming to the surface, a snake passing by snapped the plant out of his hands and swam away with his last hope of immortality. Snakes or serpents have been associated with immortality in many myths, dying and being reborn with the shedding of their skins. In the end, however, that immortality was denied to Gilgamesh.

The Gilgamesh epic, therefore, was a myth that explored the dilemmas of human mortality. Unlike the gods, human beings had to die. Mortality was an unavoidable part of the human condition. In rare cases, immortality might be a special gift bestowed by the gods. But the gift was an exception that reinforced the rule. Nevertheless, human beings were entitled to a type of immortality through ancestral and cultural transcendence. Humans could live on through offspring and through accomplishments but not in any personal immortality. Although its hero was not satisfied, the Gilgamesh epic of ancient Mesopotamia suggested that, in the end, symbolic immortality was all that was available to human beings in their confrontation with a mortality that would eventually reduce them to shadows and dust.

Ancient Persia

The Zoroastrian tradition of ancient Persia began with the teachings of the prophet Zarathustra (called Zoroaster in Greek). Uncertain exactly when he lived, scholars have recently placed the life of the prophet Zarathustra somewhere between 1400 and 1200 B.C.E. (Boyce, 1982); earlier scholars placed his life around 600 B.C.E. Whenever he lived, Zarathustra taught a religion dedicated to a cosmic principle of order, *asha,* that was similar in some respects to the ancient Egyptian ethical standard. Asha was a principle of order, truth, and righteousness that manifested in a life of good thoughts, good words, and good deeds. After death, a person was expected to be judged on the basis of his or her adherence to asha.

Upholding the principle of asha was the supreme god of Zoroastrian faith, Ahura Mazda. Assisted by six angelic beings, the Amesha Spenta, that god of light represented the forces of goodness in the universe. Ahura Mazda was locked in a cosmic struggle with an evil god, Angra Mainyu, who was dedicated to all that was false. With his demons, Angra Mainyu promoted evil in the world. The evil lie, *druj,* promoted by Angra Mainyu was manifested in a human life of wicked thoughts, wicked words, and wicked deeds. Human beings were poised at the crossroads of two ethical paths: asha or druj.

Zoroastrian religion, therefore, was a dualism based on two opposing forces in the universe. The message of the prophet Zarathustra was a cosmic dualism because he taught that two gods operated in the universe. A Zoroastrian hymn declared, "Truly, there are two primal spirits, twins, renowned to be in conflict." Zarathustra's message was also an ethical dualism because the gods Ahura Mazda and Angra Mainyu represented two ethical choices that were posed to human beings. The hymn continued, "In thought, word, and act they are two, the good and the bad." Human beings stood between these two gods and two ethical options.

Those cosmic and ethical dualisms in Zoroastrian myth were understood to operate in a historical process. Before the beginning, the two were separate; in creation they became mixed; but at the final culmination of cosmic and human history, the good and the evil would be separated. The Zoroastrian hymn concluded, "When these two spirits first encountered, they created life and not-life . . . at the end, the worst existence shall be for the followers of falsehood [druj], but the best dwelling for those who possess righteousness [asha]." The separation of the good and the evil occurred at the moment of personal judgment that each person passed through after death. That separation was finalized, however, in the victory of good over evil that was expected to happen at the end of the world. In Zoroastrian myth, the judgment of the dead had both personal and collective dimensions.

Individual Judgment After death, the soul was thought to remain at the head of its body for three days and nights, experiencing joy or pain, depending on its ethical character. The souls of the righteous—those who had been dedicated to asha in thought, word, and deed—sat at the head singing hymns, praising Ahura Mazda, and proclaiming their happiness. Righteous souls experienced more joy in those three days than they had experienced in their entire lives. However, wicked souls—those who had been dedicated in thought, word, and deed to druj—tried to run away like people fleeing a burning building. Unable to escape, they experienced intense misery during the first three days and nights after death.

Traditionally, Zoroastrian death rituals required a final disposition of the body by exposure. On the fourth day, the corpse was taken to the tower of silence, *dakhma,* to be reverently exposed for the birds (Pangborn, 1977). But the soul was thought to begin its journey toward the world of the dead also on the fourth day after death. Proceeding on its journey, the soul came to the Chinvat Bridge, the bridge of separation. Across the bridge was paradise, the House of Song that radiated a boundless light, resounded with music, and emanated a pleasing fragrance. Beneath the Chinvat Bridge, however, loomed a deep, dark abyss. On the narrow bridge that led to paradise—but was suspended over hell—the judgment of the dead took place.

If it had been righteous in thought, word, and deed, the soul first encountered the fragrant wind from paradise as it began to cross the bridge. At the middle of the bridge, the soul was met by an apparition, a lovely human form that stood before the soul. The soul asked, "Who are you?" The radiant, beautiful person responded, "I am your *daena*." The term *daena* referred to the Zoroastrian religion, but, more specifically, it signified the inner dimension of religion that had been shaped and formed by a person's thoughts, words, and deeds. In other words, the daena was the conscience. The soul and the daena embraced, and together they proceeded across the bridge into the House of Song.

If the person had been wicked, however, dedicated in thoughts, words, and deeds to druj, the soul had a very different experience on the bridge. It first encountered the foul stench rising up from the abyss of hell. This smell was so bad that it was described as the worst punishment that would be visited on the soul. As it tried to cross the bridge into paradise, the wicked soul was met in the middle by an ugly, horrible, frightful apparition. The soul asked, "Who are you?" The ugly person replied, "I am your daena." Whereas a good conscience had been made beautiful, an evil conscience had been made ugly by wicked thoughts, words, and deeds. The daena of the wicked soul declared, "I am your own bad actions. . . . You have made me worse day after day, and now you have thrown me and your own self into misery and damnation." Trying to run away, the wicked soul was embraced by its daena, and together they fell off the bridge into the hell below.

Each person, therefore, was expected to go through judgment after death. Judgment was symbolized as a crossing that could be successfully completed only by a soul dedicated to asha. Like the balance in ancient Egyptian religion, the bridge was a symbol of automatic judgment after death. Similarly, judgment occurred through a self-disclosure of the inner quality of the person that had been formed during life. The quality of a person's inner self, heart, or conscience was disclosed in death.

Zoroastrians imagined a place for people who were neither righteous nor wicked. The "Place of the Mixed Ones" held some people after death in a gray underworld in which they experienced nothing, neither sorrow nor joy. But most people after death were expected to be divided into the paradise across the Chinvat Bridge or the hell below. People went to the appropriate place after death because the ordeal of the bridge had disclosed their true natures.

The Zoroastrian myth represented that self-disclosure in aesthetic terms. The person's daena appeared in the beauty or the ugliness in which it had been formed during life. The aesthetic appearance of the daena depended on its conformity to either asha or druj. Rewards and punishments followed accordingly, as the aesthetic and ethical quality of the person was disclosed in the passage through death (Pavry, 1965).

Universal Salvation The rewards of paradise and the punishments of hell were not permanent, however. As the ugly, horrible daena plunged off the bridge with the wicked soul, it said, "We shall suffer punishment till the day of resurrection." Zoroastrian myth anticipated a final culmination of cosmic and human history at the end of time, when a general resurrection of the dead would take place. The good and the wicked would be brought back to life in their bodies for one final judgment. The last judgment, however, was not expected to result in salvation for the good and eternal damnation for the wicked. It was merely a prelude to one final purification that promised universal salvation for all human beings.

In the beginning of human history, the primordial human couple, Mashye and Mashyane, lived on a diet consisting solely of water. Gradually, human beings added plants to their diet, then milk, and finally meat. As their diet expanded, the power of gluttony became stronger and led to the involvement of human beings in the wickedness of druj. Before the end of human history, the power of gluttony was expected to diminish. Humans would stop eating meat, then milk, then plants, then even water, until finally during the last ten years human beings would live on nothing, but they would not die. The end, therefore, was expected to reverse the pattern of the beginning.

The end would be signaled by the appearance of a savior. That savior, Saoshyant, was expected to be born of a virgin who had become pregnant when she entered a pool of water that had miraculously preserved the seed of Zarathustra over the centuries. Besides being the son of Zarathustra, the savior Saoshyant was also the representative of Ahura Mazda in the last days. Saoshyant would supervise the work of resurrection. The savior would ask Ahura Mazda, "How will the dead be raised?" And the god of light would respond, "If I created what had not been, why should it be impossible to re-create what once was?" Since Ahura Mazda had created human beings in the first place, it should not be difficult to re-create them in the resurrection. Their bones would be drawn from the earth, their blood from the waters, their hair from the plants, and their spirits from the wind. All would be brought back to life through the power of Ahura Mazda and under the direction of the savior Saoshyant.

The saved and the damned would be resurrected, restored to life in their bodies. Each would rise from the place where he or she had died. Families would be reunited. People would recognize each other, but the saved and the damned would be clearly distinguishable. The entire process of resurrection was expected to take as long as fifty years. After everyone was back, the saved and the damned would be separated one last time. The saved would be taken in their bodies to paradise, while the damned were sent back in their bodies to hell. The joys of paradise and the pains of hell, made more intense by having a body, would be experienced for three days. That would be the final separation of the good and the wicked before all were purified in a universal salvation.

On that last day, the skies would open, the serpent of the moon would fall on the earth, and the fire god Atar would melt the mountains and the hills, turning them into rivers of molten metal. Human beings would be brought from paradise or hell to pass through the molten metal and be made clean. For the saved, the rivers of burning, fiery metal would seem like a bath of warm milk. For the damned, however, that bath of molten metal would seem exactly like molten metal.

After that final purification, all would be saved. All would gather to praise Ahura Mazda, to enjoy the Haoma drink of immortality, and to live forever in a transformed world. Husbands and wives would be reunited, enjoying the pleasures of companionship and sex, but no children would be born. Creation at that point would be over, but life would continue on a flat earth that had become immortal.

One final act in this cosmic drama would still be necessary. After the resurrection and purification of the dead, Ahura Mazda and his angelic forces were expected to defeat the evil demons in a cosmic battle. At the end of that battle, the evil god Angra Mainyu would be bound and thrown into the abyss of hell to be sealed up forever by the molten metal that would flow down from the earth into hell. Evil would be destroyed in the triumph of Ahura Mazda at the end of time. Although Zoroastrian myth was based on a dualism of good and evil, that dualism was expected to be dissolved in the final victory of the good god of light, Ahura Mazda, at the end of time. Only good would remain forever and ever (Boyce, 1979: 27–29). In their anticipation of universal salvation, rather than an eternal separation of the righteous and the wicked, Zoroastrian myths about death and afterlife differed from most Jewish, Christian, and Muslim understandings of the judgment of the dead.

Although only about 150,000 adhered to the faith of Zarathustra at the beginning of the twenty-first century—about 100,000 forming the Parsi community in India—the impact of the Zoroastrian myths of ancient Persia has been widespread. Zoroastrian dualism, the individual judgment of each person after death, and the general resurrection of the dead were themes that influenced the three prophetic religions: Judaism, Christianity, and Islam.

JEWISH RESURRECTION

With its roots in the ancient Near East, the Jewish tradition developed approaches to death and afterlife similar in many respects to the religions of ancient Egypt, Mesopotamia, and Persia. Like ancient Mesopotamian religion, the religion of ancient Israel assumed that a person was reduced to a shadowy, semiconscious existence after death in a dark underworld from which there was no return. The Hebrew Bible referred to that place as She'ol. At death, the spirit was thought to return to God, the flesh to the earth, and the person as a living being ceased to exist. All that remained was a trace of the person in the dim underworld of She'ol.

Gradually, however, the religion of ancient Israel developed an expectation that the dead would be raised back to life, restored to their bodies, and judged, rewarded, and punished for their past deeds. The resurrection of the dead became central to Jewish reflections on death and afterlife. That expectation became so important that anyone who denied the resurrection of the dead would be excluded from the world to come. Belief in the resurrection of the dead was supported by passages from the Hebrew Bible, but it was elaborated through the work of rabbis in the first few centuries of the common era.

Unlike reincarnation, resurrection was expected to restore the person to life in the same body. In that respect, Jewish resurrection valued the physical body just as—for different reasons and in different ways—the body was valued in the religious beliefs and practices of ancient Egypt and Persia. In the resurrection, the body would be restored as the permanent habitation of the human person in a new world. Although Jewish religious beliefs and practices tended to concentrate on this world, they nevertheless anticipated the resurrection of the dead as a prelude to a world to come when the history of this world had been brought to its close.

Ancient Israel

The story in Genesis of the Garden of Eden may have been intended as a myth of the origin of death (Gen. 2:4b–4). The primordial human couple, Adam and Eve, were placed by the creator God, Yahweh, at the center of a garden paradise, given dominion over all its creatures, and sustained by a plant of immortality. The Tree of Life was their food, but the Tree of the Knowledge of Good and Evil was forbidden to them. "When you eat of it," Yahweh told them, "surely you will die." Disobeying that divine command, Adam and Eve were driven out of the Garden of Eden and kept from the plant of immortality by an angel with a fiery sword.

From that day, the woman was cursed with pain in childbirth, the man was cursed with the necessity of work, and both were cursed with human mortality. At death, human beings would return to the earth from which they had originally been created. Although no longer immortal like gods, human beings were blessed by their curses: They exchanged personal immortality for the ancestral transcendence of children and the cultural transcendence of work. In that sense, Adam and Eve lived on in and through their offspring and the continuous human culture they began.

Jewish tradition, however, saw death not as a punishment for the primordial human couple's disobedience but as a part of God's original design for human life. From this perspective, Adam and Eve were originally created to be mortal. The first humans were fashioned from the red clay of the ground, just as every other creature was made, and they were animated by the breath of God. Life resulted when Yahweh blew his spirit into the earthen forms. With that breath of God, or *ruah,* the human beings became living creatures, a mixture of divine spirit and earthly form. The creation of human beings demonstrated the supreme power of Yahweh, the God of Israel, over all life. It did not necessarily indicate that human beings were created to be immortal.

Human Mortality In the religion of ancient Israel, a person was not understood as an immortal, eternal, or deathless soul trapped in a body but as a living mixture of breath and earth. Human beings were "earthlings," shaped from the clay and animated by the breath of God. A living person, or *nephesh*, depended on both those elements for life. When the breath of God animated a person, that spirit might be referred to as a *neshamah*, or a personalized spirit. But at death, the person dissolved as the elements of life returned to their sources. The breath went back to God, the clay returned to the earth (Ps. 104:29). The person as a living nephesh ceased to exist. Nothing remained of the person but a trace that descended to the shadowy underworld of She'ol.

The geography of She'ol was not worked out in the Bible in any detail. But it did bear a marked similarity to the underworld imagined by the ancient Mesopotamians. She'ol was like Arulla in at least three respects: She'ol was a dark, underground world; it was a place of no return; and it reduced all human beings to the same level in a ghostly, shadowy existence.

First, She'ol was beneath the ground, a dark netherworld where the dead lingered as shadows. She'ol was described as the underground pit of the dead (Ps. 6:6, 28:1, 88:5; Job 28:22, 30:23), as the dust into which the dead descended (Ps. 22:16), and as the earth that swallowed up the dead (Exod. 15:2; Jon. 2:7).

Second, that underworld was seen as a place of no return. Thinking about his own death, Job anticipated a descent into the darkness of She'ol. "I go whence I shall not return, even to the land of darkness and of the shadow of death; a land of thick darkness, as darkness itself; a land of the shadow of death, without any order, and where the light is as darkness" (Job 10:21–22).

Finally, She'ol reduced all the dead to the same level of semiconscious existence. No ethical judgment separated the righteous from the wicked, no ritual distinctions set apart the holy from the impure, and no marks of status distinguished the powerful from the weak. All the dead were reduced to the same dust. The prophet Isaiah called the attention of the rich and powerful to this common fate shared by all human beings: "She'ol beneath is stirred up to meet you when you come, it raises the shades to greet you. . . . All of them speak and say to you: 'You too have become as weak as we! You have become like us! Your pomp is brought down to She'ol . . . maggots are the bed beneath you, and worms are your covering'" (Isa. 14:9–11). In the Book of Ecclesiastes, the teacher of wisdom concluded, "Better to be a live dog than a dead lion in She'ol." Regardless of power, wealth, or accomplishments during life, all were expected to be reduced to the same condition in the dust of the underworld (Tromp, 1969).

Ancestral and Cultural Transcendence Personal immortality may have been denied, but the religion of ancient Israel placed great importance on the biological and ancestral transcendence of death. Although personal identity and social status were dissolved in death, a human being could still live on through offspring. The pattern for ancestral transcendence in the religion of ancient Israel was set by the patriarch Abraham. According to the account in Genesis, Abraham had been called by Yahweh for a special destiny. God's promise was not personal immortality but ancestral and cultural transcendence. "I will make you a great nation," Yahweh promised, "and I will bless you, and make your name great . . . and by you all the families of the earth shall bless themselves"

(Gen. 12:1–3). Abraham would become the patriarchal ancestor of a great nation that would keep him alive in its shared cultural memory from generation to generation.

The Hebrew Bible suggested that personal immortality was a rare gift given by God. Like the Mesopotamian Utnapishtim, Enoch and Elijah were said to have been given this gift. They did not die but ascended to the heavens. The patriarch Abraham, however, was promised a gift that the biblical text regarded as greater than personal immortality. As he lay dying after a long life, Abraham was not concerned about his personal survival after death. According to Genesis, his dying act was to ensure the continuity of his lineage. Calling a servant to take a vow, Abraham placed the servant's hand on his genitals—signifying the seriousness of his request but perhaps also the importance of procreation in the symbolic transcendence of death—and had his servant swear that he would find a wife for Abraham's son (Gen. 24:1–9). Only by continuing his biological line could Abraham's potential for ancestral and cultural transcendence be fulfilled. Ultimately, Abraham's life and death had their significance in the ongoing life of his offspring and their religious culture.

The central historical event in the religious culture of the ancient Israelites was their exodus from the bondage of slavery in Egypt. Under the leadership of Moses, the Israelite slaves were freed from their captivity and led through the wilderness to the promised land of Israel. The exodus from Egypt represented a transcendence of death—escaping the social death of slavery and escaping the angel of death, who miraculously passed over the children of Israel during the plagues that befell Egypt. Although all but two of the exodus generation died during the forty-year journey to the promised land, subsequent generations kept alive their liberation from the social death of slavery through the annual celebration of Passover (Pesach). In that ritual commemoration of the exodus, an ongoing, living cultural memory was nourished by encouraging all Jews to regard themselves as having been present in that liberation. Through ritual identification, a collective transcendence of death was supported every Passover, signifying that the children of Abraham lived on in a shared religious culture.

Apocalypse

The Greek term *apocalypse* signified an unveiling, pulling back the curtain of illusion to reveal the ultimate reality. An apocalypse was a revelation. As the Jewish tradition developed, reflection on death and afterlife sometimes took the form of apocalyptic visions of heavens, hells, and the resurrection of the dead expected to occur at the end of time. An apocalyptic imagination emerged in Jewish history under certain pressures: the destruction of the temple and the city of Jerusalem in 586 B.C.E., the captivity of Israelites to the political power of Babylon, and foreign influences from Persian and Greek thought. But the elaboration of afterlife imagery was also supported by elements in the biblical tradition. The God of Israel had been credited with the power to bring the dead to life if he wanted to (Deut. 32:39; 1 Sam. 2:6). The apocalyptic imagination specified more precisely how this could be expected to be accomplished (Hanson, 1979; Russell, 1964).

Visions of Resurrection The earliest biblical reference to any type of resurrection of the dead was the apocalyptic vision recounted by the prophet Ezekiel. In the wake of the destruction of Jerusalem, Ezekiel promised that through the miraculous spiritual intervention of God, the nation of Israel would be restored like the dead being brought to life. In the figurative imagery of resurrection, Ezekiel predicted that the nation of Israel would recover political autonomy in its own land.

The prophet compared the desolation of Israel with a valley of dry bones. In a vision, Ezekiel saw the bones begin to rattle and come together, bone to bone. "As I looked," Ezekiel said, "there were sinews on them, and flesh had come upon them, and skin had covered them: but there was no breath in them." Suddenly, the breath of life came from the four directions and animated all those who had been slain. They formed a great army that would restore the nation of Israel (Ezek. 37:7–10).

Ezekiel explained his vision as a symbol for the people of Israel. "These bones," he said, "are the whole house of Israel." Not a resurrection of the dead at the end of time but a restoration of the nation of Israel was the content of Ezekiel's vision. Ezekiel symbolized the recovery of independent national identity in the vivid imagery of bringing the dead back to life from their graves:

> Thus says the Lord God: Behold, I will open your graves, and raise you
> from your graves, O my people: and I will bring you home into the land
> of Israel. And you shall know that I am the Lord, when I open your
> graves, and raise you from your graves, O my people. And I will put my
> Spirit within you, and you shall live, and I will place you in your own
> land: then you shall know that I, the Lord, have spoken, and I have done
> it, says the Lord. (Ezek. 37:11–14)

Although the language was symbolic, it could easily be taken literally. Later Jewish and Christian thought could look back to the vision of Ezekiel as support for the doctrine of the resurrection of the dead. Ezekiel may have been referring to the cultural transcendence of death by the people of Israel as a whole: When their nation was restored, they would be brought back to life as a unified people. But the later tradition would tend to understand the resurrection of the dead from their graves quite literally.

The doctrine of the resurrection of the dead was elaborated during another type of political oppression in Jewish history. During the second century B.C.E., Israel came under Greek rule, and the Jews experienced persecution under foreign domination. In that context, the apocalyptic vision of the resurrection of the dead promised afterlife restoration for all those who had died in defense of Israel and the Jewish faith. Death would not be a final defeat. Death itself would be conquered in the resurrection.

The biblical Book of Daniel was written during that time of political turmoil. As an apocalyptic text, Daniel outlined a dramatic vision of the resurrection of the dead, culminating in a judgment of the dead. Probably written in the second century B.C.E., the Book of Daniel brought the themes of afterlife judgment, reward, and punishment into prominence in Jewish reflection on death.

The Book of Daniel predicted a time of trouble, very similar to the turbulent period of Jewish history in which the text was written, when a resurrection of the dead would take place. "Many of those who sleep in the dust of the earth shall awake," the text promised (12:1–2). The promise of resurrection, however, was left somewhat unclear: If *many* would awaken from the dust of death, the resurrection was probably not understood to apply to *all* who had died. The resurrected would be people whose names had been recorded in a book, but who those people would be was not specified. That book may have referred to the book of Yahweh. "Whoever has sinned against me," Yahweh had said to Moses, "I will blot out of my book" (Exod. 32:33). In that case, those who had committed serious sins against God might not be raised from the dead. Perhaps the resurrection was imagined to affect only the people of Israel or perhaps only some of the people of Israel.

Those who did come back to life in the resurrection would not all meet the same fate. Some would awaken "to shame and everlasting contempt." Specific punishments for those who deserved shame and contempt were not specified. But they were distinguished from other people who would rise from the dead to "everlasting life." Some people were expected to be glorified in the resurrection. Symbolizing their glory in the imagery of the heavens, the Book of Daniel reported that the wise and the righteous would shine like the stars forever and ever. Although their precise nature was not explained, the basis for rewards and punishments at the resurrection was identified as a judgment of the dead. The main elements of that judgment were the divine judge, the throne, and the book. Daniel described the judge as an old man, "ancient of days," with white hair and robes. The throne he sat on was in flames, its wheels were on fire, and from the throne came a fiery stream. Around the radiant, flaming throne a thousand thousands ministered to the divine judge, and ten thousand times ten thousand stood before him to be judged. "The judgment was set," the Book of Daniel declared, "and the books were opened" (Dan. 7). Judgment of the dead, therefore, was ultimately by the book.

Whereas the Egyptian and Persian judgments of the dead symbolized the process as a self-disclosure of the person's conscience in death, Jewish symbolism represented the judgment of the dead as an objective reading of what had been recorded in the book of life. The symbolism of resurrection and judgment was dominated by the specialized technology of the book. Written indelibly in the book, the judgment was already set. After awakening from the sleep of death, the dead did not have to prove themselves through an afterlife ordeal. They could only submit to the awesome power and majesty of the divine judge as the record of their lives was read.

By the second century B.C.E., the themes of resurrection and judgment had become familiar in Jewish thought. As Jewish leaders of resistance against Roman political power, the Maccabees offered sacrifices and prayers for the dead. A text that was not included in the Hebrew Bible but related the events of those times described how Judas Maccabaeus performed those rituals for the dead, asking that those who had died might be released from their sins in expectation of the resurrection (2 Macc. 12:43–44).

By the first century C.E., Jewish opinion was apparently divided on the doctrine of resurrection. Sadducees, who were responsible for temple ritual, denied the doctrine, while Pharisees held the expectation that the dead would be raised in the flesh in the messianic age. With the destruction of the temple of Jerusalem in 70 C.E., the Pharisaic position on the resurrection of the dead became normative for the rabbis who compiled the sacred texts and commentaries of the Mishnah and the Talmud. From the perspective of the rabbis, the resurrection of the dead was a nonnegotiable position within the Jewish tradition.

Visions of Immortality Also in the first century, however, another Jewish perspective on the afterlife was developed under the influence of Greek philosophical thought. The Jewish philosopher Philo Judaeus (d. 45–50 C.E.) of Alexandria worked out a very different understanding of death. According to Philo, all souls were immortal. The souls of the righteous returned after death to the heavens, while some souls that had gained philosophical insight and wisdom ascended to a realm of eternal ideas. By regarding the human soul as immortal in and of itself, Philo saw death simply as a release of that soul from a body in which it had only temporarily been imprisoned. Philo's understanding of death was developed under the influence of the Greek philosophical system of Plato.

For Plato (427–347 B.C.E.), death had simply meant the separation of the immortal soul (*psuche*) from the body (*Phaedo* 64c; Warrington, 1963: 97). In Plato's system, the soul was the immortal essence of a person, only temporarily housed in a body. That soul existed before birth, and it would continue to exist after death. While in the body, the soul was separated from an eternal realm of ideas that was its true home. Nevertheless, through philosophy the soul could recover its direct intuition of the ideal forms of reality. Because the soul returned to the eternal realm of ideas after death, Plato called the philosophy that contemplated eternal ideas during life a "rehearsal for death." Rising above the body, the soul was able to see directly the eternal forms of reality because the soul itself was eternal and immortal.

Plato's theory of the soul was based on a specialized philosophical theory of knowledge. The soul had existed before birth, according to Plato, because everything learned during life was a recollection or remembering of the world of ideas in which the soul had lived before entering a body. The soul was immortal because it could know the eternal, immortal ideas—such as the ideas of the good, the true, and the beautiful—and "nothing mortal knows what is immortal" (*Phaedo* 78a–84b; Warrington, 1963: 119–29). During life, philosophy was a rehearsal for death because it taught the soul to see immortal ideas independent of the body. When the soul ruled the body, it was like the immortal gods, independent and eternal. A soul that was attached to the body—ruled by the senses, passions, and opinions—would separate from the body at death only with violence and difficulty. But a soul that had rehearsed for death through philosophy would be released from the body at death like a prisoner released from prison to return to its true home in the eternal realm of ideas.

Although Plato's thought was a specialized philosophical system, the concept of an immortal soul was widespread in Greek and Roman thinking about death. At death, the soul might descend to the shadowy underworld Hades. But the wise and the righteous souls might ascend to the heavens, transported after death to the upper air around the stars and planets. The upper air, or *aether*, was often imagined as the home of the gods. An immortal soul that ascended to the aether after death became almost like a god (Cumont, 1922: 95; Lattimore, 1942: 32ff.). But every soul was godlike in the sense that it was understood to be immortal by nature.

Ancient Greek and Roman thought on the immortality of the soul contrasted dramatically with mainstream Jewish expectations about the resurrection of the dead. Immortality implied a dualism of body and soul in which the person was an eternal, deathless soul temporarily residing in a mortal physical body. Resurrection, however, was based on the assumption that a person was by nature a mixture of body and spirit. At death the person ceased to exist as the spirit returned to God and the body to dust. But the person could be recreated if body and breath were reunited in a special intervention by God. The resurrection of the dead, therefore, was understood as a miraculous restoration of the mixture of spirit and body that defined a human being.

In mainstream Jewish thought, a person was not an independent, immortal soul imprisoned in a body. Philo of Alexandria did argue for the immortality of the soul along Platonic lines, but he represented a minority position by trying to adapt Jewish thought to Greek philosophy. For Philo, Plato was Moses speaking Greek, providing a philosophical system that allowed Philo to interpret the Hebrew Bible as supporting the doctrine of the immortality of the soul. Philo had little effect on the emergence of the dominant position in Jewish thought that continued to understand a human person as a mixture of spirit and body. The person ceased to exist at death but might be restored to life in the resurrection of the dead.

Immortality and resurrection persisted as two ways of understanding death and dying in Western approaches to a mythic transcendence of death: the one anticipating the liberation of the immortal soul from the prison of the body, the other looking forward to the eventual reunion of spirit and body in the restoration of a complete human nature with the resurrection of the dead (Moore, 1927–30: I:295). Although sometimes combined or confused, immortality represented the Greek option, while resurrection represented the biblical option for imagining a mythic transcendence of death.

The World to Come

The rabbis who rebuilt the Jewish tradition after the destruction of the Jerusalem temple by the Romans in 70 C.E. held to the doctrine of the resurrection of the dead. The rabbis regarded the belief in resurrection as so important that anyone who denied it was expected to be excluded from the world to come. Through creative interpretations of biblical texts, the rabbis argued that the resurrection of the dead had been taught in the religion of ancient Israel. When the Bible said those who broke the commandments would be cut off and their sins placed on their heads (Num. 15:31ff.), that passage was taken to refer to punishments in the next world. When the Bible said the children of Israel shall sing their song for God (Exod. 15:1), the text was interpreted as referring to rejoicing in the world to come after the resurrection. The rabbis who compiled the Mishnah and the Talmud, therefore, understood the doctrine of the resurrection to have been an integral part of the written and oral law that stood as the foundation of Jewish tradition.

Rabbis The term "world to come" ('olam ha-ba') first appeared in an apocalyptic text—the *Apocalypse of Enoch*—sometime between 164 and 105 B.C.E. According to the Bible, Enoch had not died but had gone directly to God. Granted that exceptional gift of immortality, Enoch became an appropriate figure to which writers of apocalypses could attribute visions of the other worlds beyond death.

As the vision of the next world developed into an orthodox doctrine, the rabbis specified two places in the world to come: one place of reward for those who had followed God's law and one place of punishment for those who had violated ethical or ritual commandments of divine law. The place of afterlife reward was called Gan Eden. The term was derived from the original paradise of Eden, but it was understood as the paradise restored in the world to come after the resurrection. The place of punishment was referred to as Gehinnom. This name was derived from the name of a valley just outside the ancient city walls of Jerusalem, *ge ben hinnom,* where children had been sacrificed to the gods Moloch and Baal (Jer. 2:23; 2 Chron. 26:9; Neh. 2:13–15, 3:13). Gehinnom came to be understood as an afterlife place of eternal punishment for those who were excluded from afterlife rewards in the world to come.

The world to come was expected to appear in several stages as the culmination of human history. The end would begin with the appearance of the messiah, the anointed one of God, who would usher in the messianic age. Following a period of worldwide turmoil, the messianic age was expected to bring about an era of peace on earth. The messiah would supervise the rebuilding of the temple of Jerusalem and the restoration of the city.

At the end of the messianic age, the dead would be resurrected and subjected to a final judgment. Some would enter paradise, others would be condemned to eternal punishment in hell. A third possibility, for those not fully righteous but not completely wicked, was also considered. But there was some disagreement over whether those people would be punished with fire until they were purified or whether they would be shown mercy. For both the righteous and the wicked, however, the judgment was final: Rewards and punishments would be eternal. Permanent rewards in heaven and permanent retribution in hell attested to the absolute power of God and divine law to determine a person's destiny after death.

Rabbis differed on the details when they described the rewards of the world to come. They agreed, however, that paradise would be an afterlife in the presence of God. In the Talmud, one rabbi observed that Gan Eden would be unlike life in this world. "In the world to come, there is no eating, no drinking, no begetting of children, no bargaining or hatred or jealousy or strife; rather, the righteous will sit with crowns on their heads and enjoy the effulgence of the *shekhinah,* God's presence." The world to come might be devoted to study, or worship, or simply rejoicing in the constant presence of God.

As the tradition developed, Gan Eden was imagined to hold five different chambers for the various classes of the righteous, all transfused with the light of the shekhinah. Even non-Jews might have a place in that world if they had followed the laws that applied to all humanity, the Noachide Laws against idolatry, incest, shedding blood, profaning the name of God, injustice, robbery, or cutting flesh off a living animal. The paradise was imagined to be vast beyond all measurement, a world that extended over 2,920,000,000 miles that would take as long as 800,000 years to traverse at a rate of ten miles a day (Cohn-Sherbok, 1987: 27–28).

Hell and its torments also came to be described in greater detail as the tradition developed. In the Talmud, hell was divided into seven levels, each with seven rivers of fire and seven torrents of hail. Fire and ice were environmental punishments in which the wicked suffered for eternity. In addition, sinners were imagined to be punished by more specific forms of torture—lashed by whips, stung by scorpions, or hanged by different parts of their bodies—administered by the angels of hell (Ginzberg, 1909–38: II:310–13). These punishments were not remedial forms of purgation but eternal retribution for those who had sinned against divine law. To escape the divine retribution of punishment in hell, people had to occupy themselves with doing good deeds. Jewish symbolism of death and afterlife reinforced a commitment to observing ethical laws and to devoting life to gaining ethical merit. In this way, the Jewish way of life was supported by the symbolism of resurrection, judgment, rewards, and punishments after death.

Philosophers, Mystics, and Pietists During the medieval period, heaven and hell continued to be developed as themes in Jewish thought, often given rise to elaborate and imaginative visions of those other worlds. At the same time, however, Jewish philosophers were influenced by the Greek philosophical systems of Plato and Aristotle to view life after death in terms of the immortality of the soul. Moses Maimonides (1135/38–1204) criticized any vision of the world to come as a place of material rewards or punishments. Although he insisted on the importance of the doctrine of the resurrection of the dead, Maimonides argued that it would be a spiritual immortality rather than a restoration of spirit and flesh.

"In the world to come," Maimonides wrote, "the body and the flesh do not exist but only the souls of the righteous alone." Criticized for what seemed to be a denial of the orthodox understanding of the resurrection of the dead, Maimonides responded by distinguishing between the messianic age and the world to come. In the messianic age, souls would be restored to their bodies, but in the world to come, only the souls would enjoy an eternal spiritual afterlife (Dienstag, 1983; Maimonides, 1982).

Considerable controversy raged among Jewish philosophers in the Middle Ages over the resurrection and whether immortality would be achieved by good deeds, wisdom, or the love of God (Guttmann, 1964). At the same time,

Jewish mystics developed alternative perspectives on death and the afterlife. The mystics of the Kabbalah saw the task of life as the restoration of the soul to God. The Kabbalistic text of the *Zohar* (c. 1300) divided the soul into three parts: The nephesh and the ruah were lower souls that could be involved in sin and therefore punished after death, and the neshamah was a purely spiritual soul that came from the heavens and returned there after death. Life after death was imagined to be purely spiritual but also to involve the possibility of purgative punishments for the lower souls of human beings.

Gradually, the notion of a preexistent soul in Kabblistic thought developed into the idea of reincarnation. In Kabbalah, the concept of *gilgul* signified a process in which souls continued to be reborn until they were purified of all sins and able to return to God. Souls came to be understood as sparks of light that had been dispersed throughout the world when the heavenly sheaths around God had shattered at the beginning of creation. Through meditation, prayer, and conscientious observance of ritual, the soul could be purified in order to be restored eventually to God. Kabbalists understood the restoration of the soul to God as a restoration of the original wholeness of God's spiritual body. Since that process of purification might require many lifetimes, the notion of gilgul became an important part of Jewish mystical thought about death and afterlife (Scholem, 1961, 1973).

In addition to philosophers and mystics, Hassidic pietists formed a third movement that developed a distinctive Jewish approach to life and death. By making every thought, word, and deed a devotional service to God, the Hassidic movement beginning in Europe in the eighteenth century sought a total sanctification of life. Every act could be done to sanctify God's name, even the act of dying. The concept of dying to glorify the name of God, *Kiddush Hashem,* had particular relevance for Jewish communities in Eastern Europe and Russia that suffered persecution and pogroms in which many were killed. Such a death could be interpreted as a devotional sacrifice to God, a holy act for the faith that opened paradise for the one who died and hastened the coming of the messiah for the whole community.

The Hassidic Rabbi Nachman of Brazlav prayed that he might be ready to die if necessary in devotion to God: "May I truly be prepared to die any death and to suffer every pain and torment for the sanctification of Your great Name" (Schindler, 1977: 176). During the twentieth-century holocaust in which six million Jews were killed by the Nazi atrocities in Europe, the Hassidic concept of dying for the faith as a redemptive sacrifice to God was often drawn on as a source of courage. In the hell of the concentration camps, devotion to God provided hope that death would be redemption.

By the twentieth century, the Jewish tradition was divided into Orthodox, Conservative, and Reform movements that held different doctrines about death and afterlife yet nevertheless continued to perform rituals of mourning that showed continuing respect and concern for the dead. Traditionally, mourning was divided into five stages: (1) the three days between death and burial; (2) the three days of mourning in seclusion after burial; (3) the seven days after burial (including the first three), called *shiva,* in which mourners remained at home but started to receive visitors; (4) the thirty days following burial in which mourners gradually reentered society; and (5) the one-year anniversary of the death, which brought mourning to a close, except for the annual commemoration of the deceased.

The stages of mourning gradually released the connections between the living and the dead while renewing those bonds once a year by observing the *yizkor* or *yahrzeit* commemoration of the deceased (Lamm, 1969; Reimer, 1974). Although some variations in practice developed, Jewish rituals of mourning and respect for the dead continued to be regarded as an important part of religious reverence for human life and its divine creator.

CHRISTIAN ESCHATOLOGY

From the beginning, the death and resurrection of Jesus of Nazareth stood as the model through which Christians understood their own deaths. Like the enlightenment of the Buddha, the death of Jesus illustrated a transcendence of death. Unlike the calm deathlessness promised by the Buddha, however, the Christian transcendence of death was symbolized as a victory in combat over a dangerous enemy. In the New Testament accounts of the trial, torture, death, entombment, and restoration to life of Jesus, Christians found a symbolic model for death. Dying was an ordeal through which a human being could emerge victorious: Death was an enemy that could be conquered.

The conquest of death moved to the center of the Christian message as it spread from its Jewish base to the Greco-Roman world. According to the Gospel of Mark, Jesus had announced the arrival of the kingdom of God (Mark 1:15). Early Christians of the first century proclaimed Jesus as Lord of that kingdom. Particularly, the missionary Paul stated a promise of salvation from death through a liberating devotion to Jesus Christ. As Christ had been restored to life, Christians could expect to be resurrected from the dead. Like Hindu bhakti traditions of India, Christians expected to be saved from death through a devotional attachment to a divine savior. Therefore, Jesus not only provided a symbolic model for transcendence but was understood by Christians as the divine agent in human salvation from death.

The Christian tradition underwent a remarkable transformation in its first 300 years. From small, loosely organized, and often persecuted communities, the Christian religion was eventually adopted by the Roman Empire as state religion. Under the emperor Constantine, Christianity became the officially sponsored religion of the state; by the time of the emperor Theodosius in 381, Christianity became the only religion that was allowed to be practiced in the empire. Theodosius declared that non-Christians would be punished by the force of law. Although he was confident that non-Christians would be judged and punished after death, Theodosius wanted to ensure that they would be punished while still alive. Christians went from being a persecuted minority to a persecuting majority in the course of the fourth century.

Before Constantine, Christians were subject to persecution, torture, and even death for their faith. Bearing witness to the faith in death, martyrs willingly chose to die rather than renounce their religious commitment. Martyrdom came to be regarded as a direct path to salvation, following the example of Jesus. It was regarded as a redemptive sacrifice that transformed a dying Christian into a living saint. The spiritual influence of martyrs and other saints—the "special dead"—continued to be important in Christian burial practices. The ideal place of burial was considered to be near the remains of a martyr, saint, or holy person. A grave near saints—*ad sanctos*—was regarded as the best place for corpses to remain until the resurrection of the flesh anticipated at the second coming of Jesus. In that final conquest of death, Jesus was expected to return as savior in the resurrection of the dead.

Jesus was expected to return not only as savior but also as the judge of the dead. In the official creed for the imperial church that was adopted at the Council of Nicaea in 325, Christian faith proclaimed, "And he shall come again in glory to judge both the quick and the dead." The expectation of the return of Jesus was based on passages in the New Testament, particularly the Book of Revelation. At the end of human history, Jesus was expected to restore the dead to life as well as to act as the divine judge in the final separation of the saved and the damned.

Those two functions, savior and judge, were combined in a mythic transcendence—an unfolding narrative drama in human history—that culminated at the end of time. The Greek word for the end, *eschaton,* provided a technical term for those expectations about the ultimate, final, or last things, *eschatology.* Christian eschatology was based on the anticipation that Jesus would return in the final resurrection of the dead. As savior and judge, Jesus was expected to transform heaven and earth into the kingdom of God.

Immortality and Resurrection

Immortality and resurrection were two options in early Christian thought about death. As we have noted, in Greek thought immortality implied that the human soul was an independent conscious agent that lived temporarily in the body and was freed from the body at death. From that perspective, death released the person from the prison of the body. In Hebraic thought, resurrection implied the miraculous restoration of the human person as a living person composed of spirit and flesh. Hebraic thought imagined that death dissolved the person as the spirit returned to God and the flesh to the earth.

Although Greek and Hebraic influences can be separated for analysis, they were woven together in early Christian thought about death. Before the immortality of the soul and the resurrection of the dead became integrated, however, they stood as two different, mutually exclusive ways of symbolizing death. Many scholars have argued that these two ways of symbolizing death—immortality and resurrection—may explain the extremely different attitudes toward dying exemplified in the deaths of the ancient Greek philosopher Socrates and Jesus of Nazareth (Cullmann, 1958; Sutherland, 1966–67).

Socrates and Jesus In the year 399 B.C.E., the philosopher Socrates was condemned to death by the city of Athens. He was accused of being a traitor to Athens, extending his influence over the youth of the city, turning their attention away from practical matters of state toward the love of wisdom. Judging Socrates to be a danger to public order, the rulers of the city decided to eliminate him. Given the choice of banishment—a form of social death—or execution by poison, Socrates chose to drink the fatal cup of hemlock. The death of Socrates was regarded as an exemplary death in the Greek philosophical tradition. Convinced of the immortality of the soul, Socrates calmly welcomed death as a friend that promised to release him from the condition of temporary imprisonment in a body.

Describing the death scene of Socrates, his student Plato depicted a calm, controlled acceptance of death as Socrates spent his last moments in quiet conversation with friends. On the morning of his execution, Socrates began the day by asking the women to leave so that there would be no weeping or display of emotion. He bathed, settled his affairs, and continued speaking quietly with his friends. When the cup of hemlock arrived, Socrates prayed that his "change of residence" might be blessed with good fortune. In his last moments, Socrates reaffirmed his conviction that death was merely a change, like changing homes or changing clothes, that would release his immortal soul from the body in which it was imprisoned.

As the poison slowly moved through his body, Socrates remained calm. When death finally came, Socrates turned to his friend Crito and said, "We owe a cock to Asklepios. See that it is paid" (*Phaedo* 118a; Warrington, 1963: 175). With that last reference to the Greek god of healing, Socrates died. In his dying, Socrates exemplified an assurance that the human soul was immortal by nature. The soul was like a musical composition that would remain even if the instrument through which it was played was destroyed. Philosophy had been a rehearsal for death by allowing the eye of the soul to rise above the limitations of the body. Death finally broke the bonds of the body, releasing the soul to continue in its transcendent immortal state.

The New Testament accounts of the death of Jesus described the process of dying in very different terms. Death was not welcomed as a friend but shunned as an enemy. Instead of meeting death with calm, philosophical acceptance, Jesus fought death in an agonizing ordeal. The Gospel of Mark recounted that Jesus was greatly distressed and troubled, that he did not want to be left alone, and that he prayed to be spared from death (Mark 14:33–37). At his execution, Jesus implored God with loud cries and tears (Heb. 5:7). In his dying moment, Jesus cried out that God had forsaken him (Mark 15:34). The entire picture of the death of Jesus painted by the New Testament was one of a difficult struggle against a force that Paul referred to as the enemy of God. From the perspective of the Christian New Testament, death was God's greatest and last enemy (1 Cor. 15:26).

Although both resulted from executions, comparison of the deaths of Socrates and Jesus may be of limited value because of the different methods of execution: Death by hemlock poisoning was much less painful than the prolonged torture of crucifixion. Nevertheless, Socrates and Jesus did represent contrasting symbolic models for approaching the human encounter with death. Socrates embraced death as a friend who would assist him in his change of residence. Because he was convinced of the immortality of the soul, Socrates could calmly accept the transition death represented. From his Hebraic background, Jesus probably did not assume that the soul was inherently immortal. Therefore, he imagined death as an ordeal in which the human person was dissolved. Death might be conquered, however, not by calm acceptance but by a victory over death in the resurrection of the body. According to New Testament accounts, Jesus was miraculously restored to life in the flesh after he had been dead and in the tomb three days. That resurrection represented a victory over death and, as it was interpreted in the Christian tradition, promised a similar victory over death, the enemy, for human beings.

The Resurrection of Jesus Miraculous appearances of Jesus figured prominently in early Christian literature. The Book of Acts described a vision of Jesus that appeared to the first martyr for the faith, Stephen, as he was dying under torture and an appearance of Jesus to Paul on the road to Damascus that inspired his conversion. In addition, texts written by Gnostic Christians, such as the noncanonical Acts of John, described appearances of Jesus to some of his disciples after his death. These appearances were described as spiritual visions by martyrs, saints, and disciples.

The New Testament Gospels, however, described the return of Jesus from the dead in explicitly physical terms. The resurrection was a return to life in the flesh. This corporeality was emphasized by reports that he ate meals with his disciples (Luke 24:41–43; John 21:13), that he appeared in his same body that bore the marks of his torture and crucifixion (Luke 24:39–40; John 20:20), and that he allowed his disciples to touch him in order to verify that his return to life was real (John 20:24–29). The victory over death, therefore, was represented not as a release of an immortal soul but as a restoration of life in the flesh.

The followers of Jesus expected a similar resurrection. The resurrection of Jesus was understood as both proof of the possibility and guarantee of the eventuality that his followers would also be restored to life after death. A general resurrection became the common Christian expectation that "there will be a resurrection of both the righteous and the unrighteous" (Acts 24:15).

The only comments directly attributed to Jesus by the New Testament on the subject of the resurrection occurred in the context of a dispute with a group of priests. Denying the notion of resurrection, a group of Sadducees posed a problem for Jesus to solve: If a woman had been married to seven brothers in succession, whose wife would she be in the resurrection? Jesus responded that marriage relations would no longer be relevant after the resurrection. "The dead neither marry, nor are given in marriage," Jesus said, "but live like angels in heaven." Regarding the resurrection itself, Jesus answered the priests by quoting a passage from the Hebrew Bible specifying that God "is not the God of the dead but of the living." Implying that God had equal power to create the living as to raise the dead, Jesus argued that God's power over life extended to the resurrection (Mark 12:18–27; Matt. 22:23–33; Luke 20:27–38). After his death, Jesus' resurrection was interpreted as a demonstration of that divine power over life and death at work.

The Return of Jesus

In his letters, the first-century theologian Paul promised his fellow Christians that the second coming would happen soon. Paul assured Christians that many of them would not die before they witnessed the return of Jesus and the resurrection of the dead. Because the end was anticipated soon, Paul exhorted Christians to live as if they were already in that kingdom of God expected to be ushered in by the resurrection. As proof of an imminent general resurrection, Paul pointed to the example of Jesus. "Now if Christ is preached as raised from the dead," Paul insisted, "how can some of you say that there is no resurrection of the dead?" Jesus' resurrection was not the end but only the beginning. The raising of Jesus from the dead was understood by Paul as "the first fruits of those who have fallen asleep" (1 Cor. 15:20). A general harvest of all those asleep in death was anticipated very soon.

The Theology of Paul The theology of Paul interpreted death as an enemy, as an evil, and as the result of an original human sin. As Paul analyzed the biblical creation story of the Garden of Eden, he concluded that death had not been part of God's original design for human beings. Adam and Eve had been created immortal but had fallen into death through their disobedience. That original sin condemned Adam, Eve, and all their descendants to death.

The inheritance that Adam transmitted to all future generations was sin. "One man's trespass led to condemnation for all men," Paul argued. "By one man's disobedience many were made sinners" (Rom. 5:18–19). The human condition was universal guilt, an indebtedness that had to be paid by death. "The wages of sin," Paul concluded, "is death" (Rom. 6:23). All human beings had to pay for sin with death, unless, to complete the economic symbolism, they were redeemed—literally meaning "bought back"—by Christ.

Death was not merely the result of sin, however; it was also an element in the forces of evil that were imagined to operate in the universe. Paul's thought was marked by a certain amount of dualism. Death appeared as an enemy because it was in league with the demons that threatened human beings. As in Zoroastrian dualism, Paul declared war against devils and demons. "For we are not contending against flesh and blood," Paul warned, "but against the principalities, against the powers, against the world rulers of this present darkness, against the spiritual hosts of wickedness in the heavenly places" (Eph. 6:12). By conquering death, Paul believed, Jesus had also defeated these evil forces in the universe. In the promise of the resurrection, victory was expected to be complete over the demonic forces of evil.

According to Paul, Christians were not only armed for that cosmic battle against evil by the virtues of faith, hope, and love; they were also strengthened by ritual practices that symbolized the victory over death. The two major early Christian rituals, baptism and eucharist, both incorporated death in their symbolism. Baptism was the ritual initiation of a convert into the Christian community. But it was also a symbolic death and rebirth. Paul explained that in baptism the person was "buried into the death of Christ . . . so that as Christ was raised from the dead by the glory of the Father, we too might walk in newness of life" (Rom. 6:3–4). As a symbolic death and rebirth, baptism was a ritual rehearsal for death and for a new life in the resurrection.

In the communal meal of bread and wine of the eucharist, or the Lord's Supper, participants symbolically sacrificed and ate the body and blood of Jesus in celebration of the redemptive sacrifice of his death. "As often as you eat this bread and drink this cup," Paul instructed Christians, "you proclaim the Lord's death until he returns" (1 Cor. 10:16, 11:26). Again, the corporeality of Jesus was emphasized. By insisting that they were eating the body and drinking the blood of Jesus, Christians were even accused by Roman authorities of practicing ritual cannibalism. Although the elements of bread and wine were symbolic, they symbolized the importance of the physical body in the Christian symbolism of death.

Jesus' redemptive sacrifice had been physical, his resurrection had been corporeal, and the general resurrection of the dead was expected to be in the body. The resurrected body might be glorified and transformed into an imperishable form, but it was nevertheless expected to be a body (1 Cor. 15:35–50). Encouraged by Paul, early Christian communities expected that resurrection to occur very soon. Dying in baptism, Christians could live on the eucharist until Christ returned to raise the dead, judge the saved and the damned, and begin his kingdom on earth.

The Apocalypse of John   Christian anticipations of the return of Jesus were heavily influenced by the apocalyptic visions recorded in the Book of Revelation. The apocalypse that unfolded before the author John on the island of Patmos provided an outline for Christian eschatology. Paul had suggested that the return of Jesus would be a dramatic descent from the heavens. With a shout, the voice of an archangel, and the trumpet of God, the heavens were expected to open and Christians to rise up into the air to be with Christ among the clouds (1 Thess. 4:16–18). The apocalypse of John, however, outlined the return of Jesus in elaborate detail. In dense and complex symbolism, the Book of Revelation described a victorious battle against the forces of evil, the resurrection and judgment of the dead, and a new heaven and new earth under the reign of Christ.

The apocalyptic vision of John began with the unsealing of a book, a scroll that was closed with seven seals. The first four seals revealed visions of horses— white, black, red, and pale—riding into battle. On the last horse sat Death. The fifth seal revealed the martyrs who had been killed for their faith. They were buried beneath the altar of sacrifice. The deaths of the martyrs had been redemptive sacrifices, but in the vision of John the martyrs called out for judgment and revenge against those who had caused their deaths. The sixth seal revealed the beginning of cosmic vengeance. The sun became black, the moon became blood, and the earth shook with earthquakes as the living tried to hide from the judgment and retribution. After that cataclysm, the seventh seal revealed silence (Rev. 5:1–8:1).

The apocalyptic scroll with seven seals, therefore, revealed one of the motives for the resurrection and judgment of the dead: Final retribution would avenge the deaths of the martyrs who had died for their faith. The end promised to reverse the social order of the world—"the first shall be last, and the last shall be first." Persecuted Christians could draw strength and courage from the promise that they would be restored to life and their deaths would be avenged at the end. After a brief silence, cosmic upheavals and devastation at the sound of seven trumpets and the pouring out of seven vials of wrath on the world were the next stage of John's vision. At the end of that destruction, the kings of the earth gathered in a place called Armageddon (Rev. 16:12–16). In lightning, thunder, earthquakes, and a rain of hail from heaven, the cities of the nations fell. With the destruction of the kingdoms of the world, the apocalypse of John promised the institution of the kingdom of Christ.

Like the Zoroastrian resurrection, the Christian resurrection of the dead also involved a cosmic battle against the forces of evil in the universe. In the apocalyptic scenario outlined in the Book of Revelation, an angel would come from heaven, bind Satan, and cast him into a pit, which would be sealed for a thousand years. The thousand-year reign of Christ on earth would begin with a first resurrection, the raising of Christian martyrs who had died for the faith. "I saw the souls of those who had been beheaded for their testimony to Jesus," John reported. "They came to life again, and reigned with Christ a thousand years" (Rev. 20:4). This thousand-year reign was known as the millennium. Martyrs were not only restored to life but elevated to political power over the world in that millennial kingdom.

At the end of a thousand years, the Book of Revelation promised, Satan would be released from the pit, but, along with all his demons, he would finally be destroyed. After eliminating the devil, demons, and evil forces in the universe, Christ would supervise a second resurrection of the dead. From the sea, from the earth, and from hell, the dead would be restored to life. In that last resurrection, all the dead would stand before the throne of the divine judge.

As in the vision of Daniel, judgment was by the book. "The dead were judged by what was written in the books, by what they had done," reported the author of the Book of Revelation. "If anyone's name was not found written in the book of life, he was thrown into the lake of fire" (Rev. 20:15; cf. Mark 9:43–48). The new heaven and new earth that followed the judgment of the dead would restore the earthly paradise, but it would also transform the social and political order of the world into the kingdom of God under the rule of Christ (Collins, 1977).

The expectation of an apocalyptic end of the world has been referred to as *millennialism* or *millenarianism*. In general, millenarian movements can be defined as "religious movements that expect imminent, total, ultimate, this-worldly, collective salvation" (Talmon, 1968: 349). This expectation motivated the formation of early Christian communities. When Christ's return was delayed, Christians had to adapt to a world that showed every sign of persisting (Gager, 1975). Nevertheless, Christians continued to discern signs of the end. But after the fourth-century accommodation of the Christian religion to the state, millenarian movements tended to be movements of social protest against even the Christian social order that came to dominate Europe in the Middle Ages (Cohn, 1961).

Waiting For The End

With the delay of the return of Jesus, Christian thinking about death had to account for the interim period between an individual's death and the general resurrection of the dead. One option was to regard the interim between death and resurrection as a period of sleep to be ended by the trumpets of the last day. In the unconsciousness of sleep, no time would seem to have passed.

Early church authorities such as Justin Martyr and Tertullian taught that the soul slept after death. Justin Martyr, for example, argued that only an interim period of sleep was consistent with the Christian doctrine of resurrection. If someone should say "that when they die their souls are taken up to heaven, do not suppose that they are Christians" (Roberts and Donaldson, 1969: I:239). Rather than going to heaven or hell after death, Justin Martyr argued, souls remained in a sleeplike state of suspended animation until restored to life in the resurrection of the flesh.

Passages in the New Testament Book of Luke suggested a different option for imagining the condition of the person in the interim between death and resurrection. The afterlife conditions of two men, Dives and Lazarus, were described as being opposite to their relative wealth and social status during life. The wealthy Dives was described as suffering torment in hell, while the poorer Lazarus had been carried after death by angels to Abraham's bosom (Luke 16:19). The different conditions of Dives and Lazarus after death suggested some type of individual judgment. Likewise, Jesus was reported to have said to the penitent thief who was crucified by his side, "Today you will be with me in paradise" (Luke 23:43). Again, some type of afterlife judgment for each individual might have been implied in which some are rewarded and others punished during the interim period between death and the resurrection.

The dominant Christian resolution to the problem of what happened to the person after death combined the concepts of immortality and resurrection. Immortality was implied in the immediate judgment—with accompanying rewards or punishments—of each person after death. Human beings were regarded as immortal to the extent that they had souls that were rewarded and punished individually after death. That individual aspect of judgment, however, was ultimately imagined to be finalized in the last judgment. The general, collective resurrection and judgment of the dead certified each person's individual judgment and assigned each to eternal reward or punishment according to his or her merits.

While it was considered a likely possibility, the individual judgment of each person after death did not become an official teaching of the church until well after the twelfth century. Before that time, individual judgment was considered less important than the collective, general resurrection of the dead.

Burial Practices The importance of the general resurrection in Christian thinking about death was reflected in burial practices. In early Christian custom, the dead were buried in mass graves. No personal markers distinguished individuals. Rather, the corpses were placed in the ground together to wait for a collective resurrection of the flesh. When a cemetery became full, the bones might be taken from the ground and displayed on the walls of a church or charnel house. The entire community of Christians as a whole was expected to be raised from the dead, so Christian remains were collected in corporate graves to await that resurrection.

The best place for a corpse to await the general resurrection was in close proximity to the holy remains of a saint or martyr. Following Roman practice, Christian martyrs were buried in the cemetery, or *necropolis,* outside the city. Their tombs became important religious shrines. By the fifth century, the practice of burying Christians near the remains of saints and martyrs was already seen as an ancient practice. Maximus of Turin explained, "The martyrs will keep guard over us, who live with our bodies, and they will take us into their care when we have forsaken our bodies. Here they prevent us from falling into sinful ways, there they will protect us from the horrors of hell. That is why our ancestors were careful to unite our bodies with the bones of the martyrs" (Ariès, 1974: 16). As superhuman dead, martyrs extended their beneficial influence over Christians during life, in the grave, and at the general resurrection.

Burial in church, churchyard, or cemetery became customary during the Middle Ages, but those places were made sacred by the bones of saints interred within them. Saints and martyrs were the "special dead" (Brown, 1981). Their remains and relics were felt to emanate a special power and influence that would have a beneficial effect in the present and at the resurrection. In the corporate Christian body that awaited the resurrection, one individual in particular, the martyr, stood out for his or her sacred power. Having died a superhuman death, the martyrs were felt to radiate a sacred energy that continued even in the remains they left behind.

Martyrs The Christian martyr who died for the faith was thought to have performed a redemptive self-sacrifice. In Tertullian's phrase, martyrs were the seed of the church. Their sacrificed blood allowed the community to live and grow. Although they died for the group, martyrs were also imagined to attain instant personal salvation through their sacrificial deaths. The death of a martyr was regarded as a superhuman death. In many cases, martyrdom was sought intentionally as a sanctifying act. An almost suicidal impulse animated the preparations of many Christians for martyrdom. As a redemptive sacrifice, however, death through martyrdom was regarded as an imitation of the death of Christ.

In the first three centuries, Christians were periodically persecuted by Roman authorities, who accused them of various crimes, the most serious being atheism. Because Christians refused to sacrifice to the Roman gods, who were identified with the welfare of the Roman state, Christians were regarded as both atheists and traitors to the state (Frend, 1965). Under persecution, Christian martyrs chose to die rather than betray their faith. The stories of previous martyrs served as training manuals for future martyrs, providing examples for all Christians to imitate in preparing for death. Prospective martyrs called themselves athletes, in training for a sacrifice that would save them and their community.

One influential manual for martyrdom was the second-century story of the death of the Christian church leader Polycarp, bishop of Smyrna. Polycarp had a dream one night that his pillow was on fire. On awakening, he announced, "I must be burned alive." Although he tried to evade the Roman authorities by hiding at a nearby farm, Polycarp was betrayed by two slaves and taken into custody by the police. Under interrogation, Polycarp refused to disavow his allegiance to the Christian religion. The authorities threatened him with death by fire, but he responded, "The fire you threaten burns but an hour and is quenched after a little; for you do not know the fire of the coming judgment and everlasting punishment that is laid up for the impious." Polycarp concluded by challenging the authorities to execute him.

In the arena, Polycarp was burned at the stake. The story of his death described him as "a burnt offering ready and acceptable to God." Polycarp's execution by the Roman authorities was interpreted as a redemptive sacrifice. While his body was in the flames, Polycarp was "not as burning flesh, but as bread baking or as gold and silver refined in a furnace." When the authorities saw that his body was not being consumed by the flames, they stabbed Polycarp with a dagger. As the blood flowed from his body, it extinguished the fire surrounding him. The crowd was said to have marveled at this miracle and to have been convinced of Polycarp's sanctity at the moment of his death.

The story of the martyrdom of Polycarp suggested that a Christian martyr's death was sacred because it imitated sacred models. The martyrdom of Polycarp was sacred because it was a death just like the death of Jesus: Polycarp was betrayed to the authorities but remained steadfast under interrogation and showed courage under torture. More than that, however, his death was described as a redemptive sacrifice like the sacrifice of Jesus because it brought eternal life for himself and salvation for his community. And the death of Polycarp himself was described as a model to be followed by Christians. The day of Polycarp's death and the deaths of other martyrs were to be celebrated "in memory of those athletes who have gone before, and to train and make ready those who are to come hereafter." Following the sacrificial examples of Jesus and Polycarp, Christian martyrs died superhuman deaths: "To them the fire of their inhuman tortures was cold. They were no longer men, but already angels" (Chidester, 2000: 75–90; Roberts and Donaldson, 1969: I:39–44).

ISLAMIC MYSTICS

The prophet Muḥammad (570–632) initiated the Islamic faith by recording the revelations of Allah in the sacred text of the Qur'ān (Koran). Allah required a life of obedience, a surrender of the human will to divine will. Literally, *islam* meant surrender. An Islamic life in submission to divine will was lived in devotion to Allah as the one God. At the center of Islamic faith stood the creed *La ilaha illa Allah: Muḥammad rasul Allah* ("There is no god but Allah, and Muḥammad is his Prophet"). Allah's prophet Muḥammad instructed Muslims in the life of regular prayer, charity, fasting, and pilgrimage that would be in accordance with divine will.

A life devoted to Allah could be expected to be rewarded after death. Like other prophetic religions, the faith of Muḥammad promised a resurrection of the dead that would result in the final separation of the righteous and the wicked. In the judgment of the dead, Allah would be merciful to the righteous but vengeful against the wicked, the polytheists, and the unbelievers, who would be condemned to eternal punishment.

Qur'ān and Tradition

The Qur'ān consistently depicted Allah as the supreme power over life and death. Allah was the divine creator of the living and the re-creator of the dead at the resurrection. The Qur'ān stated, "[Allah] is the one who gave you life, then He will cause you to die, then He will give you life [again]" (Surah 22:66). Other gods had been worshiped, but they held no power over life. Those gods "create nothing but are themselves created, and . . . [they have] no power over death or life or resurrection" (Surah 25:3). The central teaching of the Qur'ān, therefore, was that Allah had total power and control over human life. Originally, Allah had created human beings from the earth; he would re-create them from the earth in the resurrection of the dead. The resurrection would be the "new creation," demonstrating Allah's absolute power over all life, even life that had been dissolved by death. Allah was proclaimed in the Qur'ān as the ultimate cause of life, death, and resurrection of the dead.

As in Jewish and Christian traditions, the Islamic doctrine of resurrection raised the question of the status of the dead during the interim period between death and the general resurrection. Did the dead merely enter into the unconsciousness of a sleeplike state while they awaited the resurrection? Or were the dead conscious after death? Perhaps they survived as disembodied souls to experience rewards or punishments before the general resurrection. Both these possibilities were considered in the Islamic understanding of death and afterlife.

Death and Sleep The Qur'ān suggested a close relationship between sleep and death. Death may have been like sleep, but sleeping and waking in the normal rhythms of life were just like death and resurrection. When a person slept, Allah took the soul, but restored it to life when the person awakened. Allah's control over sleeping and waking during the course of life demonstrated His absolute divine power over every human person. "It is he who takes you by night," the Qur'ān stated, "and He knows what you do during the day: He raises you up again by day so you may complete your appointed term" (Surah 6:60). In this sense, human beings died daily. They were taken by Allah in sleep but were restored on awakening to continue their course of life.

By comparing death and sleep, the Qur'ān not only insisted on Allah's absolute power and authority over human life but also suggested that sleep was a rehearsal for death. Every night, the soul separated from the body in sleep. Sleep prepared the person for the final separation from the body that would occur when Allah and his angelic messengers took the soul from the body at death. Therefore, death was nothing to fear because human beings died every night.

As the Islamic tradition developed, death was regarded as a peaceful sleep for the faithful as they awaited the resurrection. The angels were imagined to say to the believers, "Sleep like a bride" or "Sleep the sleep of a bridegroom" (Macdonald, 1965: 75). Death for the faithful was expected to be a well-deserved rest. The legend of seven sleepers who fell asleep in a cave and woke at the resurrection captured this notion of death as a period of peaceful sleep. This story appeared in both Christian and Islamic forms. When the sleepers awakened at the resurrection, they would ask one another, "How long have you remained asleep?" In response, they would say, "We have remained asleep for a day, or a part of a day." The Qur'ān stated that only Allah would know how long they had actually slept before the resurrection (Surah 18:18).

Since sleep and death were alike, the sleep of the living came to be imagined as a time in which the living and the dead might communicate (Smith, 1980). During sleep, the living shared the same condition as the dead. Therefore, the living could receive dreams, visions, and messages from the dead while asleep. The dead might give information to the living, perhaps even informing the living about the time of their own deaths. The communication between the living and the dead during sleep, dreams, and visions reinforced the idea that sleep was a rehearsal for death in which Allah would finally take the soul away from the world of the waking.

Death and the Soul   Islamic tradition viewed a human person as a living soul (*nafs*) animated by a spirit (*rūḥ*). The nafs of a person was identified as the soul, the self, the blood, or the living body. In other words, the nafs was the whole living person. At death, the nafs was thought to be taken from the body by Allah and his angelic messengers. "Every nafs will have a taste of death," promised the Qur'ān (Surah 3:185, 21:25, 29:57). Every person would go through the process in which the soul was extracted from the body. One passage of the Qur'ān described the soul leaping to the throat of the dying at the moment of death. Friends and relatives were incapable of keeping the soul in the body if Allah and his messengers had decided that the time had come to take it (Surah 56:83–87).

Although all souls went through the same extraction from the body, they did not all have the same experience when they were taken at death. The souls of the righteous were gently released from the body, just as they were in sleep, and entered the sleep of the faithful until they were awakened at the resurrection. But the souls of sinners, polytheists, and unbelievers were violently torn from their bodies in the agony of death (Surah 6:93).

The Qur'ān indicated that wicked souls were questioned by the angelic messengers of Allah immediately after death. Unbelievers gave damning testimony against themselves merely by their disbelief in Allah and his prophet. When the angels took souls who were living wicked lives, those souls tried to proclaim their innocence. But the angels responded, "No! Surely God knows what you have been doing! So enter the gates of Jahannam." As a place of punishment, Jahannam—like the Jewish and Christian Gehenna—was imagined as an afterlife condition of fiery torment. While that punishment would not be finalized until after the resurrection, the Qur'ān suggested that immediately after death the souls of the wicked received a taste of their fate.

Souls of the righteous, however, were not interrogated by the angels of death. Taken in the course of a good life, those souls were welcomed by the angels. "Peace be upon you!" the angels declared. "Enter the Garden [*al-jannā*] for what you have been doing!" (Surah 16:28–32). Again, rewards after death were not final until after the resurrection. But the sleep of faithful souls after death was expected to be a peaceful rest in the heavenly garden.

As the tradition developed, these rewards and punishments that followed immediately after death were often interpreted as representing the condition of the soul in the grave while it waited for the resurrection. After burial, two angels were expected to visit the soul in the grave. With black faces and piercing blue eyes, long hair that flowed to the ground, and voices like thunder, the angels Munkar and Nakir interrogated the deceased about his or her beliefs and deeds during life. That interrogation was called the "trial of the grave" (Padwick, 1961: 278–79; Wensinck, 1932: 164–66).

In preparation for that trial, mourners at the funeral might whisper instructions into the ear of the deceased concerning the proper answers to the questions that would be posed by Munkar and Nakir. If the deceased passed successfully through that trial, he or she would experience the comforts of the heavenly garden paradise while still in the grave. If the deceased was revealed as an unbeliever, however, he or she endured torments in the grave. The place of burial was exposed to the heat and smoke that rose from the fires of Jahannam, the hell below. Failing the trial of the grave, sinners and unbelievers were expected to suffer the torments of hell even while they remained in the ground waiting for the resurrection of the dead (Jeffrey, 1962: 208–10).

In the "new creation" of the resurrection, believers were expected to be awakened from the sleep of death and rewarded in paradise for eternity. The garden was imagined as a paradise of sensuous delights. Souls were established forever in a heavenly oasis among flowers and springs. They dressed in the finest robes, silks, and brocades and feasted on every delicious food imaginable. The Qur'ān even promised that lovely maidens with wide and dark eyes would be available for the enjoyment of men in that garden paradise.

The wicked, however, were expected to awaken from the sleep of death to an eternity of horrible punishment. Even if they tried to confess their faults and make amends, sinners and unbelievers would receive no relief from punishment. Those who had rejected Allah during life would suffer the tortures of Jahannam, where, the Qur'ān promised, "he is given to drink boiling slimy water which he gulps but cannot swallow: and death comes upon him from every side" (Surah 14:16). No water would be able to cool the fires of that hell. Lingering in a state between living and dying, the damned would beg to die. But no relief from suffering—not even release through a second death—could be expected.

Sufi Mystics

About 150 years after the death of the prophet Muḥammad, a loosely organized movement of mystics emerged within the Islamic tradition. Known as Sufis, perhaps for the wool (*suf*) garments they characteristically wore, they explored the central doctrine of Islam: the oneness of God. The foundation of the Islamic creed was the affirmation of belief in the one God, Allah. Sufi ascetics, renunciates, and mystics transformed the doctrine of the unity of God into a quest for union between the soul and God. The oneness of God, *tawhīd,* came to imply for Sufis the ultimate truth that nothing existed except the One

(Zaehner, 1960: 166). Tawhīd came to mean both the affirmation of the one-ness of God and the mystical quest to make the self one with God. In the ex-periential transcendence of mystical union, Sufis claimed to die to self and to continue only in the divine unity. Like a drop of water absorbed in the ocean or like a spark dancing in the fire's flames, the Sufi lived only in the divine unity of God.

Union with God In union with God, the Sufi lost all hope of heaven and fear of hell. Beyond hope for rewards and fear of punishment, the Sufi renounced all personal desires except the one consuming desire to be united with God through love. "The mark of the true Sufi," said al–Zushayri, "is that he should be indifferent to this world and the next" (Smith, 1976: 165).

The Sufi mystic's logic of desire was similar in some respects to the Bud-dhist's. Both renounced personal, selfish, or egotistical desires. As an inde-pendent ego identity bounded by desires, the self was annihilated. But whereas the Buddhist nirvāna was the *extinction* of all desires (including the desire for nirvāna), the mystical union described by the Sufis resulted from a *focus* of all desires toward one object: God. The experiential transcendence of the Sufi did not lie in the elimination of desire but in the concentration of all desires on union with God. Sufis often symbolized that union as a mystical marriage of lover and beloved. As a loving oneness to be sought for its own sake, the mys-tical union annihilated the separate self by absorbing it in the immortal, eternal unity of God.

Sufis also developed meditation practices that were similar in some ways to those of the Buddhists. Particularly with regard to death, Sufis practiced med-itations that made them mindful of their own deaths. The systematizer and de-fender of Sufi belief and practice, al-Ghazālī identified the "Remembrance of Death" as the tenth and final stage of the Sufi path to union with God. Con-templation of death was the final stage along the way to salvation (Arberry, 1950: 82). Salvation from the Sufi perspective, however, did not signify rewards in paradise, but absorption of the self in God. Meditation on death facilitated the renunciation of self that was necessary for that absorption in divine unity.

Unlike the Buddhists, however, Sufis meditated on death not only to re-nounce all attachments to the self but also to awaken the desire for God. In the early stages of Sufi discipline, meditation on death was thought to awaken fear. Afraid of afterlife punishments, the novice contemplating death was expected to renounce sinful desires and actions. But as the Sufi progressed along the mys-tical path, the remembrance of death did not awaken fear. Rather, the medita-tion on death awakened love and the desire to meet and to embrace God in complete union. The eighth-century Sufi al-Muhāsibī described the remem-brance of death (*dhikr al-mawt*) that awakened love. "As for the adept, his re-membrance of death is the love of it, and the choice of it rather than life in this world of affliction, from which the heart turns away in longing for God and the meeting with Him" (Smith, 1976: 173). In the remembrance of death, the Sufi's desires turned away from the world and toward the meeting with God that could only be consummated through love. Therefore, death was loved as a doorway to that final meeting with God.

Union with God, however, could be achieved in life. By annihilating all sense of self while alive, many Sufis claimed to have achieved a transforming union with God. In the eighth century, Sufis such as al-Bistami and al-Hallāj claimed to have been dissolved into union with God while still alive. Known as intoxicated Sufis, they described ecstatic mystical experiences of union. As if drunk on divine love, those Sufis made dramatic declarations of their unity with God. Abū Yazīd al-Bistami, for example, declared that he had ceased to exist. All that remained was God. Since he had been absorbed in God, al-Bistami announced, "Glory to Me! How great is my majesty!" (Arberry, 1950: 59). Similarly, the Sufi mystic al-Hallāj declared, "I am the Truth!" Claiming union with God through love, al-Hallāj explained that all that remained of him was God. "I have become he whom I love," al-Hallāj stated, "and he has become myself. We are two spirits in one body. When you see me you see him." This unifying love had led to a transforming self-realization. "When I saw the Lord with the eye of the heart and asked, 'Where are you?'" al-Hallāj recalled, "He replied, 'Yourself'" (Parrinder, 1976: 135).

Orthodox Muslims found this identification of the self and God difficult to accept. Even if self, in the Sufi's sense, did not mean a personal ego identity but an absorption of ego in God, mainstream Islamic orthodoxy objected to what seemed to be the heretical claims made by al-Hallāj. Claiming that he was God, al-Hallāj seemed to violate the foundation of Islamic faith—that there is no God but the one God, Allah. For his heresy, al-Hallāj was condemned to death by the orthodox Islamic authorities. At his crucifixion, al-Hallāj demonstrated a supreme detachment from life and an understanding of death as the door to final union with God. As he was nailed to the cross, he prayed for forgiveness for those who had condemned him to death. Seeing his martyrdom for the truth as a redemptive sacrifice, al-Hallāj welcomed death. "Kill me, my trustworthy friends," he invited his persecutors, "for in my killing is my life" (Massignon, 1982; Schimmel, 1975: 62–77). Al-Hallāj exemplified the ecstatic Sufi proclaiming deathless union with God as well as the Sufi martyr embracing death as a redemptive sacrifice for the truth.

Although the death of al-Hallāj resulted from a rather extreme declaration of unity with God, later Sufi tradition explained the union with God as a process by which the self died while still alive. The death of self implied that only God remained. The passing away of self (fanā') was followed by continuance (baqā') in God. By dying to self, the Sufi claimed to live on in the deathlessness of God. The Sufi teacher al-Junayd of Baghdad (d. 910) identified the passing away of self as the heart of the Sufi path. "Sufism means that God makes thee to die to thyself," Junayd observed, "and makes thee alive in Him" (Smith, 1976: 168). The passing away of self was divided by al-Junayd into three stages: obliteration of personal characteristics, obliteration of desires, and obliteration of consciousness in attaining the final ecstatic vision of God (Abdel-Kader, 1962: 81ff.).

The declaration of al-Hallāj—"I am Truth"—could be interpreted as an expression of that final stage in which even consciousness of self had been annihilated in an ecstatic union with God. Other Sufis proclaimed a similar death of self. Al-Hujwīrī, for example, described how Sufis "have of set purpose become annihilated to all desire . . . and having thus passed away [*fanā'*] from mortality, they have attained to perfect immortality." Jāmī called this immortal union with God "the state in which perishability perishes [*fanā' al-fanā'*]" (Smith, 1976: 215–17). By the eleventh century, the respected Islamic philosopher al-Ghazālī defended the Sufi quest for union with God. The end of the Sufi path, al-Ghazālī explained, was "complete absorption [*fanā'*] in God" (Watt, 1953: 60ff.). Al-Ghazālī argued that absorption in God did not violate the orthodox Islamic commitment to the unity of God. Perfect unity was in fact affirmed by Sufis, who claimed that when the self passed away in mystical union, only God remained. Alive in God, Sufis claimed to be beyond death. By dying to self, they claimed to have experienced the death of death in union with God.

The Mystical Path   Mystical beliefs and practices have appeared in many different religious traditions (Katz, 1978, 1983). In most cases, mystics have cultivated an experiential transcendence of death. Through liberating devotion or knowledge, mystics have claimed to rise above or go beyond ordinary human mortality. But the transcendence of ordinary life and death through ecstatic experience has tended to be the result of disciplined practice and preparation. Rarely has such experience occurred spontaneously. Usually, the experience of transcendence described by mystics has been cultivated and nurtured through disciplined meditation, contemplation, prayer, and other spiritual exercises.

In addition, the experiential transcendence of life and death in mystical experience has often been charted on a trajectory that passes through various stages. Sufi mystics such as al-Muhāsibī, al-Junayd, and al-Ghazālī charted the stages of the mystical path from its beginning to its final goal in the absorption of the self in God. Though they identified different stages, each suggested that the mystical path took many years of devoted practice to traverse. The mystical path in Sufi practice can be illustrated through the experience of Islam's most prominent woman mystic, Rabī'a of Basra. The stages she followed along her mystical path suggested that Sufi practice transcended death by embracing death, that is, by incorporating aspects of biological, psychological, and social death in human experience.

For years, Rabī'a lived alone in a small cave in the desert. She ate little, fasted often, stayed awake praying all night, and denied herself all sexual expression. In this ascetic denial of the body, Rabī'a demonstrated a detachment from the world in which human bodies were usually entangled. Rabī'a received many marriage proposals from Sufi men, but she refused them all. To one she explained that the marriage contract applied only to people concerned with the world. Because she had died to the world, she belonged to God. Anyone who wanted to marry her would have to ask God for her hand.

The first stage of the mystical path, therefore, involved an ascetic denial of the body. Preparation for union with God began with a denial of the most basic biological processes of the body: eating, sleeping, and sexuality. Although fasting was an important part of ritual practice in orthodox Islam, Sufis denied themselves food, sleep, and sex as a form of spiritual discipline. Sufis understood the ascetic denial of the body as a practice of purification, but it might also be understood as symbolizing biological death. As practiced in many religious traditions, ascetic discipline simulated the death of the body as a preparation for a spiritual transcendence of death.

Not only was the body denied, but human emotions and desires were sacrificed as well. Surrender to divine will was also central to orthodox Islam, but the Sufis understood that surrender to require the sacrifice of all personal needs, wants, and desires. Rabī'a was once asked by a friend what she desired. "I am a servant," she replied, "and what has a servant to do with desire?" (Smith, 1976: 221). As a servant of Allah, Rabī'a renounced all personal desires in service to the will of God. This renunciation of desire in the second stage of the mystical path also represented a symbolic death, incorporating psychological death into human experience.

Paradoxically, that psychological death promised a transcendence of death. That psychological self-sacrifice included any hope of reward in paradise or fear of punishment in hell. On a number of occasions, Rabī'a insisted that a genuine transcendence of death in union with God could be achieved only by abandoning any hope of heaven or fear of hell. An account of her life recorded that one day her friends saw Rabī'a walking along carrying a burning torch in one hand and a bucket of water in the other. When she was asked what she was doing, Rabī'a responded that the torch was to set fire to paradise and the water was to extinguish the flames of hell. Rabī'a did not want those personal motives—the desires to achieve reward or to avoid punishment—to stand in the way of union with God. Union was not achieved by hope or fear but only through a psychological self-sacrifice.

Intending to eliminate the hope of heaven and fear of hell, Rabī'a insisted that God was to be loved without any self-interested motive. "Even if Heaven and Hell were not," Rabī'a declared, "does it not behoove us to obey Him? He is worthy of worship without any motive" (Smith, 1976: 187). Sacrificing psychological motivations of hope or fear, Rabī'a suggested that a transcendent union with God could be achieved only by embracing a type of death to desire. "O my Lord," Rabī'a prayed, "if I worship Thee from fear of Hell, burn me in Hell, and if I worship Thee in hope of Paradise, exclude me thence, but if I worship Thee for Thine own sake, then withhold not from me Thine Eternal Beauty" (Smith, 1976: 224).

A third symbolic death was achieved at the next stage of the mystical path: social death. After the denial of body and desires, the person ceased to belong to herself but belonged only to God. Rabī'a consistently symbolized that transcendent life in the ironic imagery of slavery. The Sufi was a slave or servant of God. The notion that each person was a slave of Allah was also important in orthodox Islam. But a Sufi mystic such as Rabī'a understood her slavery to imply that she owned no body, desires, property, or social status; rather, she was completely owned by God. As a slave, she ceased to exist as a human person. In the social death of slavery, Rabī'a declared, "I have ceased to exist and have passed out of Self. I exist in Him and am altogether His" (Smith, 1976: 224).

Rabī'a described this slavery as the essence of her faith. If she had served God out of fear of hell or hope of heaven, Rabī'a insisted, she would have been an unfaithful slave. "But I have served Him," she concluded, "only for the love of Him and desire for Him." By embracing the social death represented by slavery, Rabī'a claimed a transcendence of death through divine love. The mystical path of Rabī'a, therefore, suggested that a Sufi transcendence of death involved a passing away of self that embraced death in the course of a life of spiritual discipline. Biological death of the body, psychological death of desires, and social death in slavery were all symbolically embraced along that mystical path. Those forms of death were incorporated in order to experience a mystical transcendence of death through an ultimate union with God.

Sufi mystics often described the union with God as a fusion of liberating devotion and liberating knowledge, in the fire of divine love and the illumination of divine knowledge. Distinctions between self and God, as the Sufi Jāmī observed, were "extinguished in the dazzling light of the Eternal Essence, and the distinction between the temporal and the eternal, the perishable and the imperishable, is taken away, and this state is called 'Union'" (Smith, 1976: 217). Ascending to that state beyond life and death, the Sufi had passed through symbolic forms of biological death, psychological death, and social death in order to achieve an ultimate transcendence of death in a unifying vision of God.

ABRAHAMIC TRANSCENDENCE

The mystical goal of achieving a vision of God—in life as well as after death— appeared in Jewish, Christian, and Islamic mysticism. A vision of God that unified the seer and the seen was an aspiration of many mystics in those religious traditions. As we will see in the next chapter, the vision of God was also the last stage of the visionary journey through the world of the dead outlined by the Italian poet Dante Alighieri in his *Divine Comedy*. Although certainly a great work of literature, Dante's *Divine Comedy* represented an imaginative transcendence of death that incorporated many elements of religious faith and the mystical path. Before exploring Dante's visionary journey, however, it might be useful to review briefly the patterns of transcendence that have appeared in Jewish, Christian, and Muslim approaches to death.

Ancestral transcendence appeared in the fact that Abraham was the common ancestor of all three religions. In the example of Abraham, Jews, Christians, and Muslims found a model for an ancestral transcendence of death: Human beings were mortal but could live on through their descendants. All three traditions claimed descent from the first ancestor, Abraham. Therefore, they participated in a continuous lineage from that first ancestor that was unbroken by death. All were children of Abraham, preserving the memory of their common father.

The example of Abraham reinforced the patriarchal, male-dominated definition of family continuity. Because a family was defined as the descendants of a father, the continuity of that family was traced along the father's line. Although less prominent than the ancestor rituals of indigenous and Asian religions, religious transcendence of death included reverence for patriarchal ancestors as a way of rising above or going beyond death. Reverence for ancestors merged into cultural transcendence when communities traced their lineage to a common "founding father," whether that father was Moses, Jesus, Muḥam-mad, or George Washington.

Experiential transcendence of death appeared most clearly in the experi-ence of mystics. In union with God, the mystic was beyond death because God was beyond death. To achieve that transcendence of death, however, mystics had to die to the world. As we saw in the case of Rabi'a, the mystic path in-volved three symbolic deaths: the denial of the body, the denial of personal de-sires, and the denial of social entanglements all simulated death in life. The Sufi mystics claimed that when the self passed away, only God remained. This pass-ing away of the self occurred while the person was still alive. In life and in death, therefore, the mystic achieved an experiential transcendence by merg-ing into the divine reality of God.

Cultural transcendence of death was achieved by funerals, cemeteries, me-morials, and regular commemorations for the dead. In addition, all three tra-ditions symbolized a cultural transcendence of death by the permanence of the book. The cultural memory of each tradition was recorded, inscribed, and pre-served in a relatively permanent form. The sacred book transcended time, linked the generations, and maintained a stable basis for cultural continuity unbroken by the deaths of individuals. While oral traditions also preserved cultural memory, the book turned memory into a visible, tangible artifact of culture.

Judaism, Christianity, and Islam were religions of the book. In each tradi-tion, the book symbolized a transcendence of death. Writing, reading, study-ing, and preserving sacred books became a cultural practice for the transcen-dence of death. However, the book not only recorded and preserved the three traditions but became a powerful symbol of the relation between God and the world in myths of the judgment of the dead. As we have seen, a successful pas-sage through the afterlife judgment depended on what had been written in the book of life. The technology of the book, therefore, entered into both the cul-tural and the mythic transcendence of death.

Mythic transcendence developed into elaborate and powerful stories about the end of human life. Those myths described not only the end of each per-son's life but the end of the entire drama of human history. In ancient myths, the afterlife was often symbolized as a semiconscious, shadowlike existence in a dark underworld: Arulla, She'ol, and Hades were such shadowy underworlds of the dead. But Judaism, Christianity, and Islam developed myths promising the possibility of salvation from such a fate after death. Although some thinkers argued along Platonic lines that human beings were immortal, the dominant position in all three traditions was that humans were mortal but would be miraculously restored to life in the resurrection of the dead.

The three religious traditions developed symbolism of the afterlife judg-ment of the dead that was similar in some respects to the judgment of the heart, conscience, or moral character found in ancient Egyptian and Persian afterlife myths. A successful passage though death depended on a person's good thoughts, words, and deeds during the course of a single lifetime. In other words, a suc-cessful passage through death depended on the formation of a moral conscience in life. As a result, myths of death reflected on life: They underscored the crucial moral status of every thought, word, and deed in that single span of life. The judgment of the dead suggested that each person's conscience stood under the scrutiny of divine judgment during the entire course of life. In different ways, religious myths promised that the moral status of the conscience would be disclosed in death.

Chapter Five: References

Abdel-Kader, A. H. (1962). *The Life, Personality, and Writings of al-Junayd*. London: Luzac.

Allen, T. G. (1960). *The Egyptian Book of the Dead*. Chicago: University of Chicago Press.

Alster, Bendt (ed.). (1980). *Death in Mesopotamia*. Copenhagen: Akademisk Forlag.

Andrews, Carol (ed.). (1972). *The Ancient Egyptian Book of the Dead*. Trans. Raymond O. Faulkner. London: British Museum Publications.

Arberry, A. J. (1950). *Sufism: An Account of the Mystics of Islam*. London: George Allen & Unwin.

Ariès, Philippe. (1974). *Western Attitudes Toward Death: From the Middle Ages to the Present.* Trans. Patricia M. Ranum. Baltimore: The Johns Hopkins University Press.

———. (1981). *The Hour of Our Death*. Trans. Helen Weaver. New York: Random House.

Badham, Paul. (1976). *Christian Beliefs About Life After Death*. London: Macmillan.

Bailey, Lloyd R. (1979). *Biblical Perspectives on Death*. Philadelphia: Fortress Press.

Boyce, Mary. (1979). *The Zoroastrians: Their Religious Beliefs and Practices*. London: Routledge and Kegan Paul.

———. (1982). *A History of Zoroastrianism*. 2 vols. Leiden: E. J. Brill.

Brandon, S. G. F. (1966). "The Origin of Death in Some Ancient Near Eastern Religions." *Religious Studies* 1: 217–28.

———. (1967). *The Judgment of the Dead: An Historical and Comparative Study of the Idea of a Post-Mortem Judgment in the Major Religions*. London: Weidenfeld and Nicolson.

Brown, Peter. (1981). *The Cult of the Saints: Its Rise and Function in Latin Christianity*. Chicago: University of Chicago Press.

Budge, E. A. Wallis. (1911). *Osiris and the Egyptian Resurrection*. 2 vols. London: Philip Lee Warner.

———. (1913). *The Book of the Dead: The Papyrus of Ani*. 2 vols. London: British Museum Publications.

Charles, R. H. (1913). *A Critical History of the Doctrine of a Future Life in Israel, in Judaism and in Christianity*. London: Adam and Charles Black.

Chidester, David. (2000). *Christianity: A Global History*. San Francisco: HarperCollins.

Clark, R. T. Rundle. (1959). *Myth and Symbol in Ancient Egypt*. London: Thames and Hudson.

Cohn, Norman. (1961). *The Pursuit of the Millennium*. 2nd ed. New York: Harper (1st ed. 1957).

Cohn-Sherbok, Daniel. (1987). "Death and Immortality in the Jewish Tradition." In Paul and Linda Badham (eds.), *Death and Immortality in the Religions of the World*. New York: Paragon House, 24–36.

Collins, John J. (1977). *The Apocalyptic Vision of the Book of Daniel*. Missoula, Mont.: Scholars Press.

Cullmann, Oscar. (1958). *Immortality of the Soul or Resurrection of the Dead?* New York: Macmillan.

Cumont, Franz. (1922). *After Life in Roman Paganism*. New Haven, Conn.: Yale University Press.

Dienstag, Jacob. (1983). *Eschatology in Maimonidean Thought: Messianism, Resurrection, and the World to Come*. New York: KTAV.

Frend, W. H. C. (1965). *Martyrdom and Persecution in the Early Church: A Study of a Conflict from the Maccabees to Donatus*. London: Basil Blackwell.

Gager, John G. (1975). *Kingdom and Community: The Social World of Early Christianity*. Englewood Cliffs, N.J.: Prentice Hall.

Gaster, M. (1893). "Hebrew Visions of Hell and Paradise." *Journal of the Royal Asiatic Society* 23: 571–611.

Gatch, Milton, McC. (1969). *Death: Meaning and Mortality in Christian Thought and Contemporary Culture*. New York: Seabury Press.

Ginzberg, Louis. (1909–38). *The Legends of the Jews*. Trans. Henrietta Szold. 7 vols. Philadelphia: Jewish Publication Society.

Gruenwald, Ithamar. (1980). *Apocalyptic and Merkavah Mysticism*. Leiden: E. J. Brill.

Guttmann, Julius. (1964). *Philosophies of Judaism: The History of Jewish Philosophy from Biblical Times to Franz Rosenzweig*. Trans. David W. Silverman. New York: Schocken.

Hanson, Paul D. (1979). *The Dawn of Apocalyptic*. Rev. ed. Philadelphia: Fortress Press.

Heidel, Alexander. (1949). *The Gilgamesh Epic and Old Testament Parallels*. Chicago: University of Chicago Press.

———. (1951). *The Babylonian Genesis*. 2nd ed. Chicago: University of Chicago Press.

Himmelfarb, Martha (1983). *Tours of Hell: An Apocalyptic Form in Jewish and Christian Literature*. Philadelphia: Fortress Press.

ibn Hishām, 'Abd al-Malik. (1955). *The Life of Muḥammad*. Trans. Alfred Guillaume. London: Oxford University Press.

James, E. O. (1958). *Myth and Ritual in the Ancient Near East*. London: Thames and Hudson.

Jeffrey, Arthur. (1962). *A Reader on Islam*. The Hague: Mouton.

Jonker, Gerdien. (1995). *The Topography of Remembrance: The Dead, Tradition, and Collective Memory in Mesopotamia*. Trans. Helen Richardson. Leiden: E. J. Brill.

Katz, Stephen (ed.). (1978). *Mysticism and Philosophical Analysis*. Oxford: Oxford University Press.

——— (ed.). (1983). *Mysticism and Religious Traditions*. Oxford: Oxford University Press.

Kramer, Samuel Noah (trans.). (1969). "Sumerian Myths and Epic Tales." In James B. Pritchard (ed.), *Ancient Near Eastern Texts Relating to the Old Testament*. 3rd ed. Princeton, N.J.: Princeton University Press, 37–59.

Lamm, Maurice. (1969). *The Jewish Way in Death and Mourning*. New York: Jonathan David.

Lattimore, Richmond. (1942). *Themes in Greek and Latin Epitaphs*. Urbana: University of Illinois Press.

Leca, Ange-Pierre. (1979). *The Cult of the Immortal: Mummies and the Ancient Egyptian Way of Death*. Trans. Louise Asmal. London: Granada.

Lieberman, Saul (1965). "Some Aspects of After Life in Early Rabbinic Literature." In Saul Lieberman et al. (eds.), *Harry Austryn Wolfson Jubilee Volume*. English Section. 2 vols. Jerusalem: American Academy of Jewish Research, II: 495–532.

Macdonald, John. (1965). "The Twilight of the Dead." *Islamic Studies* 4: 55–102.

Maimonides, Moses. (1982). *Treatise on Resurrection*. Trans. Fred Rosner. New York: KTAV.

Massignon, Louis. (1982). *The Passion of al-Hallāj: Mystic and Martyr of Islam*. Trans. Herbert Mason. Princeton, N.J.: Princeton University Press.

Moore, George Foot. (1927–30). *Judaism in the First Centuries of the Christian Era, the Age of Tannaim*. 3 vols. Cambridge, Mass.: Harvard University Press.

Morenz, Siegfried. (1973). *Egyptian Religion*. Trans. Ann E. Keep. Ithaca, N.Y.: Cornell University Press.

Nickelsburg, George W. E. (1972). *Resurrection, Immortality, and Eternal Life in Intertestamental Judaism*. Cambridge, Mass.: Harvard University Press.

O'Shaughnessy, Thomas. (1969). *Muḥammad's Thoughts on Death: A Thematic Study of the Qur'ānic Data*. Leiden: E. J. Brill.

Padwick, Constance. (1961). *Muslim Devotions*. London: SPCK Press.

Pangborn, Cyrus R. (1977). "Parsi Zoroastrian Myth and Ritual: Some Problems of Their Relevance for Death and Dying." In Frank E. Reynolds and Earle H. Waugh (eds.), *Religious Encounters with Death: Insights from the History and Anthropology of Religions*. University Park: Pennsylvania State University Press, 125–39.

Parrinder, Geoffrey. (1976). *Mysticism in the World's Religions*. London: Sheldon Press.

Pavry, Jal Dastur Cursetji. (1965). *The Zoroastrian Doctrine of a Future Life*. 2nd ed. New York: AMS Press (orig. ed. 1929).

Pelikan, Jaroslav. (1962). *The Shape of Death: Life, Death, and Immortality in the Early Fathers*. London: Macmillan.

Pritchard, James B. (ed.). (1969). *Ancient Near Eastern Texts Relating to the Old Testament*. 3rd ed. Princeton, N.J.: Princeton University Press.

Reimer, Jack. (1974). *Jewish Reflections on Death*. New York: Schocken.

Reynolds, Frank E., and Earle H. Waugh (eds.). (1977). *Religious Encounters with Death: Insights from the History and Anthropology of Religions*. University Park: Pennsylvania State University Press.

Roberts, Alexander, and James Donaldson (eds.). (1969). *The Ante-Nicene Fathers*. 10 vols. Grand Rapids, Mich.: Eerdmans.

Rohde, Erwin. (1925). *Psyche: The Cult of Souls and Belief in Immortality Among the Greeks*. New York: Harcourt, Brace.

Rush, Alfred C. (1941). *Death and Burial Customs in Christian Antiquity*. Washington, D.C.: Catholic University of America Press.

Russell, D. S. (1964). *The Method and Message of Jewish Apocalyptic*. London: SCM Press.

Schimmel, Annemarie. (1975). *Mystical Dimensions of Islam*. Chapel Hill: University of North Carolina Press.

Schindler, Pesach. (1977). "The Holocaust and the Kiddush Hashem in Hassidic Thought." In Frank E. Reynolds and Earle H. Waugh (eds.), *Religious Encounters with Death: Insights from the History and Anthropology of Religions*. University Park: Pennsylvania State University Press, 170–80.

Scholem, Gershom. (1961). *Major Trends in Jewish Mysticism*. New York: Schocken.

———. (1973). *Kabbalah*. New York: Schocken.

Sherry, Patrick. (1984). *Spirits, Saints, and Immortality*. Albany: State University of New York Press.

Smith, Jane I. (1980). "Concourse Between the Living and the Dead in Islamic Eschatological Literature." *History of Religions* 19: 224–36.

Smith, Jane I., and Yvonne Yazbeck Haddad. (1981). *The Islamic Understanding of Death and Resurrection*. Albany: State University of New York Press.

Smith, Margaret. (1928). *Rābi'a the Mystic, and Her Fellow-Saints in Islam*. Cambridge: Cambridge University Press.

———. (1976). *The Way of the Mystics: The Early Christian Mystics and the Rise of the Sufis*. London: Sheldon Press (orig. ed. 1931).

Speiser, E. A. (trans.). (1969). "Akkadian Myths and Epics." In James B. Pritchard (ed.), *Ancient Near Eastern Texts Relating to the Old Testament*. 3rd ed. Princeton, N.J.: Princeton University Press, 60–119.

Spencer, A. J. (1982). *Death in Ancient Egypt*. Harmondsworth: Penguin.

Sutherland, Stewart R. (1966–67). "Immortality and Resurrection." *Religious Studies* 3: 377–89. Reprinted in John Donnelly (ed.) (1978), *Language, Metaphysics, and Death*. New York: Fordham University Press, 196–207.

Talmon, Yonina. (1968). "Millenarism." In David L. Sills (ed.), *International Encyclopedia of the Social Sciences*. New York: Macmillan, X: 349–62.

Tromp, Nicholas J. (1969). *Primitive Conceptions of Death and the Nether World in the Old Testament*. Rome: Pontifical Biblical Institute.

Warrington, John (trans.). (1963). *The Trial and Death of Socrates*. New York: Dutton.

Watt, W. M. (1953). *The Faith and Practice of al-Ghazālī*. London: George Allen & Unwin.

Welch, Alford T. (1977). "Death and Dying in the Qur'ān." In Frank E. Reynolds and Earle H. Waugh (eds.), *Religious Encounters with Death: Insights from the History and Anthropology of Religions*. University Park: Pennsylvania State University Press, 183–99.

Wensinck, A. J. (1932). *The Muslim Creed*. Cambridge: Cambridge University Press.

Wilson, John A. (trans.). (1969). "Egyptian Myths, Tales, and Mortuary Texts." In James B. Pritchard (ed.), *Ancient Near Eastern Texts Relating to the Old Testament*. 3rd ed. Princeton, N.J.: Princeton University Press, 3–36.

Wolff, Hans Walter. (1974). *Anthropology of the Old Testament*. Trans. Margaret Kohl. Philadelphia: Fortress Press.

Wood, Richard (ed.). (1980). *Understanding Mysticism*. Garden City, N.Y.: Doubleday.

Zaehner, R. C. (1956). *The Teachings of the Magi: A Compendium of Zoroastrian Beliefs*. New York: Oxford University Press.

———. (1960). *Hindu and Muslim Mysticism*. London: Athlone Press.

———. (1961). *The Dawn and Twilight of Zoroastrianism*. New York: G. P. Putnam's.

Zandee, J. (1960). *Death as an Enemy According to Ancient Egyptian Conceptions*. Leiden: E. J. Brill.

6

The Divine Comedy

In the mythic transcendence of the Christian tradition, death was not a tragic, irrecoverable loss but an event in a larger story of redemption. The Christian story was a comedy because it anticipated a happy resolution in the resurrection of the dead and the rewards of heaven. Of course, the damned were expected to be excluded from that happy ending. Like goats separated from the sheep, tares from the wheat, darkness from the light, those condemned to eternal punishment were cut off from salvation and destined only for eternal retribution in hell.

Throughout most of Christian history, the punishment of the damned was an important element in the divine comedy celebrated by the saved. Many Christian theologians supposed that part of the joy of heaven would be derived from looking down on the eternal torments of the damned (Walker, 1964: 29). The happy condition of the saved in heaven could be measured in relation to the suffering of the damned in hell (Bernstein, 1993).

Heaven occupied two places in the Christian imagination. One location was vertical in space, the realm of heaven above in which God dwelled. The Hebrew Bible claimed by Christians as their Old Testament called on God to "look down from thy holy habitation, from heaven" (Deut. 26:15). The New Testament exhorted Christians to pray to the "Father which is in heaven" (Matt. 5:45). In spatial terms, heaven was imagined as the present abode of God and his angels. But heaven in the Christian imagination also occupied a place in time. At the end of time, heaven awaited in the promise of "a new heaven and a new earth" (Isa. 65:17, 66:22; 2 Pet. 3:10–13; Rev. 21:1). The future held the eschatological promise of a heaven on earth in which Christ's kingdom would be established for the eternal reward of his followers.

As a place of eternal punishment, hell occupied just one location in the Christian imagination: a fiery pit beneath the earth. Like She'ol, the Christian hell was an underworld to which the dead descended. In the Christian imagination, however, only the damned descended to the underworld. The New Testament referred to that place of punishment as Hades or Gehenna. It was an underground pit (Matt. 5:29–30, 18:9; Mark 9:45, 47; Luke 12:5), a place of fire (Matt. 5:22, 18:9; Mark 9:43; James 3:6), and a place of torture, torment, and retribution exacted on the damned (Luke 16:23). Hell was that place of eternal punishment "where the worm dieth not, and the fire is not quenched" (Mark 9:43–48). Punishment in hell was expected to last forever and ever (a period of time longer, for some reason, than simply forever).

In early Christian thought, the only exception to the doctrine of the eternity of hell was provided by the third-century theologian Origen. Influenced by the Platonic concept of the immortality of the soul, Origen held that souls would be refined after death until every soul was eventually saved. That refining process might require a series of disembodied lifetimes in spiritual worlds, places of purgation that Origen imagined awaited the soul after death.

Origen's doctrine of universal salvation was consistently condemned as heresy by church councils that met to define and to uphold orthodox Christian belief. The Council of Constantinople in 543, for example, condemned "whoever says or thinks that the punishment of demons and the wicked will not be eternal." Anyone who believed that all souls ultimately would be purified and saved could expect to join the number of the damned for holding that heresy.

As the Christian tradition developed, one modification to the absolute afterlife separation of the saved and the damned emerged: the doctrine of purgatory. Originally imagined as part of hell, purgatory was a place where Christians would be punished after death for their sins. Punishments in purgatory, however, were not eternal retribution; they were remedial, exacted to refine and purify the soul so that it could eventually have a place in heaven.

Medieval Christian images of hell, purgatory, and heaven culminated in the poetic synthesis of Dante's *Divine Comedy*. The Italian poet Dante Alighieri (1265–1321) produced a monumental visionary journey through the Christian worlds beyond death. Although *The Divine Comedy* may be appreciated as a work of literature, the text also focused Christian expectations about life after death: the descent to hell, purification in purgatory, and the ascent to the beatific vision of God reserved for the saints at the pinnacle of heaven. Through visionary poetic imagination, Dante traveled in all three of those afterlife worlds, witnessing the torments of the damned in the inferno of hell, struggling up the levels of purification in purgatory, and flying free from the gravitational pull of the earth to ascend through the heavenly spheres to the highest paradise of divine love. In poetic form, Dante outlined a Christian transcendence of death.

Before the age of twenty, Dante was writing poetry in his native Florence in a new style that combined romantic love with philosophy. The Italian poets of this new style addressed their philosophical verse to specific women whom they exalted as the sources of their inspiration. The object of Dante's devotion was a certain Beatrice. Dante first addressed Beatrice in the poems of his *Vita Nuova* in 1292. He described their first meeting; his pure, sacred devotion to her; and the death of his beloved two years earlier in the prime of her youth.

In the poetry of *The Divine Comedy,* Dante continued to regard Beatrice as a sacred source of inspiration and object of devotion. Even her name, suggesting "one who brings blessed joy and salvation," made Beatrice an appropriate guide in Dante's *Divine Comedy* through the celestial realms of heaven.

Active in local politics after 1300, Dante was involved in controversy and exiled from Florence. During that exile, Dante served at the courts of nobles in many different cities in Italy. Turning his attention to the study of politics, philosophy, and theology, Dante wrote on all those subjects while working for almost twenty years on his monumental epic, *The Divine Comedy.* Conceiving the poem perhaps as early as 1292, Dante did not complete it until just before his death in 1321. In 13,000 lines, Dante described a visionary journey through the Christian worlds after death that has remained one of the greatest achievements of European literature.

In a letter to one of his patrons, Dante explained that his objective in writing *The Divine Comedy* was not merely to produce a work of aesthetic pleasure or intellectual speculation but "to remove those living in this life from a state of misery, and to bring them to a state of happiness" (*Epist.* XI. 15; Latham, 1891: 199). In other words, the poem was composed with a therapeutic and transcendent intention: to encourage readers to rise above the suffering of human existence and to ascend to the celestial happiness of the vision of God. Sharing Dante's visionary journey through the afterlife, readers might direct themselves toward its ultimate goal, the supreme joy of heaven. Before entering that blessed state, however, readers first had to journey through the tortures of hell and the purification of purgatory. The way up began with the journey down.

HELL

Midway through life's journey, *The Divine Comedy* began, Dante found himself lost in a dark forest in a state of despair that was like sleep or death. Suddenly, the figure of the ancient Roman poet Virgil appeared before him and told him of the journey they would undertake together. Virgil would guide Dante through the worlds of the dead, the places of afterlife punishment for the damned and purification for Christians who were destined for heaven. As a pagan, however, Virgil was unable to guide Dante any farther. In order to enter heaven, Dante would require a different guide. In fact, that guide had been responsible for sending Dante the grace that would carry him on his visionary journey through the other worlds. On the ascent to heaven, Dante would be guided by his beloved Beatrice.

Descent

Virgil took Dante down to the gates of hell. There he read the inscription on hell's door: "Through me the way into the woeful city, through me the way to the eternal pain, through me the way among the lost people. . . . Abandon every hope, ye that enter" (III.1–9). Passing through the door of hell, Virgil and Dante came to the banks of the river Acheron. There the boatman of the dead, Charon, ferried souls into the first level of hell. Like other elements of Dante's visionary journey, Charon was a figure from classical mythology who was woven into the poet's conception of the other world (Terpening, 1985). Rivers have represented transition in many myths of the afterlife. On Dante's journey through the world of the dead, transitions were often symbolized by the crossing of rivers.

While crossing the Acheron, Dante lost consciousness only to awaken in Limbo, the place in hell assigned to good men, women, and children who were never baptized into the Christian faith. Occupants of Limbo experienced no torture except the loss of any hope of salvation. Limbo was the place that Virgil himself, as a virtuous pagan, occupied in hell. From Limbo, Virgil and Dante proceeded to the judge of the dead, identified by Dante as Minos, who assigned souls to their appropriate places of punishment in hell. Under Virgil's direction, Dante descended through each of those places of damnation.

In Dante's vision, hell consisted of nine levels in which souls received punishments appropriate to their sins. After Limbo, the second level of hell held the lustful, who were punished by being locked in embrace, tossed about on a howling wind throughout eternity. Then followed the gluttonous wallowing in mire, the greedy rolling huge rocks against each other, and the wrathful submerged in a slimy swamp. Level six contained heretics locked in fiery tombs. In level seven, the violent were trapped in a desert of burning sands under a rain of fire; the eighth level held ten different types of frauds, who were scourged and tortured by demons for their deceptions.

Finally, Dante and Virgil arrived at the lowest level of hell, which was reserved for traitors. At the bottom of hell was the archtraitor of Christian myth, the angel Lucifer, the devil Satan. Virgil and Dante had reached the center of the earth when they arrived at the depths of hell. Climbing down the body of Satan, they followed the course of another river, Lethe, that led up to the other side of the earth. Coming to the surface, they found themselves on the shores of Mount Purgatory.

Dante's journey through the other worlds was like a rehearsal for death, an extended meditation on the fate of the soul after death. Without dying, Dante was nevertheless able to see and map those other worlds as if he had died and returned to the living. The ghosts Dante met in the other worlds, however, were unable to return. Death had dissolved them as living human persons. Yet they persisted through a cognitive and forensic continuity that determined each person's survival and destiny after death.

Continuity

Dante's understanding of the process of dying was derived from both ancient pagan and Christian sources. Looking back to Aristotle, Dante understood a human person as a merger of soul and body. Aristotle (384–322 B.C.E.) had disagreed with Plato's definition of the soul as an independent, immortal consciousness temporarily imprisoned in a body. Rather, Aristotle defined the soul as the form of the body. The soul was what unified and animated the body, while the body was the raw material for the soul. In that synthesis, a human person was understood as a combination of soul and body. Both the soul's formative power and the body's raw material were required for a human person to exist.

From Aristotle's perspective, the soul had three functions: nutritive, sensitive, and intellective. The nutritive soul gave life to the body. The sensitive soul endowed it with seeing, hearing, smelling, tasting, and touching. The intellective soul provided the conscious human attributes of memory, will, and understanding. At death, only the immortal intellect continued as a form without matter. Although Aristotle held that the immortal function of the soul—the intellect—survived death, there was considerable disagreement in later Aristotelian thought regarding whether the survival of intellect should be understood as implying the continuity of any kind of personal identity after death. Intellect may survive, but the person might not.

The theologian Thomas Aquinas (1224–1274) adapted Christian thought to the framework provided by Aristotle. Aquinas held that the intellective soul survived the death of the body. "The soul continues to be," Aquinas explained, "when separated from the body by the failure of the body we call death" (Aquinas, 1968: la.xc.4, 3). The body failed when the nutritive and sensitive souls dissolved, but the intellective soul continued after death.

Since Aquinas considered the survival of a soul without a body to be an unnatural condition, however, he argued that the separation of soul from body could not last forever. "Nothing unnatural can be perpetual," Aquinas observed, "and therefore the soul will not be without the body forever." The resurrection of the dead was required to restore the surviving soul to a body and to recover what Aquinas regarded as the natural condition of a living human person in the merger of soul and body.

Because the soul sought its natural state of union with a body, Aquinas concluded, "the immortality of the soul, then, would seem to demand the future resurrection of the body" (Aquinas, 1929: IV:270–71). In this way, Aquinas combined an Aristotelian understanding of the relation between soul and body with a Christian expectation of the resurrection of the dead.

Following Aristotle and Aquinas, Dante assumed that death dissolved the union of soul and body that constituted a human person. When the soul was freed from the body, the intellective functions of memory, understanding, and will intensified. But the faculties of sensation—seeing, hearing, smelling, tasting, and touching—were temporarily dulled. On arriving at its destination in the other world, however, the soul gave shape to a body that was not of flesh and blood but nevertheless had the size, shape, and dimensions of a body. That ghost body or shade body was projected by the intellective and sensitive souls so that it could experience all the pleasurable or painful sensations of a body.

Like the thought bodies in *The Tibetan Book of the Dead,* the bodies that occupied hell, purgatory, and heaven were projections. The *Bardo Thödol* explained afterlife bodies as projections from consciousness; *The Divine Comedy* explained them as projections from the surviving intellective and sensitive functions of the soul. Dante described how the soul "rayed forth" its likeness in the form of a body, or "stamped itself" in the form of a body on the atmosphere around it (Boyde, 1981: 279–80).

The formative functions of the soul required a body for their expression. They projected a shadow body in the other world. Eventually, as Aquinas had suggested, they would require a restoration of the physical body in the final resurrection of the dead. In the meantime, souls continued to occupy a place in one of the afterlife worlds by virtue of their ability to project an immaterial body that could experience pleasure and pain.

The survival of the soul in a projected shadow body accounted for cognitive continuity after death. But the forensic continuity of a human person depended on two other factors: baptism and repentance for sin. A person's place in the other world was determined by his or her forensic status, the condition of his or her moral conscience at the time of death. Baptism washed away original sin; repentance began the process of atoning for particular sins committed during a person's lifetime. The unbaptized and unrepentant were burdened with full responsibility for a sinful past. Therefore, after death they arrived at the bank of the river Acheron to be ferried into hell without any hope of salvation. Only the baptized and repentant had any hope of a forensic continuity after death that might lead to salvation in heaven.

As a result of original sin, all humanity was assumed to share the guilt of the first human couple and to deserve damnation after death for that shared culpability. The fourth-century theologian Augustine (354–430) had referred to the corporate forensic identity of human beings when he called humanity a great fallen lump—a *massa perdita*—that as a whole deserved condemnation and punishment for sin. If forensic identity is based on responsibility for past actions, then all human beings were lumped together in a shared guilt for sinful, fallen human nature.

Dante followed a long tradition of Catholic teaching on salvation when he suggested that some could be rescued from that common fate. Their salvation depended on the ritual of baptism. Baptism was regarded as a necessary, but not always sufficient, requirement for salvation from hell. Although Dante included a few examples of pre-Christians in purgatory and heaven to illustrate the mysterious, unpredictable quality of God's grace, most were relegated to some place in hell. Even infants could not expect salvation from hell unless they had been baptized. The doctrine that unbaptized infants were condemned to hell was stressed by Augustine but was tempered to some degree as the tradition developed. The punishment for unbaptized infants was modified by imagining a place in hell, Limbo, in which unbaptized infants and virtuous non-Christians were separated from the joys of heaven but spared the tortures of hell. Since infant mortality in the course of human history may have accounted for as much as 50 percent of all deaths, Limbo must have been the most densely populated place in the other world.

Baptism, however, was not sufficient. The second requirement was repentance for sins. Even baptized Christians who died unrepentant could be expected to descend to hell with no hope of salvation. Repentance was an ethical requirement, but it was also developed into a ritual format. Within the Catholic tradition, the ritual of penance was divided into three stages: contrition, confession, and acts of penance. Christians who repented, confessed, and turned from their sins could perform acts of penance in hope of forgiveness.

The souls in hell abandoned all hope, but those who continued their penance after death in purgatory lived in hope of atoning for their sins and purifying themselves in order eventually to enter heaven. That process of purification was outlined in the second book of Dante's *Divine Comedy* in the poet's vision of purgatory.

Tours of Hell

Virgil was a particularly qualified guide to the territory of hell. As a first-century Latin poet, he had written an epic poem of Rome, the *Aeneid,* that featured a descent to the underworld. Many of the characteristics of the world of the dead that Virgil described also appeared in Dante's visionary journey. In Virgil's version of the underworld of ancient Roman religion, the dead descended to a waiting area, crossed the river Styx, entered a field of tears, and finally came to a meadow where the path forked in two directions. The left branch led to the hell of Tartarus; the right branch proceeded beyond the walls of Dis (or Pluto), the king of the underworld, to the paradise of the Elysian fields. In that paradise of rest, the river Lethe flowed as a river of forgetfulness.

Hell featured torments. Virgil described the "deep groans and the savage crack of whips and the rattle of metal from dragging shackles." In some cases, those punishments were described as purifying. "Souls are trained with punishment," Virgil explained, "and pay with suffering for old felonies." The Elysian fields, however, brought rest and perhaps release from the past in the waters of the Lethe. Torment or repose after death was understood to be based on the person's previous life. As Virgil observed, "We suffer the afterworld we deserve" (Dickinson, 1961: 141). Although Virgil was not a Christian, many elements of his vision of the afterlife were congenial with the Christian imagination.

Although Dante enlisted the pagan poet Virgil as his guide to the Christian underworld, he might also have been inspired by Jewish, Christian, and Islamic visionary journeys through hell. All three traditions produced a type of apocalyptic literature that described tours of hell. Attributed to holy persons, saints, prophets, or, in the Islamic case, to the Prophet himself, these visionary journeys through the world of the dead described the territory of hell and the punishments suffered by its inhabitants in vivid, graphic detail. In fact, some scholars have concluded that the most important Christian tour of hell during the Middle Ages, the *Apocalypse of Paul,* had a direct influence on Dante (Silverstein, 1935); others have argued that Dante's imagination was influenced by familiarity with Islamic stories of Muhammad's visions of the suffering of the damned in hell (Asín Palacios, 1926; see also Silverstein, 1952).

Like Dante, the authors of these tours of hell imagined punishments in the afterlife to be of two kinds: environmental punishments and measure-for-measure punishments. Environmental punishments were punishments of place. In the Christian imagination, the simple biblical description of the pit, the fire, and the worm was transformed into an elaborate scenario of fiery rivers flowing around the damned that gave off burning heat without necessarily providing illumination (fires that were dark); smoke, boiling pitch, and the noxious fumes of burning sulfur (fire and brimstone); and worms, snakes, lions, dragons, dogs, panthers, and three-headed beasts—not to mention beastly demons—that roamed through hell and attacked the damned. Environmental punishments were not associated with specific sins; rather, they were features of the general condition of damnation shared by all the souls in hell (Himmelfarb, 1983: 106–26).

"An eye for an eye, a tooth for a tooth" provided the basic standard of measure-for-measure punishments. Adapting the ancient law of *lex talionis* ("law of retaliation") to the judicial system of the other world, the tours of hell imagined that the damned would be punished in ways that corresponded directly to the sins they had committed. But the correspondence of measure-for-measure punishments was also a type of poetic justice. Like Dante's, the apocalyptic tours of hell imagined punishments that not only exacted retribution but also poetically showed the nature of a person's sin. Besides being a place of punishment, hell was imagined as a place of revelation in which even the most hidden and secret of sins came out. Particularly, sins of speech and sins of sex tended to be secret sins that were revealed in the punishments of hell. Divine power of judgment over even hidden sins was imaginatively demonstrated in afterlife punishments.

In many cases, the damned in hell were imagined to be punished by hanging. In keeping with the demands of measure-for-measure punishment, the victim was hanged by the part of the body associated with his or her sin. The tours of hell depicted sexual sins of lust being punished by hanging sinners from their genitals and verbal sins of lying, slander, or blasphemy by hanging the sinner from his or her tongue. Immodest women might find themselves in hell hanging by their hair, thieves hanging by their hands, gossips by their ears, and so on (Himmelfarb, 1983: 68–105). Hanging as a means of punishment in the ancient world was not merely a method of execution but also a public object lesson about the dangers of crime and the power of the political order. As a punishment in hell, hanging served the same function: The display of the body revealed the truth of sin and the truth of the power of God.

Dante echoed this understanding of hell when he described the inscription on its door declaring, "Divine power made me" (III.5). On each level of hell, punishments were exacted to fit the crime through an imaginative poetic justice. Sinners at each descending level of hell were made less and less mobile, from the swirling mass of the lustful down to the frozen traitors locked in ice at the center of the earth. At the end of *The Divine Comedy,* Dante contrasted the immobility of hell with the divine source of all movement at the pinnacle of heaven, where he beheld "the Love that moves the sun and other stars." Dante saw the greatest punishment of hell in its eternal separation of the damned from the animating power of divine love that moved the universe.

PURGATORY

Dante's journey down to the frozen center of the earth brought him out on the other side at the base of the mountain of purgatory. As Dante and Virgil began to climb up toward the majestic mountain that reached into the heavens, they turned from the hopeless condition of the damned in hell to the hope of heaven shared by all the suffering souls in purgatory, "that second kingdom where the human spirit is purged and becomes fit to ascend to Heaven" (I.4–6).

Locating purgatory on a mountain was an innovation in Christian afterlife geography introduced by Dante. Christian tradition had imagined purgatory as a temporary hell, located underground, where punishments were remedial rather than eternal. But Dante saw purgatory rising above the earth. He imagined it as the beginning of an ascent that would carry Christian souls after death into the heavens. First, however, they had to be purified.

During his tour of hell, Dante had been an observer, a relatively innocent bystander witnessing the torments of the damned. In purgatory, however, Dante participated more directly in the entire process of penance. In this respect also, Dante's visionary journey through the other world was a rehearsal for death: Dante repented, suffered, and was purified of sins as he climbed the mountain of purgatory, and that imaginary journey rehearsed a similar journey Dante expected that his soul would take after death. Attention to Dante's tour through purgatory might also assist his Christian readers in their preparations for death. A successful transition through death, Dante suggested, required a pure conscience and the willingness to be further purified through sufferings that would make the soul worthy of entry into heaven.

Purification

Dante stressed the importance of purification by recounting that Virgil had to wash Dante's face with the morning dew to remove any sinful residue from hell before Dante could climb the mountain of purgatory. After crossing another river to get to the mountain, Dante and Virgil climbed the lower slopes outside the gates of purgatory where souls waited for entrance. Apparently, some souls had to wait indefinitely: Those who had been excommunicated, those who had repented of their sins too late, those who had died without the last rites of the Church lingered on the lower terraces of the mountain. While Dante waited, he was carried asleep by an angel of light, St. Lucy, to the door of purgatory.

The guardian of purgatory invited Dante to walk up the three steps that led to the door. Perhaps those steps represented the three stages in the Catholic ritual of penance: contrition, confession, and acts of penance. Rather than confessing his sins, however, Dante knelt in humble submission to the gatekeeper who held the keys that would unlock the door to salvation. That power was held by the Church on earth but by the guardian of the door of purgatory in the other world. Before admitting Dante into purgatory, however, the guardian drew his sword and swiftly inscribed the letter P seven times on Dante's forehead. Each letter represented a different sin that would have to be purged in order for Dante to successfully climb up the mountain of purgatory. As the door clanged behind them, Dante and Virgil began the steep, narrow, zigzag climb to the first level of purgatory.

Like Dante's hell, the geography of purgatory was carefully organized in levels, on the plan of the most important medieval catalog of sins: the seven deadly sins. Dante depicted the levels of purgatory that punished souls for each of the seven deadly sins in order: pride, envy, anger, sloth, greed, gluttony, and lust. Dante explained that these were sins because they were "misdirected love." In Dante's Christian logic of desire, love was to be directed only toward God. Sin alienated the soul from God by misdirecting the soul's desires toward the world. Pride, envy, and anger were love perverted; the laziness and boredom of sloth were love defective; greed, gluttony, and lust were love excessive. These deadly sins, therefore, were not merely specific actions but were misdirected expressions of human desire that separated the soul from God.

Souls were punished in the level associated with the sins that preoccupied and misdirected them during life. Dante, for example, expected that after death he would have to return to the first level of purgatory for further purification from the sin of pride. Perhaps, he surmised, he would then be required to spend some time on the third level for the sin of anger. However, he did not expect to have to spend any time in the second level that purified souls of the sin of envy. In other words, souls were assigned to appropriate levels of purgation, passing through as many levels as necessary to purify them of any sins that would prevent them from entering heaven.

On his visionary journey, however, Dante passed through each level. Dante saw the proud burdened under enormous stones, the envious sitting like blind beggars with their eyes stitched shut, the angry immersed in a cloud of thick smoke, the slothful overcoming their laziness and boredom by running continuously, the greedy bound facing the ground, the gluttonous forced to starve within sight of food, and the lustful burning in the heat and flames of a purifying fire.

Like the punishments of hell, these were measure-for-measure punishments, designed to fit the crime they punished. But the punishments of purgatory were accepted gratefully by the suffering souls as redemptive sacrifices that would purify them of their sins and prepare them for heaven. At each stage, Dante also was purified. An angel erased one of the letters on his forehead as he made the transition to the next level of purgatory. Finally, the last P was removed from Dante's forehead as he passed through the flames of the seventh level of purgatory.

Arriving at the top of Mount Purgatory, Dante and Virgil found themselves in the meadows surrounding the earthly paradise, the Garden of Eden. Virgil pronounced Dante purified. "Free, upright, and whole is thy will," Virgil announced (XXVII.140). Explaining that he could no longer serve as Dante's guide, Virgil departed to return to his allotted place in Limbo. Dante wandered from the meadows through a forest until he came to a stream where he beheld the light and music emanating from the earthly paradise. In a pageant of angels, Dante's beloved Beatrice appeared to serve as his guide on the ascent into the heavenly realms.

Before leaving the mountain of purgatory, however, Dante had to pass through two more rivers. First, he was taken across the Lethe, the river of forgetfulness. Instead of merely crossing the river, Dante was submerged so that he drank its waters. As a result, he lost all memory of his former faults. The river of oblivion produced only forgetfulness of sins. They could now be forgotten because they had been removed in purgatory. Second, Dante was taken to the Eunoe, the river of good remembrance. When he drank from the

Eunoe, Dante recalled all his good deeds. Renewed by that memory, he was strengthened to begin his ascent to heaven.

Myth and Ritual

Most forms of mythic transcendence in the history of religions have been connected to a practical context of ritual. As we have noted, the story of purgatory was no exception.

Prayers for the Dead First, the belief in purgatory was related to ritual offerings of prayers for the dead. In the early church, prayers for the dead perhaps followed the example of Jewish practice. During the political turmoil of the second century B.C.E. in which many Jews died, the leader Judas Maccabaeus reportedly "made prayers for them that had died, that they might be released from their sin" (2 Macc. 12:39–45). Prayers for the dead, therefore, were not merely to comfort the living but to benefit the dead by releasing them from the burden of their sins in the next world.

These prayers became an important part of Christian practice during the first four centuries of the common era, providing a ritual means for maintaining contact between the living and the dead. As a form of cultural transcendence, they kept alive the memory of the deceased in the hearts and minds of survivors. But Christian rituals for the dead also came to be imagined as actually having a positive effect on the status of the deceased in the next world.

The effect of prayers for the dead was specified by the theologian and church leader Augustine. During the interim between death and the general resurrection, Augustine held, souls existed in secret storehouses, experiencing rest or tribulation depending on the merit or demerit accrued in life. Although the condition of the soul was determined according to God's justice, the living might intercede on behalf of the dead to request God's mercy. Divine mercy for departed souls might be sought through prayers, masses, or charitable donations offered in the name of the departed.

Augustine insisted, however, that such rituals for the dead would not assist all departed souls. Only those baptized souls who deserved God's mercy by virtue of the relatively good lives they had led could expect to benefit. According to Augustine, the purely good did not need help, and the purely wicked were beyond help. Rituals for the dead, therefore, might improve conditions in the afterlife for baptized Christians who had lived lives in which goodness and wickedness were mixed. Souls who were more good than wicked might win a complete forgiveness of sins; those who were more wicked than good might receive the mercy of what Augustine called a "more tolerable damnation" (Ntedika, 1966). Incidentally, it is important to remember that the vast majority of souls in human history were unbaptized and therefore firmly entrenched somewhere in that bottom region beyond the aid of prayers or any other intercession by the living.

In Augustine's thought, therefore, the basic distinction between the saved and the damned was modified into different gradations of afterlife rewards and punishments. Although Augustine did not explicitly work out a doctrine of purgatory, he did outline a middle ground in the afterlife that would develop in the Christian imagination into the world of purgatory.

Penance Development of the middle ground into a place called purgatory required a second ritual practice, the ritual of penance. The second-century church leader Clement of Alexandria (d. 215) considered the situation of Christians who repented of their sins on their deathbeds. Having confessed their sins but lacking time to make amends through good works, those souls would be given opportunities to perform acts of penance in the afterlife. Clement was the first Christian theologian to distinguish between two kinds of punishment after death: punitive and educational. Punitive punishment was absolute retribution destined for the incorrigibly wicked. But for souls capable of improvement, educational punishments might be corrective. The suffering of those souls in the other world would be a form of remedial education.

In both types of punishment, Clement imagined fire as the agent of the soul's torments. Punitive fire would devour and consume wicked souls, but educational fire would refine, purify, and sanctify souls like the fires of execution had sanctified the martyrs. Repentance for sins in this life, however, was regarded as necessary for a soul to be entitled to undergo educational, purifying punishments in the next.

As the ritual practice of penance developed, Catholic theologians decided that purifying punishments could atone only for minor, or venial, sins. According to Pope Gregory the Great (c. 540–604), minor sins included constant chattering, immoderate laughter, and attachment to private property. Gregory expected that souls would be refined of such minor sins by purifying fires in the upper regions of hell while they waited for the last judgment. More serious sins—referred to as major, capital, or mortal sins—could not be dissolved by purgatorial fires after death. This distinction between minor and major sins continued in Catholic reflections on the forensic status of the soul after death.

Like karma in Hindu and Buddhist thought, sin defined the forensic continuity of a human person during life and after death in Christian thought. Human identity was both corporate and individual. A collective human identity was formed out of a shared guilt for the original sin of Adam and Eve. Paul insisted that "all had sinned in Adam." Augustine concluded that original sin had resulted in the present state of humanity as a vast, corporate, fallen lump of degradation. From this perspective, humans lived and died as part of that mass of sin. Individual identity, however, was determined by continuous responsibility for actions during the course of a life. Those actions might produce great merit—as in the sacrificial acts of Christ and the martyrs—but they were more likely to result in the demerits of major or minor sins. In forensic terms, a human person was by definition a sinner.

Forensic human identity was synchronized with Christian ritual practices. Baptism washed away original sin; the ritual of penance cleansed minor sins that did not deserve absolute damnation. For the baptized, penance could be expected to continue after death. Since the forensic responsibility for actions continued to define the identity of a person after death, souls could expect to be punished in the next life if they were to have any hope of redemption from sin. The prayers of the living might assist the dead, but their own penitential sufferings were required for salvation.

Individual Burial In addition to the rituals of prayers and penance, a third ritual practice was related to the development of the doctrine of purgatory in Christian thought: individualized burial of the dead. Ancient Roman burial practices had required that each individual be buried in his or her own place and that the place be marked by an inscription. Inscriptions testified to personal attributes and relationships, setting each person apart as a unique individual. By the fifth century, Christians had stopped the practice of individual burials marked by tomb inscriptions. Christians were buried anonymously, close to the martyrs, in the company of the faithful, to wait as a community for the resurrection of the dead.

Only by the thirteenth century did Christians return to the practice of funeral inscriptions on personalized tombs (Panofsky, 1964). Originally designed for royalty, the practice gradually was extended to all Christians and became standard in Christian death rituals. The inscriptions recorded the deceased's name, dates, and place of death. Personalized tombs were decorated with sculpted portraits, death masks, and funeral art that preserved the memory of the deceased as a particular individual.

The Medieval Art of Dying The innovation of individualized burial was connected with a general change in attitudes toward death and dying. One last ritual practice signified that change: the medieval Christian art of dying. As described in Chapter 1, the Christian *ars moriendi* was a formalized ritual in which the dying prepared a clear conscience for the passage through death. Relatives, friends, and neighbors gathered around the deathbed, priests heard the last confession of sins, and the dying person received the last holy rites of the Church before leaving this world.

In medieval Christian understanding of the art of dying, the deathbed became an individualized location for a personal judgment of the dead. Medieval illustrations of deathbed scenes often depicted the dying as poised between two options—symbolized by Christ, Mary, and the angels on one side and Satan with his demons on the other—as if the person's destiny would be determined at the moment of death. In a sense, the judgment of the dead expected at the end of time was brought into the present at the deathbed during the moment of dying. In the ritual art of dying, the last confession of sin prepared a person's conscience for entry into the next world. Further penance, however, would have to be performed in purgatory (DuBruck and Cusick, 1999).

Catholics and Protestants

In the development of Christian thought, the doctrine of purgatory took shape gradually. It emerged out of ritual prayers for the dead and the ritual of penance and developed into the form described by Dante under the influence of increasingly individualized arts of dying and rituals of death in the thirteenth century (Le Goff, 1984). Collective waiting for the resurrection and judgment of the dead receded in importance before the concern for the fate of individuals immediately after death. Most baptized Christians could expect an afterlife of purification in purgatory before they would be ready to enter heaven. Entry into heaven might occur prior to the resurrection. Dante, for example, described how the mountain of purgatory shook like an earthquake whenever a soul completed its course of purification and was released to ascend to heaven. Apparently, however, those earthquakes were rare. Most souls in purgatory could expect to endure a regimen of educational suffering that would last a very long time.

A soul's sentence in purgatory might be reduced, however: The Church might intercede by granting a special gift of pardon from punishment. The gift of pardon was called an *indulgence*. Originally granted to release Christians from acts of penance, punishments, vows, or contracts in this world, the indulgence eventually was understood as a pardon that could be obtained from punishment in purgatory. First granted to crusaders on military expeditions to the Holy Land, indulgences were more widely dispensed during the Jubilee year of 1300. During that year, anyone who went on pilgrimage to Rome and its holy sites would receive full pardon from punishment in purgatory. Similar offers were made during subsequent Jubilees, which were declared every fifty years. By the fifteenth century, indulgences were dispensed more widely to the general public throughout Christian Europe.

The theory of indulgences was based on the idea that the Church held the keys to a storehouse of merit built up by Christ and the saints. By virtue of the sacrificial acts of Christ, the saints, and the martyrs, the Church had inherited an infinite treasury of merit. Although it belonged to the Church as a whole, the treasury of merit could be administered for the benefit of human beings by the pope and his delegated representatives. From that infinite storehouse, merit was dispensed to ordinary Christians through the sacraments and other offices of the Church. But merit was also dispensed when the pope declared special pardons that absolved people from punishments for their sins. The pardon might not erase the stain of guilt, but it would relieve the person from punishments in this life and the next.

Afterlife indulgences, therefore, were part of a cosmic accounting system administered by the Church. Individuals might have gained merit during life, but measured against absolute standards of goodness it was more likely that they would die in a state of guilt, liability, or indebtedness. For baptized and penitent Christians, debts had to be paid through sufferings in purgatory. Payments might be advanced to the deceased's account, however, from the infinite treasury of merit that was administered and dispensed by the Church. By granting an indulgence, the Church declared, "I make you a participant in the merits of the whole Church." On receiving an indulgence, a soul's torments in purgatory might be reduced.

In some cases, full payment might be offered. A *plenary* indulgence promised full pardon from punishments in purgatory. Since indulgences could be obtained by the living for the dead, the system of indulgences maintained a link between this world and the next. Seeking indulgences for the departed demonstrated the concern of medieval Christians for the suffering of souls in purgatory.

In his formulation of the theory of indulgences, Thomas Aquinas was concerned that the Church might abuse the practice by issuing pardons indiscriminately or by selling them for profit. The spiritual accounting system might easily become entangled with the material if the Church entered into the business venture of selling afterlife indulgences. In theory, indulgences were freely dispensed gifts from a treasury of merit owned by the Church as a whole. In administering that treasury, however, medieval popes frequently linked the granting of indulgences with financial benefits for the Church. They granted indulgences to raise money for wars, building projects, and charitable organizations.

Dante attacked what he regarded as abuses in the system of indulgences that occurred whenever they were granted for the purpose of financial gain (Par. XXIX.118–26). Two hundred years later, perceived abuses in the system of indulgences contributed to the Protestant break from the Catholic Church initiated by Martin Luther.

According to the sixteenth-century Protestant reformers, indulgence sellers were duping the public with extravagant sales pitches: "When a coin in the coffer rings, a soul from purgatory springs." One indulgence seller was accused of promising that even a man who had deflowered the Virgin Mary could obtain a pardon from punishment in purgatory.

In breaking with the Church, the reformer Martin Luther (1483–1546) rejected this symbolic accounting system, declaring that all considerations of credit and debt, merit and demerit, were irrelevant to salvation. God saved souls, according to Luther, only on the basis of a free, unmerited gift of grace. No ritual works could increase a person's merit or influence God. As sinners by definition, all human beings merited damnation, but Luther expected that God would demonstrate mercy in saving some from the damnation that all deserved. Therefore, Luther rejected indulgences and all other ritual connections between the living and the dead. As a result, purgatory disappeared as an afterlife possibility in Protestant thought. Souls after death were either in heaven or in hell. No middle ground of afterlife payment was imagined because in Luther's thought no conceivable payments could possibly be adequate to merit salvation.

With the elimination of purgatory, Protestant thought on death and afterlife turned to a stark division between heaven and hell. In addition, those afterlife places of reward and punishment receded in importance before the expectation of the resurrection of the dead and the Last Judgment. The sixteenth-century reformer John Calvin argued that souls after death did not sleep until the resurrection but were gathered in places of rest or torment where they remained conscious. Calvin declared, "The souls of the faithful, after completing their term of combat and travail, are gathered into rest, where they await with joy the fruition of their promised glory; and thus all things remain in suspense until Jesus Christ appears as the Redeemer."

The wicked, however, were chained like criminals until dragged to the punishments that awaited them. After the Last Judgment, the damned would suffer the incomprehensible vengeance of God. "Since no description could adequately express the horror of the vengeance of God upon the unbelievers," Calvin concluded, "the torments they have to endure are symbolized to us by corporal things: namely, by darkness, weeping, gnashing of teeth, everlasting fire and worms incessantly gnawing at their hearts" (Brandon, 1967: 132). Although the fire might not be physical, it could be expected to produce even more painful effects on the wicked in hell than physical fire.

Purgatory allowed Catholics to anticipate the afterlife as an ongoing process of salvation. Every soul released from purgatory after enduring its course of purification increased the company of the saved in heaven. By comparison, Protestants understood heaven to hold the relatively small company of the elect. In Protestant thought, the drama of life for the faithful and the wicked was essentially over at the moment of death; their fates were decided at death only to be finalized at the resurrection and Last Judgment. Protestants did not expect that the drama of life would continue after death to provide new opportunities for repentance of sins or purification through remedial, educational punishments. With the elimination of purgatory, Protestants imagined rewards in heaven and punishments in hell as an absolute division of the saved and the damned. In Protestant thought, therefore, purgatory ceased to function as it had for Dante and the Catholic tradition as a stairway to heaven.

HEAVEN

Dante's visionary journey through the Christian afterlife symbolized the progress of the soul in terms of motion. At the lowest level of the soul's progress, the bottom of hell was symbolized by the frozen immobility of ice. Climbing up the mountain of purgatory, Dante moved gradually through seven levels of purification until the wholeness of his will was restored. From the top of the mountain of purgatory, Dante flew into the celestial spheres of the heavens. Free from the gravitational pull of sin, Dante's soul moved with the freedom of flight. Hell had been immobility; heaven was perfect freedom of movement.

Most important, however, was that the movements of Dante's soul became synchronized with the will of God that moved the heavens. "The glory of Him who moves all things penetrates the universe," the last book of *The Divine Comedy* began, "and shines in one part more and in another less" (I.1–3). The book ended with Dante beholding the eternal light of God in the highest heaven, where it appeared in its greatest brilliance. At that point, Dante concluded that the movements of his heart had become harmonized with the divine will, light, and love that moved the heavens. Sin had been defined as misdirected love; salvation in heaven was symbolized by directed love, by a heart perfectly attuned to the movements of a divine love that moved the universe.

Following Ptolemaic astronomy, Dante pictured the earth as the stationary center of the universe. In concentric circles, the sun, moon, and the five visible planets revolved around the earth. Dante located heaven in those celestial spheres that encircled the earth. Each of those seven heavenly bodies comprised a sphere in which souls of the blessed lived after death. In order, the moon, Mercury, Venus, the sun, Mars, Jupiter, and Saturn represented celestial circles in the heavenly realm. Flying above the earth, Dante journeyed through each of the spheres of heaven. *The Divine Comedy* has been described as a ghost story because Dante saw, met, and talked to the spirits of the dead, but it was also a story of space flight, as he soared into outer space to travel through the planetary spheres to the stars.

Just as the seven levels of purgatory represented seven vices, each of the seven planetary spheres was associated with a virtue: faith, service, love, wisdom, courage, justice, and temperance. Above the seven planets, three further levels of heaven brought Dante to its pinnacle. On the eighth level of heaven, the fixed constellations of the zodiac formed a heavenly sphere in which the Church Triumphant resided. The ninth level of heaven was the sphere of the first mover, the *Primum Mobile,* which Dante described as a sphere that put all the others in motion. In that ninth sphere he found the angels. Finally, Dante entered the tenth sphere of heaven, the *Empyrean,* which he described as above the planets and stars, beyond time and space. In the Empyrean, God appeared eternally as the Trinity of Father, Son, and Holy Spirit, and the Virgin Mary, angels, and saints received their eternal reward in beholding the vision of God. In the concluding poetry of *The Divine Comedy,* Dante described his own ascent to that beatific vision.

Ascent

While still on top of the mountain of purgatory, Beatrice gazed up directly at the sun. Dante found that he could tolerate looking into the sun for only a brief moment. Suddenly, the heavens became even brighter, as if another sun had appeared in the sky. Beatrice continued to gaze directly into the dazzling light, but Dante could only see it reflected in her eyes. As he looked into Beatrice's eyes, Dante was transformed, "passing beyond humanity" (I.70). Hearing new sounds and surrounded in a great light, Dante lifted off from the earth. Enveloped in the sound and light of the heavenly spheres, Dante and Beatrice ascended to the first level of heaven.

Like the moment of dying in *The Tibetan Book of the Dead,* Dante's transition into heaven was symbolized as an entry into light and sound. In medieval thought, the heavenly spheres were believed to turn in melodious harmony, each luminous body giving off its own music. Combining light and sound in a single symbol, the radiant music of the planetary spheres was an important medieval image of transcendence.

The music of the spheres had figured prominently in an ancient Roman text by Cicero, *The Dream of Scipio,* that served as one of the inspirations for Dante's ascent. Cicero had described the vision of the Roman general Scipio Africanus in which he ascended through the celestial spheres and beheld their light and sound. Following that example, Dante described his own ascent into heaven as an emergence into the light and sound of the celestial spheres.

As he ascended, Dante passed beyond humanity through each of the planets in succession. Along the way he received instruction from the blessed in each heavenly realm about many of the finer points of Christian doctrine. When he reached the eighth heaven in the sphere that represented the Church Triumphant, Dante was tested for his understanding of the three Christian virtues, faith, hope, and love. Saint Peter examined Dante concerning faith, Saint James regarding hope, and Saint John on the subject of love. Dazzled by the light of Saint John, Dante was temporarily blinded. In his blindness, Dante demonstrated sufficient understanding of divine love to pass his test and rejoice with the assembly of saints.

Rejoining Beatrice, Dante's eyes were healed by looking into hers. As he did so, Dante noticed an infinitely tiny point of light reflected in them. Turning around, he beheld a small, indivisible light surrounded by nine rings. Beatrice explained that he was seeing the light of God's essence surrounded by the nine orders of angels on which heaven and earth depended for their existence. Passing through the ninth level of heaven occupied by the angels, Dante and Beatrice ascended to their final destination, the Empyrean. Entering the highest heaven, Dante crossed one final river, a river of light, in which he bathed his eyes. Immediately, Dante beheld the angels and the souls of the blessed in heaven in a vision of the celestial rose.

The blessed appeared as if they had bodies, manifesting before Dante's eyes in human forms. They appeared as they would at the time of the resurrection. In the meantime, however, the blessed rested in the supreme joy of heaven. The blessed souls in the highest heaven were seated on thrones on more than a thousand tiers that were arranged to form the petals of a magnificent snow-white rose. Angels flew in and out of the celestial rose like bees ministering to the assembly of the blessed. At one edge of the rose, the Virgin Mary sat attended by countless angels.

Directing Dante's attention to the great assembly, Beatrice declared, "See our seats so filled that few souls are now wanting there" (XXX.131–32). In an earlier work, *The Convivio*, Dante had stated his conviction that "we are already in the last age of the world." Implying that the second coming of Jesus and the resurrection would occur when all the seats in heaven were filled, Beatrice suggested that the end of the world was near.

As Beatrice assumed her seat in the celestial rose, Dante was granted the vision of God. In that ultimate vision, he beheld the pure light of God. The luminous essence of the Christian Trinity appeared as three circles of light. Noting that words were inadequate to describe what he saw, Dante nevertheless recounted that "in the profound and clear ground of the lofty light appeared to me three circles of three colors and of the same extent, and the one seemed reflected by the other as rainbow by rainbow, and the third seemed fire breathed forth equally from the one and the other" (XXXIII.115–20). Dante described the Trinity as a rainbow procession of light, recalling the afterlife experiences promised by *The Tibetan Book of the Dead*. Dante was given the opportunity to merge into the rainbow light of the divine form through loving devotion.

Dante identified that light as pure love, the beginning and end of all human desire. Earlier, Dante had observed that if anything else kindled love in the human heart, it was nothing more than a misunderstood trace of that light of God shining through the objects of desire (V.10–12). The seven deadly sins had been explained as misdirected love. From Dante's heavenly vantage point, however, any love not directed toward God was misdirected. Any desire other than the desire for God misunderstood the traces of light for their source.

Understanding all loves and desires as traces of the light of God, Dante turned his heart toward the source of all love and the end of all desires. In the culmination of his visionary journey, Dante declared, "My desire and will, like a wheel that spins with even motion, were revolved by the Love that moves the sun and other stars" (XXXIII.143–45). Merging into the "glory of Him who moves all things," Dante described the ultimate transcendence of death in the Christian heaven as a vision of God in which the soul was synchronized with the divine love that moved the universe.

The Vision of God

The primary Christian concern in the transcendence of death was the forensic continuity of the human person. Responsibility for past actions determined the status of the person in the next world. A successful passage through death depended on a clear conscience. In order to successfully transcend death, Christians had to be saved from sin and redeemed from the punishments of hell. All these forensic considerations defined human persons in terms of their continuous moral responsibility for actions.

Nevertheless, a concern for the cognitive continuity of the human person also appeared in Christian reflections about the pains of hell and the pleasures of heaven. Pain and pleasure were forms of conscious awareness. Although the fires of hell might not be physical, they could still be expected to produce an intense awareness of pain in the surviving consciousness. Likewise, the pleasures of heaven were not physical. They involved some higher level of conscious awareness and enjoyment than ordinary human awareness. Dante was consistent with a long tradition of Christian thought about heaven when he described the highest form of conscious awareness and enjoyment after death as the vision of God.

In the Christian New Testament, Paul had described the state of human consciousness in the world as "seeing in a glass darkly." While living in the world, human beings knew the truth in distorted reflections, but after death, Paul promised, Christians would see "face to face" (1 Cor. 13:12). As early as the second century, the theologian Irenaeus proposed that Christians would behold God face to face in the heaven that awaited them after death. Christians "shall see God, that they may live, being made immortal by that sight" (Irenaeus, 1969: 489). The life of heaven was imagined to be sustained by a transcendent vision of God that made the dead immortal. To see God was to be in some sense like God, immortal in the heaven beyond death. In the relationship between seer and seen, Christians could anticipate their closest approximation to divinity after death.

By the time of Dante, Thomas Aquinas had defined this vision of God as a purely intellectual knowledge. In the heavenly vision of God, the potential of the human intellect for knowledge was completely fulfilled. Seeing God also meant that the human intellect in heaven would be able to see like God. The intellect would know everything. It was expected to share God's knowledge by knowing all things simultaneously from the vantage point of eternity. Although divine knowledge could be attained all at once, that vision of God also was imagined to continue for eternity.

The human intellect in heaven attained its highest state of consciousness in the perpetual wonder of the vision of God. Aquinas promised that the intellect would never become bored with that vision because "nothing that is contemplated with wonder can be tiresome, since as long as the thing remains in wonder it continues to stimulate desire" (Aquinas, 1956: 205). As the supreme pleasure of heaven, the vision of God remained a desirable knowledge that would satisfy the intellect throughout eternity. As we have seen, Dante also described the vision of God as a merger of knowledge and desire in the soul's highest state of consciousness in heaven.

Throughout the Christian mystical tradition, the vision of God was an experience to which mystics aspired in this lifetime. After death, however, the vision of God was promised to all Christians as their highest fulfillment. A modern summary of Catholic teachings on the subject described the vision of God as an afterlife union between the human mind and God. God would be seen not as something outside but as a divine reality within the mind: "God will not remain outside us. He will be within our mind itself, and there we shall see him" (Arendzen, 1956: II:1253–54). Like self-knowledge in this life, the vision of God in heaven was expected to be achieved by looking within. Since God would be alive in the surviving soul, the afterlife vision of God could be achieved only by looking into the essence of the soul and seeing the presence of God. In that sense, the transformation of consciousness after death promised a heavenly union with God through divine knowledge.

Great diversity may be found in Christian expectations about heaven. Heaven might remain a vague, unspecified hope, or its dimensions might be specified in precise details such as pearly gates and streets of gold, but heaven has been under constant reinterpretation in the Christian tradition. In recent Catholic thought, for example, the theologian Karl Rahner created considerable controversy by introducing an innovative reinterpretation of heaven that suggested it was not a place but every place. When the soul departed the body at death, it ceased to be tied to a particular location as it had been when it was in a body. Instead, the soul survived death to become "pancosmic," open to the entire universe of which its body had been only one part.

"Since the soul is united to the body," Rahner argued, "it clearly must also have some relationship to that whole of which the body is a part, that is, to the totality which constitutes the unity of the material universe" (1961: 18). In death the soul's relationship to the whole material universe was perfected, "becoming a fully open, pancosmic relationship, no longer mediated by the individual body" (1961: 23–24). Although it might be hard to tell what such a pancosmic existence would be like, Rahner's reinterpretation of Christian life after death certainly departed from more conventional notions of heaven as a particular otherworldly place of afterlife reward.

In the twentieth century, Christian theologies of death and afterlife displayed a significant shift in their interpretation of the vision of God. Rather than promising Christians that they would see God, some theologians argued that the only afterlife Christians could expect would be the vision of God in which God saw them. From this perspective, souls survived death only to the extent that God remembered them. The Spanish Catholic Miguel de Unamuno suggested that human beings survived death as ideas in the divine mind. "If there is a Universal and Supreme Consciousness, I am an idea in it; and is it possible for any idea in this Supreme Consciousness to be completely blotted out? After I have died, God will go on remembering me, and to be remembered by God, to have my consciousness sustained by the Supreme Consciousness, is not that, perhaps, to be?" (1954: 149). Life after death, therefore, consisted in having one's life on earth remembered by God.

Although this line of thought was not pursued by Catholics, a few significant Protestant theologians developed it in the twentieth century. Paul Tillich argued that human beings survived death by remaining in the eternal memory of God. In God's perfection, however, only the good was retained in memory. Therefore, heaven might be understood as God's perfect memory of the goodness of his creation (Tillich, 1963: III:394–414). Similarly, Charles Hartshorne concluded that human immortality could mean only that when human beings died they would be eternally remembered by God. Just as cultural transcendence of death kept alive a person's memory in the hearts and minds of the living, Hartshorne's definition of immortality depended on the memory of God. "The true immortality," Hartshorne insisted, "is everlasting fame before God" (1962: 259). Human beings might not achieve personal immortality after death, but their lives would continue to be remembered by God. "In this sense," Hartshorne concluded, "we can interpret 'heaven' as the conception which God forms of our actual living" (1962: 258).

The argument that human beings survived death only by continuing in the memory of God has been criticized by other Protestant theologians (Hick, 1976: 213–27). Under the pressures of modern materialist philosophy, this position demonstrated a significant reversal in the traditional doctrine of the vision of God: Heaven was not the soul's vision of God; rather, it was God's eternal vision of the soul.

THE DIVINE COMEDY

In poetic form, Dante focused Christian concerns about death and afterlife. As we noted, he claimed to have had a practical objective in writing *The Divine Comedy:* to remove the living from their misery and to bring them to a state of happiness. By directing his readers away from the misery of sin, Dante exhorted them to ascend to the eternal happiness of salvation. As did medieval sermons, Dante used the vivid imagery of punishment in hell both to terrify and to instruct. Hell's most horrible aspect, however, was its utter hopelessness. Abandoning all hope, souls in hell entered an eternity of separation from God. Souls in purgatory also suffered, but their torments were made bearable by the hope of salvation. That hope would ultimately be fulfilled in the music, light, and love of heaven. Imaginatively ascending with Dante to the supreme vision of God, readers might also share the hope of salvation after death.

Dante brought his readers to the hope of salvation, but he also conducted them through an imaginary rehearsal for death. By descending to the depths of hell and ascending to the highest heaven, readers could imaginatively traverse the entire Christian afterlife universe in ways they could not expect to after their own deaths. In Dante's purgatory, Christian readers could rehearse their own repentance and purgation for sins. Because the most important factor in determining a person's destiny in the afterlife was the status of his or her moral conscience at the time of death, Dante's visionary tour of purgatory provided an opportunity to rehearse and to prepare for the purification of moral conscience that would be required for a successful passage through death.

By depicting the moral structure of the afterlife, Dante outlined the context for a transcendence of death in keeping with the concerns of the Christian tradition. In conclusion, we can briefly summarize some of those basic concerns in a Christian transcendence of death.

1. The primary emphasis was on conscience. As in most forms of Jewish, Christian, and Muslim transcendence, *The Divine Comedy* focused on the status of the moral conscience of the person making the transition through death. The balance in ancient Egypt had revealed the status of the person's heart, the bridge in ancient Persia had disclosed the status of a person's inner character, the book in ancient Israel had read out the status of a person's moral deeds—all these myths of judgment shared a common preoccupation with the moral conscience as the primary requirement for a successful passage through death. Death was symbolized not as a change in consciousness but as a test of conscience. Likewise, Dante followed this concern with conscience in his depiction of Christian death and afterlife. The destiny of the soul was determined by the status of its moral conscience. During life, ritual penance may have prepared that conscience for death by absolving it of sins. But life after death was an ongoing drama of penance and purification, as most Christians could expect to endure suffering in purgatory until their consciences were cleansed and their souls could ascend to heaven. Life and death, therefore, were symbolized as tests for the human conscience.

2. The physical body was valued. Because the fate of the soul was determined primarily by a person's moral character formed in a single lifetime, life in the physical body was valued as the primary testing ground for the soul. In addition, however, Christians assumed from a number of different perspectives that a body was an essential ingredient in personal identity. Early Christians had inherited the Hebraic assumption that a person was a mixture of breath and body. Later, Christians influenced by the philosophy of Aristotle held that a body was necessary for personal identity because the soul was the form of the body rather than something that could exist forever independent of a body. The doctrine of resurrection anticipated a reunion with the same physical body a person had occupied during a single lifetime. That body might have been expected to be glorified, transfigured, or spiritualized, but it would be the same recognizable form that the person had animated during life.

Like the Tibetan Buddhists, Dante imagined that the person survived during the interim period after death in a projected body. The Buddhists imagined a body projected by consciousness, whereas Dante pictured a body projected by the formative power of the surviving soul. A more important difference, of course, was the length of the interim: forty-nine days until consciousness entered a different body for the Buddhists and an indefinite period of waiting until the soul rejoined its body in the resurrection for the Christians. That projected body in hell, purgatory, or heaven could experience pain or pleasure, but it was only a temporary arrangement. As Thomas Aquinas had insisted, it was an unnatural state that could not last forever. In the end, the soul would be reunited with its resurrected body to recompose the natural union of soul and body that was thought to constitute a living person. In that glorified condition after the resurrection, the full value of the human body was expected to be realized.

3. Emotions blocked the ultimate transcendence of death. In Dante's vision of the moral architecture of the otherworld, the deadly sins that alienated the soul from God were not usually described as specific actions, such as stealing, lying, cheating, and so on; rather, they were emotions that blocked the progress of the soul because they led away from God. The seven deadly sins—pride, envy, anger, sloth, greed, gluttony, and lust— were basic forms of human desire. During the Middle Ages they were called *deadly* sins because they were usually assumed to be punished in hell. Dante, however, placed their punishment in purgatory in order to demonstrate his Christian logic of desire. These seven sins were misdirected desire. Unlike the Buddhists, Dante argued not for the elimination of desire but for the redirection of desire. Misdirected love was perverted desire, but love might be converted and directed toward its true object, God. A successful Buddhist passage through death required the extinction of desire, but a successful Christian death depended on the direction of emotion, love, and desire toward God.

4. The moral dimension in the symbolism of death was represented by the symbolism of judgment. In the Buddhist case, karma provided a continuous, ongoing mechanism of cause and effect that exacted the moral consequences of every person's past actions. In the Christian tradition, however, those consequences were paid only as a result of the judgment of the dead. By the time of Dante, the soul's judgment at the moment of death had become the primary determinant of its afterlife destiny. The dying's deeds had all been recorded in the book of life, and judgment was exacted accordingly. Unlike the continuous cause-and-effect process of karma, judgment was an absolute, final division of the saved and the damned. After the moment of death, the fate of the soul was generally sealed. With the exception of the Catholic hope for improvement in purgatory, the soul was consigned to a condition of rewards or punishments immediately after death that would merely be confirmed at the Last Judgment. Although the wicked might certainly prosper during life, the moral symbol-

ism of divine judgment assured Christians that they would be thoroughly punished after death.

5. Punishments for past deeds were remedial only in the case of purgatory. Otherwise, punishments were retribution. Retributive punishments in hell were vivid demonstrations of God's power. Dante followed a long tradition of Christian, Jewish, and Islamic tours of hell when he had the inscription over the door of hell announce that "divine power made me." The ultimate truth of the power of God was revealed in the punishments exacted on the wicked in hell. Tibetan Buddhists regarded afterlife punishments as remedial forms of shock therapy. Revealing the truth about those punishments, the *Bardo Thödol* explained them as projections from the surviving consciousness designed to awaken it to its true nature. From the Christian perspective, however, afterlife punishments were revealed as manifestations of God's absolute power. A consciousness in hell could only awaken to an eternal torment of pain and suffering under the vindictive judgment of God. With no hope of relief, souls in hell stood in the Christian imagination as demonstrations of God's final and absolute power of retribution.

6. Afterlife places of reward and punishment were permanent. Unlike the six temporary places of rebirth in Tibetan Buddhist thought, the Christian heaven and hell had a kind of permanence. They promised to be places of reward and punishment forever and ever. Two exceptions, however, modified the permanence of Christian afterlife places. First, the Catholic purgatory provided a temporary abode for purification from which souls could expect eventual release. Second, heaven and hell might be regarded as temporary in the sense that souls remained there only until the general resurrection of the dead. The expected resurrection, however, was only expected to certify the afterlife judgment that had already separated the saved from the damned. After the resurrection, heaven might be transposed into a new heaven on earth, but the damned would be eternally excluded by being confined in hell. The Buddhist afterlife lokas were temporary places of rebirth that provided further opportunities for the liberation of consciousness. Christian afterlife lokas, however, sealed the afterlife salvation or damnation of the soul in places of eternal reward or punishment.

7. The symbolism of death gave shape to life. As we found in the Tibetan Buddhist case, the way in which Christians imagined death provided a basic orientation toward life. If death was symbolized as God's last enemy, life became constant warfare against the forces of evil in preparation for that final battle against death. If death was imagined as a trial, ordeal, or contest in which the moral conscience was tested, life's priority was to prepare for that test. In Dante's world, the soul was prepared for death by a life of moral discipline. The ritual of penance trained the conscience to recognize, confess, and atone for sins in this life in order to be prepared for the passage through death.

Beyond the ritual cycle of penance, however, Dante suggested that the human soul might best prepare for death by conforming its desires to the divine will. Perverted desires directed toward the world had to be converted into desire for God during life in order for the soul to successfully pass through death. Life's priority, therefore, was the redirection of desire demanded by the Christian symbolism of death. If heaven was the attunement of the human heart to the "love that moves the sun and other stars," life might be lived in the present in a similar harmony. In that respect, the shape of life might approximate heaven while still on earth.

Chapter Six: References

Aquinas, Thomas. (1929). *Summa Contra Gentiles*. New York: Benziger Brothers.

———. (1956). *On the Truth of the Catholic Faith*. Trans. Vernon J. Bourke. New York: Image Books.

———. (1968). *Summa Theologiae*. New York: McGraw-Hill.

Arendzen, J. P. (1956). *The Teachings of the Catholic Church*. 2 vols. New York: Macmillan.

Ariès, Philippe. (1974). *Western Attitudes Toward Death: From the Middle Ages to the Present*. Trans. Patricia M. Ranum. Baltimore: The Johns Hopkins University Press.

Armour, Peter. (1983). *The Door of Purgatory: A Study of Multiple Symbolism in Dante's Purgatorio*. Oxford: Clarendon Press.

Asín Palacios, D. Miguel. (1926). *Islam and the Divine Comedy*. Trans. Harold Sunderland. London: John Murray.

Auerbach, Erich. (1961). *Dante: Poet of the Secular World*. Trans. Ralph Manheim. Chicago: University of Chicago Press (orig. ed. 1929).

Becker, Ernest Julius. (1899). *A Contribution to the Comparative Study of the Medieval Visions of Heaven and Hell with Special Reference to the Middle English Versions*. Baltimore: J. Murphy.

Bernstein, Alan E. (1993). *The Formation of Hell: Death and Retribution in the Ancient and Early Christian Worlds*. London: UCL Press.

Bloomfield, Morton. (1967). *The Seven Deadly Sins: An Introduction to the History of a Religious Concept, with Special Reference to Medieval English Literature*. East Lansing: Michigan State University Press.

Boase, T. S. R. (1972). *Death in the Middle Ages*. London: Thames and Hudson.

Boyde, Patrick. (1981). *Dante Philomythes and Philosopher: Man in the Cosmos*. Cambridge: Cambridge University Press.

Brandon, S. G. F. (1967). *The Judgment of the Dead: A Historical and Comparative Study of the Idea of a Post-Mortem Judgment in the Major Religions*. London: Weidenfeld and Nicolson.

Camporesi, Piero. (1991). *The Fear of Hell: Images of Damnation and Salvation in Early Modern Europe*. Oxford: Polity Press.

Carroll, John S. (1971). *Exiles of Eternity: An Exposition of Dante's Inferno*. Port Washington, N.Y.: Kennikat Press (orig. ed. 1904).

Cavendish, Richard. (1977). *Visions of Heaven and Hell*. New York: Harmony Books.

Culianu, Ioan Petru. (1983). *Psychanodia I: A Survey of the Evidence Concerning the Ascension of the Soul and Its Relevance*. Leiden: E. J. Brill.

Dickinson, Patric (trans.). (1961). *The Aeneid*. New York: New American Library.

DuBruck, Edelgard, and Barbara J. Cusick (eds.). (1999). *Death and Dying in the Middle Ages*. New York: Peter Lang.

Fergusson, Francis. (1953). *Dante's Drama of the Mind: A Modern Reading of the Purgatorio*. Princeton, N.J.: Princeton University Press.

———. (1966). *Dante*. New York: Collier.

Hartshorne, Charles. (1962). *The Logic of Perfection*. Lasalle, Ill.: Open Court.

Hick, John. (1976). *Death and Eternal Life*. San Francisco: Harper & Row.

Himmelfarb, Martha. (1983). *Tours of Hell: An Apocalyptic Form in Jewish and Christian Literature*. Philadelphia: Fortress Press.

Irenaeus. (1969). *Against Heresies*. In Alexander Roberts and James Donaldson (eds.), *Ante-Nicene Fathers*. Vol. 1. Grand Rapids, Mich.: Eerdmans.

Kohler, Kaufmann. (1923). *Heaven and Hell in Comparative Religion, with Special Reference to Dante's Divine Comedy*. New York: Macmillan.

Lang, Bernhard. (1987). "The Sexual Life of the Saints: Towards an Anthropology of Christian Heaven." *Religion* 17: 149–71.

Latham, Charles Sterrett (trans.). (1891). *A Translation of Dante's Eleven Letters*. Boston: Houghton Mifflin.

Le Goff, Jacques. (1984). *The Birth of Purgatory*. Trans. Arthur Goldhammer. Chicago: University of Chicago Press.

McDannell, Colleen, and Bernhard Lang. (1988). *Heaven: A History*. New Haven, Conn.: Yale University Press.

Ntedika, Joseph. (1966). *L'Évolution de la doctrine du purgatoire chez Saint Augustin*. Paris: Études augustiniennes.

Panofsky, Erwin. (1964). *Tomb Sculpture*. New York: H. N. Abrams.

Patch, Howard Rollin. (1950). *The Other World According to Descriptions in Medieval Literature*. Cambridge, Mass.: Harvard University Press.

Rahner, Karl. (1961). *On the Theology of Death*. London: Burns & Oates.

Reade, W. H. V. (1969). *The Moral System of Dante's Inferno*. Port Washington, N.Y.: Kennikat Press (orig. ed. 1909).

Reeves, Margaret. (1969). *The Influence of Prophecy in the Later Middle Ages: A Study in Joachimism*. Oxford: Oxford University Press.

Russell, Jeffrey Burton. (1997). *A History of Heaven*. Princeton, N.J.: Princeton University Press.

Segal, A. F. (1977). *Two Powers in Heaven*. Leiden: E. J. Brill.

Silverstein, Theodore. (1935). *Visio Sancti Pauli: The History of the Apocalypse in Latin, Together with Nine Texts*. London: Christophers.

———. (1952). "Dante and the Legend of the Mi'rāj: The Problem of Islamic Influence on the Christian Literature of the Other World." *Journal of Near Eastern Studies* 2: 89–110, 187–97.

Simon, Ulrich. (1958). *Heaven in the Christian Tradition*. London: Rockliff.

Sinclair, John D. (ed. and trans.). (1961). *The Divine Comedy of Dante Alighieri*. 3 vols. London: Oxford University Press.

Terpening, Ronnie H. (1985). *Charon and the Crossing: Ancient, Medieval, and Renaissance Transformations of a Myth*. Lewisburg, Pa.: Bucknell University Press.

Tillich, Paul. (1963). *Systematic Theology*. 3 vols. Chicago: University of Chicago Press.

Toynbee, Paget (ed. and trans.). (1966). *Dantis Alagherii Epistolae*. 2nd ed. Oxford: Oxford University Press.

Unamuno, Miguel de. (1954). *The Tragic Sense of Life*. Trans. J. E. C. Flitch. New York: Dover (orig. ed. 1913).

Walker, D. P. (1964). *The Decline of Hell: Seventeenth-Century Discussions of Eternal Torment*. Chicago: University of Chicago Press.

Zaleski, Carol. (1987). *Otherworld Journeys: Accounts of Near-Death Experience in Medieval and Modern Times*. Oxford: Oxford University Press.

7

Living Transcendence

In the mid-twentieth century, British author Geoffrey Gorer observed that death had become a forbidden subject in modern societies. What sex had been to the Victorians, death had become for people in the modern West—a topic that had to be hidden from view, excluded from conversation, and purged from public awareness. Death was the new pornography. Dying was a dirty business. If death and dying were ignored, perhaps they would go away. Even if death refused to take a holiday, however, at least people could participate in the mutually supported pretense that death was not part of personal and social life. Reinforced by modern medical and funeral institutions, human beings in modern Western societies could pretend that death was not a basic fact of life (Gorer, 1965: 169–75).

More recently, David Wendell Moller reinforced this assumption that modern relations with the process of dying and the fact of death have been based on a fundamental denial. "The traditional orientation to death with its essential patterns of religion, ritual and community," according to Moller, "has been replaced by the denial, confusion, contradiction, and meaninglessness of the modern styles of death and dying" (Moller, 1996: 22).

These judgments have tried to establish a stark contrast between a traditional acceptance and a modern denial of death. Certainly, relations between acceptance and denial are much more complicated than these historical judgments might suggest. From a psychological perspective, as Robert Jay Lifton argued, any denial of death is not merely denial since it involves ways of thinking and acting that inevitably acknowledge the reality of death even in the midst of denial.

At the same time, from a sociological perspective, the attempt to construct a historical divide between traditional and modern ways of relating to death ignores an important feature of modernization. Although people reportedly have maintained traditional beliefs in God, death, and afterlife in the modern world,

they have had difficulty in locating those traditional beliefs within modern social arrangements (Walter, 1996). On both psychological and sociological
grounds, therefore, it is difficult to support the simple historical opposition between traditional and modern religious engagements with death.

From a variety of religious perspectives, the preceding chapters of this book
have concentrated on religious ways of thinking and acting about one's own
death. In this chapter, the focus shifts to the living, to the thoughts and feelings, the rituals and memorials, of the survivors who remain in the world of the
living to deal with the loss of beloved relatives and friends. As the historian
Philippe Ariès argued, this attention to the death of others is itself a modern development, signaling a dramatic shift in European thinking about death during
the nineteenth century (Ariès, 1974: 56). In the history of religions, however,
many ways have been found to regard the death of others. Both traditional and
modern, religious relations with the death of others have been at the heart of a
living transcendence of death.

GRIEVING

In the history of religions, rituals for the dead, such as the ancestral rituals of
indigenous religions, the twelve-day *śrāddha* rites of Hindu tradition, or the
yearlong mourning observances in Jewish tradition, are obviously not only performed for the dead. They are also important rituals for the living. As a crucial
part of the religious life of a household, these rituals reaffirm the integrity of
family and kinship relations. For participants, these rituals provide practical avenues for expressing powerful emotions of grief, pain, and anger. Many analysts
have argued that the formalized expression of intense emotion in these rituals
can be therapeutic (Imber-Black, 1991; Jacobs, 1992). While providing occasions for displaying the personal effects of loss, these rituals also reaffirm continuing personal, kinship, and social bonds between the living and the dead
(Klass et al., 1996). By affirming unbroken connections linking ancestors and
offspring, rituals of mourning enact an ancestral transcendence of death.

Traditionally, religion has shaped the experience of grief, its socially legitimate forms of expression in bereavement, and the formalized processes of
mourning. In the embodied language of emotion, grief can take many forms.
As an intense emotional encounter with loss, the experience of grief can range
from sorrow and sadness to pain and anger. Grief can appear in colors, as fiery
red or freezing blue, for example, producing blindness or insight. It can regis-
ter as a solid obstacle that blocks everything or as a fluid, dizzying, and disori-
enting sense of being dissolved into nothing. Encompassing an extraordinarily
wide range of emotional experience, grief finds many expressions, from chok-
ing off all communication into silence to bursting the bounds of language in
anguished sound.

Anthropologist Clifford Geertz has observed that emotions, like everything
else in human experience, are "cultural artifacts" (1972; Corrigan et al., 2000).
In response to death, cultural styles of bereavement organize the experience
of grief. According to ethnographic reports, the indigenous Ilongot living in
the highlands of the Philippines experienced an intense grief at the loss of a

member of their community that took the form of anger. As anthropologist Renate Rosaldo reported, an Ilongot man's "rage, born of grief, impels him to kill his fellow human beings." By taking revenge on enemies, the Ilongot warrior was able "to vent and throw away the anger of his bereavement" (Rosaldo, 1993: 1).

By contrast, indigenous people on the Pacific island of Ifaluk reportedly responded to the death of a loved one not in anger but in profound sadness, experiencing an emotional state more like deep depression than like vengeful fury. In the loneliness of that feeling of sadness, immersed in the emotional state of *lalomweiu,* a person was thoroughly and completely absorbed in thoughts and feelings about the missing person. As a result, grieving islanders neglected social duties to the living. They did not pay attention to others, for example, when they spoke. Nevertheless, even while they were disrupting the normal order of social recognition and exchanges, people in grief could rely on a common understanding that their sadness was an expression of *fago,* a blend of sadness, love, and compassion (Irish et al., 1997; Lutz, 1985; Rosenblatt et al., 1976).

In the experience of grief, people seek to establish a common understanding, whether that understanding is expressed in anger and pain or sadness and silence. Although any grieving person might feel lost and alone, desolate and abandoned, the emotional life of grief is inevitably embedded in social, cultural, and religious connections. For the living, the pain and sadness of grief can be crucial ingredients in maintaining connections with the dead.

Grief, Bereavement, and Mourning

Among the indigenous Toraja villagers living on one of the islands of Indonesia, complex religious issues were at stake in feelings of grief. Generally, the villagers tried to maintain an emotional balance. They believed that any intense feelings of personal sorrow risked the harmony of the family and the community. Accordingly, they tried to avoid getting into an overheated emotional state, trying not to become either frenzied or choked by the heat of strong feelings. Such an overheated condition was dangerous since it could cause the displeasure of ancestors and other spirits, who upheld the harmony of the world, and might result in illness, misfortune, or even death. To avoid the risk of displeasing the ancestors and spirits, Toraja villagers developed strategies for cooling their emotions. Reminding themselves of the dangers involved in strong emotions, they consciously suppressed certain thoughts. In relation to friends or relatives experiencing strong emotions, they spoke quietly, politely, and respectfully in an effort to avoid upsetting the person (Hollan, 1992; Hollan and Wellenkamp, 1994; Wellenkamp, 1988).

At the same time, socially permitted forms of bereavement allowed for the expression of intense emotion during the limited time of the funeral and place of the burial. Within this ritual context, emotional displays of grief, through sobbing, shaking, and calling out to the dead, were not only permitted but were actually desired as an appropriate response to death. Ritualized bereavement, therefore, provided a religious channel for strong emotions of grief, sorrow, and loss that might otherwise destroy the community. For individuals, families, and the larger society, socially sanctioned forms of bereavement represented an emotional catharsis that purged strong, hot feelings that threatened the harmony among the living and between the living and the dead. After the prescribed period of mourning, however, people were expected to return to a state of equilibrium and go on with their lives.

Human beings, of course, do not always do what they are supposed to do. When his wife died, a Toraja villager, Ambe' na Doko, suffered intense and prolonged grief. Overwhelmed by sorrow at the loss of his beloved partner, he underwent extreme disorientation. "My feelings are like a crazy person," he said. "My head isn't thinking in a fixed way. My heart is very full" (Wellenkamp, 1991: 127). In the relations between head and heart, his heart had overwhelmed his thinking, not only making him feel crazy but also making him violate Toraja cultural standards of emotional balance.

After the prescribed period of mourning, Ambe' na Doko continued to grieve for his wife. Wanting him to continue with his life, neighbors who came to visit encouraged him to remarry. Preoccupied with his wife's death, however, Ambe' na Doko refused to consider any prospect of marrying again. In his grief, his wife's absence had left a presence in his life. "I think within my heart, I imagine in my eyes or in my heart," he said, "that my wife is probably within the house" (Wellenkamp, 1991: 132; Rosenblatt, 1997).

Although he did not fit into Toraja cultural expectations, Ambe' na Doko nevertheless demonstrated important features of grieving. The intensity of emotion that he described as a full, crazy heart suggests that grief is an overwhelmingly powerful emotion that does not easily conform to religious management or control. As we have seen in *The Tibetan Book of the Dead* and *The Divine Comedy,* both Buddhists and Christians could regard emotions as obstacles to a successful transition through death. In both religious traditions, human emotions of anger, pride, greed, and so on prevented people from realizing their full human potential in the face of death. Generally, the unpredictability and instability of emotions have presented problems for religious discipline. In the case of the intense feelings experienced at the loss of a loved one, survivors might draw comfort from religion, but they also might come into conflict with the requirements of religious disciplines.

Like the indigenous people of Toraja, the Hindu tradition has regarded grief a hot emotion that needs to be cooled. Classified as the hot, fiery energy of *rajas* rather than as the tranquility of *sattva* or the solidity of *tamas,* grief registers in this traditional Hindu system of classification as an unstable emotional state that needs to be transformed. In other cases, as in Orthodox Jewish mourning, grief might be regarded as a cold feeling that needs to be comforted but also as a warm feeling that needs to be cultivated at regular intervals in memory of the deceased. In a variety of ways, religious rituals provide means for transforming, channeling, and managing emotions. In response to death, socially legitimated forms of emotional expression take the form of bereavement.

Although grief is a personal emotion, bereavement, by definition, is a socially legitimate avenue for expressing feelings of loss, sorrow, or anger in the grieving process. Religious styles of bereavement, of course, vary in their determination of what is socially acceptable. Even in one religion, styles of bereavement can diverge. In the world of Islam, for example, the same religion can provide the framework for different cultural styles of bereavement. As anthropologist Unni Wikan (1988) has documented, Muslims in Egypt observed long periods of grieving. An Egyptian mother, grieving the loss of her child by spending seven years in the depths of depression, was observing acceptable standards of bereavement.

By contrast, Muslims in Bali, although they shed tears, seemed to express joy and even laugh at death during bereavement. In this regard, a Balinese mother, displaying a lighthearted acceptance of the death of her child, was also observing the standards of bereavement in her cultural context. Although both mothers were Muslims, they nevertheless displayed different cultural styles in dealing with grief within socially accepted forms of bereavement (Wikan, 1988, 1990).

In channeling emotions of grief, cultural styles of bereavement are crucial resources for religion. As the contrast between Muslims in Egypt and Bali suggests, styles of bereavement might vary by geography. But they can also vary by social class and gender. Islamic tradition has supported two classic reactions to loss. On the one hand, the tradition has allowed for an intense display of emotions, with crying, breast beating, scratching of the face, and other dramatic expressions of emotional torment. As these expressions of grief escalate, they can be shaped into song, a prolonged dirge that merges crying, singing, and poetry in recalling the departed. In these songs of grief, the singers recall details of the deceased's life, the cause of death, and the agony of dealing with the loss.

On the other hand, Muslim tradition has encouraged emotional restraint, supporting the survivors in letting go of the dead, separating their lives from the deceased, so that the dead can go to their reward and the living can go on living. In counterpoint to the songs of death, Muslims can recite the sacred text of the Qur'ān, reading selected passages not only for themselves but also for the departed, a calm, quiet, but also powerful engagement with the dead.

Although it is impossible to generalize, women have generally assumed responsibility for crying and men have taken responsibility for reciting the sacred text (Abu Lughod, 1993). In theological controversy, some Muslim scholars, preferring the calm, quiet control of reciting the Qur'ān, have argued that crying holds the dead back from their journey into paradise. In practice, however, people have found a variety of religious ways of moving between the intense expression and quiet restraint in Islam.

In a Lebanese village, while a professional male singer performed with quiet dignity for the men outside the house, the women inside cried and clapped to the song of grief composed by the mother. In the city of Cairo, a family erected a large tent in the middle of the street, inviting neighbors to support their grief, but they also set up amplifiers to broadcast a recitation of the Qur'ān so that people all over the neighborhood could also benefit.

Encompassing both personal emotions of grief and social styles of bereavement, religious rituals of mourning represent ways of timing and placing the living in relation to the dead. In the case of the Toraja, religious rituals of mourning defined the period of time in which the living could grieve and the place that the deceased would occupy in the spiritual world. As Ambe' na Doko found, however, things are not always so simple. While he continued to grieve the death of his wife beyond the prescribed period of mourning, he also defied the prescribed spatial separation of the living and the dead by locating his wife not in the spirit world but in the home that they had shared.

In Muslim rituals of mourning, the counterpoint of disciplined restraint and intense expression of emotion has often been evident at funerals. On some occasions, mourners have refrained from touching the body, maintaining a discipline of quiet dignity but also observing standards of ritual purity, for example, that required keeping tears from falling on the corpse for fear of defiling the body of the deceased. On other occasions, mourners have touched the body, kissing the face and lips and holding on to physical contact, but have gradually come under control.

· At many Muslim funerals, however, intense expression and dignified restraint of emotions have been integrated. The integration of intensity and restraint, however, has often depended on a gendered division of ritual labor. In saying farewell to the deceased, the loud crying and singing by women has often been performed in counterpoint to the restraint of men. At a turning point in the ritual, women withdrew from the room, leaving men to form three rows facing the body of the deceased. As the religious leader, the Imam asked, "Was this a good person?" all the men answered, "Good." By reciting the prayer for the dead, which consisted of four praises of God, each punctuated by the men declaring, "*Allahu akbar*" ("God is great"), the goodness of the deceased was certified.

Within the process of mourning, however, the funeral is not the end but only the beginning for the living. The funeral marks the beginning of a defined period of mourning for the survivors, a period in which they are also called to express and discipline their emotions. As that process develops, a gendered division of labor might also be observed. In Muslim tradition, for example, women have been responsible for maintaining the appropriate styles of clothing, food, and other considerations during the time of mourning. Women have assumed responsibility for preparing special food for the third, the seventh, and the fortieth day after the funeral. On the fortieth day, as the story of the prophet's birth is read aloud, men take primary responsibility, but both men and women join in shedding tears, consoling each other, comforted in many cases by the belief that the deceased has returned to the world of the living on that day to listen to the recitation (Jonker, 1997).

Although feelings of grief may very well be private, operating in an intimately personal world of emotions, religious rituals transform private feelings into public performances. According to many cultural analysts, that transformation is potentially therapeutic. In transcribing and interpreting the mourning songs of the Yolmo Sherpas of Tibet, for example, one commentator observed that the ritualized performance of songs of death was healing. In singing these songs of loss, sorrow, and grief, "wounds are exposed and hearts are cleansed." As in African-American spirituals or the "Delta Blues, pain is affirmed" (Desjarlais, 1991: 405; 1993). In the process of affirming pain, however, human solidarity is also affirmed, the solidarity of family, kinship, and community. Unbroken by death, the continuing bonds of the living with the dead are affirmed in and through the pain (Hagman, 1995; Stroebe et al., 1992, 1993).

Modern Management

In modern societies, expressions of grief, the cultural styles of bereavement, and the rituals of mourning have been shaped by a funeral industry that has assumed global proportions. Regardless of beliefs about death and afterlife, modern funerals tended to include four basic elements: the rapid removal of the corpse to a funeral parlor, the embalming of the corpse, the viewing of the restored body, and the final disposition of the corpse by earth burial. Although cremation has also been a method of disposition, it has been a small but growing option in modern funerals (Prothero, 2000). Professional specialists in the funeral industry have supervised and conducted these rituals. Although individuals had little control over the process or choice in the methods, the American public often indicated in surveys and opinion polls that they were satisfied with the basic format of modern funerals.

Although many people have assumed that these funeral rituals were a long-standing tradition, modern funeral practices were a recent development that resulted largely from the emergence of a professional funeral industry at the beginning of the twentieth century. During the nineteenth century in the United States, funerals were simple and relatively inexpensive. The funeral was a ceremony conducted by family and friends. They washed and dressed the corpse, preserved it on ice, placed it in a simple pine coffin, and carried it to the graveyard. Professionals involved in the funeral ritual might include a carpenter to make the coffin, the sexton who guarded the graveyard, and a minister or priest who performed any religious service at the burial.

Originally, the undertaker's primary skill was carpentry. When cemeteries came to be located at a distance from town, undertakers also provided horses and carriages to transport the body. By the twentieth century, however, undertakers had become funeral directors (Pine, 1975).

The first stage of almost all modern funerals was the rapid removal of the corpse from the place of death in order to transfer it to a professional funeral parlor. Instead of the simple nineteenth-century washing, dressing, and preserving of the corpse on ice, funeral parlors offered over sixty-five different services in the preparation and disposal of the corpse. The primary service was the embalming and restoration of the deceased's body. Funeral specialists embalmed the corpse by removing the blood and injecting the body with a fluid mixed from formaldehyde, glycerin, borax, phenol, alcohol, water, and perfume. Embalming was originally performed in America on the corpses of soldiers killed during the Civil War so they could be transported home over long distances. The practice was popularized when the corpse of Abraham Lincoln was embalmed and taken on a national tour to be viewed all over the United States (Laderman, 1996). Although not required by law, embalming became a standard practice of funeral directors in the twentieth century.

Embalming methods did not produce a permanent mummification of the body as practiced in ancient Egypt. Rather, the embalmed body was disinfected and temporarily preserved so that it could be handled by funeral specialists and viewed by mourners during the interim period before burial. The first reason for embalming was hygiene because hygiene and sanitation had come to dominate the modern way of life. The embalmed body was disinfected so it would not present a health risk for morticians or mourners.

The second reason for embalming was preservation of the body so it could be prepared for display. After the corpse was embalmed, it was restored to a semblance of life through funeral arts of cosmetics and costume. Funeral cosmetics, including such products as "Nature-Glo" makeup and "Lyf-Lyk" tint, created the illusion of beautiful life in death. Facial features were also arranged in an image of life. For example, the lips were parted, as if the deceased were still breathing, with the upper lip slightly protruding to give a more youthful appearance. All the features of the deceased were arranged to form what the funeral industry called a "memory picture" for surviving friends and relatives.

Replacing the traditional shroud, funeral costumes provided a wide variety of burial clothes for the dead. Funeral parlors advertised "handmade original fashions—styles from the best in life for the last memory—dresses, men's suits, negligees, and accessories." Even a range of burial footwear was provided. A company like Practical Burial Footware, for example, designed shoes for the dead that were advertised as both stylish and comfortable. The deceased could wear the "Fit-A-Fut Oxford" or the "Ko-Zee" with its "soft cushioned soles and warm, luxurious slipper comfort, but true shoe smartness."

Decorated and dressed, the corpse could be displayed for viewing in a casket. Instead of the simple wooden box, modern caskets became elaborate and expensive constructions for the deceased's final appearance. Funeral parlors were the showrooms for caskets. They offered a selection of metal caskets that promised almost permanent protection for the deceased in the grave. Symbolizing death as sleep, caskets were equipped with foam rubber or inner-spring mattresses. Casket companies advertised "the revolutionary Perfect-Posture Bed" and the "Beautyrama adjustable soft-foam bed" for guaranteed comfort in the deceased's eternal rest. Adding to the beauty of the deceased's final display, caskets could be lined in a choice of more than sixty different color-matched shades. The entire display sought to achieve an effect of beauty and repose for the viewing and final disposal of the corpse.

The practices of the modern funeral industry inspired occasional criticism and even ridicule (Mitford, 1963, 2000; Waugh, 1948). The restoration of the body was elaborate, expensive, and controlled by a funeral industry that had become a big business with a steady market for its services. The funeral industry defended its practices as necessary for the emotional well-being of surviving relatives and friends. The embalming, restoration, and display of the corpse provided what funeral directors called "grief therapy" for mourners. While bidding farewell to the dead, survivors could retain a beautiful and lifelike "memory picture" that would help them deal with their bereavement.

Critics of the industry, however, argued that funeral directors were more interested in capitalizing on the emotional vulnerability of clients than providing ritualized therapy for their grief. A mortuary management guide, for example, gave advice to funeral directors on selling techniques, telling them never to preconceive what products or services a grieving family might purchase because "you cannot possibly measure the intensity of their emotions, undisclosed insurance or funds that may have been set aside for funeral expenses." In this sense, a family's emotions were equated with its financial resources—both could be exploited by funeral directors to sell products and services. Placing death rituals on a business basis, the modern funeral industry seemed to many critics to be more concerned with profits than people.

Other critics argued that modern funeral practices were symptoms of a more general denial of death (Becker, 1997). Embalming, restoration, and display seemed designed to avoid all appearance of death and to simulate an illusion of life. The dead were not dead but only sleeping. Even language was controlled in modern funeral practices to avoid direct references to death. People did not die; rather, they expired, departed, or passed away. Euphemisms dominated the discourse that surrounded modern funerals: When undertakers became funeral directors or morticians, coffins became caskets, hearses became coaches, flowers became floral tributes, and corpses became loved ones. Funeral homes kept corpses in preparation rooms, reposing rooms, or slumber rooms. Finally, corpses were not buried but interred, graves were not dug and filled but opened and closed, and burials were performed not in cemeteries but in memorial parks. The entire funeral vocabulary seemed designed to avoid the fact of death.

Professional control over funerals and the ritual services of embalming, restoration, and display persisted in modern rites of death. While funeral professionals defended their value—stressing the hygiene, beauty, and therapy of their funerals—critics cited these practices as evidence of an avoidance of death. The ritual preparation of corpses was taken out of the hands of family and friends only to return the body to them disguised in illusion. Part of the appeal of these funeral practices may have been the protective buffer they placed between the living and the dead: People could avoid direct contact with corpses that had not been embalmed, restored, and costumed. Perhaps those practices also enabled people to avoid a more direct awareness and acknowledgment of death (Littlewood, 1993).

Mediating Grief

In the midst of this modern avoidance of the hard facts and harsh realities of death, the public outpouring of grief in response to the sudden, tragic death of Princess Diana in 1997 was remarkable. Although the modern funeral industry helped people avoid dealing with death in their personal lives, the death of Diana inspired an extraordinary public participation in grief, bereavement, and mourning for the "People's Princess." At Kensington Palace, mourners brought 10,000 tons of flowers and a million cards and other tokens. An estimated 2.5 billion people witnessed her funeral by television. All over the world, people were devastated by grief in response to her death.

Over the Internet, people poured out their emotions. "It absolutely breaks my heart to know the Princess is dead!" cried one correspondent from the United States. "I feel like I have lost a friend," said a person from New Zealand.

"We are utterly devastated," reported a family in Australia. "I don't know how many tears I have cried," a person confessed from Norway, "and I don't know how many tears I will cry." In assessing these widespread feelings of pain, a correspondent from Germany declared, "What a grievous loss for mankind" (Dyrud, 1997). The death of Princess Diana represented a public deluge of grief that seemed to overwhelm personal considerations. "I cried more at her death," as one mourner revealed, "than at my own father's" (Kear and Steinberg, 1999; Walter, 1999).

As many critics argued, Princess Diana was a "Media Saint," with an image that had been carefully manipulated by public relations experts (Richards et al., 1999). Nevertheless, the feelings of loss, sorrow, and pain reported by people all over the world suggest that media provide avenues for grief. From depictions of violent death to dramatizations of heartbreaking loss, entertainment media have played a formative role in shaping modern experiences of grief.

For many people, not only in America but also throughout the world, film has provided a powerful medium for imagining death and experiencing grief. In the "Disney way of death," for example, the "classic" animated films produced by the Walt Disney Company generally represented death within the context of dramatic battles between forces of good and evil. In those conflicts, death was something to be feared because it represented a tragic loss in the war against evil. By the end of any Disney movie, however, that loss marked by the evil of death had been redeemed by affirming the continuity of a family, whether that family was human, animal, or something in between (Laderman, 2000). Within this overarching myth of life against death, Disney films evoked powerful images of dying that had an impact on generations. As one commentator observed, the 1942 Disney animated film *Bambi,* which depicted the death of the young deer's mother, "is often recalled as the most memorable film of people's youth, not only for its charm and natural wonders, but because there children learned about death" (Payne, 1995: 140). In the world of movies, television, and other media, audiences have absorbed enduring images of death that often become primary reference points for the experience and expression of grief.

At the same time, people have sought avenues for expressing grief in socially sanctioned styles of bereavement and religious rituals of mourning. While expressing the emotions of the living, bereavement and mourning also provide occasions for communicating with the dead, for mediating the divide that seems to separate the dead from the living. In the case of Princess Diana, several people claimed to have received communications from beyond the grave. For example, Hazel Courteney, a former columnist on health issues for the *Sunday Times* in London, reported that she had been possessed by the spirit of Diana while shopping for croissants in Harrods department store. Based on her ongoing conversations with Princess Diana, Hazel Courteney wrote a book, *Divine Intervention,* to share Diana's spiritual wisdom about religion, ecology, and health (Courteney, 2000). Although Courteney's claims about her conversations with the deceased princess have been met with considerable skepticism, the idea of communicating with the dead is extremely common in the history of religions. When grieving has not been entirely silent, grief has sought communication with the dead.

COMMUNICATING

In a variety of ways, people communicate with the dead. Within indigenous religious life, the shaman has operated as a specialist in communicating with spirits in other worlds. But many other forms of religious practice speak with the dead. As we recall, the ancestral rituals of indigenous African religion provided ways of communicating with the deceased. Repairing the damage that had been done by the original communication breakdown, by the mixed messages that had brought death to human beings, ancestral ritual restored the lines of communication between material and spiritual worlds.

Many Asian religious practices, such as Vedic sacrifice, Buddhist afterlife guidance, and the Chinese ritual of offering spirit money for the dead, have all been accompanied by prayerful speaking across the gap separating the living and the dead. Similarly, Jewish prayers for the dead, Christian masses for the dead, and Muslim recitations of the sacred text of the Qur'ān for the dead have created communication links between worlds. For the living, participation in ritual communication with the dead represents an experiential transcendence, going beyond the limit of death in the here and now, to engage in powerful forms of conversation with the dead.

While opening up lines of communication, ritual enables the living to enter into exchanges with the dead. Offering sacred words and objects, participants can transfer support, benefit, or merit to the deceased. In the case of Chinese spirit money, that ritual exchange was symbolized by offering a symbol of monetary value as a transfer of spiritual value. The highly charged ritual speech of prayer has often been regarded as being beneficial for the dead. The purpose of Orthodox Jewish prayers for the dead, for example, has been explained as an intervention in their suffering in the other world in order "that they might be released" (2 Mac. 12:39–45). Catholic masses for the dead, whether performed for a deceased individual or for all Christian dead, have been regarded as benefiting those in purgatory by reducing the severity or duration of their suffering. In rituals of communication, exchange, and service, therefore, these religious practices keep relations between the living and the dead alive in the present.

In some cases, religious limits have been placed on communicating with the dead. Within the religion of ancient Israel, for example, any necromancer who consulted with the spirits of the dead was condemned (Deut. 18:11). As an experiential transcendence of death, however, communicating with the dead has taken many different forms in the history of religions. People speak to the dead in many ways, whether in love, in anger, or in the deep, resounding silence that spans the gulf between the living and the dead. By considering only a few examples of religious communication with the deceased, we can nevertheless gain some idea of the religious potential for entering into meaningful relationships with the dead. As illustrated in these examples of Haitian, Japanese, and Muslim religious communication with the dead, we find relations of exchange, mutual recognition, and beneficial assistance in which the living have found ways to interact creatively with the dead.

Exchanging

During the twentieth century, one of the most misunderstood forms of religious life in the world was the Haitian religion of Vodou. Drawing together aspects of African indigenous religion and Catholic Christianity, Vodou represented a dynamic New World religion. As practiced on the Caribbean island of Haiti and among Haitian Americans living in the United States, Vodou was a religious way of life devoted to communicating with the spiritual world. Although it was often stigmatized as magic or superstition, the religion of Vodou cultivated the values of family, community, and African spiritual identity by keeping open the lines of communication between the living and the dead. As an important religious development of the African diaspora, Vodou derived its name from *vodu,* a west African term meaning "spirit." For its adherents, this religion was simply called "serving the spirits."

Serving the spirits linked the concerns of the living with the resources of the spiritual world. In the account provided by Karen McCarthy Brown, the Vodou religious leader, Alourdes, "Mama Lola," was an expert in spiritual communication. Having passed through the necessary stages of initiation, Alourdes was able to serve as a vehicle for the spirits. Entering into trance, she allowed her body to be a meeting place between the living and the dead. As Alourdes described her experience of spirit possession, she felt dizzy, lightheaded, as if passing out of consciousness. She knew nothing. Suddenly entering the room, a spirit would begin addressing the people who were present. Speaking through Alourdes, the dead returned to be with the living. Talking and laughing, eating and drinking, the living and the dead participated in a spiritual exchange. Regularly, these sessions took the form of birthday parties for the spirits, celebrating the lives of the dead who were not really dead.

By communicating with the living, the spirits revealed their distinctive personalities. They also comprised an extended family that included the living. Among the spirits who communicated through Alourdes, the frequent presence of Azaka, who had been a mountain man and a peasant farmer in Haiti, reminded people of their roots. Also known as Kouzen—"Cousin"—Azaka represented the connections of kinship. While the life of a family depended on caring, sharing, and mutual reciprocity, the modern economy placed the family at risk in an environment of scarcity and competition. In that adversarial context, money was both a material problem and a symbol of spiritual potency. Acting as the "banker" for Azaka, the female country cousin, Kouzinn Zaka, handled money, addressing people's concerns about poverty. By serving the spirits of these cousins from the old country, people also dealt with their current problems with family and money, with health and well-being.

Although all the spirits linked the living with the world of the dead, one spirit, Gede, was the great authority on death. "Papa Gede," as Alourdes explained, "is a cemetery man" (Brown, 1991: 330). Gede presided over the rituals of burial and mourning for the dead. When Gede spoke, however, he displayed a raucous sense of humor, joking and laughing loudly with the people. Consistently, his humor was laced with explicit sexual references. Boasting of his sexual prowess, Gede, the "cemetery man," showed a keen interest in the world of the living. As the master of humor, sex, and death, Papa Gede encouraged people to cultivate a spirit of playfulness in relation to both life and death.

In its central religious practices, this Haitian religion of serving the spirits demonstrated a style of religious communication that was based on a spiritual exchange. Serving the spirits depended on a lively give-and-take between the living and the dead. At regular ritual occasions, the living offered food, drink, and other gifts for the spirits. These ritual offerings could be understood as a kind of spiritual work, as religious labor that was necessary to maintain the spiritual economy of both the living and the dead. Through the voice of Papa Gede, however, the living were reminded that both religious ritual and productive labor could be a kind of spiritual play. In the face of death, that spiritual playfulness promised an experience of transcendence for the living.

Apologizing

In the emotional complexity of grieving, the sadness of loss can merge with feelings of regret, remorse, or guilt. In communicating with the dead, those feelings might come into focus as an apology.

During the 1970s in Japan, a popular religious ritual developed in which women apologized to unborn children who were miscarried, stillborn, or aborted. This ritual was known as *mizuko kuyō,* which could be translated as service (*kuyō*) to the "water child" (*mizuko*). In practice, *mizuko kuyō* was a ritual performed for the unrealized, fluid signs of life of a fetus, a human potential in the waters of the womb, which might have been born as a human child (LaFleur, 1992). Drawing inspiration from traditional Buddhist services for the dead, the performance of *mizuko kuyō* was a new ritual, an innovation in religious practice that responded to changes in the economic stability of the family and the social roles of women. According to critics, religious entrepreneurs promoting the ritual capitalized on the sense of guilt that many women felt for miscarrying or aborting a fetus (Hardacre, 1997). Although traditional Buddhist temples and new religious movements benefited financially, many women apparently found the ritual of *mizuko kuyō* valuable in providing an opportunity for communicating with their unborn child.

In traditional Buddhist rituals for the dead, ancestral spirits were served with ritual speech and ritual objects. While praying, chanting, and reciting sacred texts, participants also offered money, food, flowers, and incense. Both types of offerings, the verbal and the tangible, provided nourishment, the literal meaning of *kuyo,* for the dead. In these ancestral rituals, however, the unborn fetus had no place since the unborn was not part of the human family. A miscarried, stillborn, or aborted fetus had no role in these services. Legalized in Japan since the 1940s, abortion was generally accepted. No organized religious campaigns emerged to mobilize support for its criminalization. Nevertheless, the popularity of *mizuko kuyō* suggested that many women in Japan were concerned about their relationship with their unborn fetus, perhaps experiencing the emotional distress of shame or guilt, and wanted to clarify that relationship.

Essentially, the ritual process of *mizuko kuyō* involved giving a name, a form, and a human identity to the unborn. Under the spiritual patronage of the Boddhisattva Jizo, who moves among all the six lokas extending compassion, the ceremony extended human recognition to the fetus. First, the fetus was given a name. In some cases, that name was a Buddhist death name (*hōmyō* or *kaimyō*), a ritual title that was consistent with the practice in Buddhist funeral services of bestowing a new name on adults when they passed from this world. By receiving a Buddhist death name, the fetus was recognized as having a legitimate status in the ongoing spiritual cycle of birth, death, and rebirth. Accordingly, the fetus might also have legitimate standing in Buddhist rituals for the dead. In other cases, the name was an ordinary name that might be given to any child, a name that acknowledged the fetus as a member of a human family.

Second, the fetus was given a visible, tangible form. By definition, the unborn *mizuko*—as water child, as unseen child—had no form in the world. In the ceremony of the *mizuko kuyō,* however, the fetus was provided with a form, usually a statue of Jizo, which represented the location of the unborn in the world. Ranging from a three-inch figure made out of cloth to a four-foot figure carved in stone, these images of Jizo gave the fetus a material reality. The statues represented a crucial meeting point for parents, the unborn, and their spiritual protector, the compassionate Boddhisattava, Jizo. Long after the ceremony, women returned to that site to communicate with the unborn.

Finally, giving a name and form to the fetus enabled communication. The ritual involved prayers and petitions to Jizo to protect the *mizuko,* but it also encouraged speeches that addressed the fetus directly. When addressing the fetus, the predominant style of communication with the unborn was apology. For many women, feelings of loss were mixed with regret, remorse, or guilt. By extending a formal apology to the unborn, they worked to come to peace with those feelings. At the same time, many participants in the ceremony believed that the unborn were angry, vengeful ghosts who could cause illness, misfortune, and suffering among the living. They needed to be assuaged by being brought into the circle of human recognition. Asking for forgiveness, therefore, was a powerful form of religious communication with the dead. While easing personal feelings of guilt, the apology formally extended human recognition to the unborn as an equal, worthy of respect, to any other human being. According to promoters of the ritual, the unborn heard and responded to this apology. "Taking the hand of the gentle Jizo," as one woman reported, "they can clearly hear their mother's voice" (Harrison, 1995: 79). In this Japanese ritual of religious communication with the dead, therefore, an apology represented healing for both the living and the unborn.

Teaching

In other religious contexts, communication with the dead has focused on giving instruction. If life can be regarded as an educational process, religious traditions have found ways of teaching that are based on the assumption that education does not stop at death. As we recall, the Tibetan Buddhist religious teacher, relying on the map of the *Bardo Thödol,* was able to instruct people about the journey through the afterlife not only by teaching them while they were alive but also by reading the text into their ears after death. In many other religious traditions, teaching the deceased is an important feature of the ongoing communication between the living and the dead.

Muslim tradition, for example, has supported a range of practices of communicating with the dead intended to expand the wisdom of the deceased. At the graveside, family members have read passages from the Qur'ān over the grave. Following the teachings of the prophet Muḥammad, one chapter from the sacred text has often been singled out as the preferred reading for the dead, the chapter titled *Ya Seen* (Surah 36), which the prophet identified as "the heart of the Qur'ān," the heart of forgiveness, with its celebration of the glory of God and its promise that all believers will be brought back to God. "Read it over your dying and deceased," the prophet advised. But reading any passage from the Holy Qur'ān over the grave has been valued as an important communication with the dead. As many Muslim authorities have held, a dead person in the grave hears the words of the living. Although the deceased might also be aware of many other sounds from the world above, the afterlife sense of hearing of the dead should be focused on the redemptive words of the Holy Qur'ān.

While comforting the living, the recitation of the Qur'ān has also been regarded as providing assistance for the dead. Reading the Qur'ān over the grave, as many Muslim authorities have argued, benefits the dead in two ways: by transferring merit and by conveying instruction. As a transfer of merit, reciting the Qur'ān over the grave recalls other Muslim ways for assisting the dead. According to the legal scholar Ibn Taymiyya, "the deceased gets the benefit of all kinds of bodily worship, whether prayer, fasting, or recitation, just as he gets the benefits of acts of monetary worship such as *sadaqa* [charity] and its like and just as if one supplicated on his behalf." In submission to the supreme will of God, Muslims could ask to transfer any merit gained by these ritual activities from themselves to the deceased.

At the same time, reciting the Qur'ān over the grave provided a direct way of dealing with the urgent need of the deceased for religious knowledge in the afterlife. While the deceased was being interrogated in the grave, questioned by the angels Munkar and Nakir, the living could stand by the grave and provide support. According to one account of the teachings of the prophet, Muḥammad said, "When one of you dies and you have settled the earth over him, let one of you stand at the head of his grave and then address the deceased by name." At this first call, the prophet advised, the deceased would hear but would not necessarily respond. So he advised a second call, at which the deceased would sit up in the grave, and a third call, at which the deceased would say, "Instruct me, and may Allah grant me mercy!" For the friends and relatives standing over the grave, this responsibility of addressing and instructing the deceased clearly called on them to cross the divide that separated the living and the dead. As such, the Muslim practice of teaching the dead was a kind of experiential transcendence of death, a transcendence experienced by the living in the here and now in bridging the barrier of death (Smith and Haddad, 1981).

By instructing, encouraging, and exhorting the soul in the grave, Muslim communication with the deceased reinforced ongoing connections between the living and the dead. As in many forms of religious ritual, teaching was regarded as a religious gift, in this case as a sacred offering given by the living to the deceased. Modern spiritualists have also cultivated methods of teaching and learning in relation to the dead. In modern spiritualism, however, the lines of communication have been reversed. Instead of assuming responsibility for teaching the deceased in matters of religion, modern spiritualists have sought to receive instruction from the spirits of the dead. Nevertheless, a variety of initiatives within modern spiritualism have worked to open the channels of direct communication between the worlds of the living and the dead.

Channeling

In the early nineteenth century, spiritualism emerged as a modern movement that had much in common with the archaic practices of the shaman. Spiritualist mediums claimed to be specialists in contacting and communicating with the dead. They suggested that an experiential transcendence of death was possible by receiving messages from spirits beyond the grave. The messages were of several different types—rappings, knockings, strange sounds, voices, and even apparitions of the dead. In the spiritualist séance, participants could share in an experiential transcendence of death under the direction of a skilled medium. Although many mediums were caught in carefully stage-managed deceptions, spiritualism captured the modern imagination. Not only claiming evidence for life after death, spiritualism promised the living that they could transcend death by experiencing direct contact and communication with the dead.

During the eighteenth-century European Enlightenment, coinciding with the rise of rational skepticism, the visionary Emmanuel Swedenborg claimed to have explored the territory beyond death. In his reports from Spirit-Land, Swedenborg recounted that he regularly conversed with the spirits of the dead and the angels living in the heavens (Schmidt, 2000: 199–245). As he documented those spiritual conversations in a series of books, Swedenborg advanced a spiritualism that was relatively restrained by comparison to the more dramatic performances by spirit mediums during the nineteenth century. Moving from literary conventions to theatrical demonstrations, spiritualism entered a new arena of public media.

In the United States, spiritualism began in 1848 in northern New York when the Fox sisters, Maggie (age thirteen) and Katie (age eleven), were proclaimed as mediums for mysterious rapping noises that seemed to come from an unknown source. Although the girls later admitted that they made the raps by cracking the joints of their toes against hardwood floors, their mother was certain at the time that the rappings were spirit messages from the dead. "We were led on unintentionally by my good mother," Maggie later explained. "We would 'rap' just for the fun of the thing, you know, and mother would declare that it was the spirits that were speaking" (Brandon, 1983: 2).

In sessions organized by Mrs. Fox and her married daughter Leah Fish, the sisters were posed questions, and the spirits answered by rapping. Leah Fish worked out a numerical alphabetic code so the spirits could rap out more

detailed messages from the dead. Soon the spirit séances of the Fox sisters became a famous attraction in concert halls and auditoriums, a kind of spiritualist road show. Investigations by doctors and public officials failed to expose the
Fox sisters as frauds. As public interest in spiritualism increased, the Fox sisters
became the center of a new religion and a lucrative business based on communication with the world of the dead.

For all its mystery and deception, spiritualism produced phenomena that
appealed to the emerging scientific interests of the nineteenth century. Like science, spiritualism claimed to deal in facts. Spiritualists cited the séances, strange
noises, and odd disturbances as scientific proof of life after death. While scientists were making discoveries in the field of electricity, spiritualists claimed to
have discovered a spiritual electricity that allowed the dead to communicate
with the living via the supernatural telegraph of the spiritualist medium. A
number of professional scientists even devised experimental tests in an effort to
verify spiritualist claims that they had discovered proof of life after death (Brandon, 1983: 77–97).

Through rapping, table tipping, levitation, automatic writing, mysterious
music, and other spiritualist arts, mediums produced phenomena that were interpreted as messages from the dead. By the end of the nineteenth century, spiritualist mediums were conducting increasingly elaborate programs in which
spirits from the dead took an even more active role in séances. Spirits spoke
from closets or mysteriously manifested in the room when summoned by the
medium. By the 1870s, spirit manifestations in which participants could even
shake hands with the dead had become common in spiritualist séances. Although many of these spirit manifestations were exposed as hoaxes, public enthusiasm for spiritualist communications with the dead continued into the
twentieth century to promise a direct experiential transcendence of death.

At the end of the twentieth century, enthusiasm for spiritualist contact with
the dead was revived in the widespread popularity of trance channeling. Promoted by the celebrity Shirley MacLaine, trance channeling attracted considerable media attention and gained a fairly large following. MacLaine drew particular attention to the channeler Kevin Ryerson, who went into trance to
communicate messages in the strange accents of two spirits, a certain John of
the first century and an eighteenth-century Irish pickpocket by the name of
Tom MacPherson. Their messages provided useful information and guidance
from the world of the dead for the benefit of the living. Ryerson was only one
among many enterprising trance channelers who claimed an experiential transcendence by directly transmitting voices from the dead (Chandler, 1988).

For skeptics, the direct contact with the dead claimed by all these spiritualists, from mediums to channelers, from Swedenborg to Shirley MacLaine, must
appear as extraordinary delusion or fraud. Certainly, such an experiential transcendence of death is not possible. Nevertheless, ordinary people have reported
contacts with the dead. According to surveys conducted in the United States,
when people were asked if they had ever had an experience in which they
"were really in touch with someone who had died," 25 percent of the respon-
dents in 1972 and 40 percent in 1984 answered that they had experienced such
direct contact with the dead (Greeley, 1987). A sense of communicating with

deceased friends or relatives, which one analyst called "Idionecrophanies," private appearances of the dead, was not uncommon among Americans (MacDonald, 1992). In one respect, this frequency of claims to having communicated with the dead is not surprising since human beings have found many ways for keeping alive their ongoing conversations with the dead. In the history of religions, those conversations have depended on establishing sacred times and sacred places for memorialization that affirms the ongoing presence of the dead in the world.

MEMORIALIZING

In many religious traditions, regular festivals have celebrated the memory of the dead. As we recall, in Native American religion the Algonkian Feast of the Dead was an occasion for remembering all the deceased of the community. As an annual festival, the Mexican Day of the Dead has reverently, playfully provided an occasion for involving the deceased in a Christian celebration for the dead. Likewise, throughout Asia, Buddhist festivals for the dead, such as the annual Obon festival for all the spirits of the dead in Japan or the annual Zhanyuan festival for all the hungry ghosts in China, have marked important ritual times for remembering all who have departed this world (Gilday, 1993).

Certainly, these festivals are about more than memory. By calling back the dead, they provided occasions for the living to enter into contacts, conversations, and exchanges that transcend the grief of loss. In many cases, festivals for the dead have been regarded as necessary for extending support to those forms of life that cannot be seen by the living. The annual Buddhist festival for hungry ghosts in China, for example, has offered food and drink as spiritual nourishment for disembodied spirits consumed by desire. According to Chinese Buddhist tradition, a disciple of the Buddha by the name of Mulian, grieving the loss of his mother, learned that she had been reborn in the realm of the hungry ghosts, the *loka* of the *preta,* and was being tormented by those spirits. The Buddha advised that Mulian should set aside one day a year to present offerings of nourishment for the hungry ghosts. By introducing this annual feast, Mulian assisted not only his mother but also all the conscious beings in that realm (Teiser, 1988). Nevertheless, even if these festivals produced tangible benefits for spirits in other worlds, they also marked out a sacred time for the living to remember the dead.

While reinforced through regular festivals, the memory of the dead is also situated in special places. Within the religious practices of aboriginal Australia, specific sites were associated with the heroic deeds of the dead. A water hole, a rock face, or a grove of trees, for example, could bear powerful spiritual traces left by the ancestors. In tracking those traces, the living cultivated an ongoing memory of the dead. By honoring the specific sites associated with the ancestors, people entered the Dreamtime that represented both a memory of the primordial past and the reality of a spiritual present. In different ways, religious traditions locate the memory of the dead in specific places. Shrines of saints, tombs of martyrs, battlefields of heroic warriors, and many other sacred sites have been established as places of memory. One of the most pervasive religious impulses has been this effort to keep alive the memory of the dead. As a cultural transcendence of death, this work of setting apart special times and places for memory rises above death's limit by keeping alive the presence of the dead among the living.

Although this cultural transcendence of death has been an important feature of every religious tradition, it has also been crucial in the modern world. During the nineteenth century, the rise of modern states, with their flags, territories, and invented histories, led to increased activity in creating memorial spaces and memorial times to reinforce a sense of national solidarity. In the ideology of nationalism, which, as Ninian Smart argued, has operated like a religion, the sacred space and the sacred time of memory has been crucial to the political project of forming a sense of shared nationality (Smart, 1999). Not only supposed to be uniform in the present, that identity is imagined to be continuous with the past, linking the living and the dead in an ongoing cultural transcendence of death. As a powerful force in the modern world, nationalism has set the terms and provided the conditions for remembering the dead in space and time.

Memorial Space

In the modern world, even the cemetery has been affected by nationalism. Although cemeteries have continued to provide locations for expressing grief, conversing with the dead, and performing religious rituals, they have also taken on specific social roles in modernity. In the United States, sociologist W. Lloyd Warner (1959) called the American cemetery the "city of the dead" in which the dead continued to live as social persons. The cemetery was a sacred space because it was set apart from the ordinary, mundane, or profane activities of daily life, providing a sacred location for maintaining ritual contact with the dead. Visits to the cemetery were pilgrimages to a sacred site that kept alive the memory of the dead.

Although visits to the graves of relatives were ancestral rituals, the cemetery achieved a cultural transcendence for the larger community of the living. The cemetery idealized a community's beliefs, values, and enduring continuity. It stood as a visible symbol of a community's commitment to transcend death. Analyzing one American community, W. Lloyd Warner observed that its cemetery symbolized a shared, collective, cultural transcendence of death: "Yankee City cemeteries are collective representations that reflect and express many of the community's basic beliefs and values about what kind of a society it is . . . and where each [person] fits into the secular world of the living and the spiritual society of the dead" (1959: 280). The city of the dead was a replica of the city of the living: Family relations, social status, displays of wealth, honor, respect, and reverence that were important in the secular world of the living were duplicated in the sacred world of the cemetery.

As the visible, tangible symbol of an agreement made by human beings not to allow each other to die, the cemetery gave individuals an opportunity to come to terms with their own deaths in relation to the lives and deaths of relatives, friends, and the larger community. Ultimately, each individual could be assured by the presence of the cemetery that he or she would be kept alive after death in the cultural memory of the community.

Between 1830 and 1855, the rural cemetery flourished in America. Replacing the churchyard or graveyard as a place of burial, the rural cemetery was like a public park where the living commemorated the dead's return to nature. Prior to the practice of embalming, the corpse buried in a rural cemetery dissolved in "the embrace of nature" or returned to "the bosom of Mother Earth." Elaborate sentimental monuments attested to these romantic attitudes toward death (French, 1974).

In 1855, the first of a new type of cemetery was founded in Cincinnati, Ohio—the lawn cemetery. Modeled after Central Park in New York City, this new style of cemetery, a large, flat expanse of carefully manicured grass, became the dominant model for American cemeteries. Its main characteristic was uniformity: Grave mounds were leveled, gravestones were limited in size, grave inscriptions were reduced, and fences or stone boundaries around grave plots were eliminated. Features that had been prominent in earlier cemeteries were removed because they were felt to violate uniformity by emphasizing status distinctions in the city of the dead. But grave mounds, stones, and fences were also eliminated because they obstructed the view of the park and made lawn mowing difficult. Ultimately, however, these features of earlier cemeteries were eliminated because they reminded people of death.

By the early twentieth century, the lawn cemetery was dedicated to the denial of death. In 1910, one cemetery administrator wrote an article called "The Cemetery Beautiful," in which he celebrated the removal from the modern cemetery of anything that might remind people of death. "Today cemetery making is an art," he observed, "and gradually all things that suggest death, sorrow, or pain are being eliminated." American cemeteries achieved a cultural transcendence of death through the art of denial. In support of the modern cemetery, a 1910 issue of *Ladies Home Journal* declared that "there is nothing to suggest the presence of death." Eliminating symbolic references to death, the modern cemetery promised perpetual care and permanent maintenance in a uniform, peaceful, and beautiful environment designed to comfort the living (Farrell, 1980: 120–21; Sloane, 1991).

The best example of the cultural transcendence of death achieved by lawn cemeteries was Forest Lawn in California. Forest Lawn was designed by a former mining engineer, Hubert Eaton. After losing a gold mine in Nevada, Eaton accepted a job in 1917 as manager of a run-down, weed-infested cemetery in Glendale, California. Eaton decided that Americans had a "memorial impulse" to commemorate their dead and that he would provide them with the proper environment to express that basic impulse. He dreamed of a place "filled with towering trees, sweeping lawns, splashing fountains, singing birds, beautiful statues, cheerful flowers, noble memorial architecture . . . a garden that seems next door to Paradise itself, an incredibly beautiful place, a place of infinite loveliness and eternal peace."

Forest Lawn continued the American tradition of romantic sentimentality. Sections of the cemetery were given sentimental names: Whispering Pines,

Everlasting Love, Kindly Light, Haven of Peace, Triumphant Faith, Brotherly Love, Ascension, and Babyland. Status distinctions were reintroduced by setting aside Gardens of Memory that were locked to the public but could be entered by relatives with the use of a golden key. In any section, however, plots at Forest Lawn represented some of the most expensive real estate in the country. Prices included the ground, the vault, opening and closing of the grave, and permanent care. But Forest Lawn was not merely a cemetery but a living monument to American culture.

Forest Lawn combined religious and patriotic themes into a uniquely American cultural transcendence of death. Religious chapels were constructed for worship, ranging in size from the Wee Kirk o' the Heather to the enormous Great Mausoleum Columbarium, and religious sculpture—including copies of Michelangelo's Moses, David, and Pietà—were on display for religious devotion and aesthetic appreciation. American patriotism was glorified in the Memorial Court of Honor, the Hall of History, the Freedom Mausoleum, and the Court of Patriots. More than merely a place of burial, Forest Lawn was a sacred space for the expression of the distinctive mixture of religious and patriotic sentiments that has been called American civil religion (Chidester, 1988: 81–109). Forest Lawn stood as both an idealized city of the dead and a monumental memorial to the American way of life.

Memorial Time

National monuments, patriotic shrines, and war memorials have represented sacred spaces for cultural transcendence in all modern nations. When citizens visited those places, they celebrated the ongoing continuity of their national culture by remembering the heroic deeds of the dead. By entering the shrines of a national religion, they participated in the sacred time of founding events, heroic accomplishments, and redemptive sacrifices that were felt to be responsible for the life of their nation. A sense of sacred time, therefore, was also important in the spaces set aside for memorializing the dead.

In the United States, a sense of sacred time was achieved in annual commemorations for America's dead. The most important holy day in the American memorial calendar was Memorial Day. Growing out of regional holidays dedicated to the war dead after the Civil War, Memorial Day became a national legal holiday in the United States after World War II. Although many Americans regarded the holiday as nothing more than a vacation from work, American communities—particularly smaller towns—celebrated Memorial Day as a holy day set aside to commemorate America's dead.

In his analysis of Memorial Day in one New England city during the 1950s, W. Lloyd Warner observed, "Memorial Day is a cult of the dead which organizes and integrates the various faiths and ethnic and class groups into a sacred unity" (1959: 249). Through collective ritual action, Americans who participated in Memorial Day celebrated a cultural transcendence of death. Memorial Day acted out American beliefs in a sacred cultural unity that was undivided by death—the unity of all the living among themselves, the unity of the living with the dead, and the unity of both the living and the dead as one nation under God.

Warner divided Memorial Day rituals into four phases. First, voluntary organizations such as the American Legion, the Boy Scouts, men's and women's groups, and various church-related associations performed memorial ceremonies for America's war dead over the course of the year. Second, these organizations intensified their efforts during the three to four weeks prior to Memorial Day. Meetings were held to plan for the holiday. Schools and churches put on patriotic programs and pageants that would lead up to Memorial Day. Memorial associations paid particular attention to preparing the cemetery: The grounds were cleaned, graves were decorated with flags, and new grave markers were installed.

Third, the few days before Memorial Day were devoted to religious and patriotic rituals performed at schools, churches, association halls, and cemeteries. Speeches, sermons, and ceremonies wove together religious and patriotic themes. Most speeches, for example, referred to Abraham Lincoln, "the martyred President of that great crisis in American life" (Capps, 1977; Warner, 1959: 251). Lincoln was the model for redemptive sacrifice in American civil religion: In the vocabulary of religious patriotism, Lincoln's death symbolized a sacrifice on the altar of national unity. Lincoln died so America might live as one nation.

In the fourth phase of the Memorial Day cult of the dead, the community gathered on the holy day itself in the center of the business district. Affirming the unity of the entire community, the various churches, associations, and groups joined together to parade to the cemetery. On the way, the parade stopped at shrines and monuments in the city dedicated to America's heroic dead who had sacrificed their lives in times of war. Entering the cemetery, everyone participated in highly symbolic and formalized rituals that commemorated the dead.

As Warner concluded, Memorial Day celebrations at the cemetery unified the community. They symbolized the oneness of the total group in a shared cultural transcendence of death. All the different religious, political, and social groups in the community participated in the same ritual with their common dead. The community affirmed itself through the rituals of Memorial Day as an all-inclusive unity sharing a common, transcendent relationship with the dead.

Moving Memorials

At the end of the twentieth century, many nations experienced conflict over creating the inclusive unity that could be woven out of the sacred space and time of memory. In the former Soviet Union, the memory of the revolutionary founder, Vladimir Lenin, which was preserved at the site of his embalmed body and reinforced through regular pilgrimages, posed a problem. During the 1990s, while leaders of the new Russian state sought to erase the memory of a communist past, in some cases tearing down monuments of communist heroes, Russian pilgrims continued to visit the body of Lenin as a reference point for a shared cultural memory that their leaders wanted them to forget.

In the United States, the Vietnam War Memorial in Washington, D.C., which recalled an intensely divisive era in American history, was eventually accepted by the American public as an authentic memorial for the dead that could be integrated into the broader landscape of memorial architecture in the nation's capital. As the Vietnam memorial was assimilated into conventional patriotic practices for remembering the dead, it became what historian James Young has called a "forgetful monument," joining other national monuments that "efface as much history from memory as they inscribe in it" (Young, 1986: 105). Although it could appear to be firmly established in sacred space and time, any cultural transcendence of death remained a struggle of memory against forgetting.

As historian Edward Tabor Linenthal has shown, memorials for the dead, whether the sacred ground of American battlefields, the Holocaust Memorial Museum in Washington, D.C., or the Federal Building in Oklahoma City, have been produced out of complex negotiations over space, time, and memory (Linenthal, 1991, 1995, 2001). In all these cases, survivors have struggled to find a sacred place, a place set apart from the ordinary, everyday world in which they might focus their grief and continue their conversations with the dead.

In the worldwide epidemic of acquired immune deficiency syndrome (AIDS), however, people who lost partners, friends, or family members had no place in the world to memorialize their dead. As a widely stigmatized disease, AIDS has generated many reactions, including a range of religious responses, that have blamed the victims. AIDS appeared suddenly as a medical crisis of unprecedented proportions but also as a social crisis in which those most directly affected by the disease tended to be ostracized. In the United States, victims of the disease have felt the pressures of exclusion from mainstream American society, a rejection that has only added to their burden of suffering and certain death (Altman, 1986). In other parts of the world, people suffering with the syndrome have also been stigmatized and ostracized. As an official of the World Council of Churches, the Reverend Joan Campbell, noted, "Death can then be accompanied by rejection, and this becomes the most painful symptom of all" (McCarthy, 1988: 167). That social exclusion, however, acquired particular force through the failure of government, the private sector, and the scientific community to respond effectively to the AIDS epidemic (Panem, 1988; Shilts, 1987).

Since 1987 the Names Project AIDS Memorial Quilt has provided a vehicle for focusing grief and celebrating the dead. Made up of three-by-six-foot panels, each commemorating someone who had died of AIDS, the Quilt was an expanding memorial that by 2000 had grown to nearly 50,000 panels. Although the Quilt was developed and most consistently displayed in the United States, panels were contributed from thirty countries. The Quilt was permanently touring around the world. By the beginning of the twenty-first century, sections of the Quilt were being displayed at 2,000 events annually. As the project grew, it became impossible to view the entire Quilt at once, except at the rare public displays that were organized in Washington, D.C. While the first public display in 1987 laid out 1,920 panels, the fifth display in 1996, when the Quilt included 40,000 panels, extended the length of the Washington Mall from the U.S. Capitol building to the base of the Washington Monument. As a memorial that was growing beyond control, as Peter Hawkins observed, the AIDS Quilt worked "to dramatize a present reality over which we have no control" (Hawkins, 1996: 169).

Although the Quilt attracted religious support, including an Interfaith Quilt Program, the memorial itself involved myths, rituals, and powerful symbols that worked like religion. In the myth of origin of the Names Project, Cleve Jones, the originator of the Quilt, has traced its inception back to a candlelight march in San Francisco on November 27, 1985, following the murders of Mayor George Moscone and Harvey Milk, the first openly gay city official. During this vigil, people covered walls of the old Federal Building with placards bearing the names of those who had died of AIDS. "It was such a startling image," recalled Cleve Jones. "The wind and rain tore some of the cardboard names loose, but people stood there for hours reading names. I knew then that we needed a monument, a memorial" (Ruskin, 1988: 9).

That monument, however, would not take the form of conventional memorial architecture. Instead of being constructed of cold, hard stone, the memorial would be woven out of warm, soft fabric. When the idea of a quilt occurred to him spontaneously, Jones immediately remembered being tucked into bed as a child by his grandmother with a quilt that had been made by his great-great-grandmother and had been preserved and mended by generations of women in his family. "I immediately had a very comforting, warm memory," Jones recalled (Abrams, 1988; Sturken, 1997: 191). By this account, therefore, the AIDS Quilt symbolized the ongoing, unbroken ancestral continuity of an extended family.

As volunteers joined the project, making memorial panels for the dead, they demonstrated an intensely personal involvement with the Quilt. In intimate and often elaborate detail, the panels created a new memorial name, form, and location for the dead. When the Quilt was displayed, formalized rituals were developed for unfolding the panels, reading out the names, and guiding people through the viewing of the panels. As part of the ritual, people were invited to write their own messages to the dead on a signature panel. The entire Quilt, however, provided an opportunity for conversations with the dead. According to cultural analyst Marita Sturken, "There, the dead are spoken to; there, the dead are perceived to hear and respond" (Sturken, 1997: 196). Not only providing a ritual context for expressing feelings of grief and loss, the AIDS Quilt enabled communication between the living and the dead. For survivors, these ongoing conversations represented an experiential transcendence, bridging the gulf between the living and the dead by weaving them together in a single community.

In the struggle of memory against forgetting, the AIDS Memorial Quilt achieved a cultural transcendence of death, keeping alive the memory of the departed in the present. As a mobile, changing, and growing memorial, however, the Quilt marked an innovation in ritualizing cultural memory. Since this moving memorial was not fixed in any one place, it could be anywhere. Because every part of the expanding Quilt was understood to represent the entire memorial, it could be entirely present everywhere its panels were on display. Although the AIDS Memorial Quilt was not explicitly religious, it nevertheless memorialized those who had died from AIDS in ways that recalled ancestral, experiential, and cultural ways of transcending death in the history of religions. Certainly, many other motives were evident, from mourning to militancy, that were not necessarily religious in character. Still, when Cleve Jones was asked to identify the point of the AIDS Quilt, he observed that its "message is that human life is sacred" (Brown, 1988; Sturken, 1997: 195).

In the face of death, loss, and grief, the sacrality of life comes into a particular focus. For the sake of the dead, the living have consistently performed religious rituals of mourning, communication, and memorialization that reinforce a sanctity of life transcending death. In the process, they have found their own ways to live with death.

LIVING

In March 1985, author Paul Monette learned that his partner, Roger Horowitz, had been diagnosed with HIV. From that moment, Paul and Roger had to live with the reality of death advancing into their world. During the eighteen months before Roger's death, they worked to invest that time with meaning. Living in the face of death, they moved through different emotional stages that they experienced as different territories of the human spirit. In living with death, as Monette recounted in his memoir *Borrowed Time,* they journeyed through the spaces of the moon, the battlefield, and the sanctuary.

At first, when they learned the diagnosis, Paul and Roger felt isolated and alone, as if they had been sent into outer space. On that day, Monette recalled, "we began to live on the moon" (1988: 2). Estranged from the ordinary cares, concerns, and human connections of life, they felt as if they were living in "a parallel universe, lunar and featureless," that was devoid of all hope (1994: 239). Gradually, this sense of despair turned into anger. Adopting a new militancy, they moved into an emotional space they experienced as a battlefield. On the front lines of the fight against AIDS, they joined with other activists, other "warriors in pitched battle" (1988: 75). Finally, they entered a space they called the sanctuary, a place of emotional safety that was produced by the power of imagination. Although Roger was too weak to travel, they went on imaginary journeys, picturing and talking about tours of Greece, Africa, and other destinations. Regarding these imaginary journeys as spiritual pilgrimage, they formed "a common geography of the mind" in their sanctuary surrounded by death (Connor, 2000).

Certainly, this journey through a spiritual geography recalled the emotional stages of dying outlined by Elisabeth Kübler-Ross. From the denial and depression of isolation on the moon, through the anger of fighting against death on the battlefield, to the peace of the sanctuary, this "geography of the mind" charted an emotional progression toward an acceptance of death. By understanding this process in terms of qualitatively different experiences of space, however, Paul and Roger directly addressed the way in which HIV has been represented in popular culture as desecrating the sacred space of the human body. In popular imagery, HIV enters the cell's "innermost sanctum"; the virus invades the body's "sacrosanct environment" (Connor and Kingman, 1988: 2;

Dwyer, 1990: 39). Not only facing death, therefore, they had to deal with this perceived violation of the sanctity of their living space. As they moved into their sanctuary, Paul and Roger found ways to reconsecrate the space of their lives, as Kimberly Rae Connor has observed, "by means of ritual demonstrations of love, empathy, and endurance" (2000: 47).

Although Paul Monette and Roger Horowitz were not religious in any conventional sense, they faced death through creative forms of ritual pilgrimage and sacred space that recalled religious ways of transcending death. By creating a shared "geography of the mind," they also demonstrated a quality of human compassion that has appeared as a spiritual goal in many religious traditions. Literally meaning "suffering together," compassion has been cultivated in the unconditional love of *agape* within the Christian tradition and in the infinite compassion of *karuna* within the Buddhist tradition.

As the ability to suffer with those who suffer, compassion has also been identified as a crucial feature of medical care. In recent thinking about caring for the terminally ill, a growing number of medical practitioners have identified compassion as central to the spirituality of living and dying. Recognizing that death is not merely a physiological event, they have argued for greater attention to the spiritual needs of patients. In this attention to spirituality, advocates have distinguished between the realms of religion, with its diverse, specific traditions, and spirituality, which is defined as a universal dimension of human life. As Kenneth J. Doka has proposed, "While individuals may not profess a religion, all have spiritual needs and concerns that must be considered" (Doka and Morgan, 1999: 2). Without being religious, people can nevertheless grow spiritually in moving through the final stage of life (Bernard and Schneider, 1996). By removing spirituality from the domain of religion, the hospice movement has developed new ways of caring, showing compassion, and being human in the face of death.

Secular Spirituality

Founded in 1967 by the British physician Cicely Saunders, the hospice movement has been dedicated to providing compassionate care for the dying. Beginning with St. Christopher's Hospice outside of London, the movement rapidly expanded worldwide (Clark, 1998). In the United States, the first hospice was established in 1974. By the end of the twentieth century, over 3,000 programs were operating throughout the country. As a movement rather than a specific place, hospice programs all over the world have organized care not only in established centers but also in private homes and nursing homes. Nevertheless, by its very name, the movement recalled a sacred place, a kind of sanctuary, drawing the term "hospice" from the medieval *hospitium,* the way station where Christian pilgrims could stop for food and shelter on their sacred journeys. By evoking that religious place of hospitality, Cicely Saunders intended to stress the relations of giving and receiving in caring for the dying. On the basis of mutual recognition, givers received and receivers gave in building bonds of compassion (Du Boulay, 1984).

By contrast to conventional medical practice, which has been both celebrated and criticized for waging a war against death (Dutton, 1992: 351–52;

Jonsen, 1992: 51), hospice developed a regimen of care that was designed to reduce pain and increase the quality of life. As Cicely Saunders found, "The greatest fear of the dying and their families is the fear of pain." Providing ways of managing pain, therefore, was essential for dealing with the fear of death. At the same time, hospice was dedicated to improving the quality of life. As a matter of principle, the terminally ill were regarded not as dying patients but as living persons. According to Saunders, hospice served "not only to help you die peacefully, but to live until you die" (Saunders, 1995). In this affirmation of life, hospice took the family as the basic unit of care, recognizing that life and death were matters of human relations.

Pioneered by hospice programs, this approach to treating the terminally ill, with its emphasis on caring rather than curing, became known as palliative care. As methods of palliative care were increasingly integrated into conventional medicine, the World Health Organization (WHO) in 1990 formally supported this practice of easing pain and providing spiritual support. In recommending this standard of treatment, WHO advocated "the active total care of patients whose disease is not responsive to curative treatment. Control of pain, of other symptoms, and of psychological, social, and spiritual support is paramount. The goal of palliative care is the achievement of the best quality of life for patients and their families" (World Health Organization, 1990: 11–12).

Like the hospice movement, WHO referred to a spiritual dimension of living and dying that was not found only in religion. Adopting a broad definition, WHO assumed that spirituality was a basic dimension of human identity. In providing spiritual support, therefore, health care workers were not expected to engage in explicitly religious activity. For Cicely Saunders, however, an explicitly religious motivation ran throughout her work in the hospice movement. Referring to her colleagues at St. Christopher's Hospice, Saunders observed, "We are not all Christians here, by any means, but our work is done in the obedience to the Christian imperative. For me personally, it could not be done otherwise" (James and Field, 1992). According to medical historian Roy Porter, the hospice movement provided a specifically Christian context for giving meaning to the process of dying. "Given scientific medicine's inability to give any meaning, and maybe any dignity, to dying," Porter observed, "the hospice movement has arisen, as an essentially Christian framework to cope with our going out" (Porter, 1997: 1465). Instead of addressing the needs of a universal human spirituality, therefore, the hospice movement apparently advanced specifically Christian religious goals.

According to the founder of a Buddhist hospice program in Brisbane, Australia, however, the hospice movement enacted the highest ideals of Buddhist compassion. Established by the Buddhist monk Pende Hawter, the Karuna Hospice Center provided the full range of palliative care, counseling, and spiritual support for the dying and their families. Putting compassion into practice, the hospice pursued the Buddhist mission to be of service to all living beings. In explicitly Buddhist terms, providers of care understood the hospice to be serving the peaceful transition of consciousness. "We have to remind ourselves that the dying process is of great spiritual importance, and we don't want to disturb the mind of the dying person, which is in an increasingly clear and subtle state," Pende Hawter advised. "We have to do whatever we can to allow the person to die in a calm, happy, and peaceful state of mind." Based on a Buddhist understanding of death as a transition of consciousness, the hospice lent its spiritual support to that transition. Buddhist rituals were performed, but participation was entirely voluntary. Buddhist principles of tolerance, harmlessness, and compassion prevented imposing those rituals on anyone who did not want to participate. Nevertheless, at the Karuna Hospice Center, care providers understood the quality of care for the dying that was developed in the hospice movement as essentially Buddhist (McGrath, 1998).

By highlighting spirituality, the hospice movement has appeared as Christian to Christians and as Buddhist to Buddhists (Collett, 1999; Heller et al., 2000). Insisting on its independence from organized religion, however, representatives of the hospice movement have frequently repeated the basic distinction between spirituality and religion. According to the Hospice of North Central Florida, for example, "Hospice views spirituality as being different from religion." By religion, the hospice movement understood the various religious affiliations of the living and the dying. As a matter of free choice, a person might identify with any religious group. In responding to this religious diversity, hospice workers were advised to refer people to the chaplains or clergy of their faith whenever it became necessary to address specifically religious concerns. With respect to spirituality, however, hospice workers were called to recognize and respond to the psychological, social, and human dimensions of living and dying. Every member of the hospice team, whatever their religious backgrounds, could contribute to providing spiritual care.

According to some commentators, this spiritual support, with its distinctive rites of passage, actually functioned like a new religion (Froggat, 1997). Incorporating characteristically religious beliefs and practices, the hospice movement appeared to be doing a kind of religious work. By contrast, other analysts have argued that the spiritual vision of the hospice movement became increasingly secularized as the movement grew (Bradshaw, 1996; James, 1994). That process of secularization, however, was necessary for achieving the religious goals of the movement's founder. As a secular spirituality, without any reference to religion, palliative care was assimilated into a wide range of caregiving, including conventional medical practice, as a humane commitment to humanizing the process of dying.

Ordinary Transcendence

In providing care for the dying, modern medicine has been dedicated to sustaining life. Modern medical technology, however, has dramatically altered the process of dying by providing heroic interventions and artificial means for maintaining the vital signs of life, even for people lingering in unrelievable pain. Statistically, most people in modern societies could anticipate a bad death, in extreme pain, after spending at least ten days in an intensive care unit (Horgan, 1996). As philosopher Elaine Scarry argued, intense and prolonged physical pain, an experience beyond words, effectively dissolves a person's meaningful world (Scarry, 1985). In addition to physical suffering, as Cicely Saunders observed, people who know they are dying often undergo the torment of a "spiritual pain," a "desolate feeling of meaningless" (Saunders, 1988). In response to both physical and spiritual pain, therefore, the dying must confront the problem of the meaning of life.

According to advocates of euthanasia, choosing to die with dignity is one way of recovering meaning in life. As a "good death," euthanasia is the intentional termination of life, at the request of the dying, to end unrelievable pain, irreversible debilitation, or permanent coma. Always voluntary, a self-selected death can take the form of passive euthanasia, as in those cases in which medical personnel allow a person to die by removing life support equipment, or it can take the form of active euthanasia, such as directly causing death by administering a lethal injection. By directly causing death, the practice of active euthanasia has appeared to critics as less like medical care than like murder or suicide. Advocates of euthanasia, however, have argued that choosing to die can represent a positive, life-affirming response to a situation in which it is no longer possible to maintain any meaning or quality of life by living (Keown, 1997).

Generally, religious traditionalists have opposed euthanasia. As a mysterious gift, they have argued, life cannot be taken or given away. In response to the unrelievable pain of the dying, adherents of religious traditions have drawn on powerful religious imagery of redemption through suffering, such as Jesus on the cross, or redemption from suffering, such as the Buddha's insight into nirvāṇa. For Christians and Buddhists, these engagements with human suffering have been signs of transcendence.

At stake in the controversy over dying with dignity, euthanasia, or physician-assisted suicide, therefore, was the meaning of transcendence in the face of the harsh realities of death and dying. In recent research, considerable attention has been directed to the ways in which people experience transcendence by rising above and going beyond the limit of death. At the Center to Improve Care of the Dying at George Washington University, for example, research was conducted into the role of spirituality in "the dying person's achievement of the developmental task of transcendence." From this perspective, transcendence was not an extraordinary breakthrough in consciousness or an extraordinary redemption of conscience but an ordinary stage in the development of a human life. As a central ingredient in that normal developmental process of achieving transcendence, spirituality was recommended as something "important for health care providers to recognize and foster" (Center to Improve Care for the Dying, 2001).

In recognizing and fostering spiritual transcendence, health care providers could use a test known as the Death Transcendence Scale. Asking a carefully selected set of questions, this scale measured five ways of transcending death—religious, mystical, biosocial, creative, and natural. According to researchers who applied this test, people in their survey tended to transcend death through their biosocial relationships and their creative accomplishments. Although not explicitly religious, as we have seen, these ways of rising above and going beyond death have played a significant role in the history of religions. As ancestral and cultural transcendence, these ways of transcending death have featured prominently in many religious traditions. In the Death Transcendence Scale, however, these modes of transcendence were explicitly distinguished from religion. Nevertheless, both were integrated into the set of indicators that revealed the specific ways in which a person transcended death. Along with other tests, such as the Meaning of Life Scale and the Spiritual Well-Being Scale, health care providers could use the Death Transcendence Scale to gain a better understanding of the spirituality of their patients who were facing death (VandeCreek and Nye, 1993).

Following recent research on aging and spirituality, health care providers could recognize and foster the spirituality of their patients by understanding that the aging process brought its own signs of transcendence. From gerontology, the study of aging, one researcher, Lars Tornstam, moved into the study of "gerotranscendence," the transcendent capacities of the elderly. According to Tornstam, gerotranscendence represented the final stage in the developmental progression toward mature wisdom (Tornstam, 1994).

As older people entered this transcendent stage, they gradually shifted from a rational, materialistic view of life to a more spiritual, cosmic, and transcendental perspective on their own lives and the world. On the cosmic dimension, people experienced changes in their sense of time, easily crossing the borders separating past and present, while undergoing a transformation of their sense of space by experiencing, for example, the presence of absent friends or relatives. As their fear of death decreased, they looked for enduring connections in genealogy or nature. Accepting the fact of death, they found joy in the mystery of life.

On the personal level, people confronted themselves, assessing their good and bad features, but regarded those characteristics with a new detachment. No longer the center of the universe, the self could be experienced as part of the larger fabric of life. In maintaining that perspective, people often needed to be alone for quiet contemplation.

On the social level, people became less interested in superficial relationships. Distinguishing between one's self and one's social roles, they felt liberated from arbitrary social conventions and binding ethical norms. Understanding the debilitating weight of material wealth, they moved into a new spiritual asceticism. Adding innocence to their maturity, the elderly who achieved gerotranscendence became like children in the wisdom of their old age (Tornstam, 1997).

From aging to death, people have displayed signs of transcendence. Moving toward the end of the human life cycle, people have shown evidence of emotional and spiritual growth. The "true work of dying," as Bernard and Schneider have proposed, is to respond creatively to those dimensions of human growth and development within the dying process (Bernard and Schneider, 1996). In all these efforts to recognize and foster the spirituality of aging and dying, researchers, hospice workers, and health care providers have struggled to refute the verdict that modern styles of death and dying are necessarily characterized by "denial, confusion, contradiction, and meaninglessness" (Moller, 1996: 22). Instead, they have found coherent, meaningful patterns of transcendence in modern engagements with death.

LIVING TRANSCENDENCE

Death apparently stands as the ultimate limit situation in human life. Clearly, human beings have refused to stop at that limit. In grieving, communicating, and remembering, they have found many ways to rise above and go beyond death's limit. Regularly, as we have seen in this chapter, that line is crossed. Something important about the porous boundary of death—as a limit situation—might be suggested by the etymology of the word "limit." From the Latin *limen,* meaning wall, door, or threshold, the limit of death has appeared as a solid wall that blocks human progress, the final obstacle to realizing hopes, dreams, and aspirations in life. But death has also appeared as a door to open or as a threshold to cross into another world. Up against the wall of death, people have found ways to open the door and cross the threshold. Keeping that door open, they have affirmed ongoing relations, connections, and exchanges with the dead. Going back and forth across that threshold, they have developed ways of imagining a human community that includes both the living and the dead. By virtue of being a limit, therefore, as a wall, a door, and a threshold, death invites transcendence.

Much has changed since Geoffrey Gorer issued his verdict that modern societies refused to acknowledge death as a fact of life. In the secular spirituality of care and compassion, modern approaches to death and dying have increasingly accepted that fact of life. A number of new approaches have even found ways of incorporating illness, suffering, aging, and death into a developmental process that leads toward a normal, ordinary transcendence by acknowledging and accepting death.

A lot of the credit for this increased acceptance of the reality of death must certainly go to the pioneering work of Elisabeth Kübler-Ross. Beginning with her early work *On Death and Dying* (1969), Kübler-Ross charted a developmental progression—from denial to acceptance—that served as a map not only for the personal experience of dying but also for a greater acceptance of the reality of death in the larger society. For both individuals and social institutions, Kübler-Ross has had a profound impact on overcoming the modern denial of death.

In her later work, Kübler-Ross showed an interest in developing a spirituality of death and dying that was similar to the spirituality of many "New Age" religious movements (Walter, 1993). Following in the footsteps of Kübler-Ross, the transpersonal psychologist Kathleen Dowling Singh, based on many years of experience in working with the dying, developed a spirituality of death and dying that explicitly drew on the resources of the history of religions. As she explored the "grace in dying," Singh reflected on the symbolic, ritual, and mythic resources of religious traditions.

As an ordinary person, working with ordinary people who were undergoing ordinary deaths, Singh reported that she had regularly observed things that were "profound, transcendent, and extraordinary." How should we understand this ordinary, extraordinary transcendence in the process of dying? As reference points for understanding, Singh cited the psychologist of religion William James and the historian of religions Mircea Eliade. As James proposed, ordinary, waking consciousness is only one type of consciousness, separated by a thin film from other types of consciousness. Occasionally, James argued, those different types of consciousness intersected in religious mysticism. Similarly, Eliade proposed that the spiritual realm of the sacred, a spiritual reality of transcendent meaning and power, occasionally erupted into the everyday, ordinary world as a hierophany, a manifestation of the sacred, that broke through levels of existence, causing "a rupture of planes," as the extraordinary entered the ordinary. According to Singh, the process of dying was marked by such events—a breakthrough in consciousness, an eruption of the sacred—that transformed ordinary death into an extraordinary revelation of reality.

Turning to religious ritual, Singh referred to the practical wisdom enshrined in traditional arts of dying in the history of religions. In the Christian tradition, she found the medieval Catholic art of dying, the *ars moriendi,* to contain this wisdom of psychospiritual transformation in the dying process. Likewise, in the Buddhist tradition, she found that the art of dying in the *Bardo Thödol* provided psychologically sound guidance and spiritually liberating practice for moving through the process of dying. As Singh discovered, these traditional rituals of dying, whether Christian or Buddhist, held enduring insights into death that remained relevant for ordinary people in modern societies.

Considering religious myths of death and afterlife, Singh pointed to the ways in which the religious imagination has produced maps of other worlds, developing a kind of spiritual cartography, that has given meaning to the process of dying. In facing the reality of death, these religious maps have been crucial for achieving an acceptance of death. In one respect, religious myths have operated as mirrors, reflecting back images of human identity and human potential. "When we look into the 'mirror' of death and dying," Singh observed, "we get a clearer image of ourselves, a clearer image of the inherent possibilities of human consciousness." At the same time, religious myths have worked like picture frames to provide a framework for locating, encompassing, and accepting the reality of death. By framing and mirroring human possibility, the medium of religious myth has played a crucial role in giving meaning to the process of dying.

Religious myths, rituals, and symbols of transcendence, however, have not merely pointed to the acceptance of death. As Singh argued, acceptance was only the beginning of the process of transformation in dying. Although Kübler-Ross had made acceptance the culmination of her five-stage process of dying, Singh argued that even the psychological adjustments necessary for reaching acceptance were still part of the swirling chaos of human suffering in the process of dying. "The transformational possibilities inherent in suffering," she proposed, "demand a context of meaning, a framework that creates sense and order out of chaos" (Singh, 1998: 56). By consciously embracing "dying's transformative and transcendent power," Singh argued, people could move through the chaos of suffering into a stage that she called transcendence.

Exploring patterns of transcendence in the history of religions, this book has outlined the basic ways in which people have engaged death and dying through religious symbols, myths, rituals, and traditions. Even in modernity, as Kathleen Dowling Singh has suggested, the traditional remains relevant, even though its relevance might be recast in new ways. If nothing else, this survey of religious patterns of transcendence has shown that death is intimately woven into the fabric of religion. If death appears as a limit, religion registers as the ways human beings have found to rise above or go beyond that limit. Religion has not always functioned merely as a way of avoiding death; it has generated a complex array of strategies for facing and embracing death as the ultimate challenge to the meaning, power, and purpose of human life. The history of religions provides one avenue into the many different ways that human beings have encountered death and have negotiated some sense of transcendence in the face of that ultimate limit. In the end, human beings have been most human when they have been working out those patterns of transcendence.

Chapter Seven: References

Abrams, Gary. (1988). "AIDS Quilt Comforting U.S. Grief," *Los Angeles Times,* March 22.

Abu Lughod, Lila. (1993). "Islam and the Gendered Discourses on Death." *International Journal of Middle Eastern Studies* 25: 187–205.

Altman, Dennis. (1986). *AIDS in the Mind of America.* Garden City, N.Y.: Doubleday.

Ariès, Philippe. (1974). *Western Attitudes Toward Death: From the Middle Ages to the Present.* Trans. Patricia M. Ranum. Baltimore: The Johns Hopkins University Press.

Becker, Ernst. (1997). *The Denial of Death.* New York: Free Press.

Bernard, Jan Selliken, and Miriam Schneider. (1996). *The True Work of Dying: A Practical and Compassionate Guide to Easing the Dying Process.* New York: Avon Books.

Bradshaw, Ann. 1996. "The Spiritual Dimension of Hospice: The Secularisation of an Ideal." *Social Science and Medicine* 43, no. 3: 409–19.

Brandon, Ruth. (1983). *The Spiritualists: The Passion for the Occult in the Nineteenth and Twentieth Centuries.* New York: Alfred A. Knopf.

Brown, Joe. (1988). "The Quilt." *Washington Post,* October 2.

Brown, Karen McCarthy. (1991). *Mama Lola: A Vodou Priestess in Brooklyn.* Berkeley and Los Angeles: University of California Press.

Capps, Donald. (1977). "The Death of Father Abraham: The Assassination of Lincoln and Its Effect on Frontier Mythology." In Frank E. Reynolds and Earle H. Waugh (eds.), *Religious Encounters with Death: Insights from the History and Anthropology of Religions.*

University Park: Pennsylvania State University Press, 233–44.

Center to Improve Care for the Dying. (2001). *Spirituality* (http://www.gwu .edu/~cicd/toolkit/spiritual.htm).

Chandler, Russell. (1988). *Understanding the New Age.* Dallas: Word Publishing.

Chidester, David. (1988). *Patterns of Power: Religion and Politics in American Culture.* Englewood Cliffs, N.J.: Prentice Hall.

Clark, David. (1998). "Originating a Movement: Cicely Saunders and the Development of St. Christopher's Hospice, 1957–67." *Mortality* 3, no. 1: 43–63.

———. (1999). "'Total Pain,' Disciplinary Power, and the Body in the Work of Cicely Saunders." *Social Science and Medicine* 49: 727–36.

Collett, Merrill. (1999). *At Home with Dying: A Zen Hospice Approach.* Boston: Shambhala Publications.

Connor, Kimberly Rae. (2000). "'A Common Geography of the Mind': Creating Sacred Space in the Autobiographical Writings of Paul Monette and The NAMES Project." *Journal of the American Academy of Religion* 68: 47–68.

Connor, Steve, and Sharon Kingman. (1988). *The Search for the Virus: The Scientific Discovery of AIDS and the Quest for a Cure.* New York: Penguin.

Corrigan, John, Eric Crump, and John Kloos. (2000). *Emotion and Religion: A Critical Assessment and Annotated Bibliography.* Westport, Conn.: Greenwood Press.

Courteney, Hazel. (2000). *Divine Intervention: The True Story of How One Woman Walked Between Worlds and Returned with Messages of Hope from Diana.* London: Cima Books.

Desjarlais, Robert R. (1991). "Poetic Transformation of Yolmo Sadness." *Culture, Medicine, and Psychiatry* 15: 387–420.

———. (1993). *Body and Emotion: The Aesthetics of Illness and Healing in the Nepal Himalayas*. Philadelphia: University of Pennsylvania Press.

Doka, Kenneth J., and John D. Morgan (eds.). (1999). *Death and Spirituality*. Amityville, N.Y.: Baywood Publishing.

Du Boulay, Shirley. (1984). *Cicely Saunders: Founder of the Modern Hospice Movement*. London: Hodder & Stoughton.

Dutton, Diana B. (1992). *Worse Than the Disease: Pitfalls of Medical Progress*. Cambridge: Cambridge University Press.

Dwyer, John M. (1990). *The Body at War: The Miracle of the Immune System*. New York: Penguin.

Dyrud, Marilyn A. (1997). "Di(e)ing on the Net: The Global Village Revisited" (http://www.theabc.org/WesternRegion/papers/dyrud.html).

Farrell, James. (1980). *Inventing the American Way of Death, 1830–1920*. Philadelphia: Temple University Press.

French, Stanley. (1974). "The Cemetery as Cultural Institution: The Establishment of Mount Auburn and the 'Rural Cemetery' Movement." In David E. Stannard (ed.), *Death in America*. Philadelphia: University of Pennsylvania Press, 69–91.

Froggat, Katherine. (1997). "Rites of Passage and the Hospice Culture." *Mortality* 2, no. 2: 123–48.

Geertz, Clifford. (1972). *Interpretation of Culture*. New York: Basic Books.

al-Ghazāli. (1989). *The Remembrance of Death and Afterlife*. Trans. T. J. Winter. Cambridge: Islamic Text Society.

Gilday, Edmund. (1993). "Dancing with the Spirit(s): Another View of the Other World in Japan." *History of Religions* 32: 273–300.

Gorer, Geoffrey. (1965). *Death, Grief, and Mourning*. New York: Doubleday.

Greeley, Andrew M. (1987). "Hallucinations Among the Widowed." *Sociology and Social Research* 71, no. 4: 258–65.

Hagman, George. (1995). "Mourning: A Review and Reconsideration." *International Journal of Psychoanalysis* 76: 909–25.

Hardacre, Helen. (1997). *Marketing the Menacing Fetus in Japan*. Berkeley and Los Angeles: University of California Press.

Harrison, Elizabeth G. (1995). "Women's Responses to Child Loss in Japan: The Case of *Mizuko Kuyō*." *Journal of Feminist Studies in Religion* 11, no. 2: 67–93.

Hawkins, Peter S. (1996). "*Ars Memoriandi:* The NAMES Project AIDS Quilt." In Howard M. Spiro, Mary G. McCrea Curren, and Lee Palmer Wandel (eds.), *Facing Death: Where Culture, Religion, and Medicine Meet*. New Haven, Conn.: Yale University Press, 166–79.

Heller, Jan C., et al. (eds.). (2000). *Faithful Living, Faithful Dying: Anglican Reflections on End of Life Care*. Harrisburg, Pa.: Morehouse Publishing.

Heyse-Moore, L. H. (1996). "On Spiritual Pain in the Dying." *Mortality* 1, no. 3: 297–316.

Hockey, Jenny. (1995). "The View from the West: Reading the Anthropology of Non-Western Death Ritual." In Glennys Howarth and Peter C. Jupp (eds.), *Contemporary Issues in the Sociology of Death, Dying, and Disposal*. London: Macmillan, 3–16.

Hollan, Douglas Wood. (1992). "Emotion, Work, and Value of Emotional Equanimity among the Toraja." *Ethnology* 31: 45–56.

———, and Jane C. Wellenkamp (1994). *Contentment and Suffering: Culture and Experience in Toraja*. New York: Columbia University Press.

Homans, Peter (ed.). (2000). *Symbolic Loss: The Ambiguity of Mourning and Memory at Century's End*. Charlottesville: University Press of Virginia.

Horgan, John. (1996). "Right to Die." *Scientific American*, May: 8–9.

Houlbrooke, Ralph (ed.). (1989). *Death, Ritual, and Bereavement*. London: Routledge.

Imber-Black, Evan. (1991). "Rituals and the Healing Process." In Froma Walsh and Monica McGoldrick (eds.), *Living Beyond Loss: Death in the Family*. New York: North, 207–23.

Irish, Donald P., Kathleen F. Lundquist, and Vivian Jenkins Nelson (eds.). (1997). *Ethnic Variations in Dying, Death, and Grief*. Washington, D.C.: Taylor and Francis.

Jacobs, Janet L. (1992). "Religious Ritual and Mental Health." In John F. Schumacher (ed.), *Religion and Mental Health*. New York: Oxford University Press, 291–99.

James, Nicky (1994). "From Vision to System: The Maturing of the Hospice Movement." In Robert Lee and Derek Morgan (eds.), *Death Rites: Law and Ethics at the End of Life*. London: Routledge, 102–30.

———, and David Field. (1992). "The Routinization of Hospice: Charisma and Bureaucratization." *Social Science and Medicine* 34: 1363–75.

Jonker, Gerdien. (1997). "The Many Facets of Islam: Death, Dying and Disposal Between Orthodox Rule and Historical Convention." In Collin Murray Parkes, Pittu Laungani, and Bill Young (eds.), *Death and Bereavement Across Cultures*. London: Routledge, 147–65.

Jonsen, Albert R. (1992). *The New Medicine and the Old Ethics*. Cambridge, Mass.: Harvard University Press.

Kear, Adrian, and Deborah Lynn Steinberg (eds.). (1999). *Mourning Diana: Nation, Culture, and the Performance of Grief*. London: Routledge.

Keown, John (ed.). (1997). *Euthanasia Examined: Ethical, Clinical, and Legal Perspectives*. Cambridge: Cambridge University Press.

Klass, Dennis, Phyllis R. Silverman, and Steven L. Nickman (eds.). (1996). *Continuing Bonds: New Understandings of Grief*. Washington, D.C.: Taylor & Francis.

Kübler-Ross, Elisabeth. (1969). *On Death and Dying*. New York: Macmillan.

Laderman, Gary. (1996). *The Sacred Remains: American Attitudes Toward Death, 1799–1883*. New Haven, Conn.: Yale University Press.

———. (2000). "The Disney Way of Death." *Journal of the American Academy of Religion* 68: 27–46.

LaFleur, William R. (1992). *Liquid Life: Abortion and Buddhism in Japan*. Princeton, N.J.: Princeton University Press.

Lifton, Robert Jay. (1979). *Broken Connection*. New York: Simon & Schuster.

Linenthal, Edward Tabor. (1991). *Sacred Ground: Americans and Their Battlefields*. Urbana: University of Illinois Press.

———. (1995). *Preserving Memory: The Struggle to Create America's Holocaust Museum*. New York: Viking.

———. (2001). *The Unfinished Bombing: Oklahoma City in American Memory*. New York: Oxford University Press.

Littlewood, Jane. (1993). "The Denial of Death and Rites of Passage in Contemporary Societies." In David Clark (ed.), *The Sociology of Death: Theory, Culture, Practice*. Cambridge, Mass.: Blackwell, 69–84.

Lutz, Catherine. (1985). "Depression and the Translation of Emotional Worlds." In Arthur Kleinman and Byron J. Good (eds.), *Culture and Depression: Studies in the Anthropology and Cross-Cultural Psychiatry of Affect and Disorder*. Berkeley and Los Angeles: University of California Press, 63–100.

MacDonald, William L. (1992). "Idionecrophanies: The Social Construction of Perceived Contact with the Dead." *Journal for the Scientific Study of Religion* 31, no. 2: 215–23.

McCarthy, Charles R. (1988). "Toward Greater Religious Participation in the Struggle to Combat AIDS." *Religious Education* 83: 163–69.

McGrath, Pam. (1998). "Buddhist Spirituality: A Compassionate Perspective on Hospice Care." *Mortality* 3, no. 3: 251–64.

Mitford, Jessica. (1963). *The American Way of Death*. New York: Simon & Schuster.

———. (2000). *The American Way of Death Revisited*. New York: Vintage Books.

Moller, David Wendell. (1996). *Confronting Death: Values, Institutions, and Human Mortality*. New York: Oxford University Press.

Monette, Paul. (1988). *Borrowed Time: An AIDS Memoir*. New York: Avon Books.

———. (1994). *Last Watch of the Night*. New York: Harcourt Brace.

———. (1997). *Sanctuary: A Tale of Life in the Woods*. New York: Scribner.

Panem, Sandra. (1988). *The AIDS Bureaucracy*. Cambridge, Mass.: Harvard University Press.

Parkes, Collin Murray, Pittu Laungani, and Bill Young (eds.). (1997). *Death and Bereavement Across Cultures*. London: Routledge.

Payne, David. (1995). "*Bambi*." In Elizabeth Bell, Lynda Haas, and Laura Sells (eds.), *From Mouse to Mermaid: The Politics of Film, Gender, and Culture*. Bloomington: Indiana University Press, 137–47.

Pine, Vanderlyn R. (1975). *Caretaker of the Dead: The American Funeral Director*. New York: John Wiley & Sons.

Porter, Roy. (1997). "Religion and Medicine." In William F. Bynum and Roy Porter (eds.), *Companion Encyclopedia of the History of Medicine*. London and New York: Routledge, II: 1449–69.

Prothero, Stephen. (2000). *Purified by Fire: A History of Cremation in America*. Berkeley and Los Angeles: University of California Press.

Richards, Jeffrey, Scott Wilson, and Linda Woodhead (eds.). (1999). *Diana: The Making of a Media Saint*. London: IB Tauris.

Rosaldo, Renate. (1993). *Culture and Truth: The Remaking of Social Analysis*. Boston: Beacon Press.

Rosenblatt, Paul C. (1997). "Grief in Small-Scale Societies." In Collin Murray Parkes, Pittu Laungani, and Bill Young (eds.), *Death and Bereavement Across Cultures*. London: Routledge, 27–51.

———, R. P. Walsh, and D. A. Jackson. (1976). *Grief and Mourning in Cross-Cultural Perspective*. Washington, D.C.: HRAF Press.

Ruskin, Cindy. (1988). *The Quilt: Stories from the NAMES Project*. New York: Pocket Books.

Saunders, Cicely. (1988). "Spiritual Pain." *Hospital Chaplain* 102: 30–39.

———. (1995). *Living with Dying: A Guide to Palliative Care*. New York: Oxford University Press.

———. (1996). "Hospice." *Mortality* 1, no. 3: 317–22.

Scarry, Elaine. (1985). *The Body in Pain: The Making and Unmaking of the World*. New York: Oxford University Press.

Schmidt, Leigh Eric. (2000). *Hearing Things: Religion, Illusion, and the American Enlightenment*. Cambridge, Mass.: Harvard University Press.

Shilts, Randy. (1987). *And the Band Played On: Politics, People, and the AIDS Epidemic*. New York: St. Martin's Press.

Singh, Kathleen Dowling. (1998). *The Grace in Dying: How We Are Transformed Spiritually as We Die*. San Francisco: HarperSanFrancisco.

Sloane, David Charles. (1991). *The Last Great Necessity: Cemeteries in American History*. Baltimore: The Johns Hopkins University Press.

Smart, Ninan. (1999). *Worldviews: Cross-cultural Explorations of Human Beliefs*. 3rd ed. Englewood Cliffs, N.J.: Prentice Hall.

Smith, Jane I., and Yvonne Yazbeck Haddad. (1981). *The Islamic Understanding of Death and Resurrection*. Albany: State University of New York Press.

Spiro, Howard M., Mary G. McCrea Curnen, and Lee Palmer Wandel (eds.). (1998). *Facing Death: Where Culture, Religion, and Medicine Meet*. New Haven, Conn.: Yale University Press.

Stroebe, Margaret S., Mary M. Gergen, Kenneth J. Gergen, and Wolfgang Stroebe. (1992). "Broken Hearts or Broken Bonds: Love and Death in Historical Perspective." *American Psychologist* 47: 1205–12.

———, Wolfgang Stroebe, and Robert O. Hansson. (1993). *Handbook of Bereavement: Theory, Research, and Intervention*. Cambridge: Cambridge University Press.

Sturken, Marita. (1997). *Tangled Memories: The Vietnam War, the AIDS Epidemic, and the Politics of Remembering.* Berkeley and Los Angeles: University of California Press.

Teiser, Stephen F. (1988). *The Ghost Festival in Medieval China.* Princeton, N.J.: Princeton University Press.

Tornstam, Lars. (1994). "Gerotranscendence: A Theoretical and Empirical Exploration." In L. Eugene Thomas and Susan A. Eisenhandler (eds.), *Aging and the Religious Dimension.* Westport, Conn.: Greenwood Press, 203–29.

———. (1997). "Gerotranscendence: The Contemplative Dimension of Aging." *Journal of Aging Studies* 11, no. 2: 143–54.

VandeCreek, Larry, and Christina Nye. (1993). "Testing the Death Transcendence Scale." *Journal for the Scientific Study of Religion* 32, no. 3: 279–83.

Walter, Tony. (1993). "Death in the New Age." *Religion* 23: 127–45.

———. (1996). *The Eclipse of Eternity: A Sociology of the Afterlife.* New York: St. Martin's Press.

———(ed.). (1999). *The Mourning for Princess Diana.* London: Berg.

Warner, W. Lloyd. (1959). *The Living and the Dead: A Study of the Symbolic Life of Americans.* New Haven, Conn.: Yale University Press.

Waugh, Evelyn. (1948). *The Loved One.* Boston: Little, Brown.

Wellenkamp, Jane C. (1988). "Notions of Grief and Catharsis Among the Toraja." *American Ethnologist* 15: 486–500.

———. (1991). "Fallen Leaves: Death and Grieving in Toraja." In David R. Counts and Dorothy Ayers Counts (eds.), *Coping with the Final Tragedy: Cultural Variation in Dying and Grieving.* Amityville, N.Y.: Baywood Publishing, 113–34.

Wikan, Unni. (1988). "Bereavement and Loss in Two Muslim Communities: Egypt and Bali Compared." *Social Sciences and Medicine* 27: 451–60.

———. (1990). *Managing Turbulent Hearts: A Balinese Formula for Living.* Chicago: University of Chicago Press.

Worden, James William. (1991). *Grief Counseling and Grief Therapy: A Handbook for the Mental Health Practitioner.* New York: Springer.

World Health Organization. (1990). *Cancer Pain Relief and Palliative Care.* Geneva: World Health Organization.

Young, James. (1986). "Memory and Monument." In Geoffrey Hartman (ed.), *Bitburg in Moral and Political Perspective.* Bloomington: Indiana University Press, 103–13.

Index